kare kano

his and her circumstances

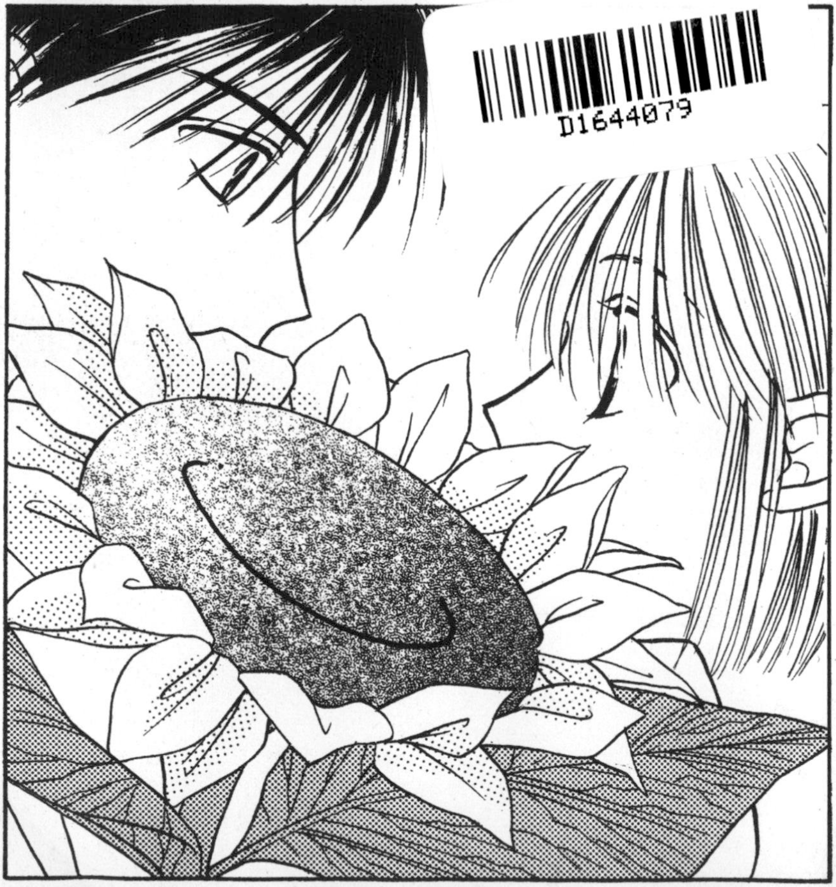

ALSO AVAILABLE FROM

MANGA

*INDICATES TITLE IS IN 100% AUTHENTIC MANGA FORMAT

ACTION

ANGELIC LAYER*
CLAMP SCHOOL DETECTIVES* (April 2003)
DIGIMON
DUKLYON: CLAMP SCHOOL DEFENDERS* (September 2003)
GATEKEEPERS*
GTO*
HARLEM BEAT
INITIAL D*
ISLAND
JING: KING OF BANDITS* (June 2003)
JULINE
LUPIN III*
MONSTERS, INC.
PRIEST
RAVE*
REAL BOUT HIGH SCHOOL*
REBOUND* (April 2003)
SAMURAI DEEPER KYO* (June 2003)
SCRYED*
SHAOLIN SISTERS*
THE SKULL MAN*

FANTASY

CHRONICLES OF THE CURSED SWORD (July 2003)
DEMON DIARY (May 2003)
DRAGON HUNTER (June 2003)
DRAGON KNIGHTS*
KING OF HELL (June 2003)
PLANET LADDER*
RAGNAROK
REBIRTH (March 2003)
SHIRAHIME: TALES OF THE SNOW PRINCESS* (December 2003)
SORCERER HUNTERS
WISH*

CINE-MANGA™

AKIRA*
CARDCAPTORS
KIM POSSIBLE
LIZZIE McGUIRE
POWER RANGERS (May 2003)
SPY KIDS 2

ANIME GUIDES

GUNDAM TECHNICAL MANUALS
COWBOY BEBOP
SAILOR MOON SCOUT GUIDES

ROMANCE

HAPPY MANIA* (April 2003)
I.N.V.U.
LOVE HINA*
KARE KANO*
KODOCHA*
MAN OF MANY FACES* (May 2003)
MARMALADE BOY*
MARS*
PARADISE KISS*
PEACH GIRL
UNDER A GLASS MOON (June 2003)

SCIENCE FICTION

CHOBITS*
CLOVER
COWBOY BEBOP*
COWBOY BEBOP: SHOOTING STAR* (June 2003)
G-GUNDAM*
GUNDAM WING
GUNDAM WING: ENDLESS WALTZ*
GUNDAM: THE LAST OUTPOST*
PARASYTE
REALITY CHECK

MAGICAL GIRLS

CARDCAPTOR SAKURA
CARDCAPTOR SAKURA: MASTER OF THE CLOW*
CORRECTOR YUI
MAGIC KNIGHT RAYEARTH* (August 2003)
MIRACLE GIRLS
SAILOR MOON
SAINT TAIL
TOKYO MEW MEW* (April 2003)

NOVELS

SAILOR MOON
SUSHI SQUAD (April 2003)

ART BOOKS

CARDCAPTOR SAKURA*
MAGIC KNIGHT RAYEARTH*

TOKYOPOP KIDS

STRAY SHEEP (September 2003)

kare kano

his and her circumstances

volume two
by Masami Tsuda

LOS ANGELES • TOKYO

Translator - Amy Forsyth
English Adaption - Darcy Lockman
Editor - Bryce P. Coleman
Retouch and Lettering - Fawn Lau
Cover Artist - Gary Shum
Graphic Designer - Anna Kernbaum

Senior Editor - Julie Taylor
Production Managers - Jennifer Miller and Jennifer Wagner
Art Director - Matthew Alford
VP of Production & Manufacturing - Ron Klamert
President & C.O.O. - John Parker
Publisher - Stuart Levy

Email: editor@TOKYOPOP.com
Come visit us online at www.TOKYOPOP.com

A **TOKYOPOP** Manga
TOKYOPOP® is an imprint of Mixx Entertainment, Inc.
5900 Wilshire Blvd. Suite 2000, Los Angeles, CA 90036

KARE KANO 2 •
KARESHI KANOJO NO JIJYO by Masami Tsuda © 1996 Masami Tsuda
All Rights Reserved. First published in Japan in 1997 by HAKUSENSHA, INC., Tokyo
English language translation rights in the United States of America
and Canada arranged with HAKUSENSHA, INC.,Tokyo
through Tuttle-Mori Agency Inc., Tokyo

English Edition
English text © 2003 by Mixx Entertainment, Inc.
TOKYOPOP is a registered trademark of Mixx Entertainment, Inc.

ISBN: 1-931514-80-1

First TOKYOPOP® printing: March 2003

10 9 8 7 6 5 4 3 2 1

Printed in Canada

kare kano
volume two

TABLE OF CONTENTS

ACT 4 / THE DAY I FELL IN LOVE / 5

ACT 5 / SCHOOL MAZE / 55

ACT 6 / HIS AMBITION / 87

ACT 7 / CRAZY FOR YOU / 119

UNDER THE CHERRY TREES / 152

TSUDA DIARY / 185

KARE KANO: THE STORY SO FAR

Yukino Miyazawa is the perfect model student: kind, athletic, super smart. But she's not all she seems. She is really the self-confessed "queen of vanity," and her only goal in life is winning the praise and admiration of everyone around her. Therefore, she makes it her business to always look and act perfect during school hours. At home, however, she lets her guard down and lets her true self show.

When Yukino enters high school, she finally meets her match: Soichiro Arima, a handsome, popular, and ultra-intelligent guy. Ever since he stole the top seat in the class from her, Yukino has hated him and has been furiously plotting on how to reclaim her place in the spotlight. Then one day, Soichiro drops by Yukino's house and finds her in sweats and glasses. A-ha: So she's not the "perfect" girl she pretends to be! He blackmails her with this info, and soon solicits her to do all his extra schoolwork and errands. Of course, she's furious—but, before long, her anger turns to amazement when she discovers that she and Soichiro have more in common than they ever imagined. In the end, they stop being enemies and start being friends...and soon much more. As their love blossoms, they promise to stop pretending to be perfect and just be true to themselves.

SUNFLOWER = ADORATION

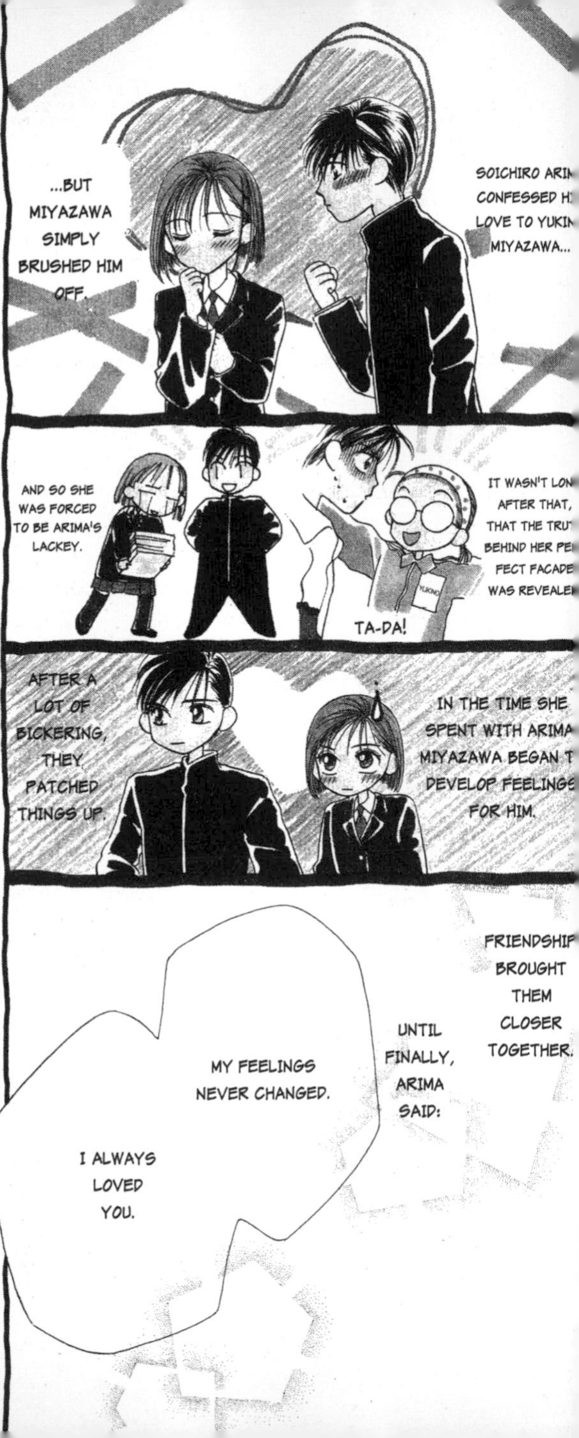
SOICHIRO ARI
CONFESSED H
LOVE TO YUKI
MIYAZAWA...
...BUT MIYAZAWA SIMPLY BRUSHED HIM OFF.
IT WASN'T LON
AFTER THAT,
THAT THE TRU
BEHIND HER PE
FECT FACADE
WAS REVEALE
YUKINO
TA-DA!
AND SO SHE WAS FORCED TO BE ARIMA'S LACKEY.
IN THE TIME SHE SPENT WITH ARIMA MIYAZAWA BEGAN T DEVELOP FEELINGS FOR HIM.
AFTER A LOT OF BICKERING, THEY PATCHED THINGS UP.
FRIENDSHIP BROUGHT THEM CLOSER TOGETHER.
UNTIL FINALLY, ARIMA SAID:
MY FEELINGS NEVER CHANGED.
I ALWAYS LOVED YOU.

And so, what will become of the two of them now?

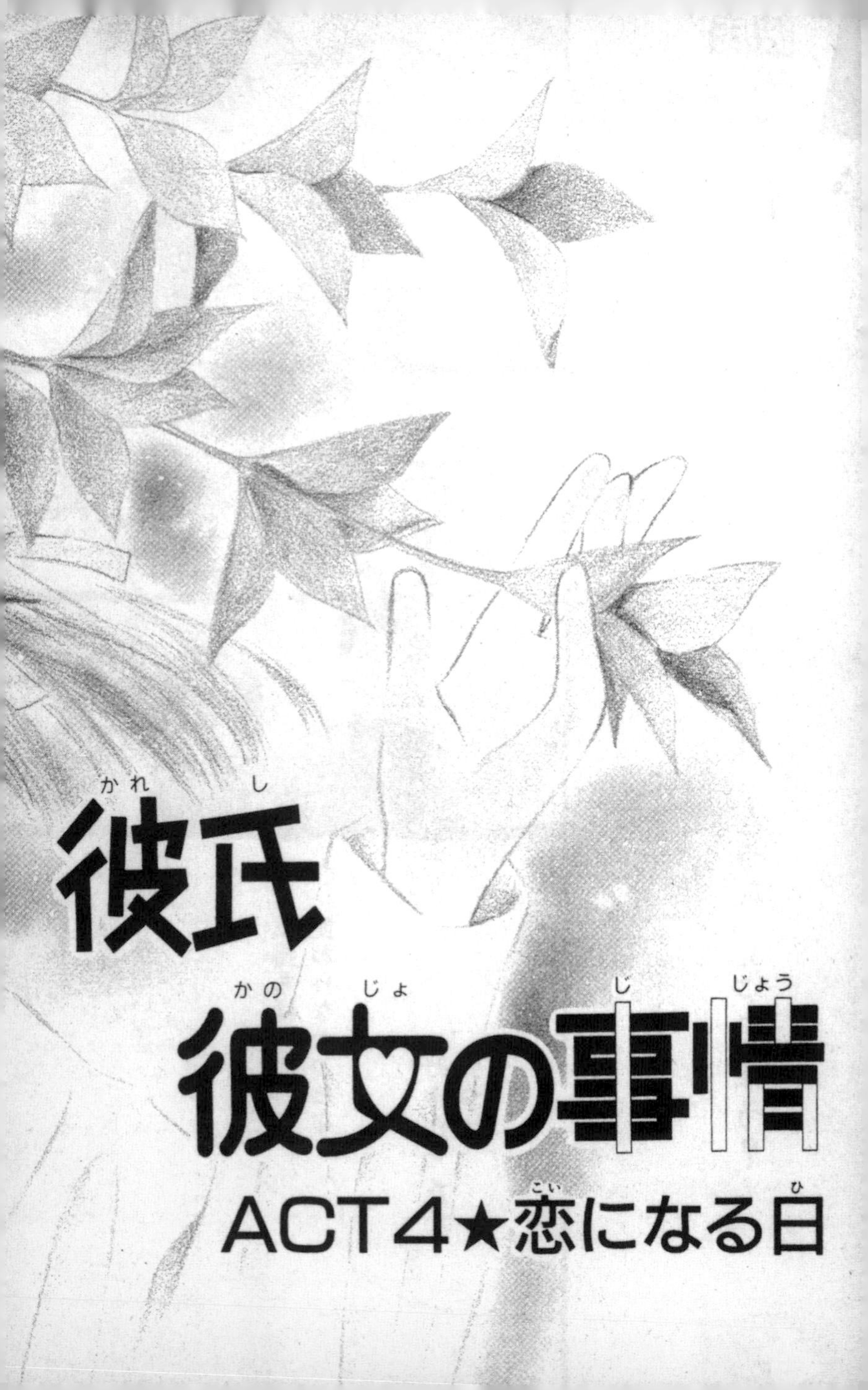

彼氏彼女の事情

ACT4★恋になる日

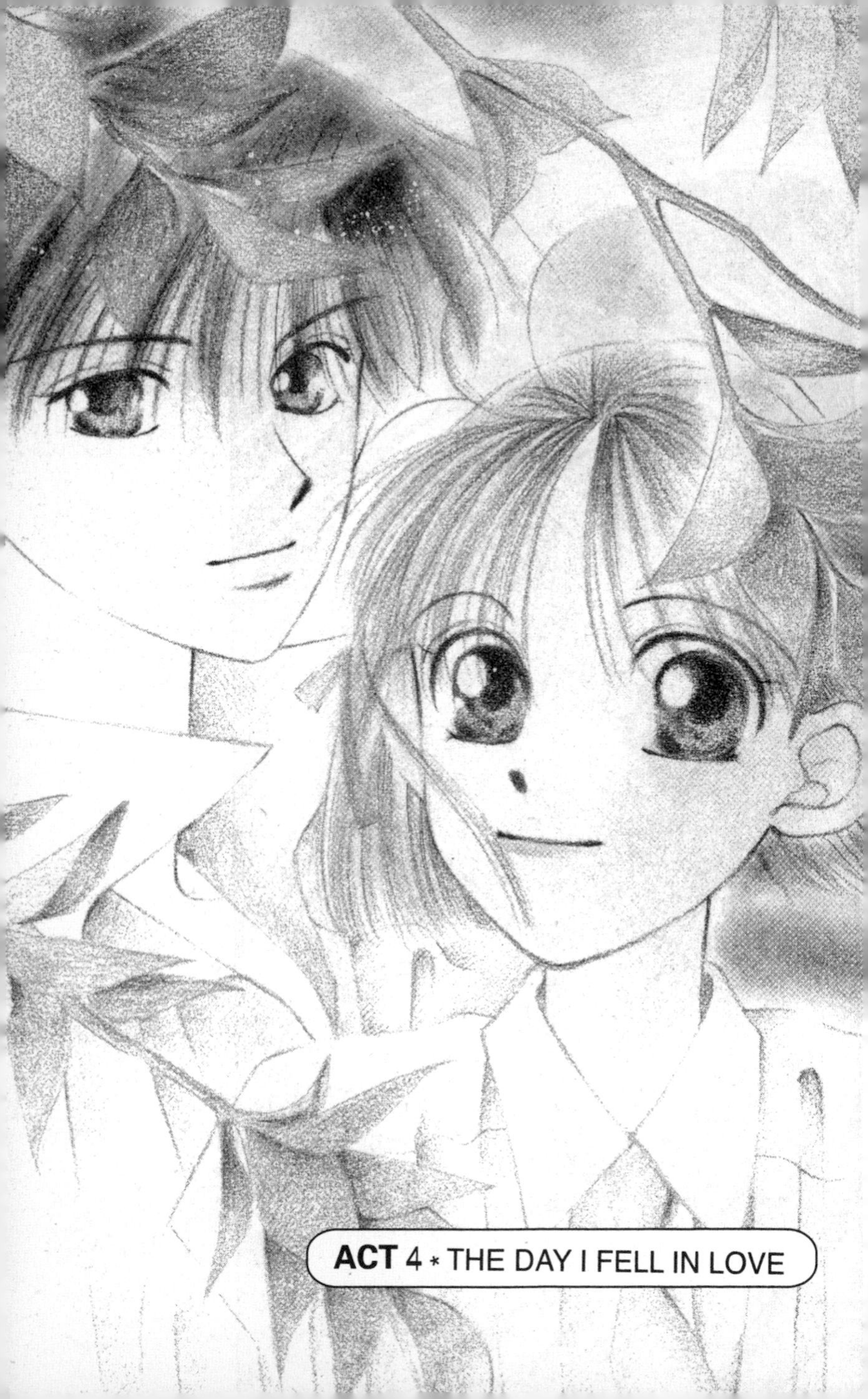
ACT 4 * THE DAY I FELL IN LOVE

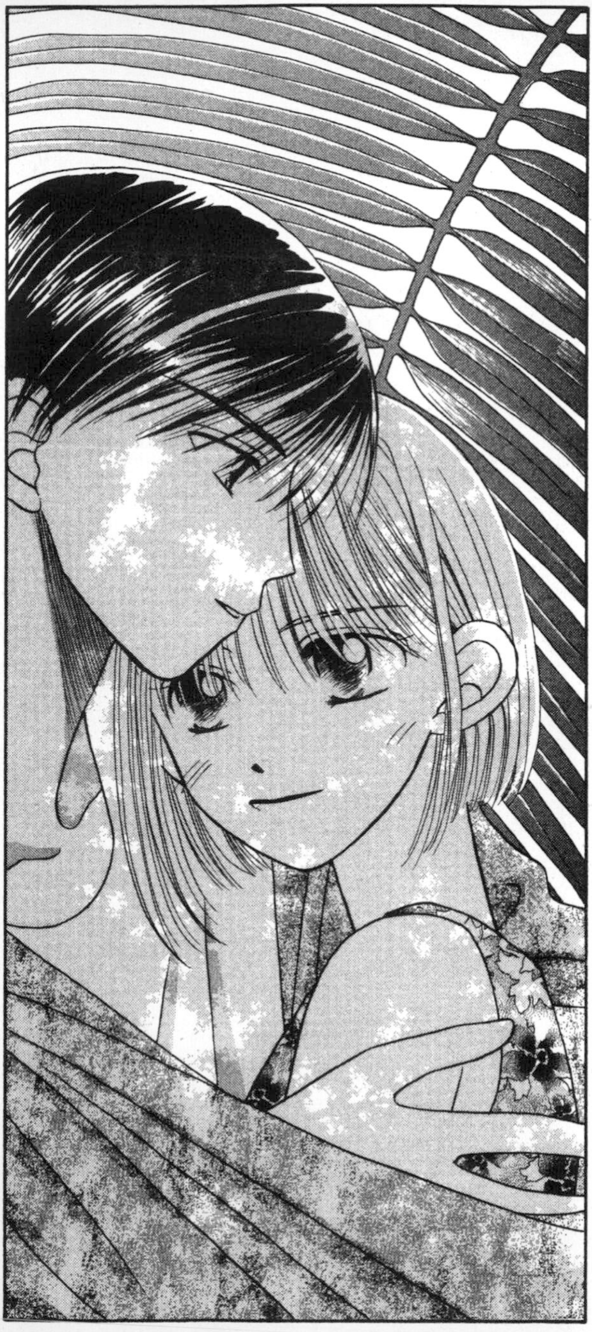

His and her romance

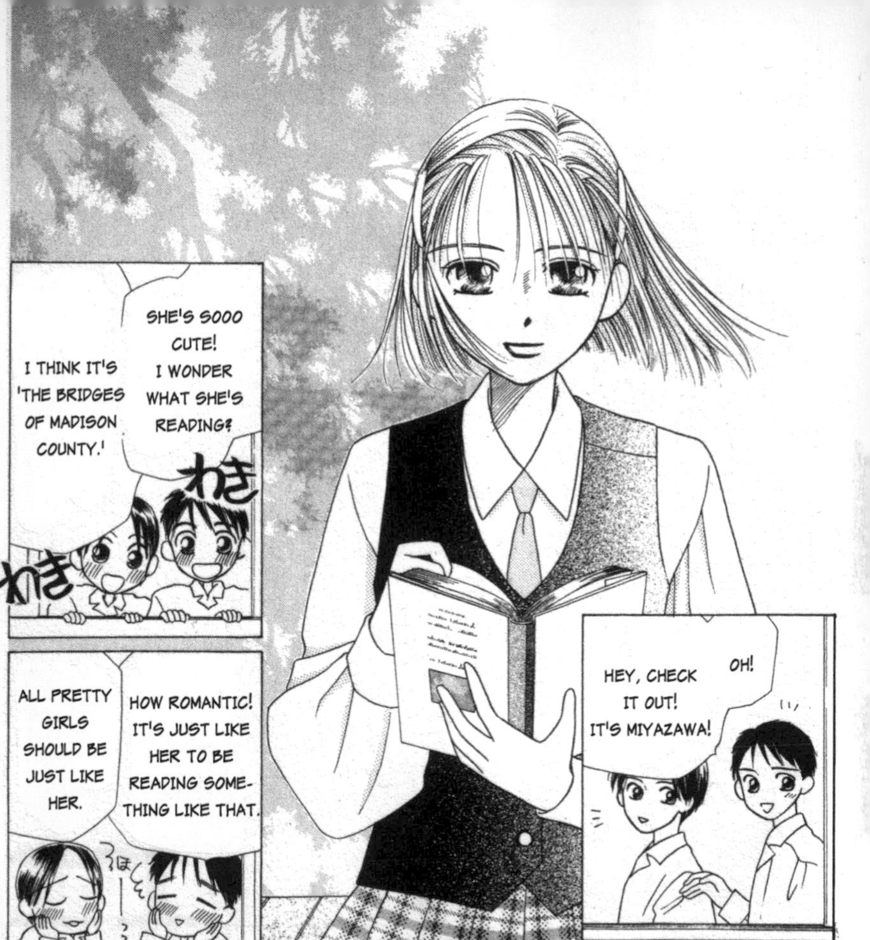
OH!
HEY, CHECK IT OUT! IT'S MIYAZAWA!
SHE'S SOOO CUTE! I WONDER WHAT SHE'S READING?
I THINK IT'S 'THE BRIDGES OF MADISON COUNTY.'
わき
わき
HOW ROMANTIC! IT'S JUST LIKE HER TO BE READING SOME-THING LIKE THAT.
ALL PRETTY GIRLS SHOULD BE JUST LIKE HER.

UNIFORM

THIS IS HOW IT LOOKS FOR NOW.

GIRLS' WINTER UNIFORM

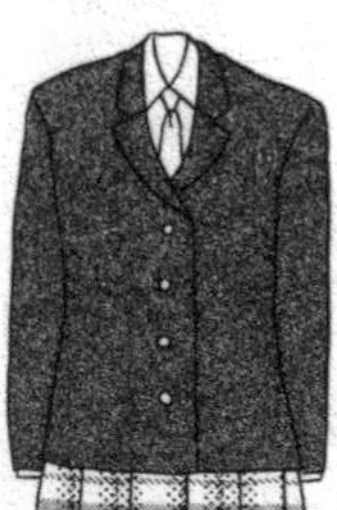

- BLAZER (BLACK)
- SKIRT (BLUE/PURPLE CHECKED)
- NECKTIE (LIGHT BLUE)
- BLOUSE

* STUDENTS ARE FREE TO WEAR THE COAT IF THEY WISH. IT'S A HEAVY COAT IN DARK CAMEL-BROWN.

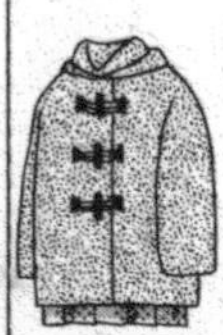

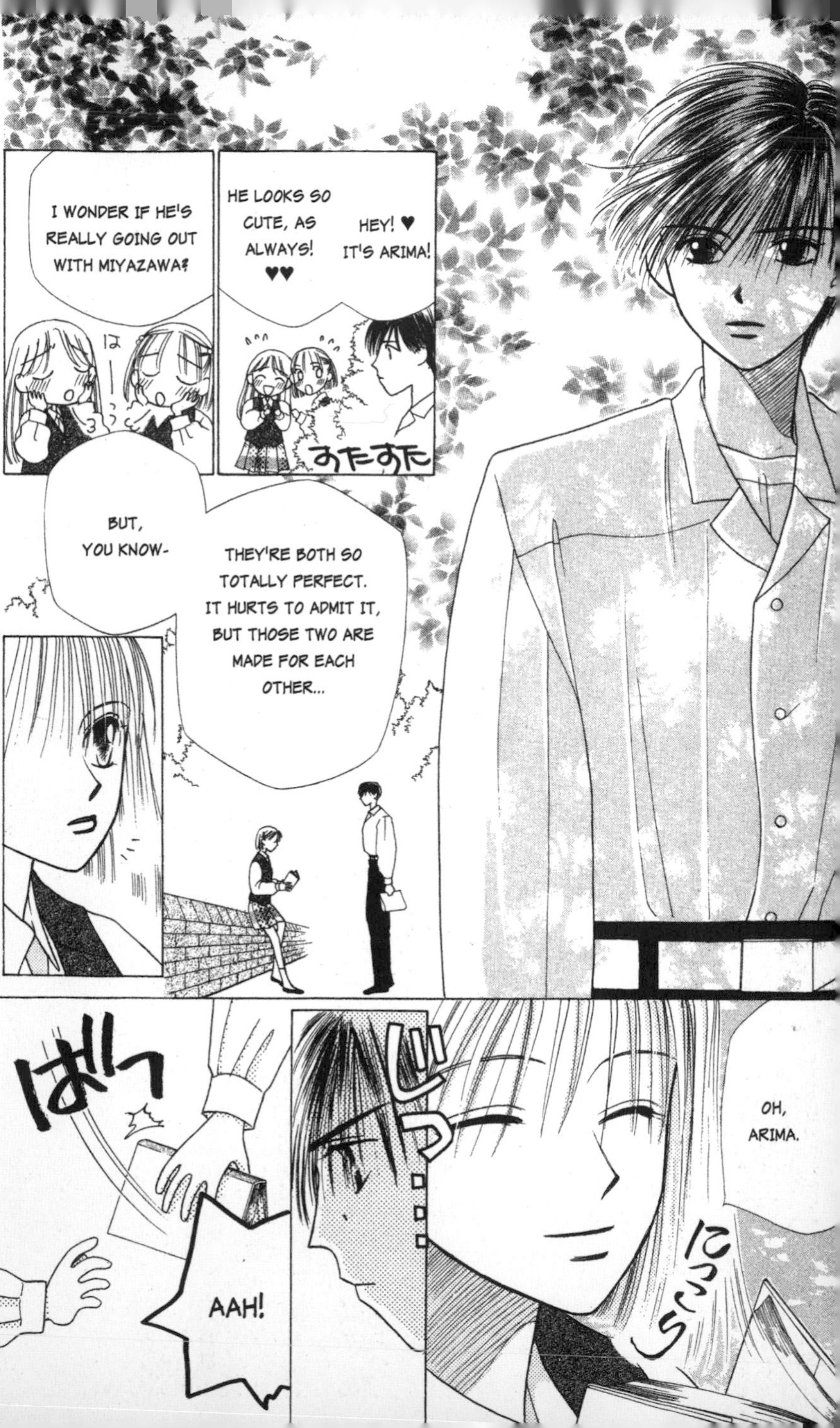
HEY! ♥ IT'S ARIMA!
HE LOOKS SO CUTE, AS ALWAYS! ♥♥
すたすた
I WONDER IF HE'S REALLY GOING OUT WITH MIYAZAWA?
は～っ
BUT, YOU KNOW-
THEY'RE BOTH SO TOTALLY PERFECT. IT HURTS TO ADMIT IT, BUT THOSE TWO ARE MADE FOR EACH OTHER...
OH, ARIMA.
にっこり
じっ
ぱっ
AAH!

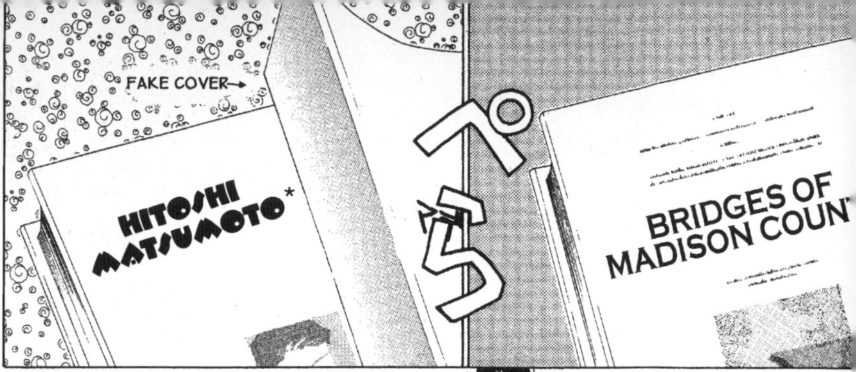
BRIDGES OF MADISON COUN
FAKE COVER→
HITOSHI MATSUMOTO*

*Hitoshi Matsumoto is a well-known comedian and humor author in Japan.

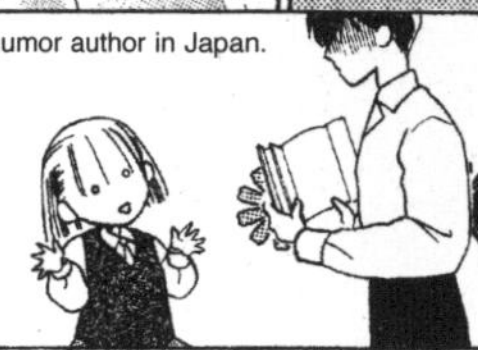

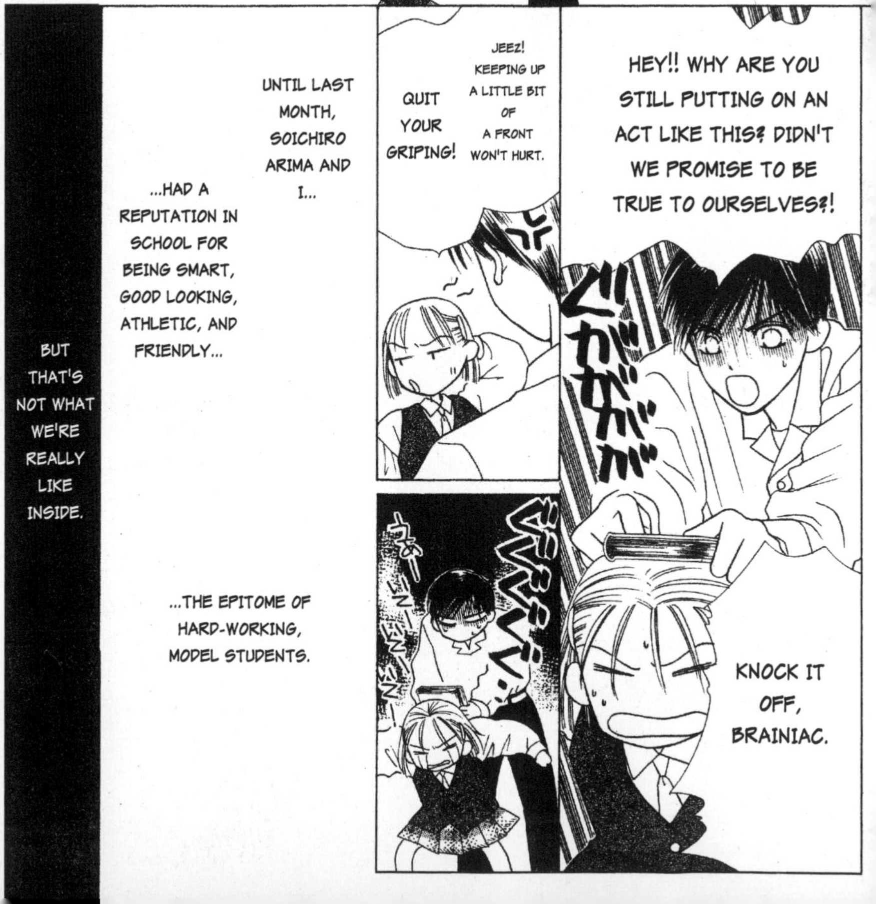
HEY!! WHY ARE YOU STILL PUTTING ON AN ACT LIKE THIS? DIDN'T WE PROMISE TO BE TRUE TO OURSELVES?!
KNOCK IT OFF, BRAINIAC.
JEEZ! KEEPING UP A LITTLE BIT OF A FRONT WON'T HURT.
QUIT YOUR GRIPING!
UNTIL LAST MONTH, SOICHIRO ARIMA AND I...
...HAD A REPUTATION IN SCHOOL FOR BEING SMART, GOOD LOOKING, ATHLETIC, AND FRIENDLY...
...THE EPITOME OF HARD-WORKING, MODEL STUDENTS.
BUT THAT'S NOT WHAT WE'RE REALLY LIKE INSIDE.

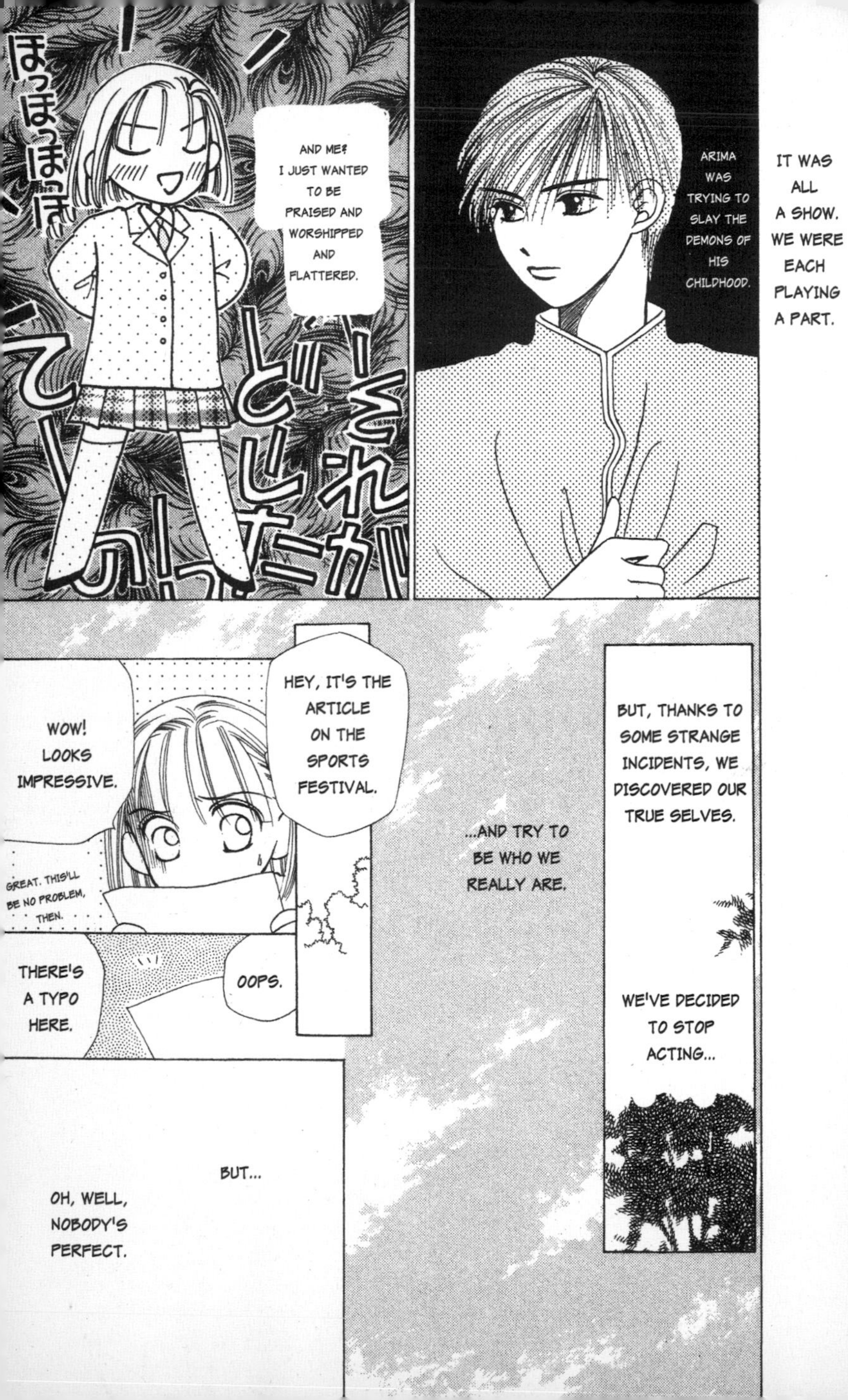
IT WAS ALL A SHOW. WE WERE EACH PLAYING A PART.
ARIMA WAS TRYING TO SLAY THE DEMONS OF HIS CHILDHOOD.
AND ME? I JUST WANTED TO BE PRAISED AND WORSHIPPED AND FLATTERED.
BUT, THANKS TO SOME STRANGE INCIDENTS, WE DISCOVERED OUR TRUE SELVES.
WE'VE DECIDED TO STOP ACTING...
...AND TRY TO BE WHO WE REALLY ARE.
HEY, IT'S THE ARTICLE ON THE SPORTS FESTIVAL.
WOW! LOOKS IMPRESSIVE.
GREAT. THIS'LL BE NO PROBLEM, THEN.
OOPS.
THERE'S A TYPO HERE.
BUT...
OH, WELL, NOBODY'S PERFECT.

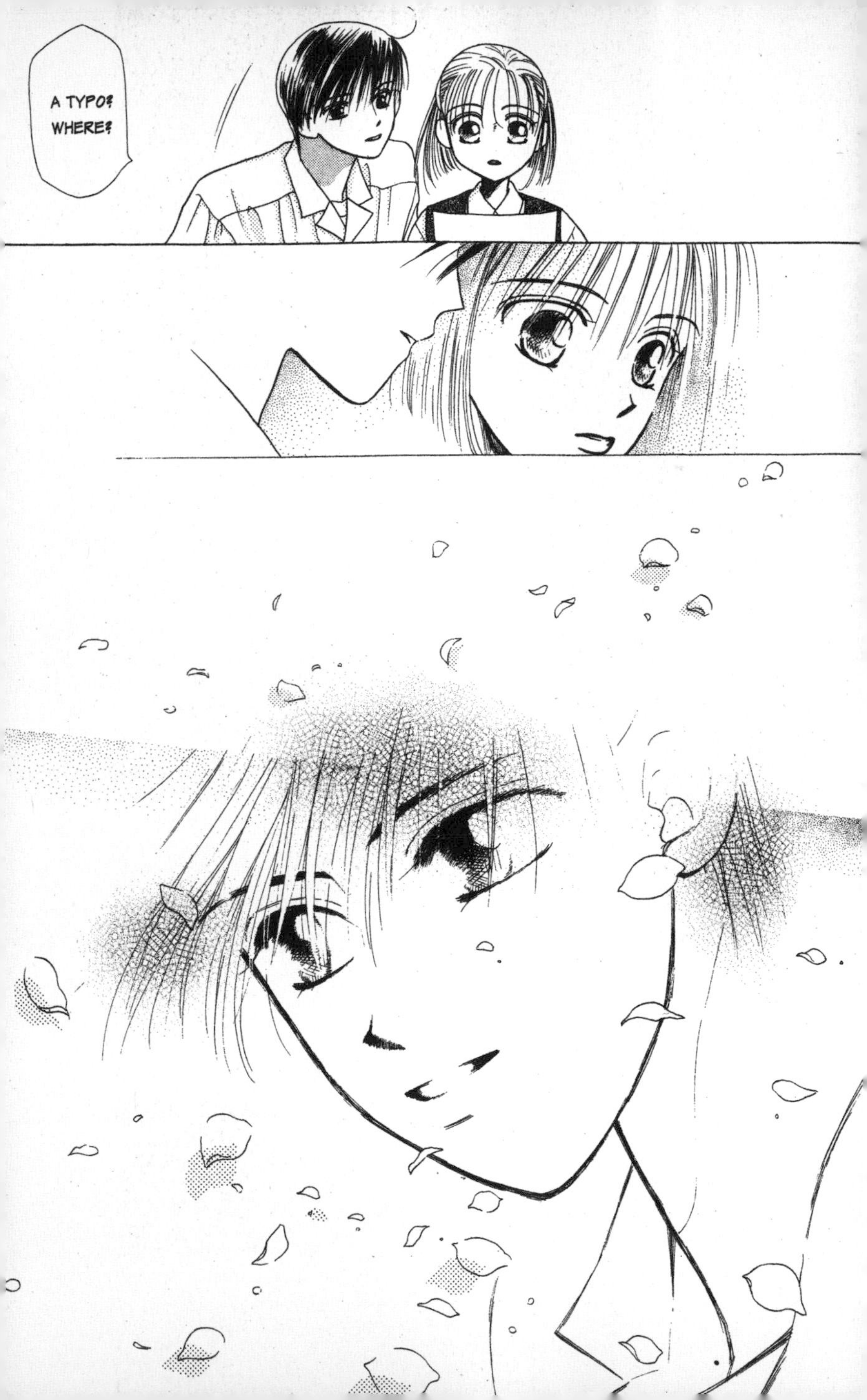
A TYPO? WHERE?

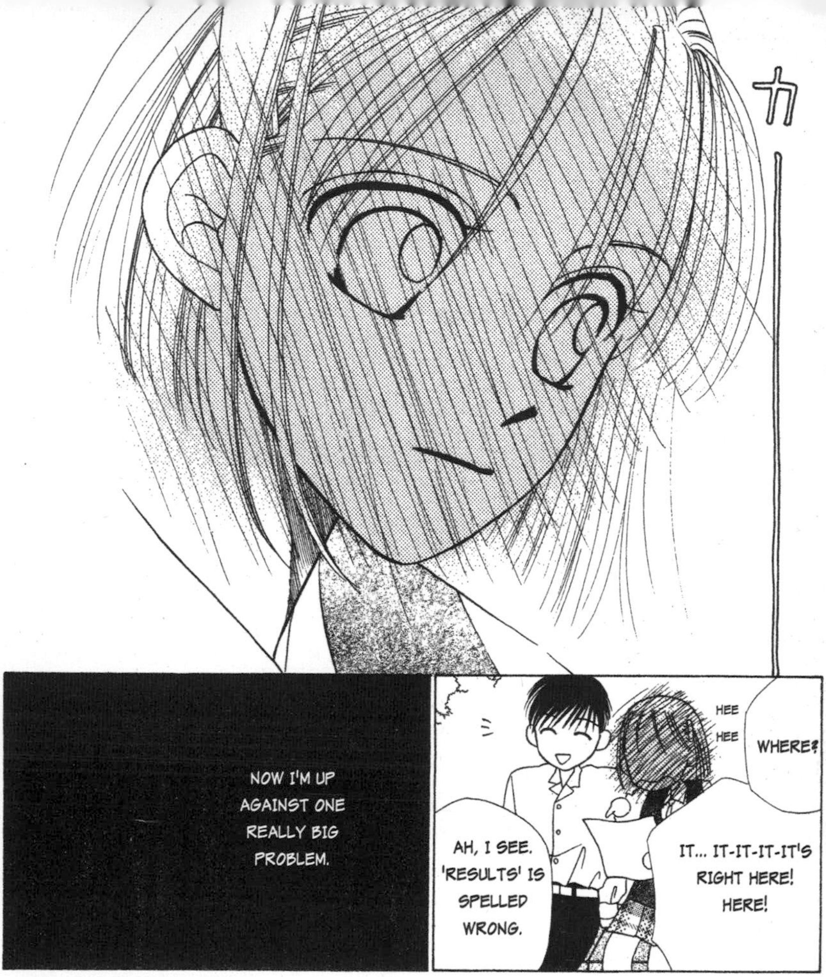
カー
WHERE?
HEE HEE
IT... IT-IT-IT-IT'S RIGHT HERE! HERE!
AH, I SEE. 'RESULTS' IS SPELLED WRONG.
NOW I'M UP AGAINST ONE REALLY BIG PROBLEM.

WE STILL HAVEN'T GONE ON AN OFFICIAL DATE.

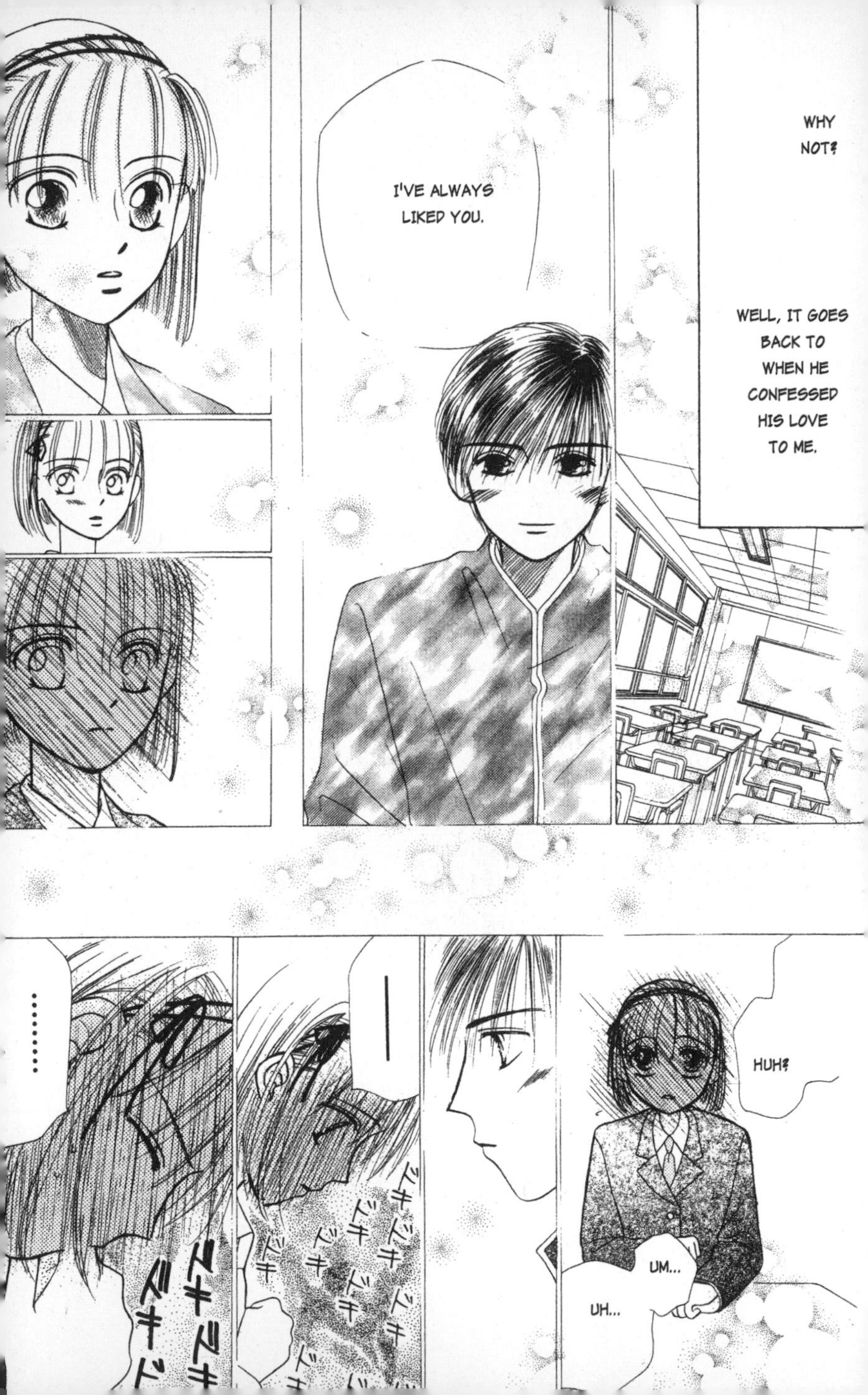
WHY NOT?
WELL, IT GOES BACK TO WHEN HE CONFESSED HIS LOVE TO ME.
I'VE ALWAYS LIKED YOU.
HUH?
UM...
UH...
—
....

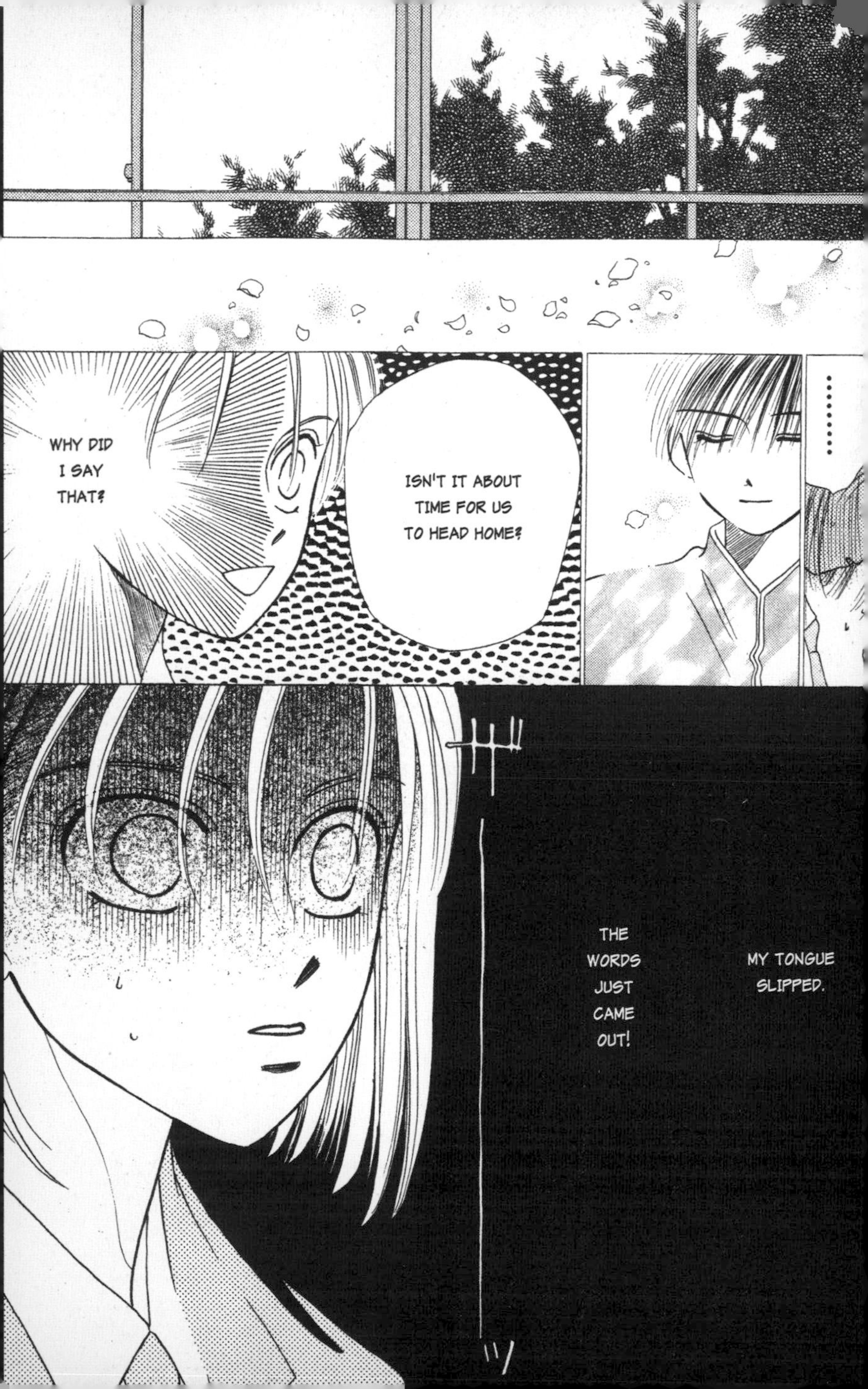
....
ISN'T IT ABOUT TIME FOR US TO HEAD HOME?
WHY DID I SAY THAT?
MY TONGUE SLIPPED.
THE WORDS JUST CAME OUT!

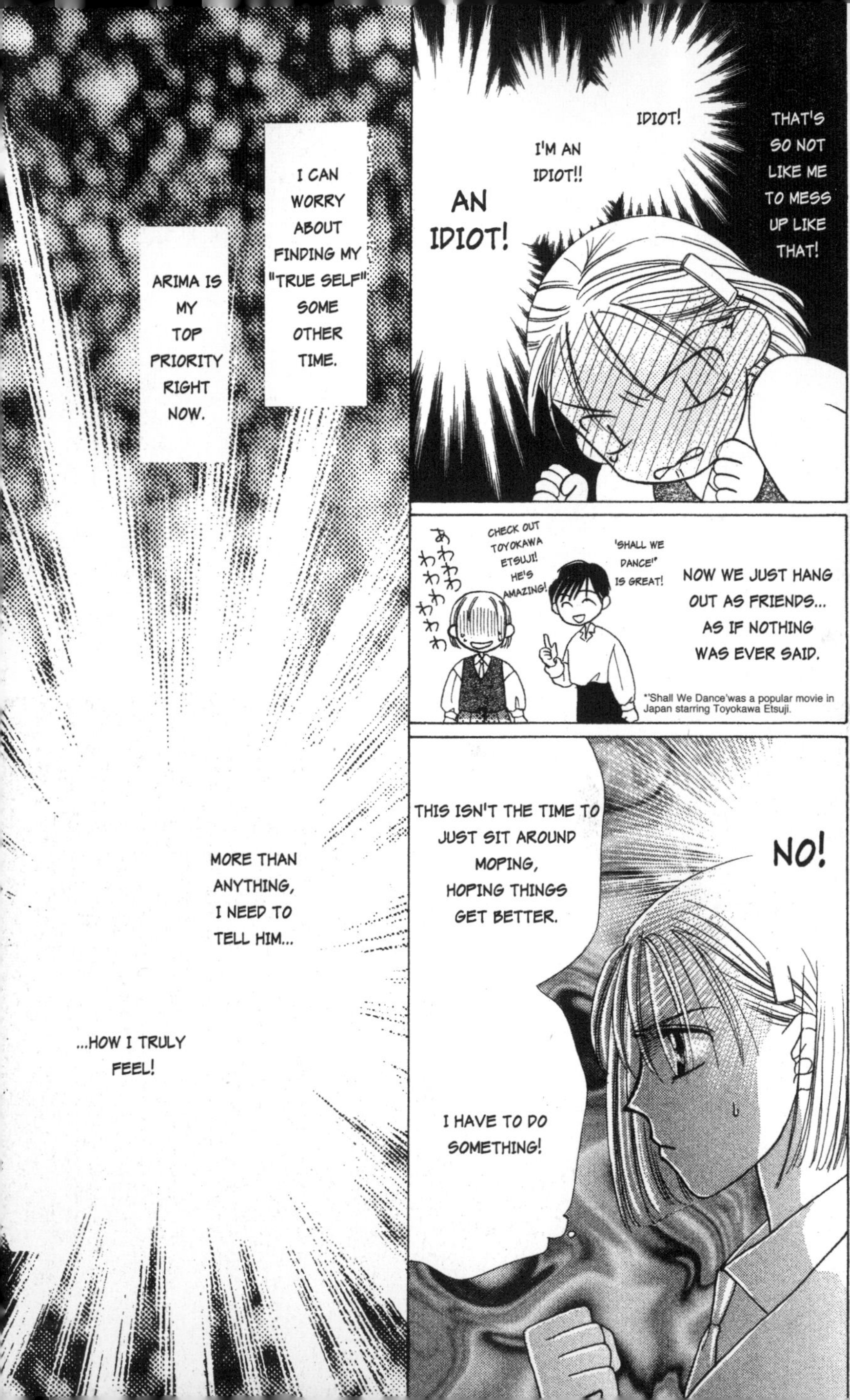

THAT'S SO NOT LIKE ME TO MESS UP LIKE THAT!
IDIOT!
I'M AN IDIOT!!
AN IDIOT!
NOW WE JUST HANG OUT AS FRIENDS... AS IF NOTHING WAS EVER SAID.
'SHALL WE DANCE!' IS GREAT!
CHECK OUT TOYOKAWA ETSUJI! HE'S AMAZING!
*'Shall We Dance'was a popular movie in Japan starring Toyokawa Etsuji.
NO!
THIS ISN'T THE TIME TO JUST SIT AROUND MOPING, HOPING THINGS GET BETTER.
I HAVE TO DO SOMETHING!
I CAN WORRY ABOUT FINDING MY "TRUE SELF" SOME OTHER TIME.
ARIMA IS MY TOP PRIORITY RIGHT NOW.
MORE THAN ANYTHING, I NEED TO TELL HIM...
...HOW I TRULY FEEL!

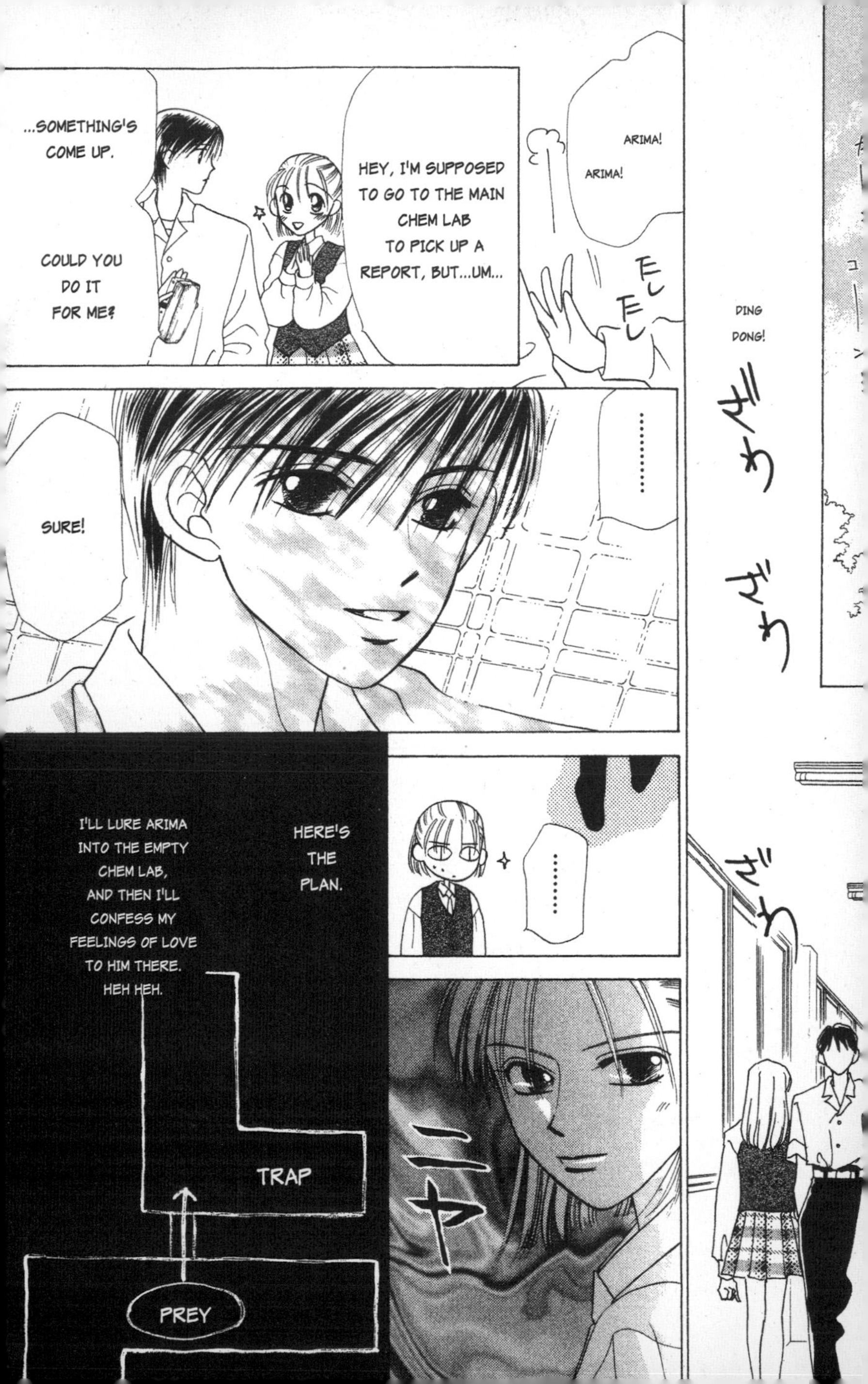
DING DONG!
ざわ
ざわ
ARIMA! ARIMA!
テレ テレ
HEY, I'M SUPPOSED TO GO TO THE MAIN CHEM LAB TO PICK UP A REPORT, BUT...UM...
...SOMETHING'S COME UP.
COULD YOU DO IT FOR ME?
......
SURE!
ざわ
......
ニヤ
HERE'S THE PLAN.
I'LL LURE ARIMA INTO THE EMPTY CHEM LAB, AND THEN I'LL CONFESS MY FEELINGS OF LOVE TO HIM THERE. HEH HEH.
TRAP
PREY

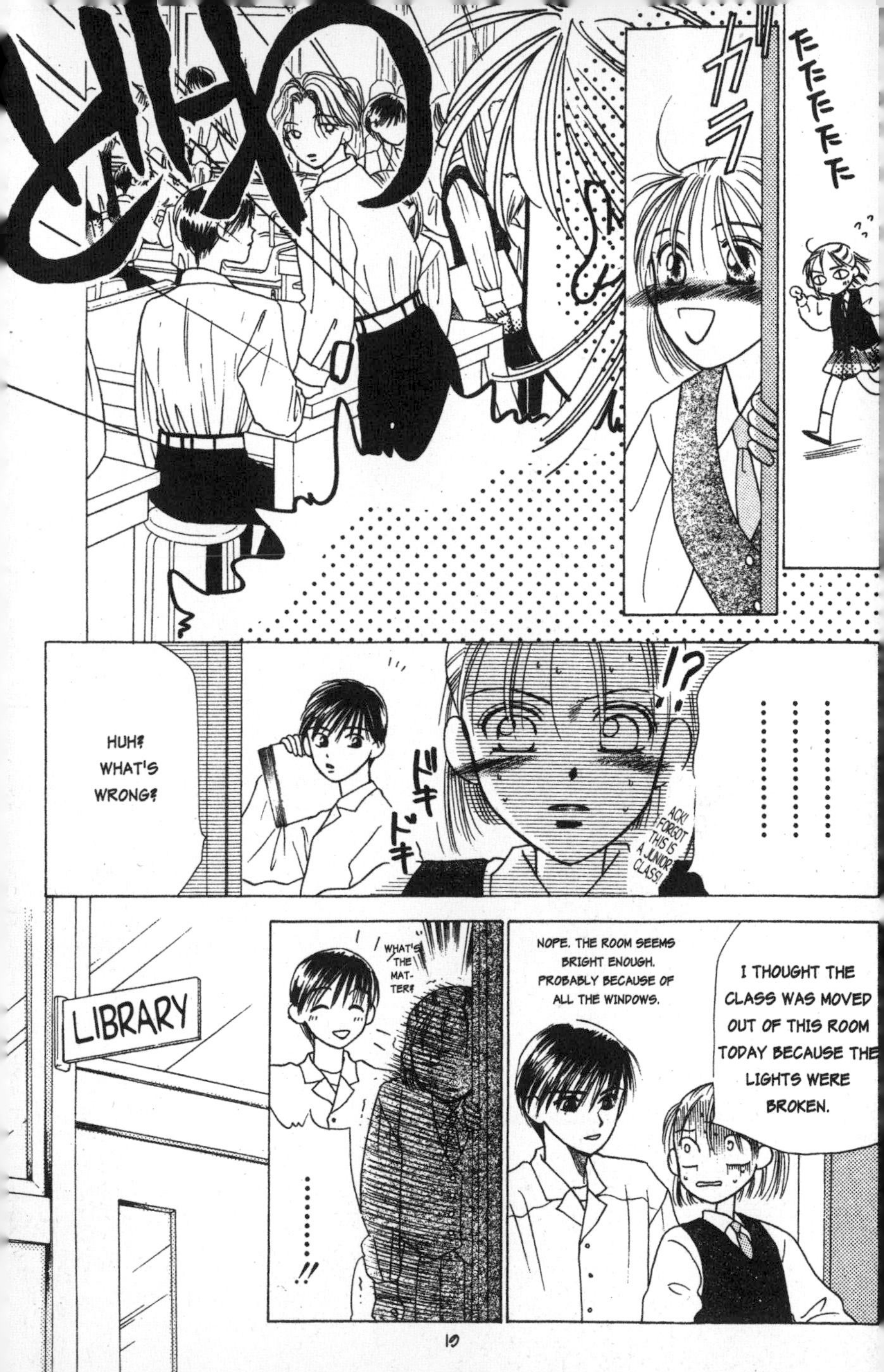
ガラ
......
!?
ACK! I FORGOT THIS IS A JUNIOR CLASS!
ドキ ドキ
HUH? WHAT'S WRONG?
I THOUGHT THE CLASS WAS MOVED OUT OF THIS ROOM TODAY BECAUSE THE LIGHTS WERE BROKEN.
NOPE. THE ROOM SEEMS BRIGHT ENOUGH. PROBABLY BECAUSE OF ALL THE WINDOWS.
WHAT'S THE MAT-TER?
......!!
LIBRARY

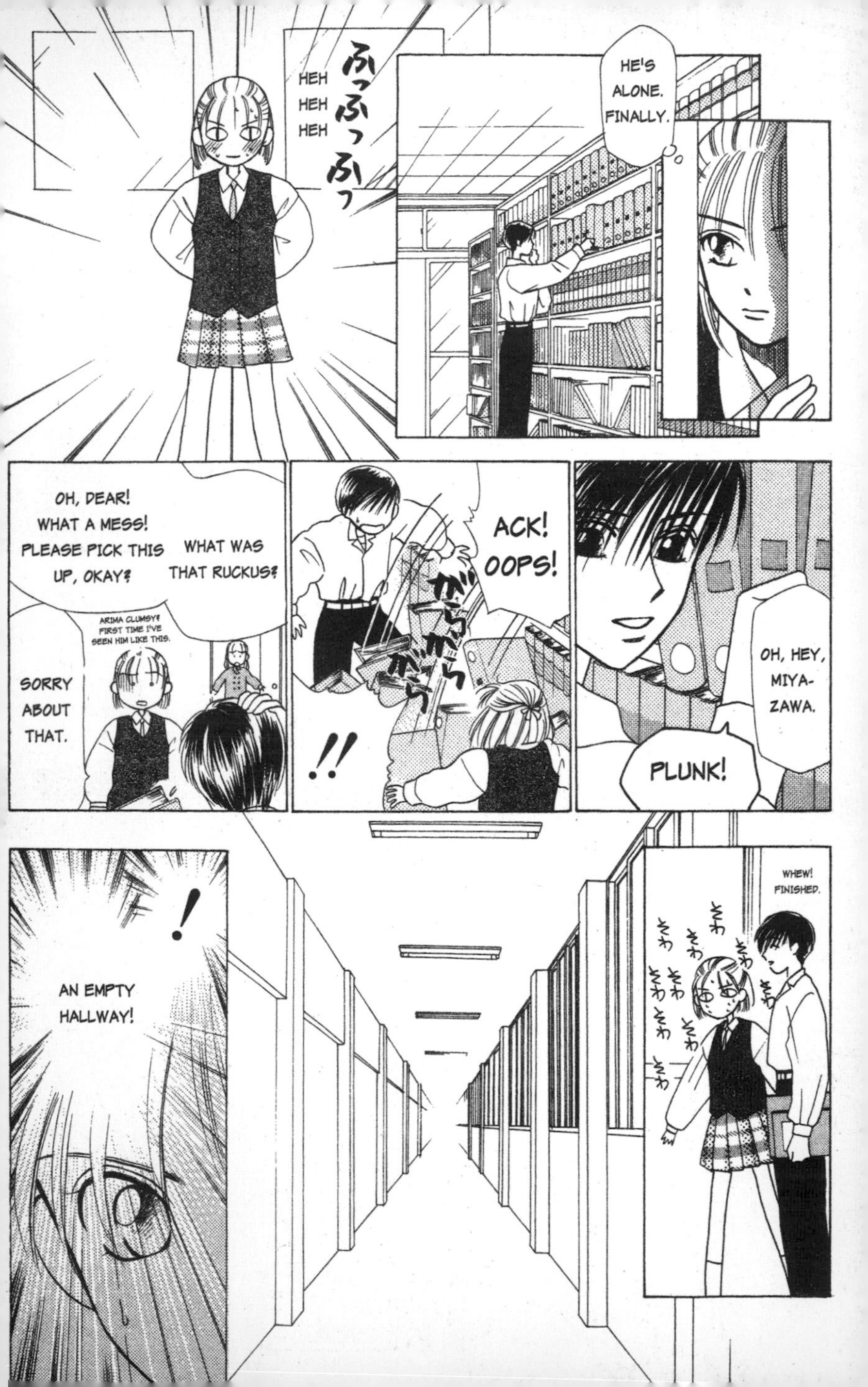

HE'S ALONE. FINALLY.
HEH HEH HEH
ふっふっふっ
OH, HEY, MIYA-ZAWA.
PLUNK!
ACK! OOPS!
がらがらがら
!!
WHAT WAS THAT RUCKUS?
OH, DEAR! WHAT A MESS! PLEASE PICK THIS UP, OKAY?
ARIMA CLUMSY? FIRST TIME I'VE SEEN HIM LIKE THIS.
SORRY ABOUT THAT.
WHEW! FINISHED.
そわそわそわそわそわそわそわそわ
!
AN EMPTY HALLWAY!

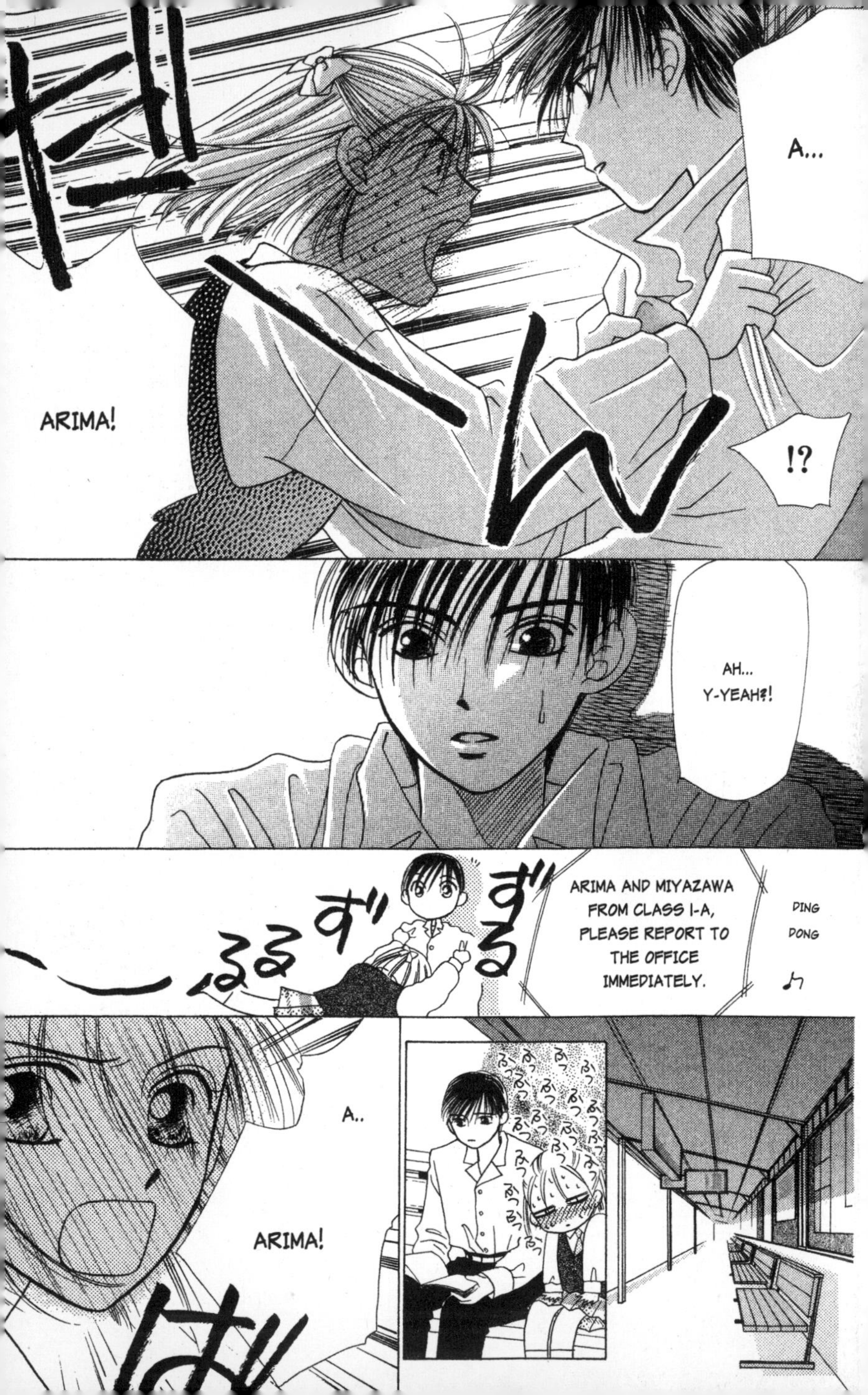
A...
!?
ARIMA!
AH... Y-YEAH?!
DING DONG ♪
ARIMA AND MIYAZAWA FROM CLASS I-A, PLEASE REPORT TO THE OFFICE IMMEDIATELY.
A..
ARIMA!

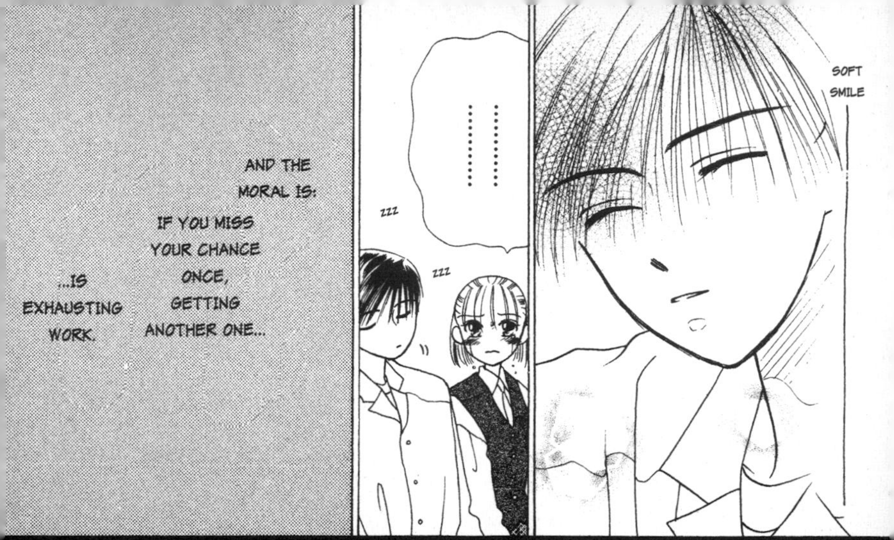
SOFT SMILE
......
ZZZ
ZZZ
AND THE MORAL IS:
IF YOU MISS YOUR CHANCE ONCE, GETTING ANOTHER ONE...
...IS EXHAUSTING WORK.

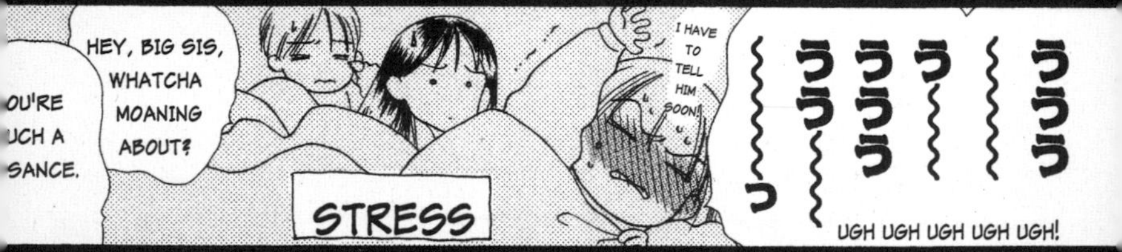
UGH UGH UGH UGH UGH!
I HAVE TO TELL HIM SOON!
STRESS
HEY, BIG SIS, WHATCHA MOANING ABOUT?
OU'RE UCH A SANCE.

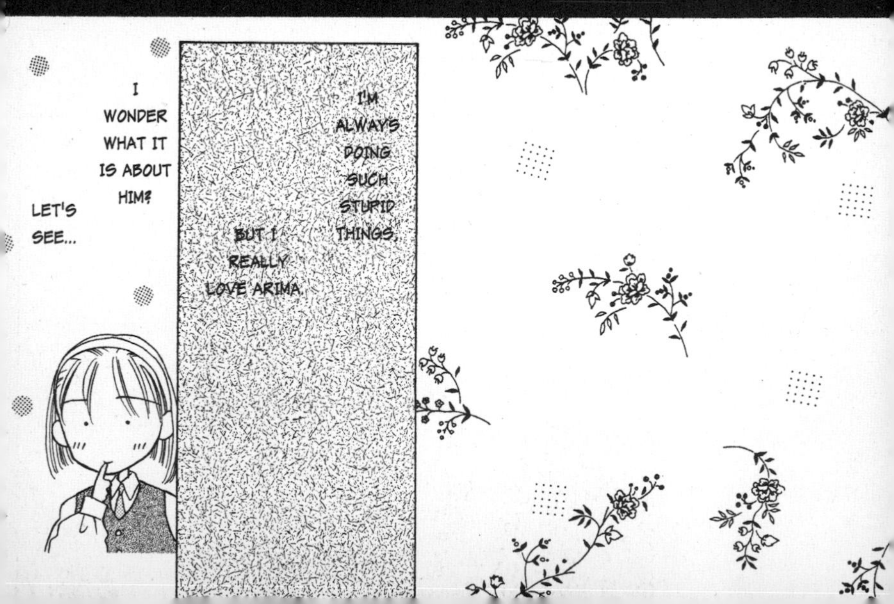
I'M ALWAYS DOING SUCH STUPID THINGS,
BUT I REALLY LOVE ARIMA.
I WONDER WHAT IT IS ABOUT HIM?
LET'S SEE...

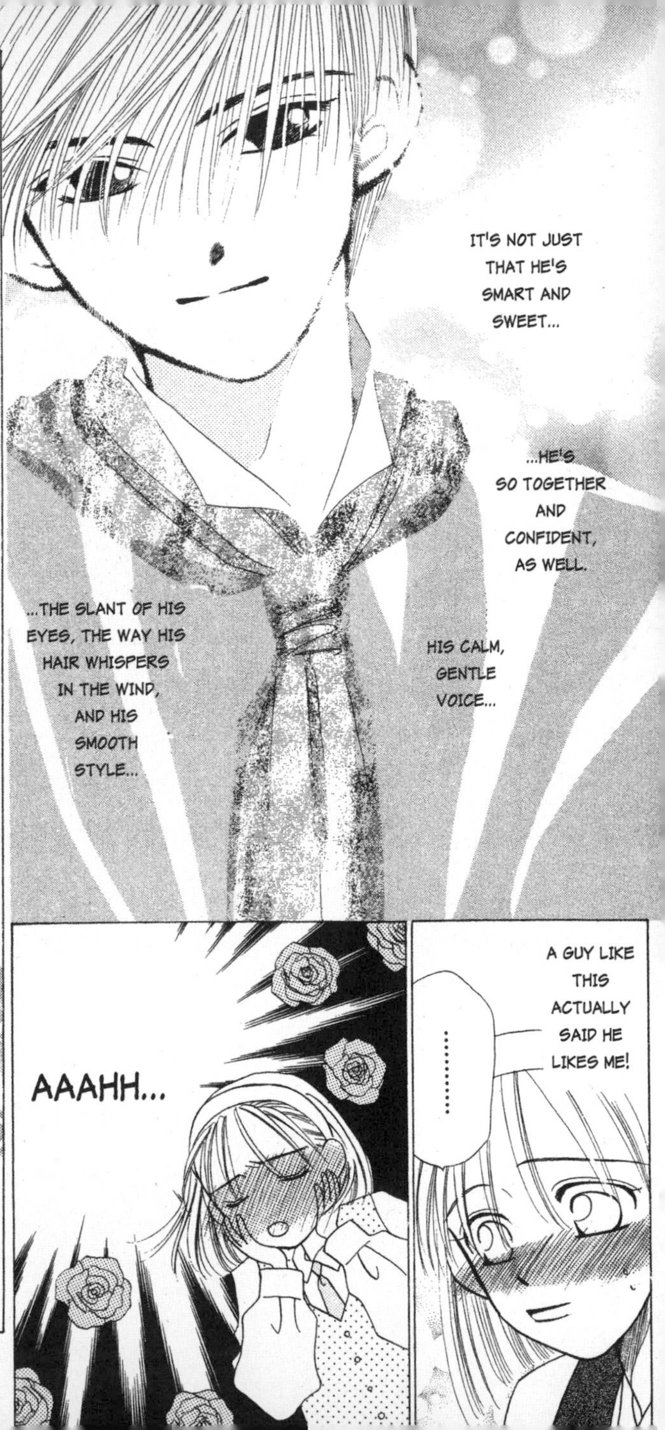
IT'S NOT JUST THAT HE'S SMART AND SWEET...
...HE'S SO TOGETHER AND CONFIDENT, AS WELL.
HIS CALM, GENTLE VOICE...
...THE SLANT OF HIS EYES, THE WAY HIS HAIR WHISPERS IN THE WIND, AND HIS SMOOTH STYLE...
A GUY LIKE THIS ACTUALLY SAID HE LIKES ME!
....
AAAHH...

1

Hello. This is my fifth comic. But this is the first time one has reached the "second volume."

SECOND VOLUME!!!!

Things were a bit thorny up until this point, but I'm happy now.

Yippee!

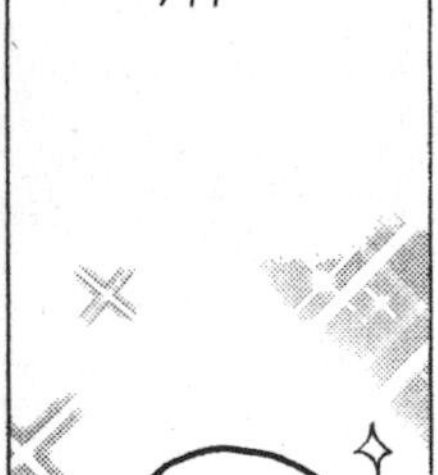

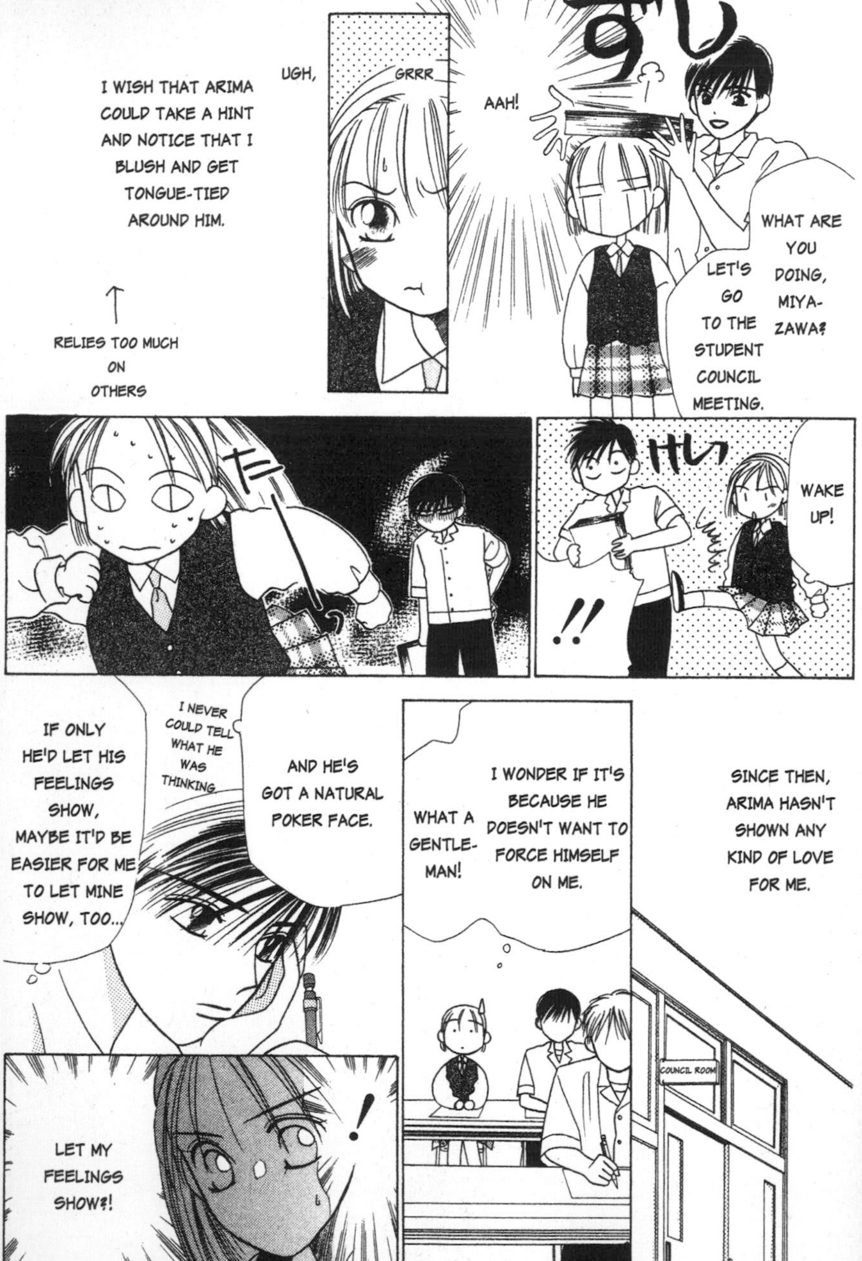
AAH!
WHAT ARE YOU DOING, MIYA-ZAWA?
LET'S GO TO THE STUDENT COUNCIL MEETING.
UGH,
GRRR
I WISH THAT ARIMA COULD TAKE A HINT AND NOTICE THAT I BLUSH AND GET TONGUE-TIED AROUND HIM.
RELIES TOO MUCH ON OTHERS
WAKE UP!
!!
SINCE THEN, ARIMA HASN'T SHOWN ANY KIND OF LOVE FOR ME.
I WONDER IF IT'S BECAUSE HE DOESN'T WANT TO FORCE HIMSELF ON ME.
WHAT A GENTLE-MAN!
COUNCIL ROOM
AND HE'S GOT A NATURAL POKER FACE.
I NEVER COULD TELL WHAT HE WAS THINKING
IF ONLY HE'D LET HIS FEELINGS SHOW, MAYBE IT'D BE EASIER FOR ME TO LET MINE SHOW, TOO...
!
LET MY FEELINGS SHOW?!

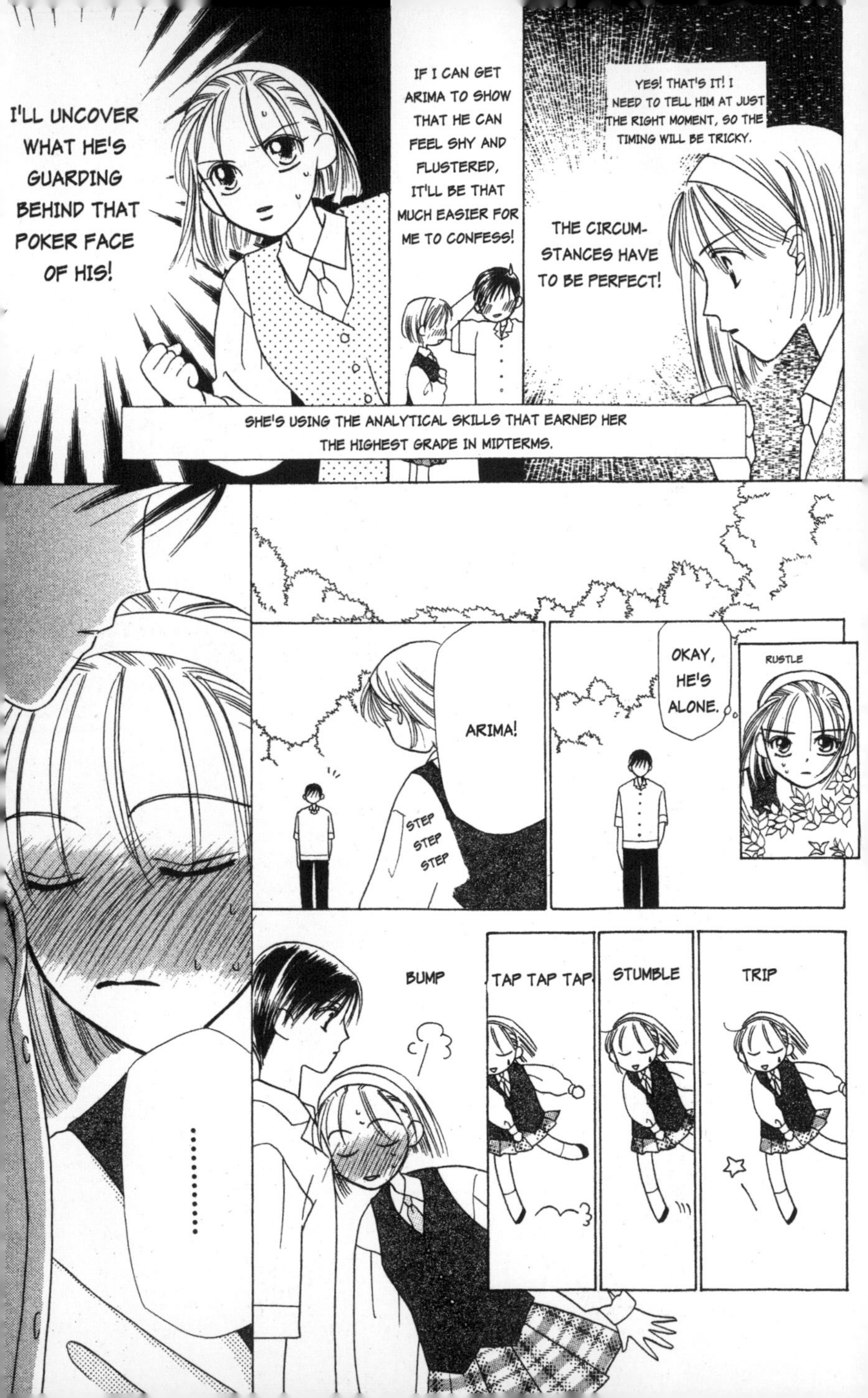
YES! THAT'S IT! I NEED TO TELL HIM AT JUST THE RIGHT MOMENT, SO THE TIMING WILL BE TRICKY.
THE CIRCUMSTANCES HAVE TO BE PERFECT!
IF I CAN GET ARIMA TO SHOW THAT HE CAN FEEL SHY AND FLUSTERED, IT'LL BE THAT MUCH EASIER FOR ME TO CONFESS!
I'LL UNCOVER WHAT HE'S GUARDING BEHIND THAT POKER FACE OF HIS!
SHE'S USING THE ANALYTICAL SKILLS THAT EARNED HER THE HIGHEST GRADE IN MIDTERMS.
RUSTLE
OKAY, HE'S ALONE.
ARIMA!
STEP STEP STEP
TRIP
STUMBLE
TAP TAP TAP
BUMP
....

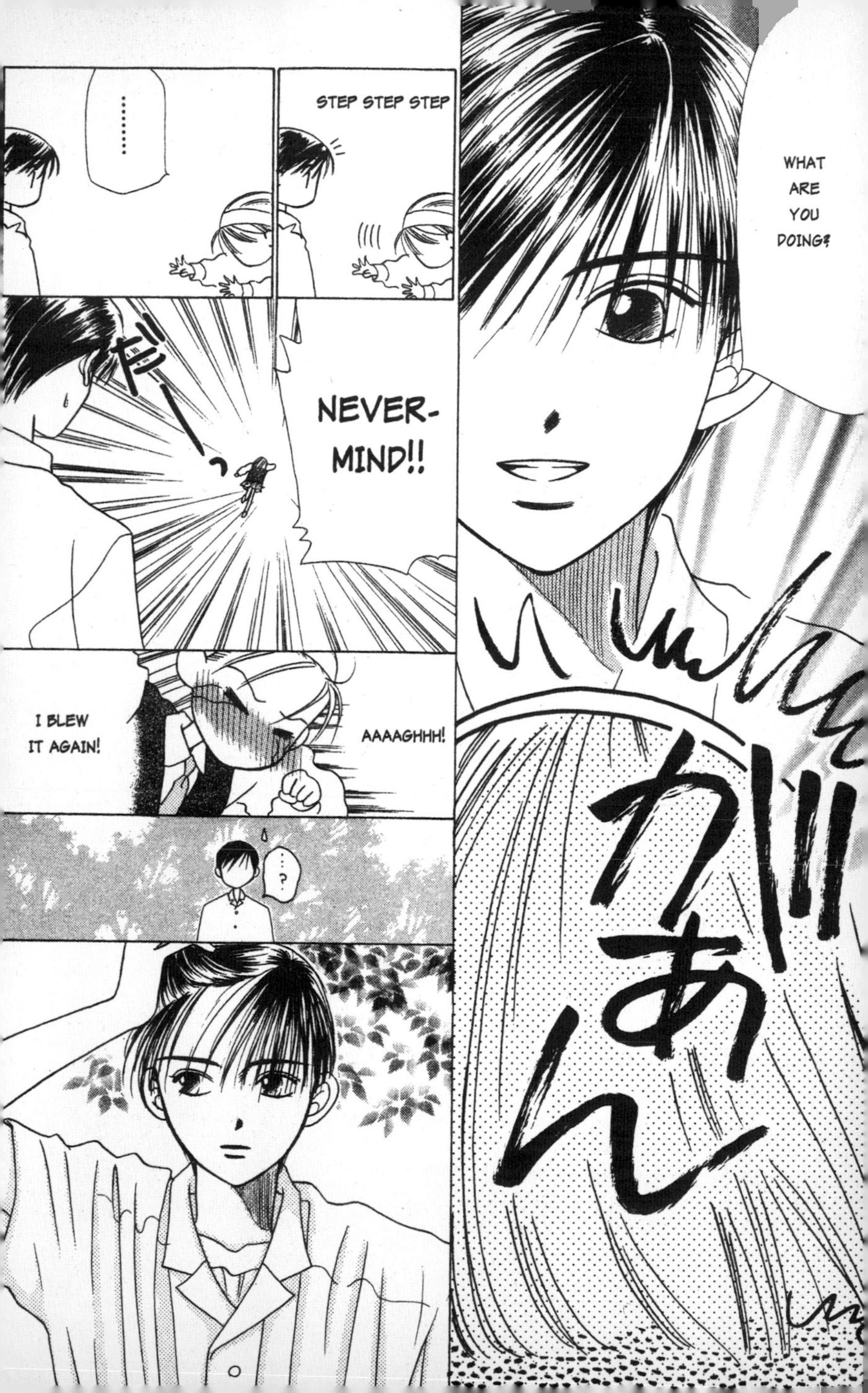
WHAT ARE YOU DOING?
STEP STEP STEP
......
NEVER-MIND!!
AAAAGHHH!
I BLEW IT AGAIN!
...?

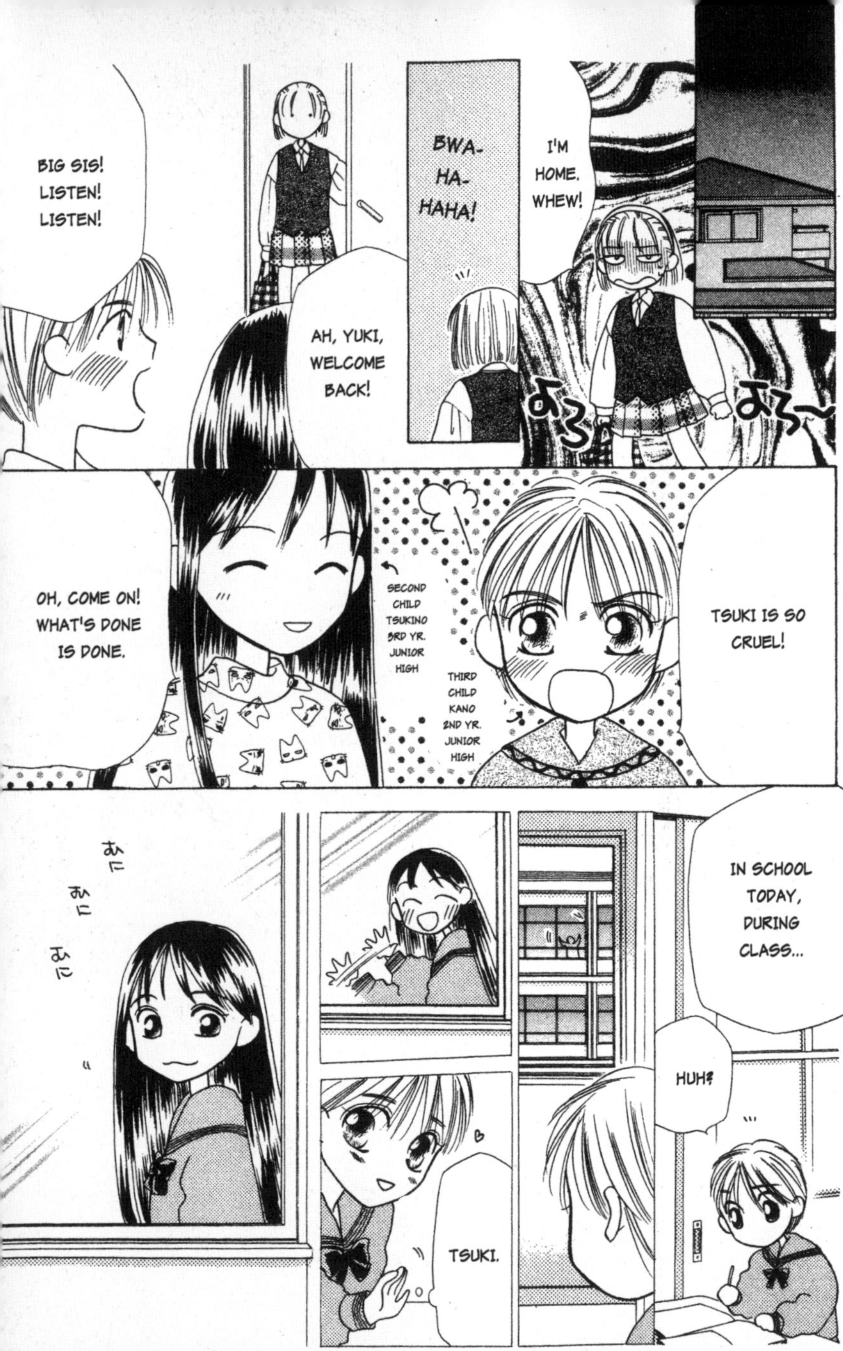

I'M HOME. WHEW!
よろ
よろ~
BWA-HA-HAHA!
AH, YUKI, WELCOME BACK!
BIG SIS! LISTEN! LISTEN!
TSUKI IS SO CRUEL!
THIRD CHILD KANO 2ND YR. JUNIOR HIGH
SECOND CHILD TSUKINO 3RD YR. JUNIOR HIGH
OH, COME ON! WHAT'S DONE IS DONE.
IN SCHOOL TODAY, DURING CLASS...
HUH?
TSUKI.
むに むに むに

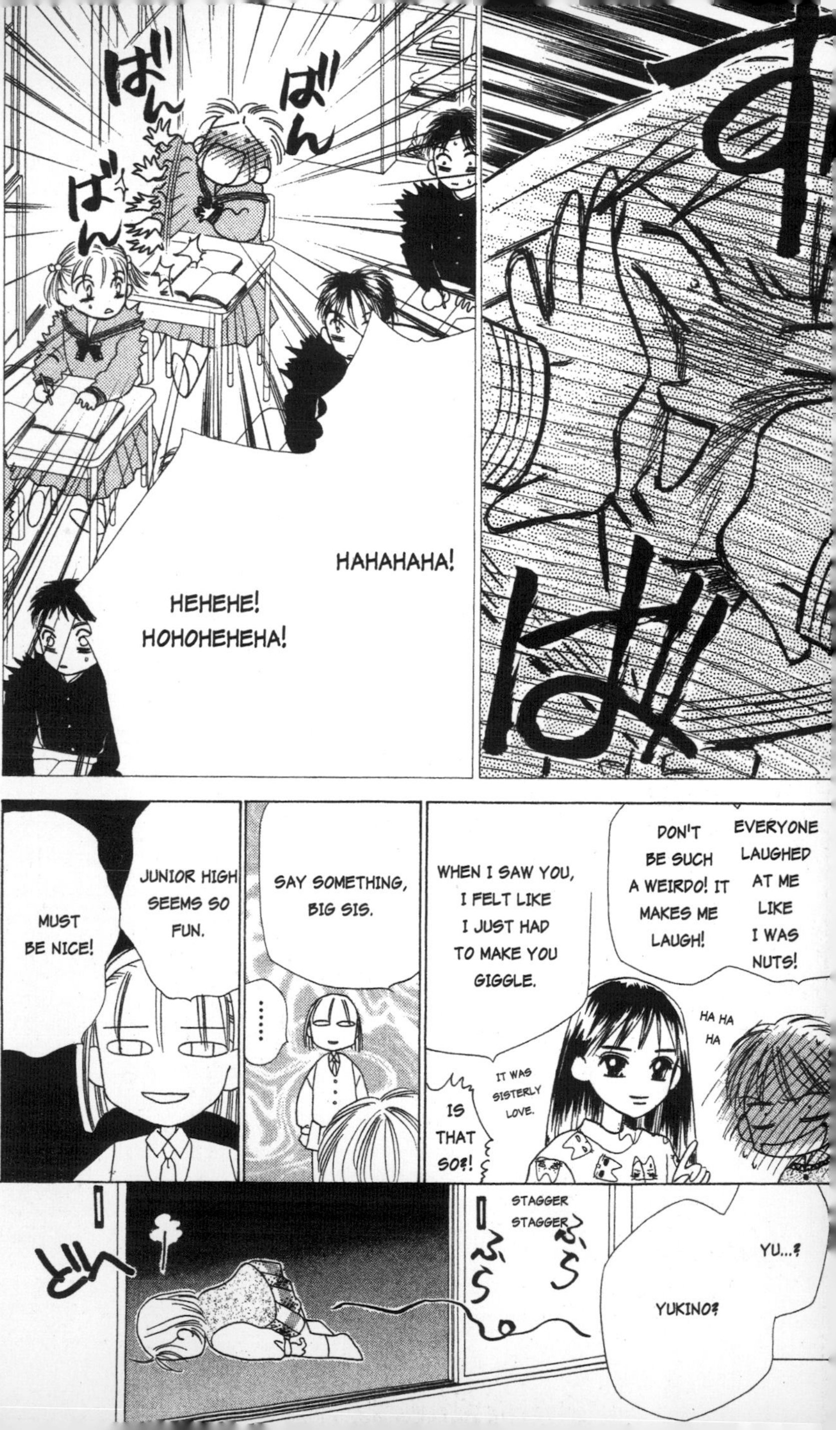
ばん
ばん
ばん
HAHAHAHA!
HEHEHE! HOHOHEHEHA!
EVERYONE LAUGHED AT ME LIKE I WAS NUTS!
DON'T BE SUCH A WEIRDO! IT MAKES ME LAUGH!
HA HA HA
WHEN I SAW YOU, I FELT LIKE I JUST HAD TO MAKE YOU GIGGLE.
IT WAS SISTERLY LOVE.
IS THAT SO?!
SAY SOMETHING, BIG SIS.
......
JUNIOR HIGH SEEMS SO FUN.
MUST BE NICE!
YU...?
YUKINO?
STAGGER STAGGER
ふら
ふら

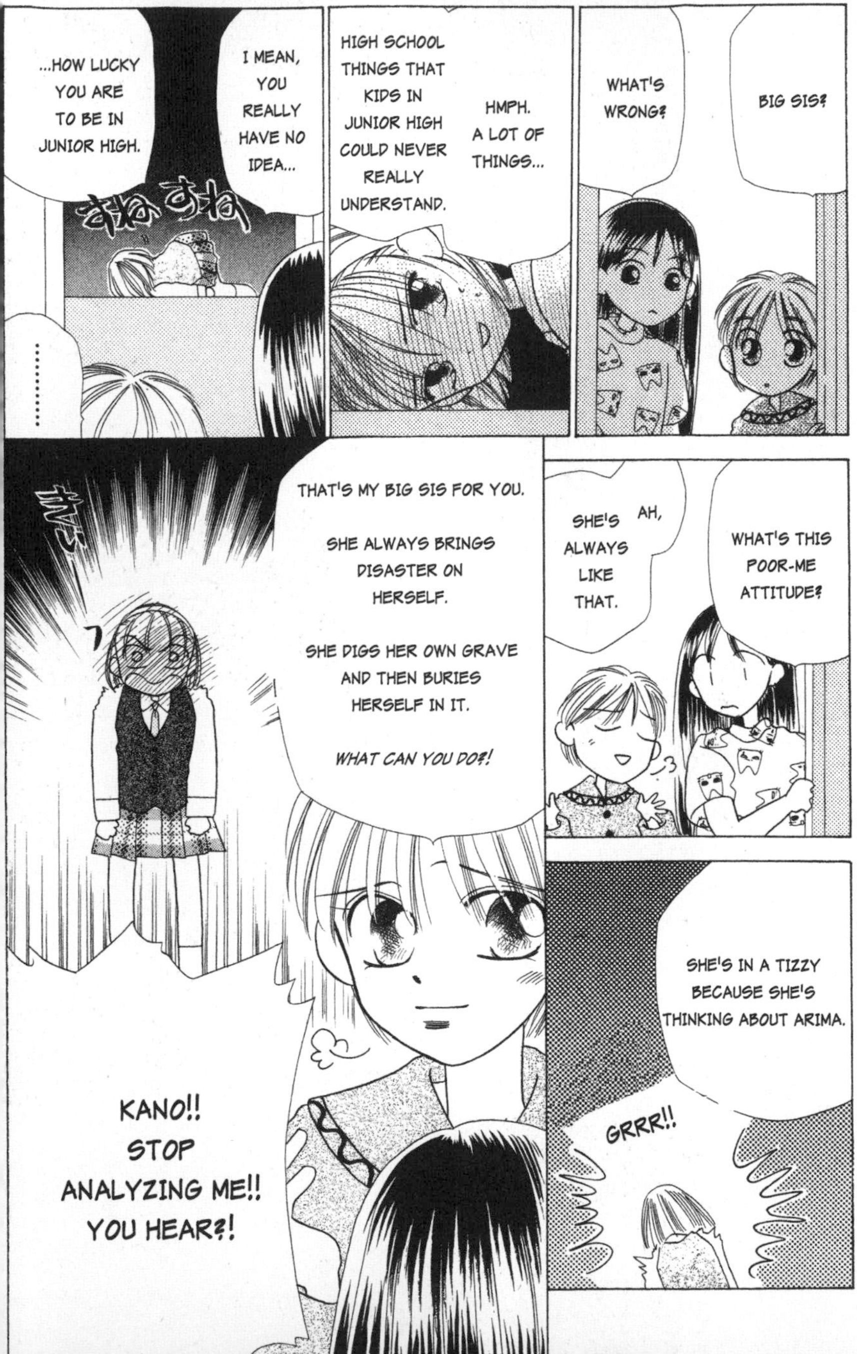
BIG SIS?
WHAT'S WRONG?
HMPH. A LOT OF THINGS...
HIGH SCHOOL THINGS THAT KIDS IN JUNIOR HIGH COULD NEVER REALLY UNDERSTAND.
I MEAN, YOU REALLY HAVE NO IDEA...
...HOW LUCKY YOU ARE TO BE IN JUNIOR HIGH.
......
WHAT'S THIS POOR-ME ATTITUDE?
AH,
SHE'S ALWAYS LIKE THAT.
SHE'S IN A TIZZY BECAUSE SHE'S THINKING ABOUT ARIMA.
GRRR!!
THAT'S MY BIG SIS FOR YOU.
SHE ALWAYS BRINGS DISASTER ON HERSELF.
SHE DIGS HER OWN GRAVE AND THEN BURIES HERSELF IN IT.
WHAT CAN YOU DO?!
KANO!! STOP ANALYZING ME!! YOU HEAR?!

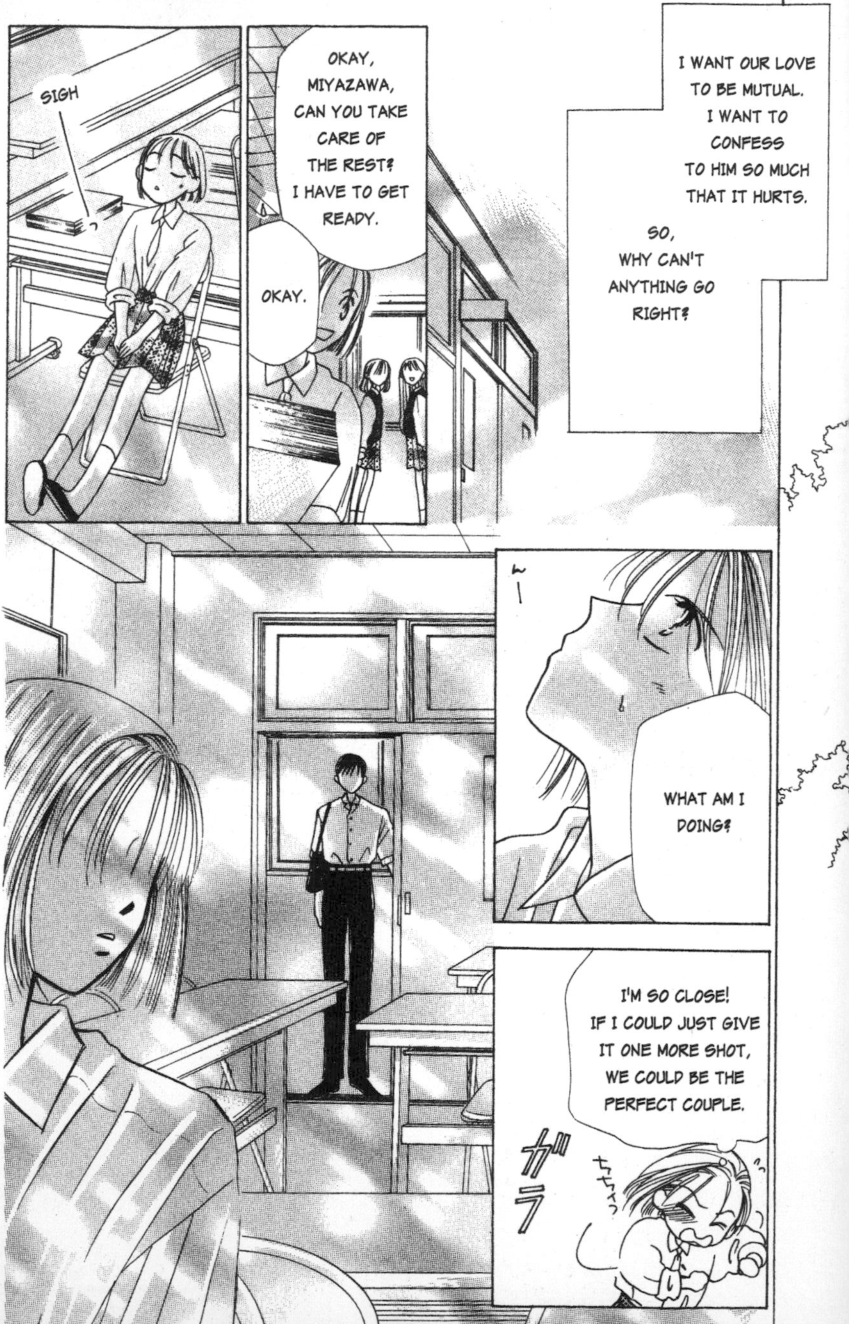
I WANT OUR LOVE TO BE MUTUAL. I WANT TO CONFESS TO HIM SO MUCH THAT IT HURTS.
SO, WHY CAN'T ANYTHING GO RIGHT?
OKAY, MIYAZAWA, CAN YOU TAKE CARE OF THE REST? I HAVE TO GET READY.
OKAY.
SIGH
WHAT AM I DOING?
I'M SO CLOSE! IF I COULD JUST GIVE IT ONE MORE SHOT, WE COULD BE THE PERFECT COUPLE.
ガラ

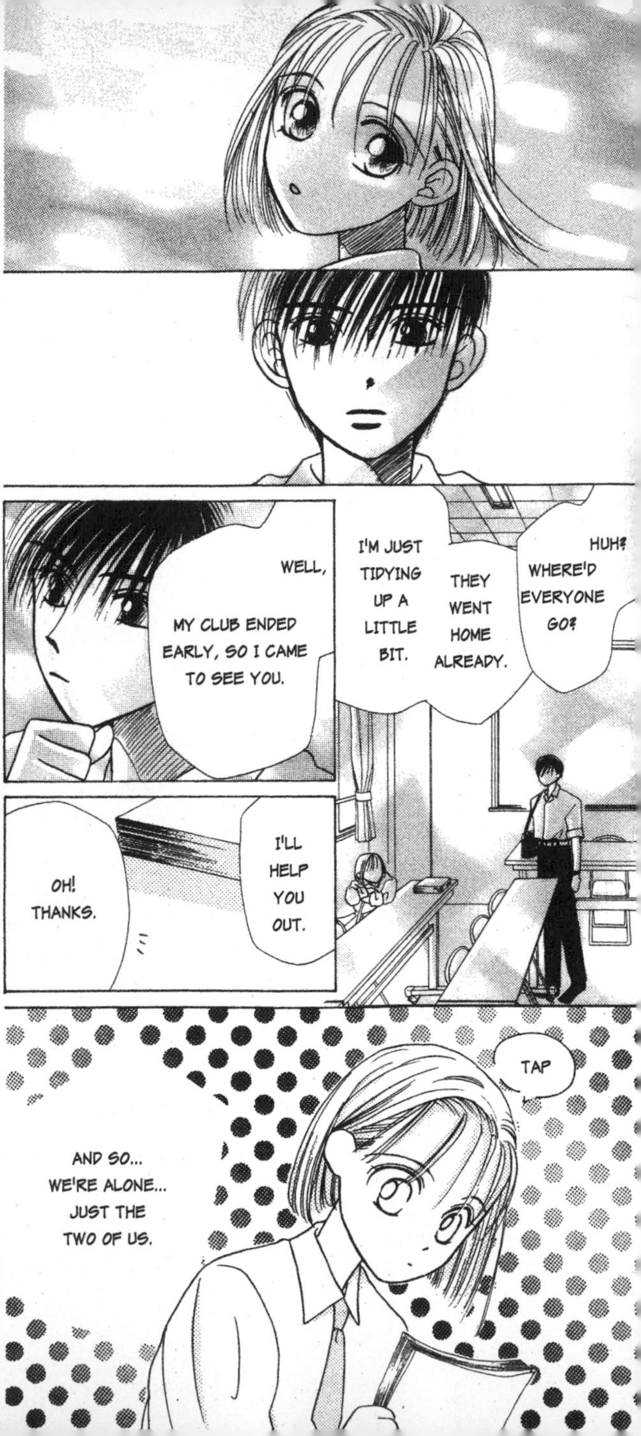
HUH? WHERE'D EVERYONE GO?
THEY WENT HOME ALREADY.
I'M JUST TIDYING UP A LITTLE BIT.
WELL, MY CLUB ENDED EARLY, SO I CAME TO SEE YOU.
I'LL HELP YOU OUT.
OH! THANKS.
TAP
AND SO... WE'RE ALONE... JUST THE TWO OF US.

2

They say that children turn out to be a lot like their parents. But can a person who's drawing a character turn out to be a lot like that character?

I'm afraid that lately I've become insanely vain and obstinate. It's her! I'm turning out to be a lot like her!!

And who would that be?

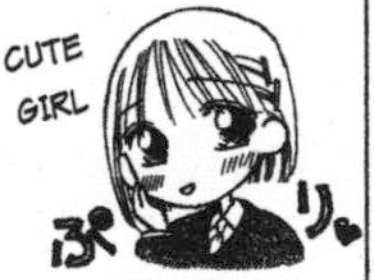
CUTE GIRL
ぷり

At first, I thought she wasn't anything like me.

Darn it. Was this part of me really hiding inside me the whole time?! Did my writing bring it out?!

Gaah! This is scary.

It's supposed to be fiction!!

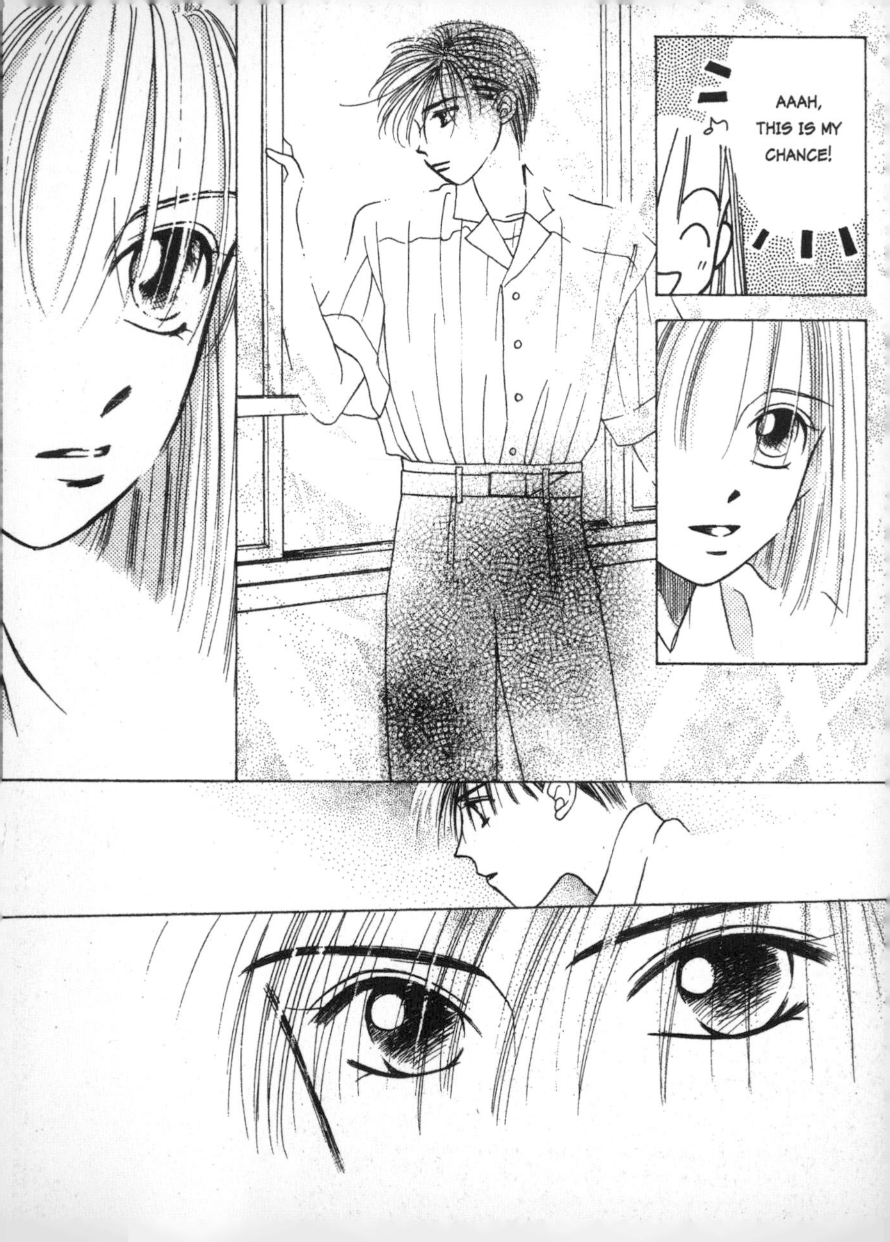
AAAH, THIS IS MY CHANCE!

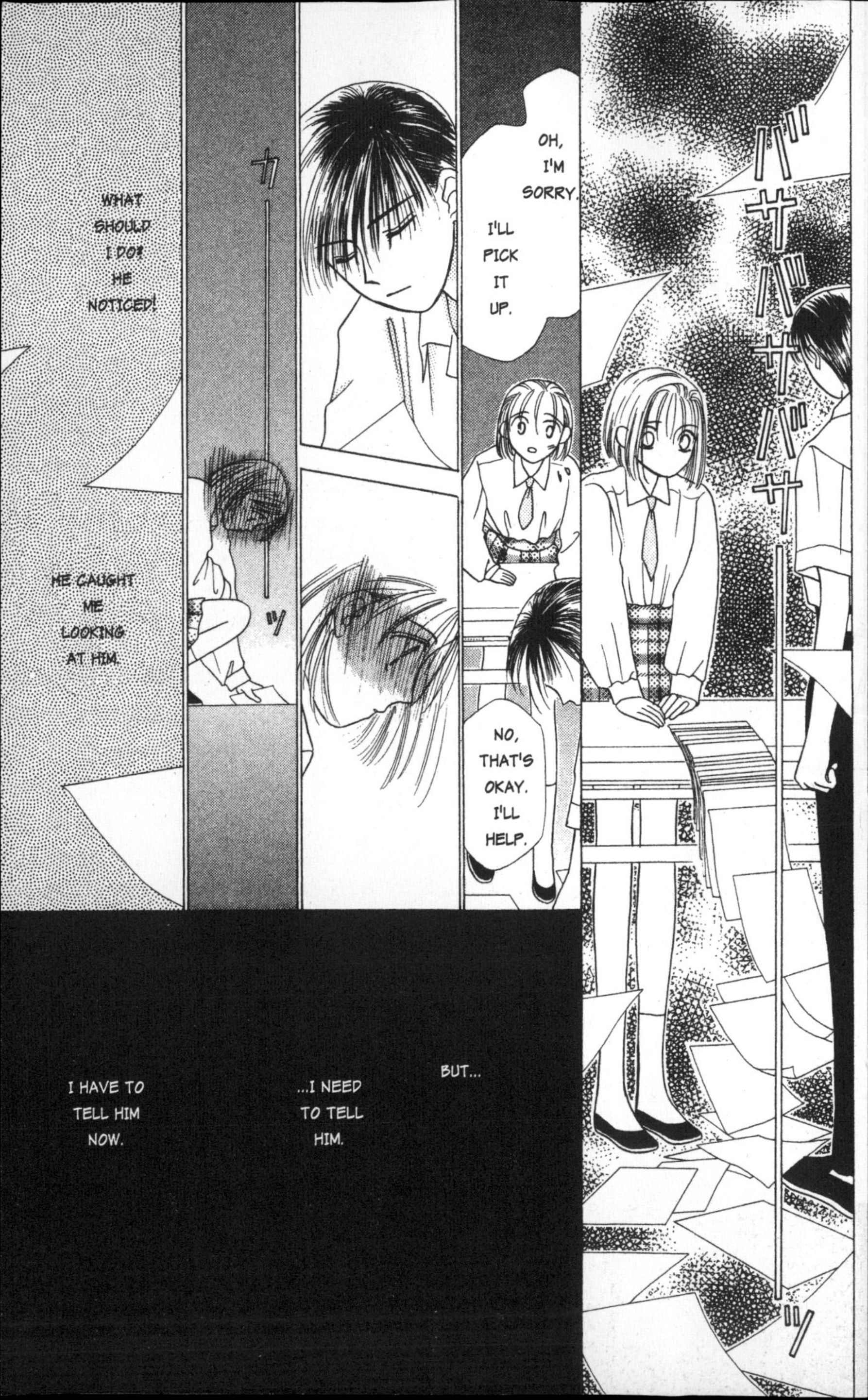
バサバサバサーッ
OH, I'M SORRY.
I'LL PICK IT UP.
NO, THAT'S OKAY. I'LL HELP.
カーッ
WHAT SHOULD I DO? HE NOTICED!
HE CAUGHT ME LOOKING AT HIM.
BUT...
...I NEED TO TELL HIM.
I HAVE TO TELL HIM NOW.

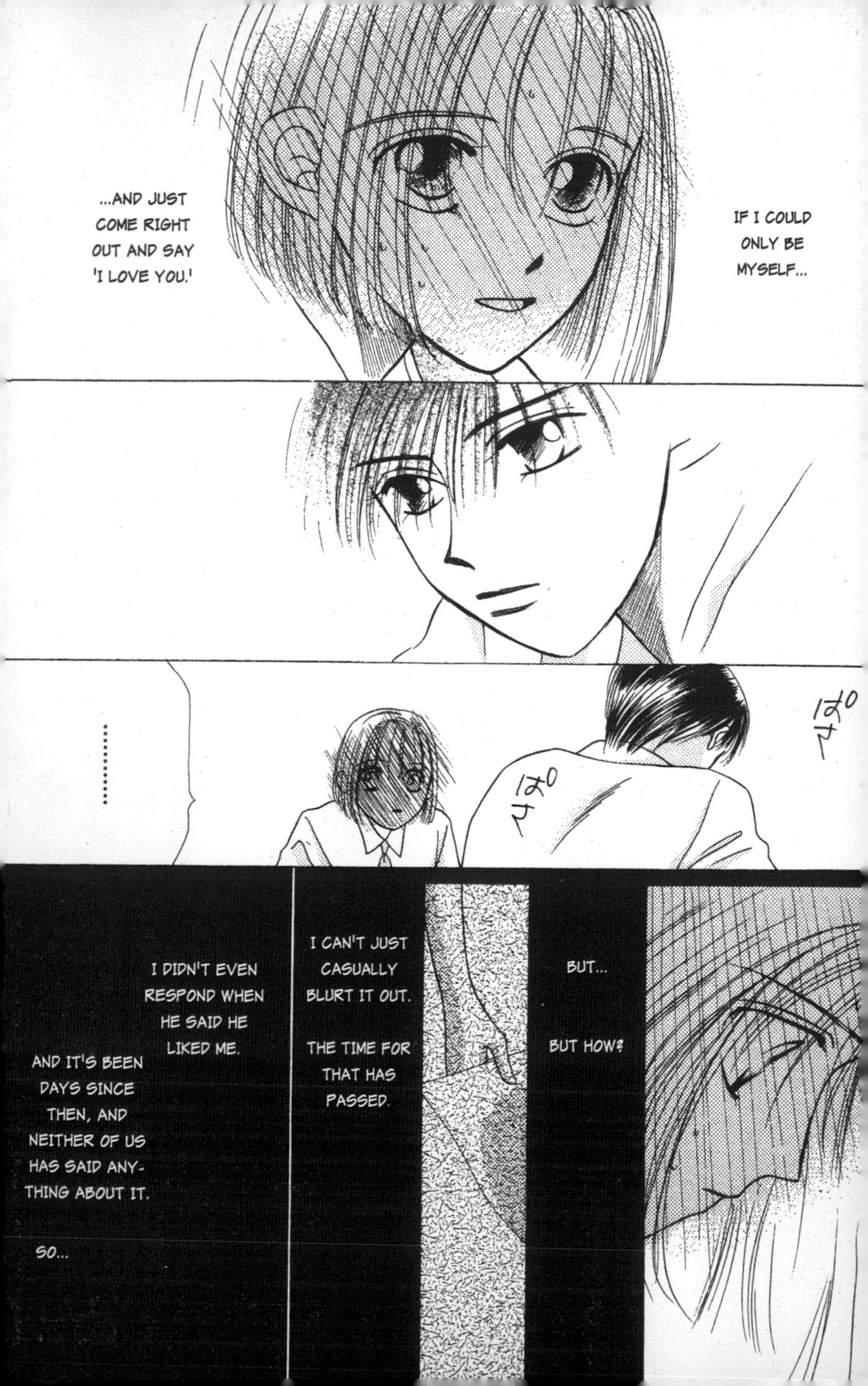
IF I COULD ONLY BE MYSELF...
...AND JUST COME RIGHT OUT AND SAY 'I LOVE YOU.'
ぱさ
ぱさ
....
BUT...
BUT HOW?
I CAN'T JUST CASUALLY BLURT IT OUT.
THE TIME FOR THAT HAS PASSED.
I DIDN'T EVEN RESPOND WHEN HE SAID HE LIKED ME.
AND IT'S BEEN DAYS SINCE THEN, AND NEITHER OF US HAS SAID ANY-THING ABOUT IT.
SO...

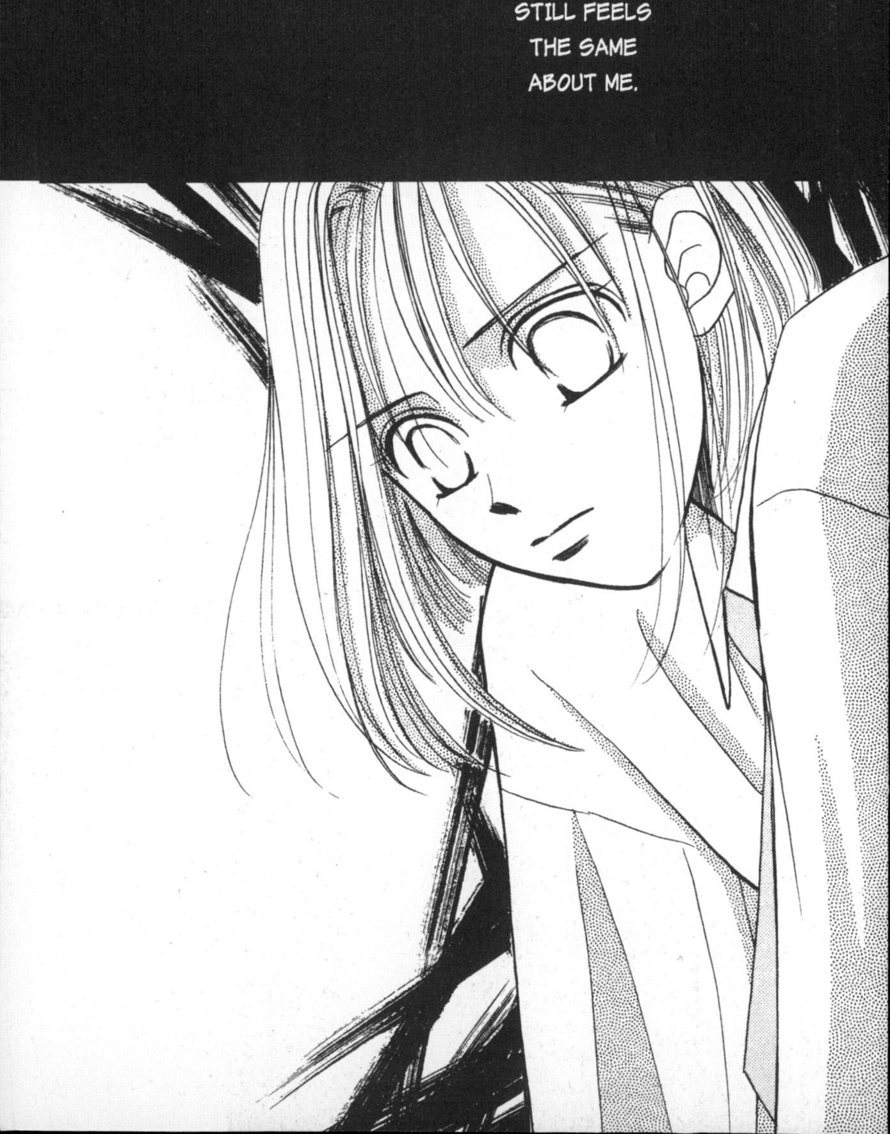
STILL FEELS THE SAME ABOUT ME.

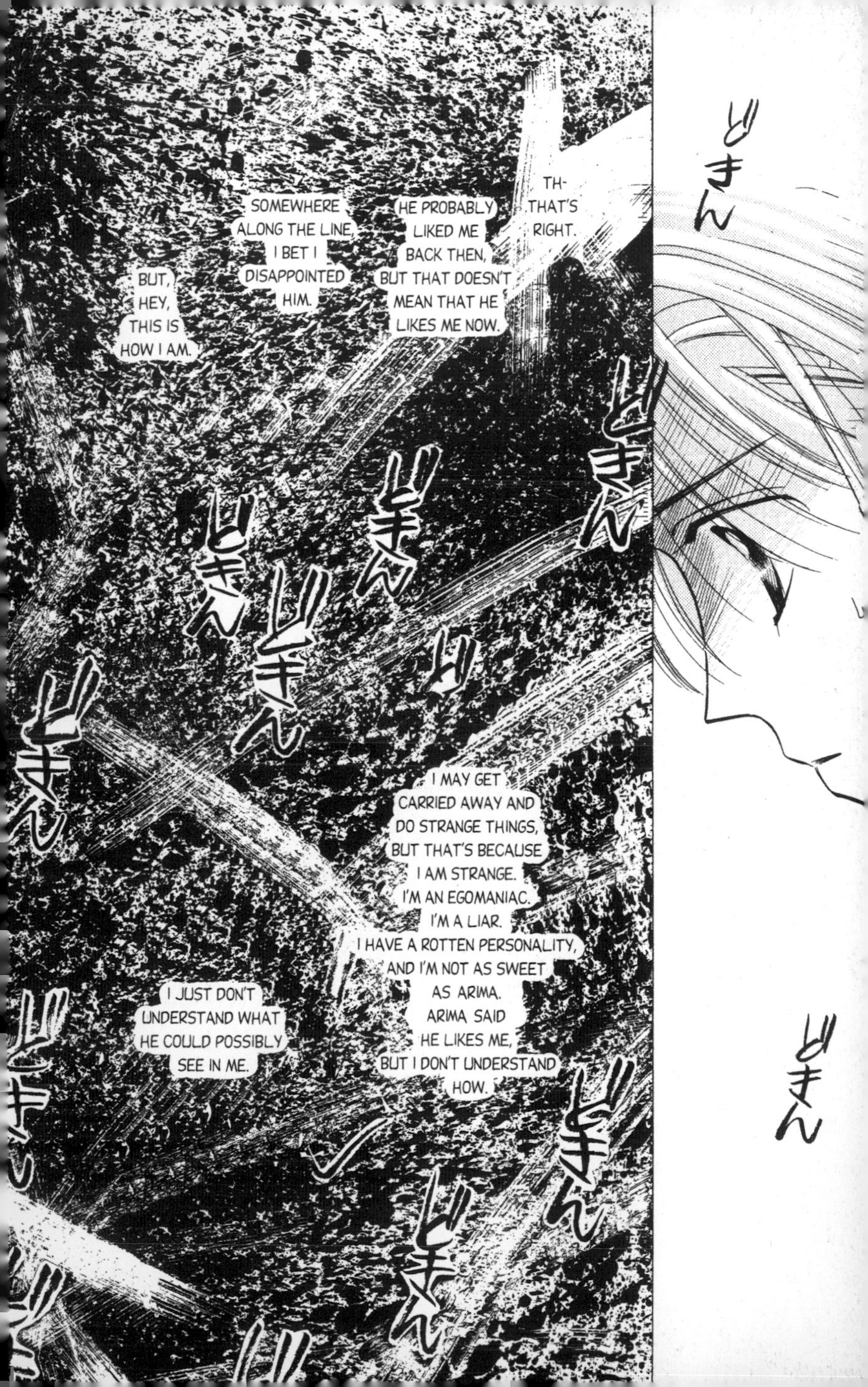

どきん
どきん
TH- THAT'S RIGHT.
HE PROBABLY LIKED ME BACK THEN, BUT THAT DOESN'T MEAN THAT HE LIKES ME NOW.
SOMEWHERE ALONG THE LINE, I BET I DISAPPOINTED HIM.
BUT, HEY, THIS IS HOW I AM.
どきん
どきん
どきん
どきん
I MAY GET CARRIED AWAY AND DO STRANGE THINGS, BUT THAT'S BECAUSE I AM STRANGE. I'M AN EGOMANIAC. I'M A LIAR. I HAVE A ROTTEN PERSONALITY, AND I'M NOT AS SWEET AS ARIMA. ARIMA SAID HE LIKES ME, BUT I DON'T UNDERSTAND HOW.
I JUST DON'T UNDERSTAND WHAT HE COULD POSSIBLY SEE IN ME.
どきん
どきん

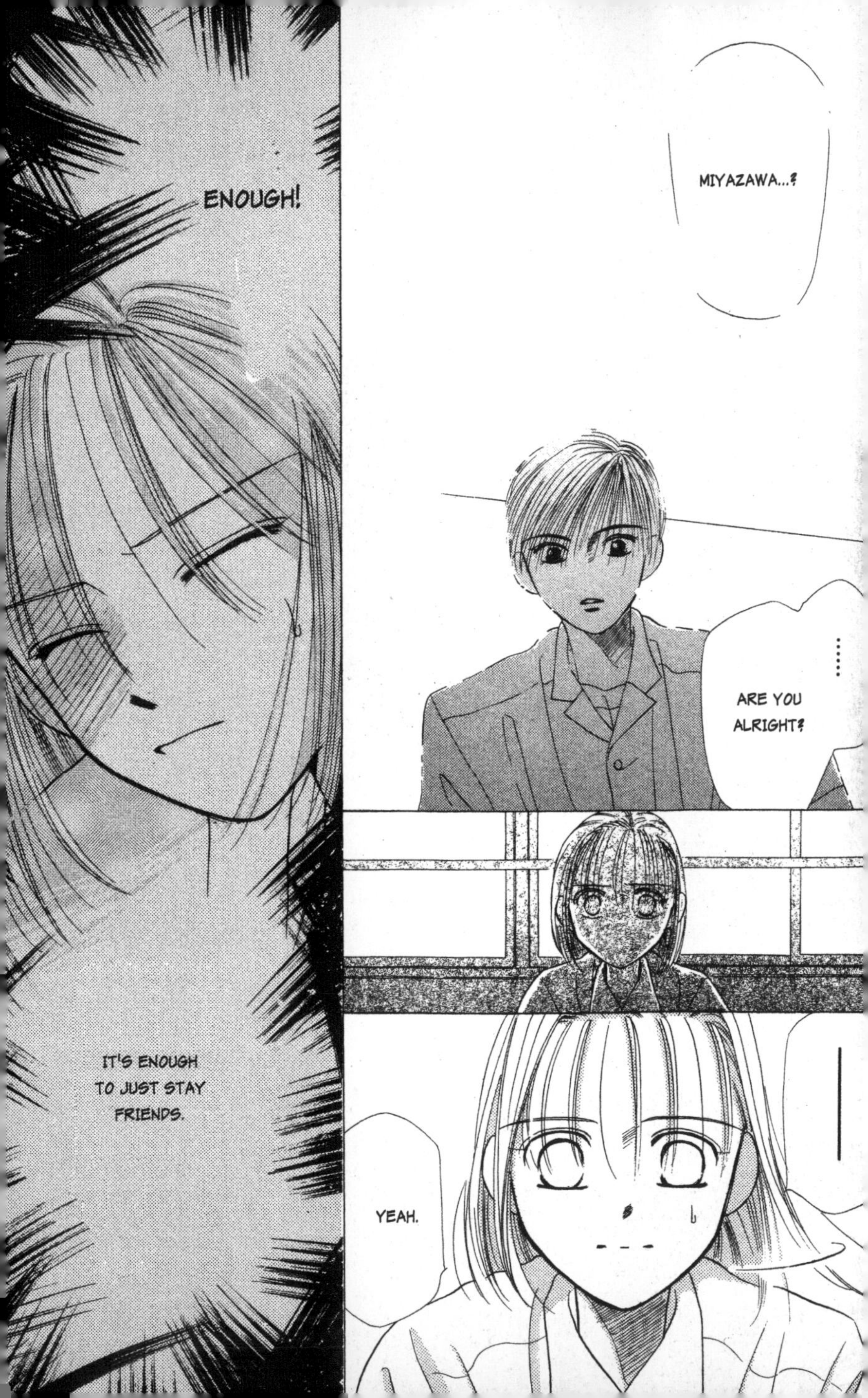
MIYAZAWA...?
...... ARE YOU ALRIGHT?
YEAH.
ENOUGH!
IT'S ENOUGH TO JUST STAY FRIENDS.

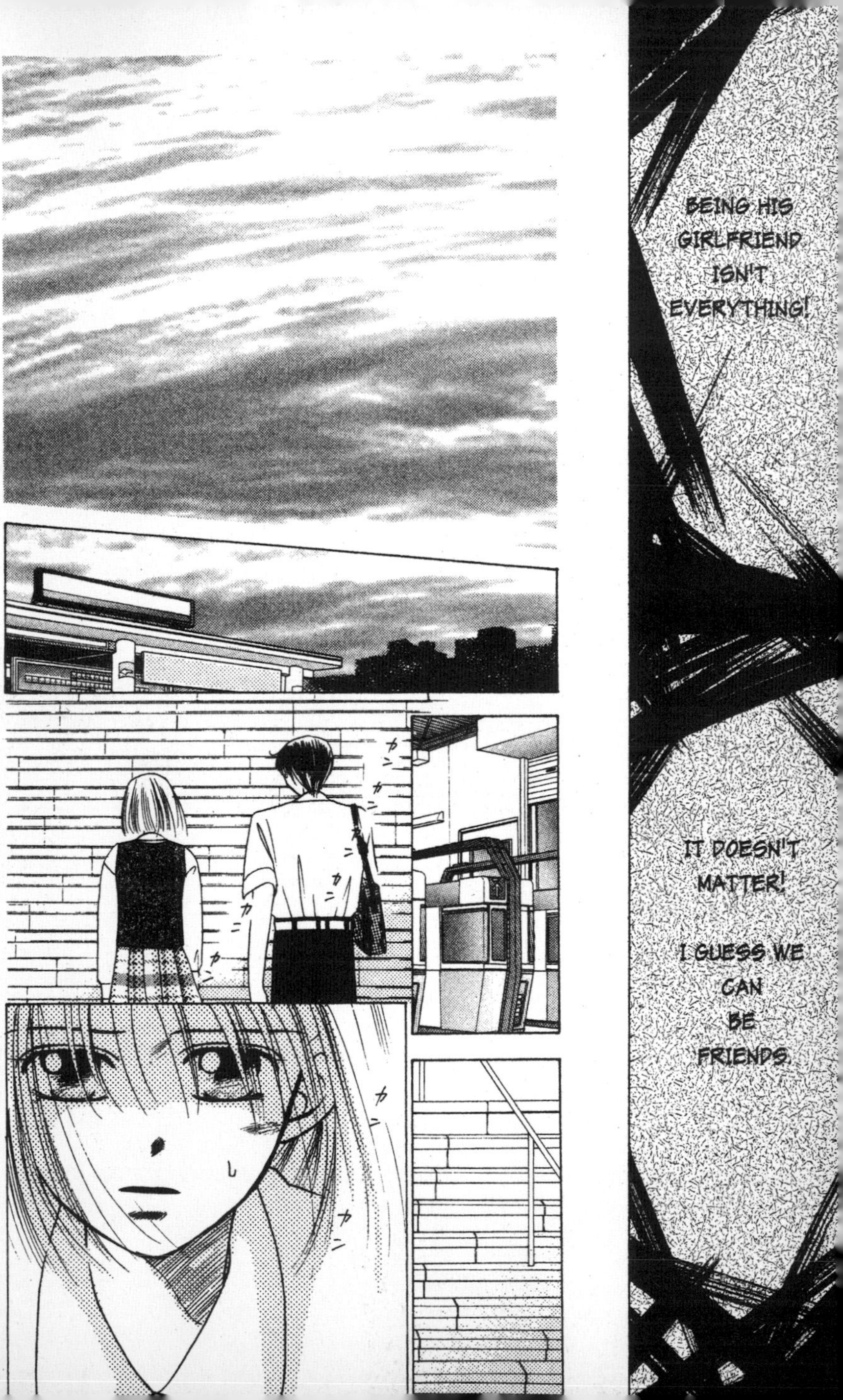
BEING HIS GIRLFRIEND ISN'T EVERYTHING!
IT DOESN'T MATTER!
I GUESS WE CAN BE FRIENDS.

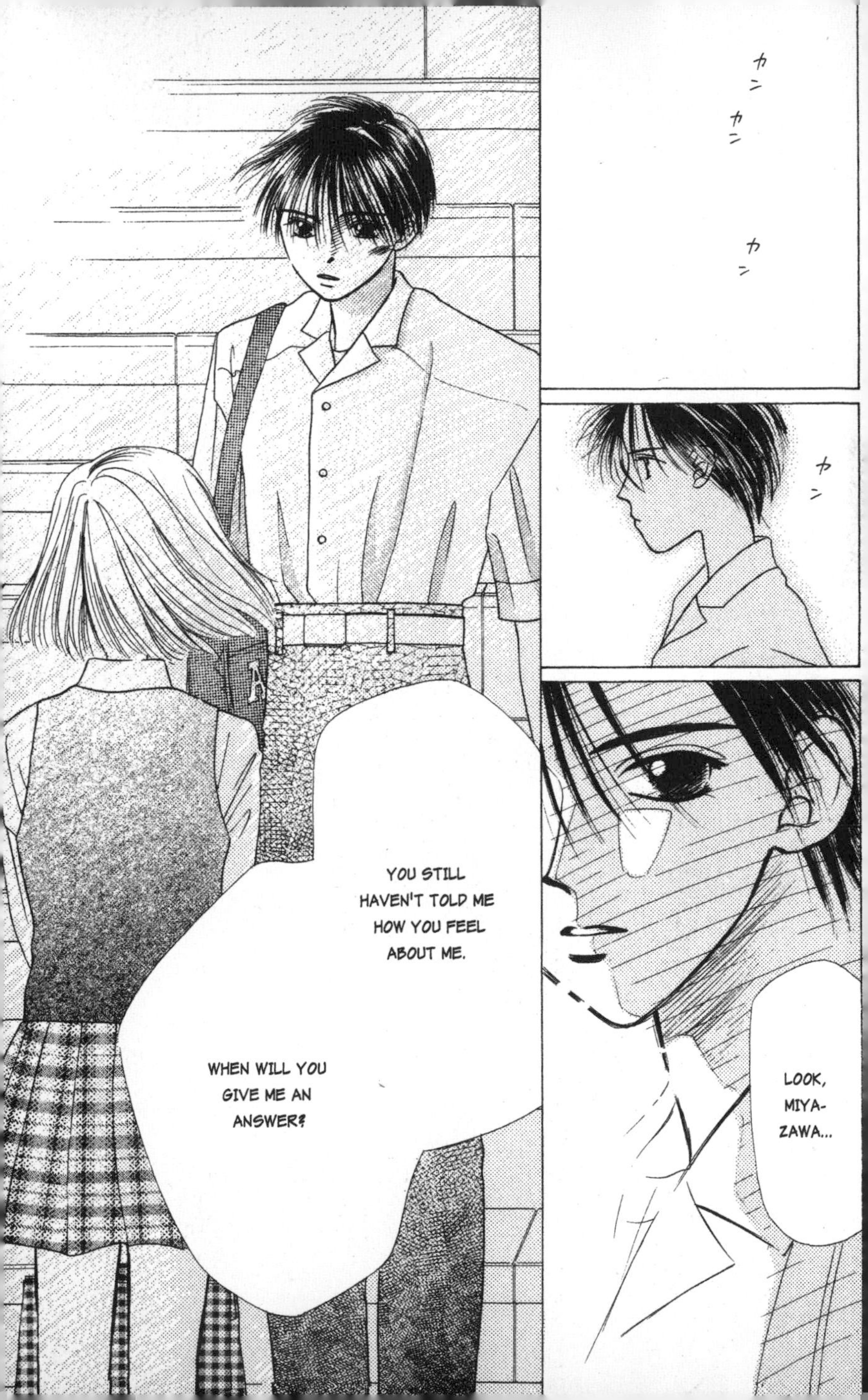
カン
カン
カン
カン
LOOK, MIYA-ZAWA...
YOU STILL HAVEN'T TOLD ME HOW YOU FEEL ABOUT ME.
WHEN WILL YOU GIVE ME AN ANSWER?

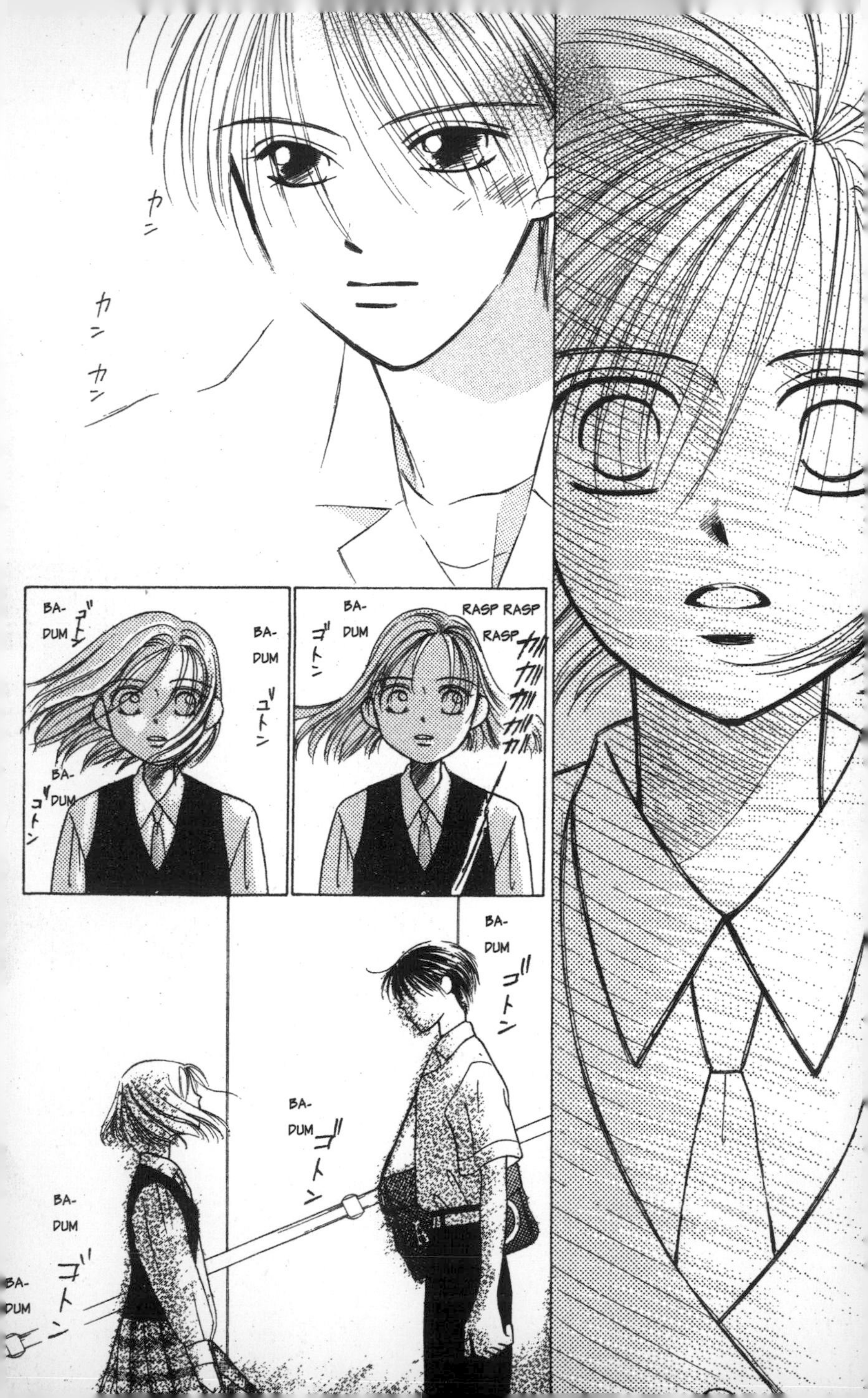
カン
カン
カン
BA-DUM
ゴトン
RASP RASP RASP
ガガガガガ
BA-DUM
コトン
BA-DUM
ゴトン
BA-DUM
コトン
BA-DUM
ゴトン
BA-DUM
ゴトン
BA-DUM
ゴトン
BA-DUM

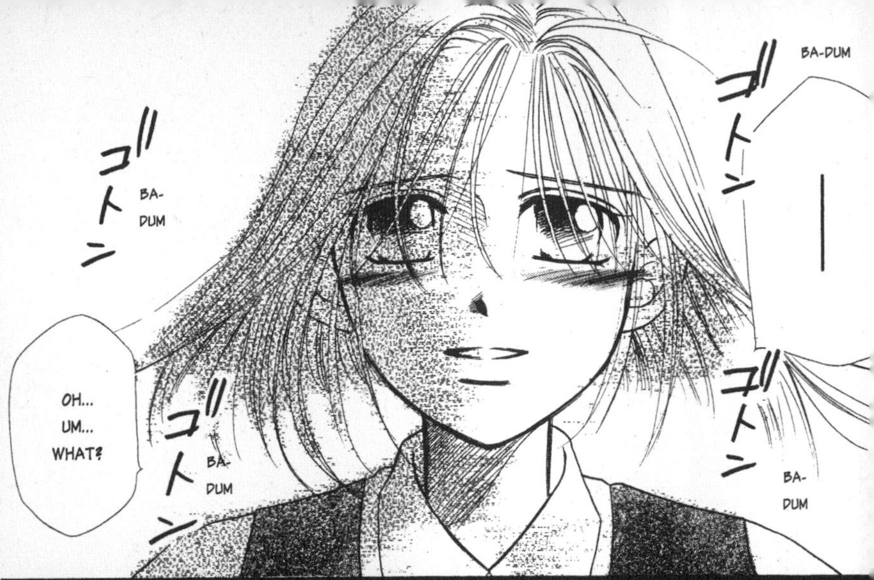
ゴトン
BA-DUM
ゴトン
BA-DUM
ゴトン
BA-DUM
ゴトン
BA-DUM
OH... UM... WHAT?
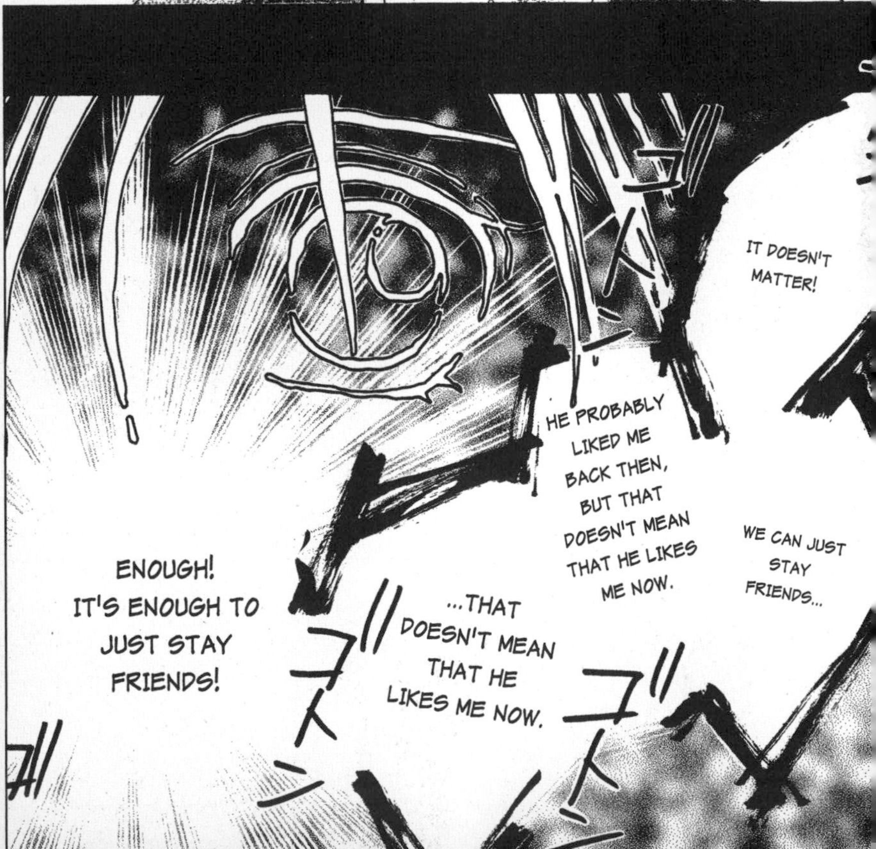
IT DOESN'T MATTER!
WE CAN JUST STAY FRIENDS...
HE PROBABLY LIKED ME BACK THEN, BUT THAT DOESN'T MEAN THAT HE LIKES ME NOW.
ゴトン
...THAT DOESN'T MEAN THAT HE LIKES ME NOW.
ゴトン
ENOUGH! IT'S ENOUGH TO JUST STAY FRIENDS!

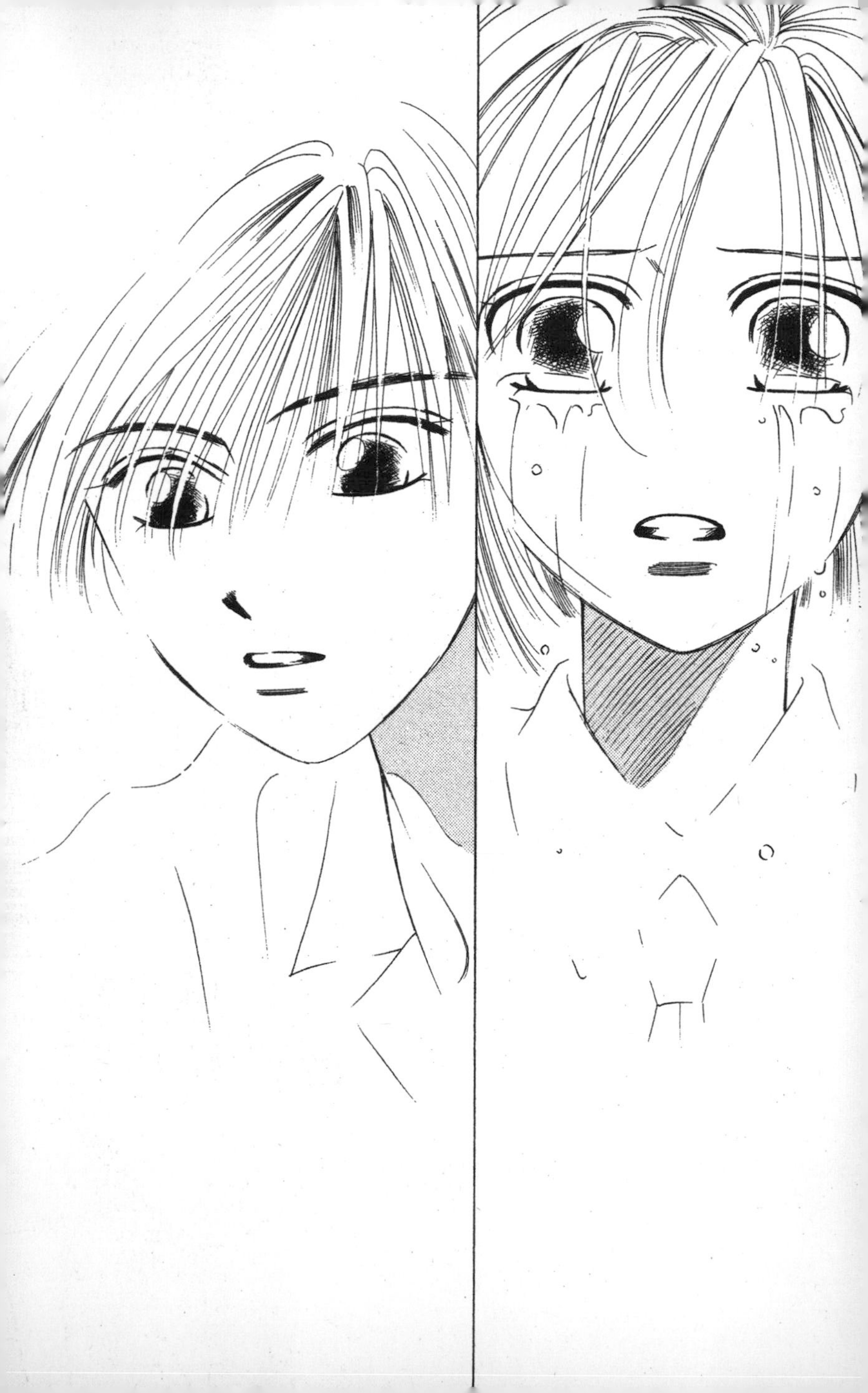

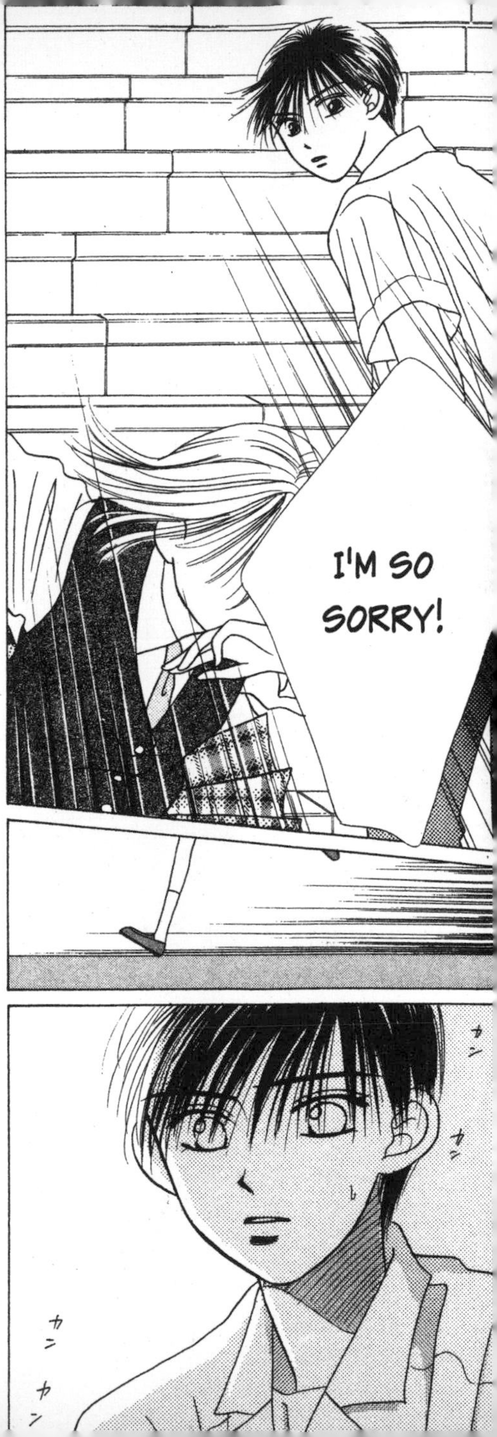
I'M SO SORRY!
カン
カン
カン
カン

MY FACE MUST LOOK HORRIBLE RIGHT NOW.

BUT THAT'S NOT WHY I'M RUNNING.

I AM
RUNNING
AWAY...
FROM
LOVE.

I CHOSE TO PROTECT
MYSELF AND MY
FEELINGS. I RAN
AWAY SO I
WOULDN'T GET HURT.

I'M SO
SELFISH.

BOO
HOO

I DIDN'T TRUST
ARIMA.

SNIFFLE

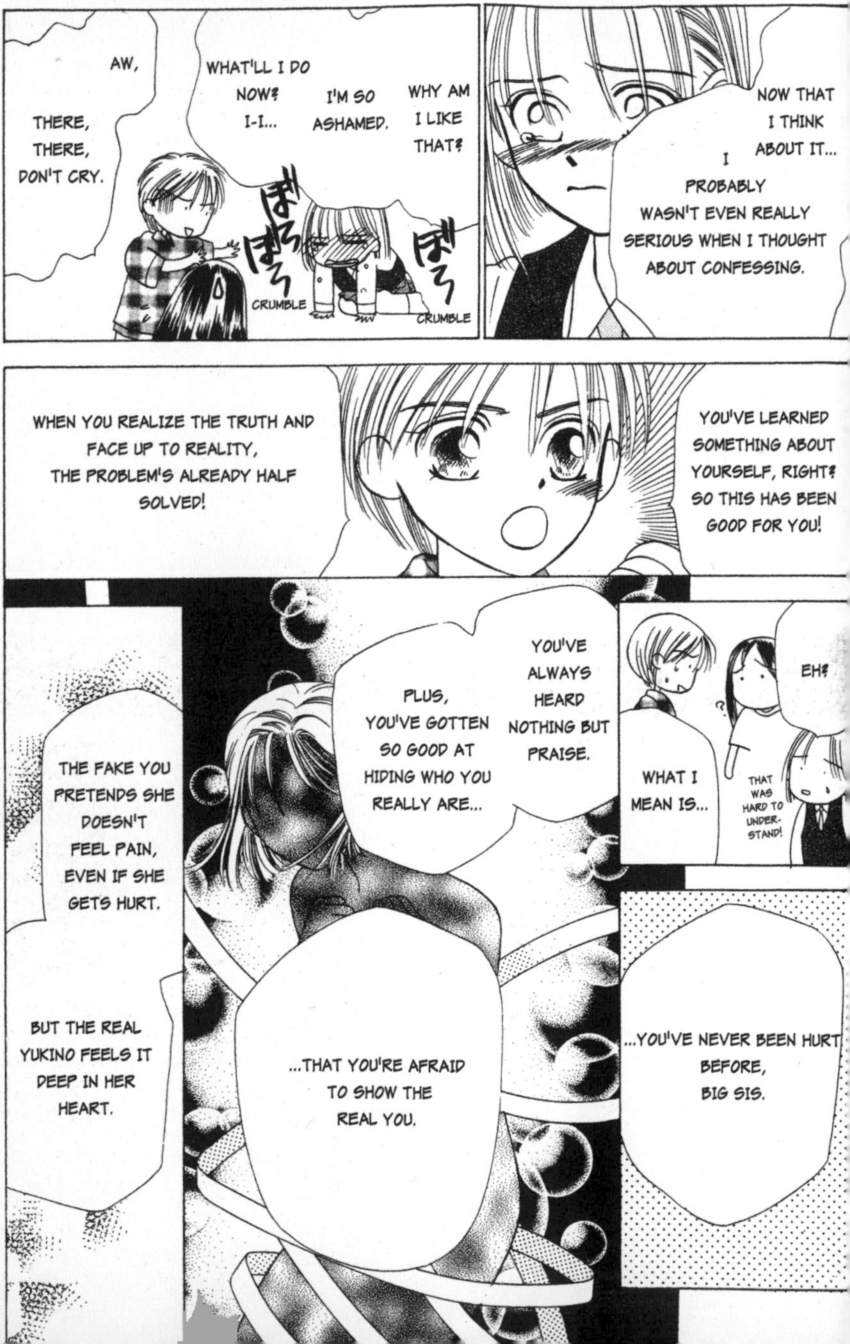
NOW THAT I THINK ABOUT IT...
I PROBABLY WASN'T EVEN REALLY SERIOUS WHEN I THOUGHT ABOUT CONFESSING.
WHY AM I LIKE THAT?
I'M SO ASHAMED.
WHAT'LL I DO NOW? I-I...
ぼろぼろ
CRUMBLE
ぼろぼろ
CRUMBLE
AW, THERE, THERE, DON'T CRY.
YOU'VE LEARNED SOMETHING ABOUT YOURSELF, RIGHT? SO THIS HAS BEEN GOOD FOR YOU!
WHEN YOU REALIZE THE TRUTH AND FACE UP TO REALITY, THE PROBLEM'S ALREADY HALF SOLVED!
EH?
THAT WAS HARD TO UNDER-STAND!
WHAT I MEAN IS...
...YOU'VE NEVER BEEN HURT BEFORE, BIG SIS.
YOU'VE ALWAYS HEARD NOTHING BUT PRAISE.
PLUS, YOU'VE GOTTEN SO GOOD AT HIDING WHO YOU REALLY ARE...
...THAT YOU'RE AFRAID TO SHOW THE REAL YOU.
THE FAKE YOU PRETENDS SHE DOESN'T FEEL PAIN, EVEN IF SHE GETS HURT.
BUT THE REAL YUKINO FEELS IT DEEP IN HER HEART.

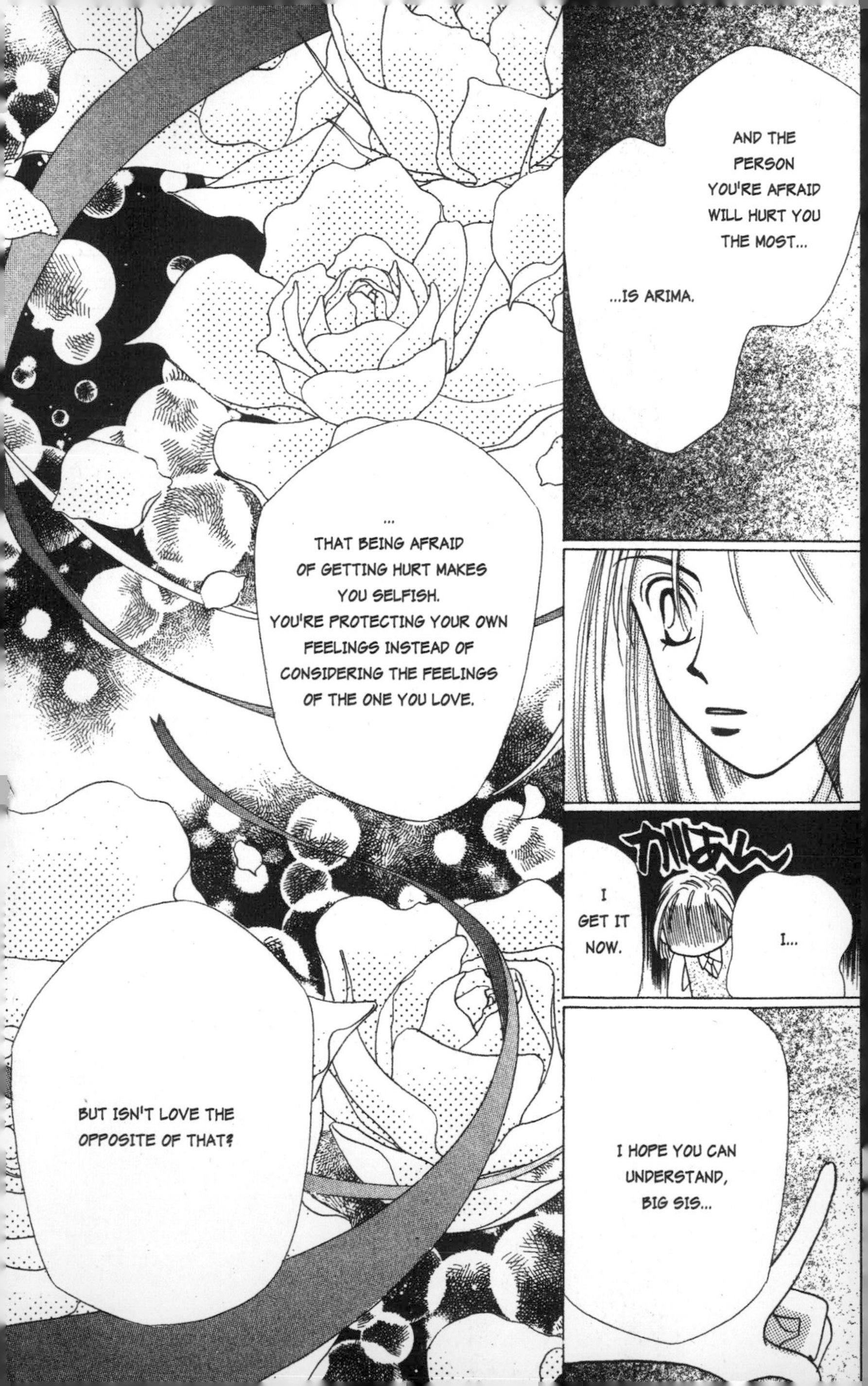
AND THE PERSON YOU'RE AFRAID WILL HURT YOU THE MOST...
...IS ARIMA.
I GET IT NOW.
I...
I HOPE YOU CAN UNDERSTAND, BIG SIS...
... THAT BEING AFRAID OF GETTING HURT MAKES YOU SELFISH. YOU'RE PROTECTING YOUR OWN FEELINGS INSTEAD OF CONSIDERING THE FEELINGS OF THE ONE YOU LOVE.
BUT ISN'T LOVE THE OPPOSITE OF THAT?

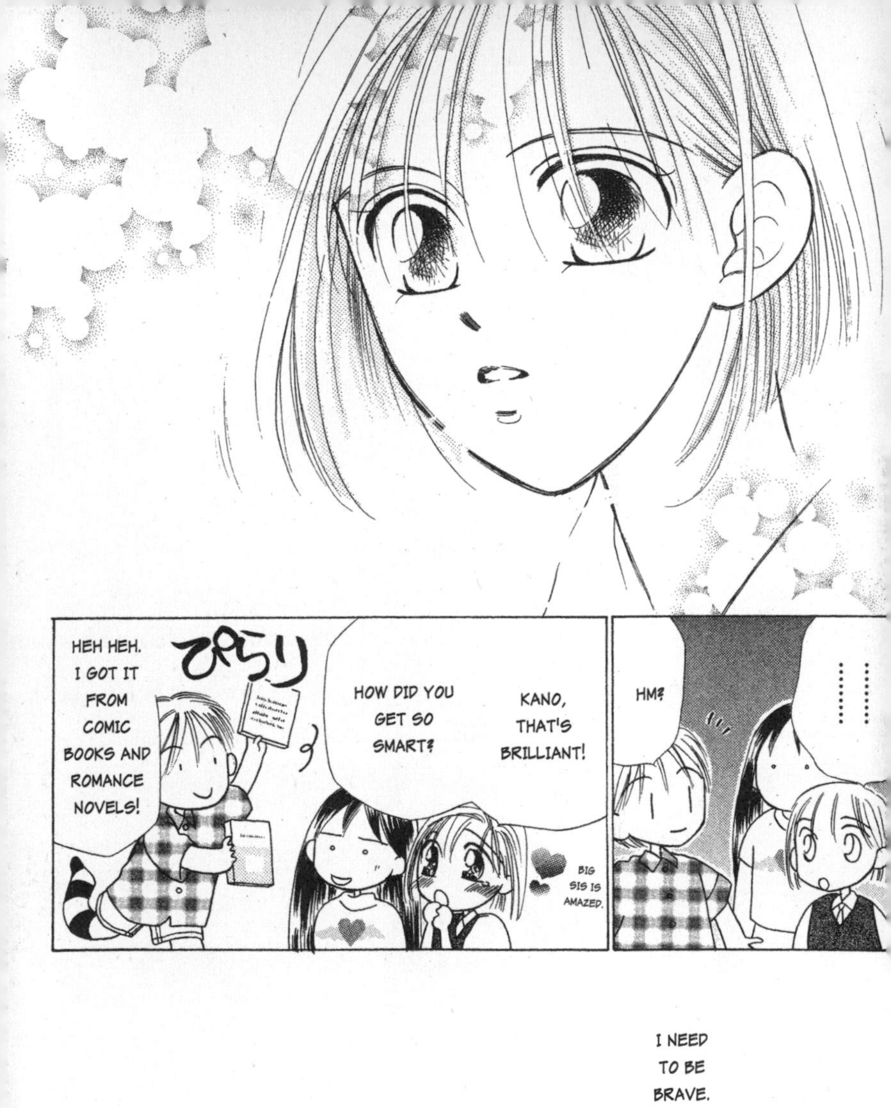
......
HM?
KANO, THAT'S BRILLIANT!
HOW DID YOU GET SO SMART?
BIG SIS IS AMAZED.
ぴらり
HEH HEH. I GOT IT FROM COMIC BOOKS AND ROMANCE NOVELS!
I NEED TO BE BRAVE.

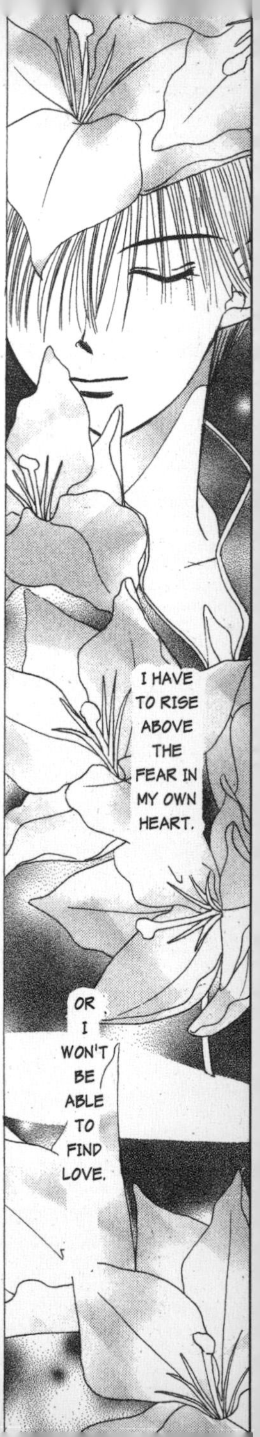
I HAVE TO RISE ABOVE THE FEAR IN MY OWN HEART.
OR I WON'T BE ABLE TO FIND LOVE.

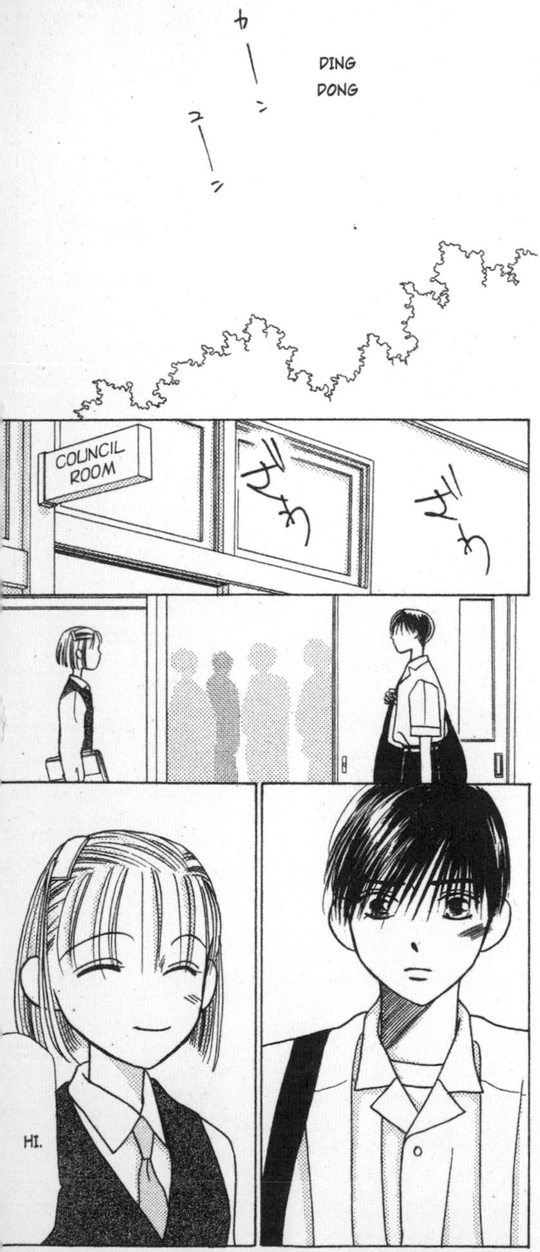
カーン
コーン
DING DONG
COUNCIL ROOM
ざわ
ざわ
HI.

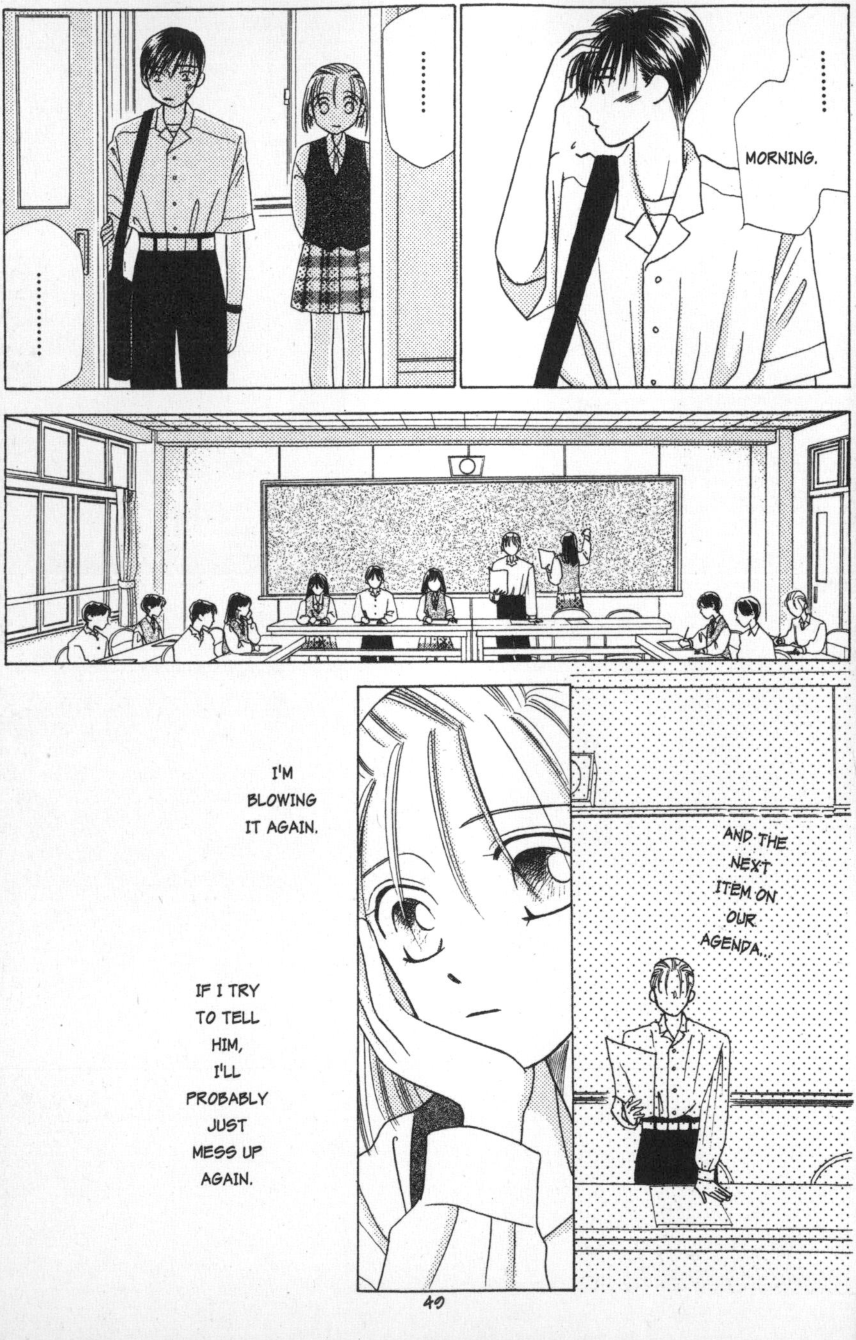
......
MORNING.
......
......
AND THE NEXT ITEM ON OUR AGENDA...
I'M BLOWING IT AGAIN.
IF I TRY TO TELL HIM, I'LL PROBABLY JUST MESS UP AGAIN.

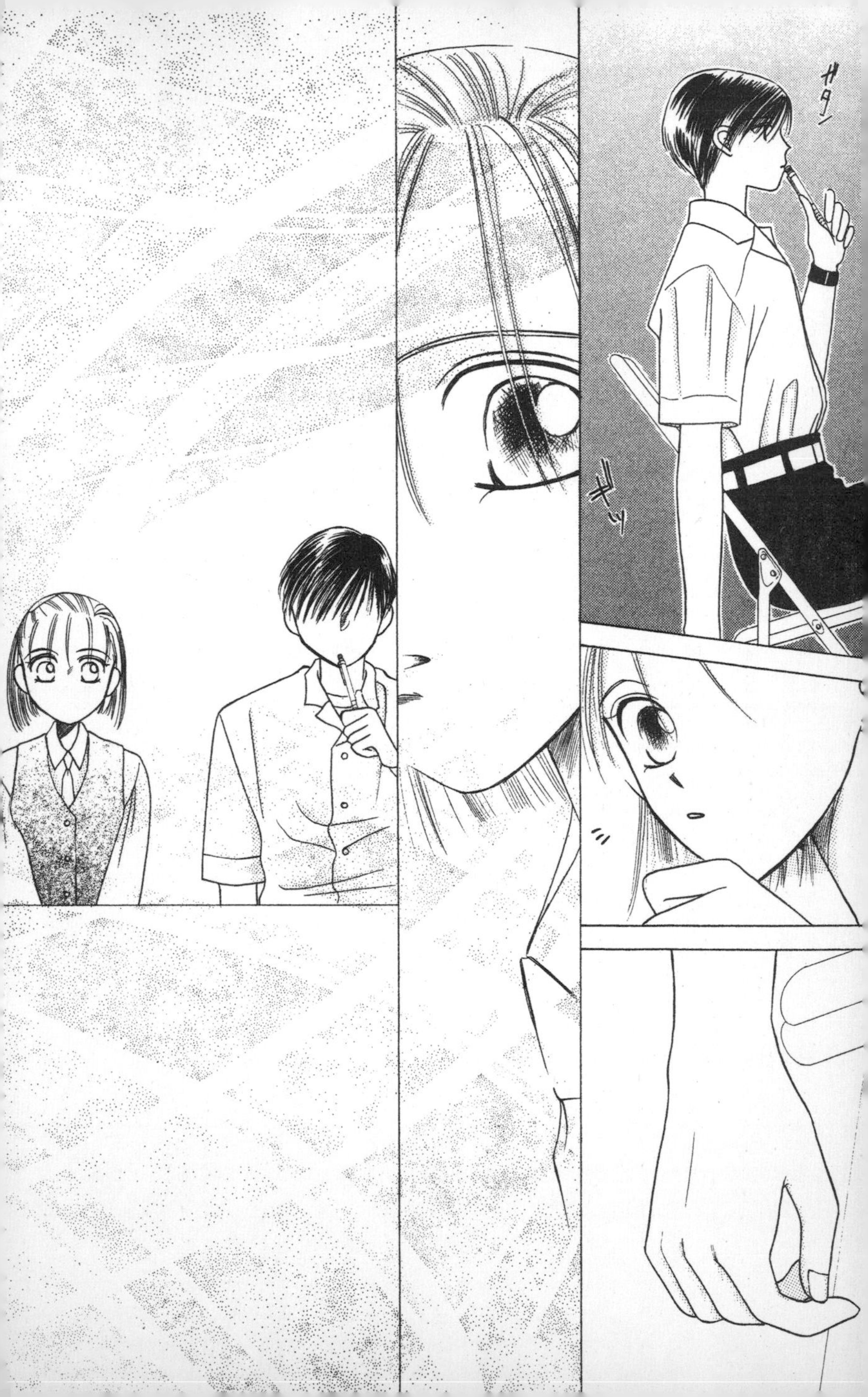
ガタン
ギッ

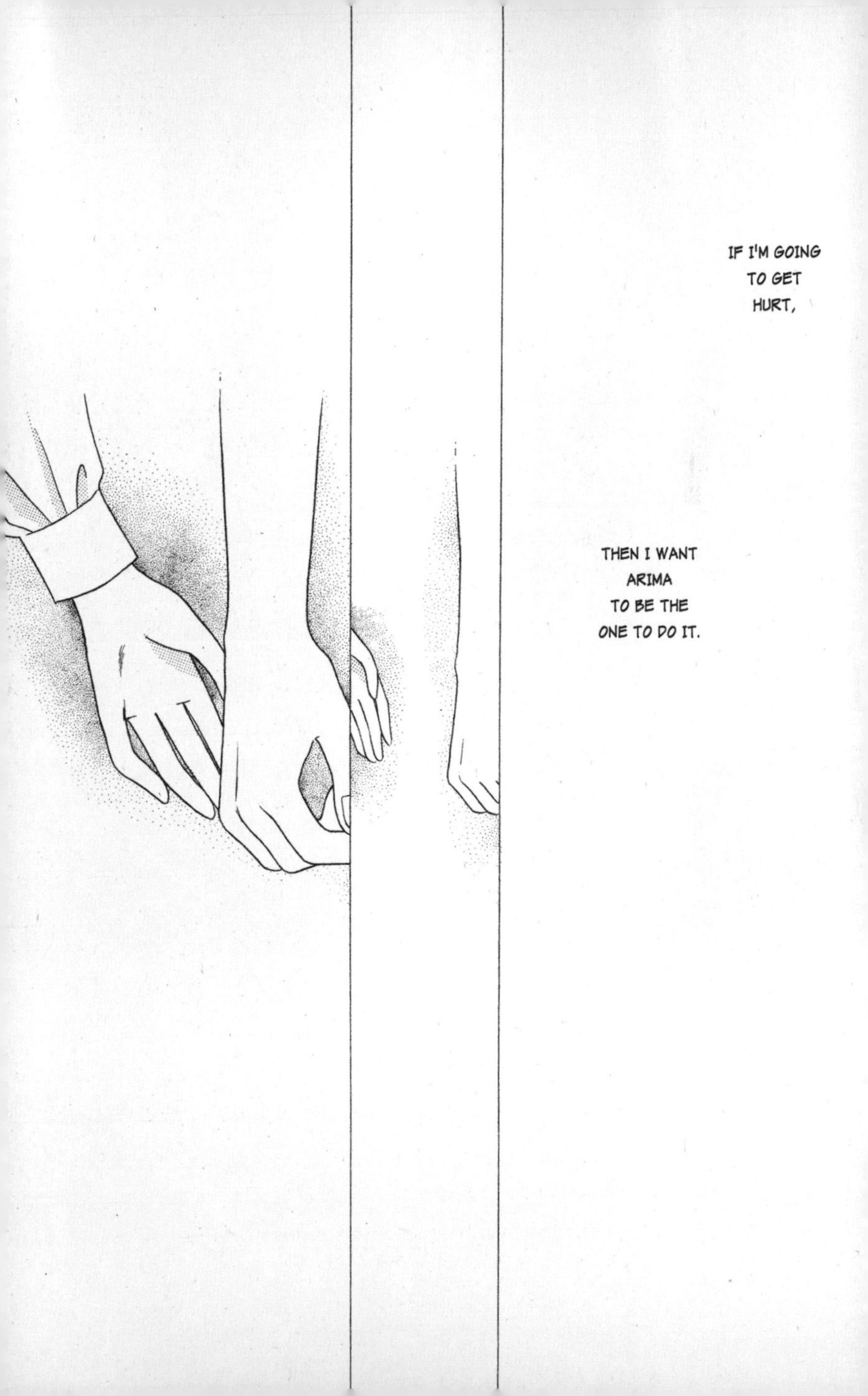

IF I'M GOING
TO GET
HURT,

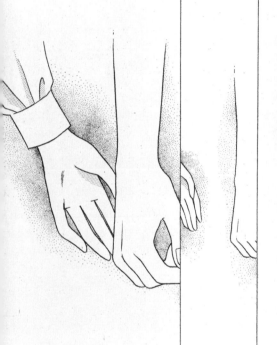

THEN I WANT
ARIMA
TO BE THE
ONE TO DO IT.

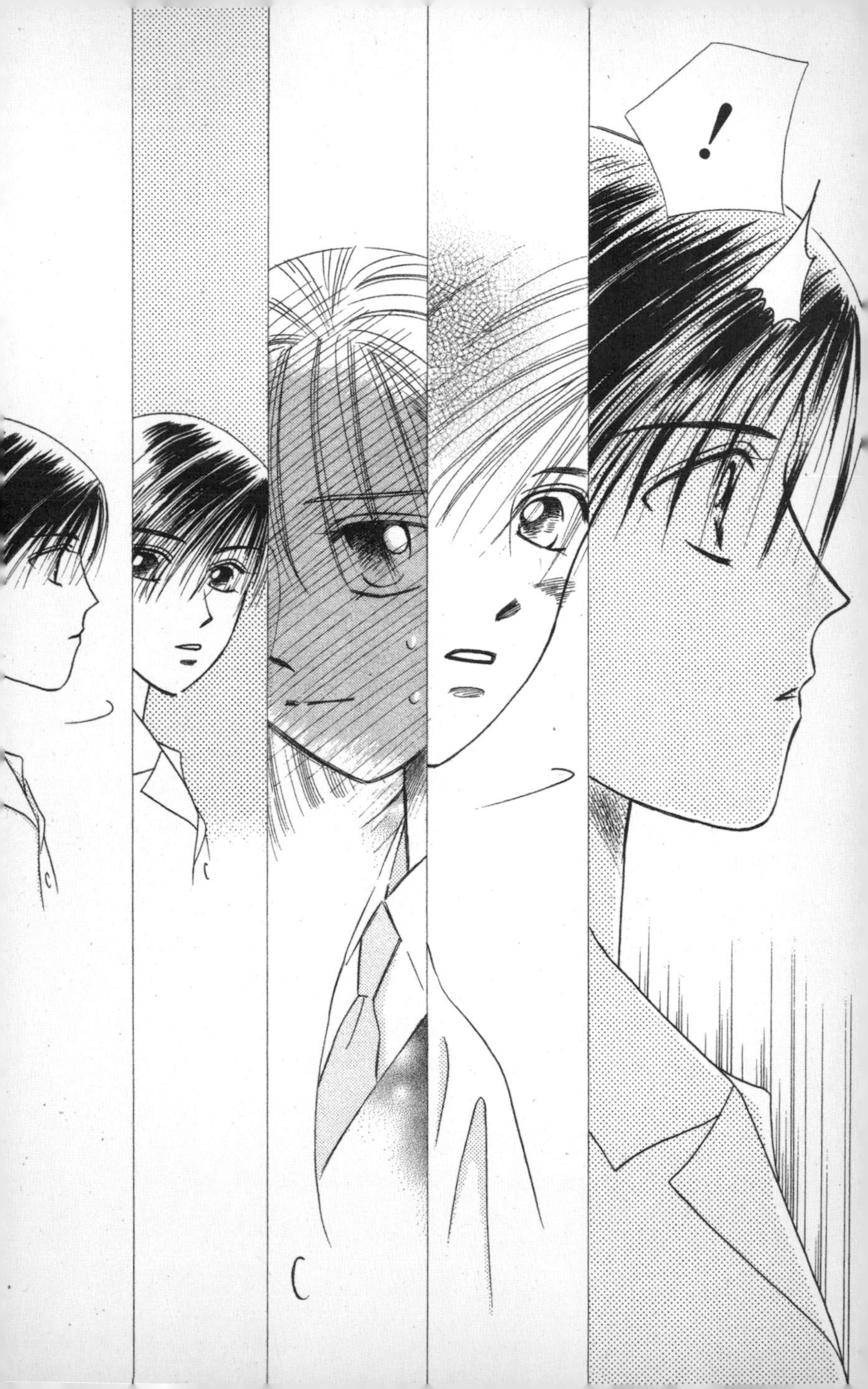
!

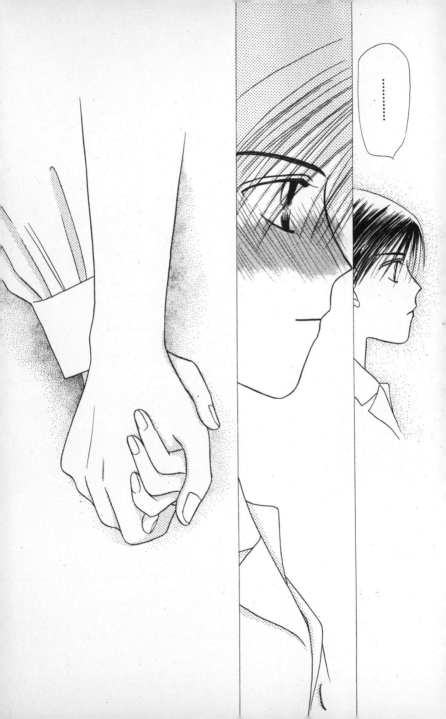

ON THAT
DAY...

...WE BECAME
"BOYFRIEND"
AND
"GIRLFRIEND."

ACT 4 ✳ THE DAY I FELL IN LOVE - THE END

彼氏彼女の事情

ACT. 2 THE SECRET

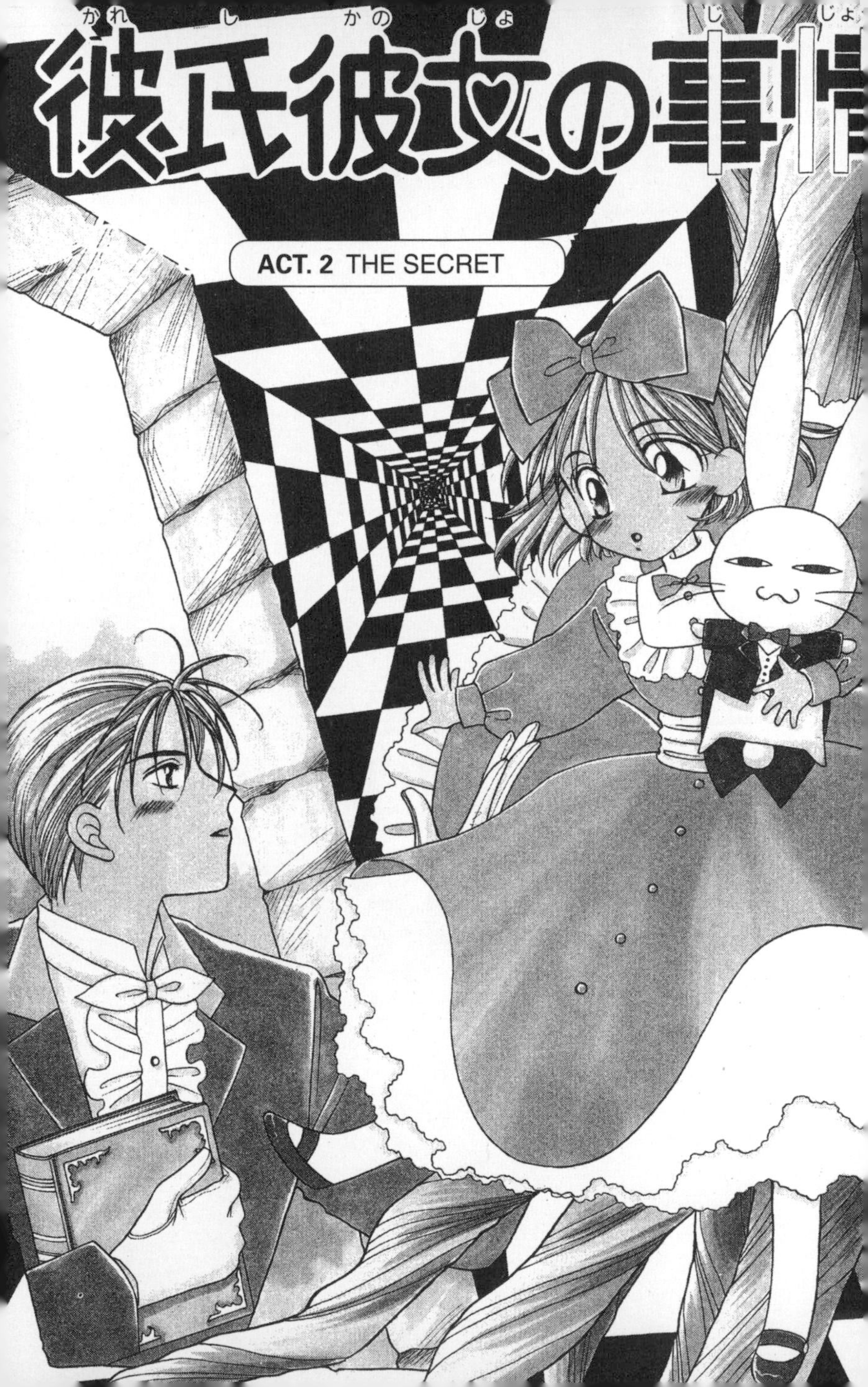

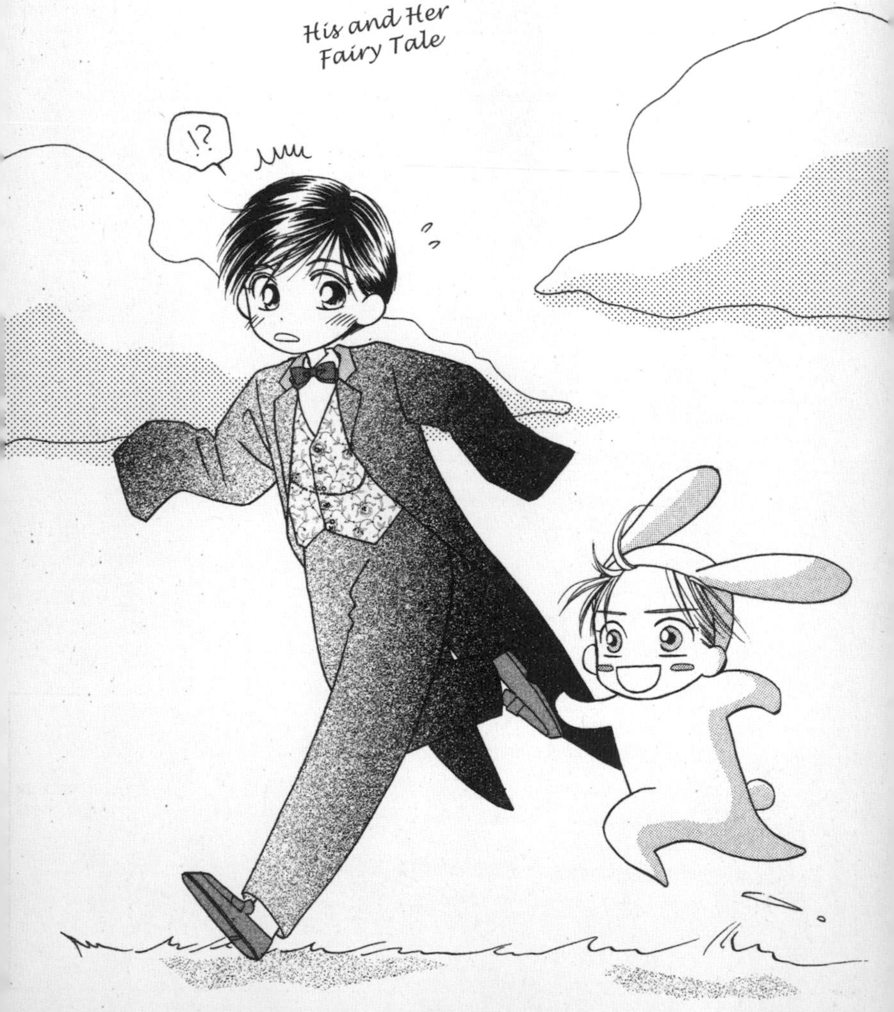
His and Her
Fairy Tale
!?

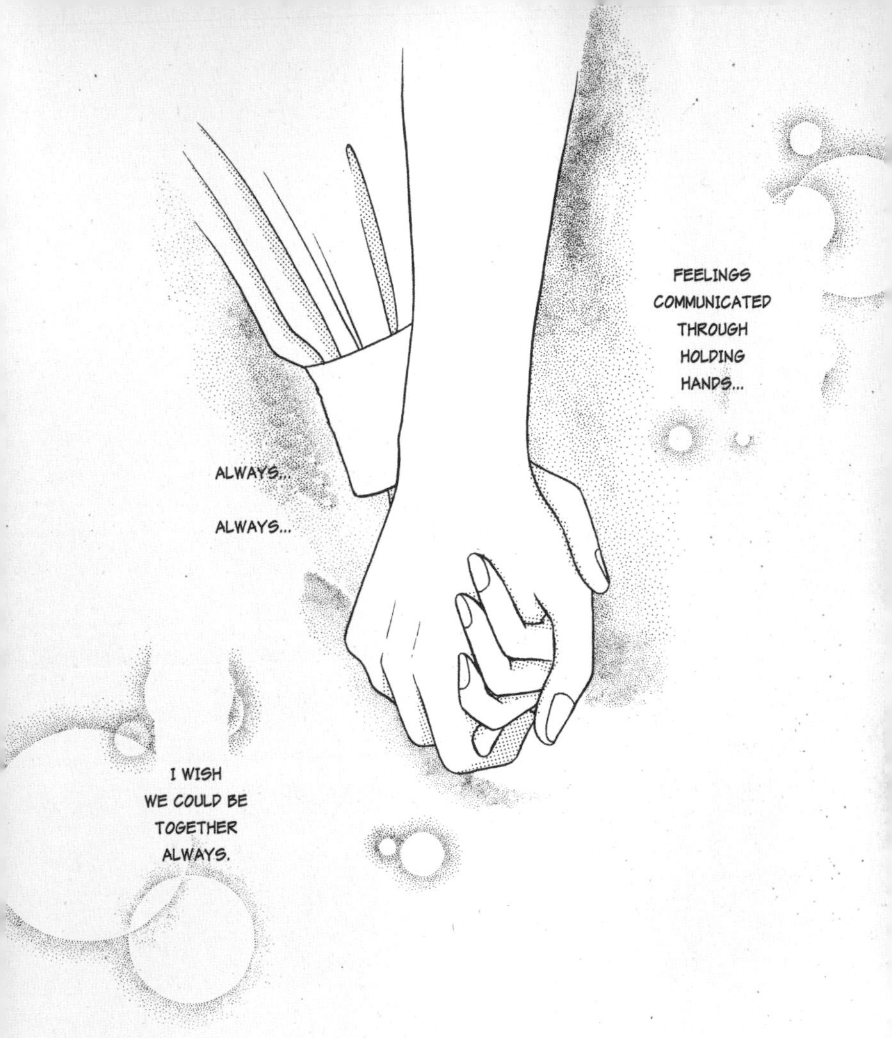
FEELINGS COMMUNICATED THROUGH HOLDING HANDS...
ALWAYS...
ALWAYS...
I WISH WE COULD BE TOGETHER ALWAYS.

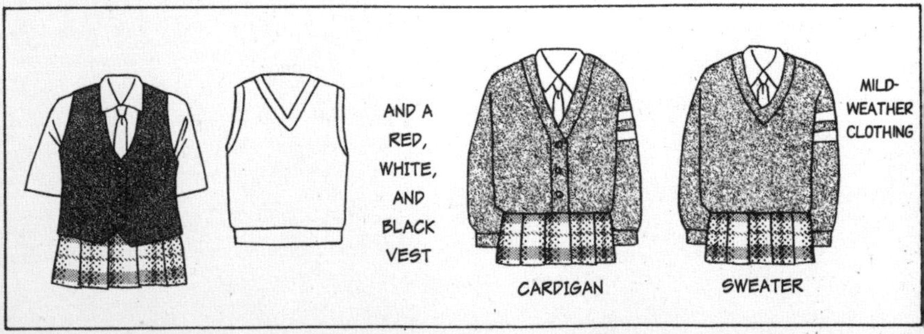
MILD-WEATHER CLOTHING
SWEATER
CARDIGAN
AND A RED, WHITE, AND BLACK VEST

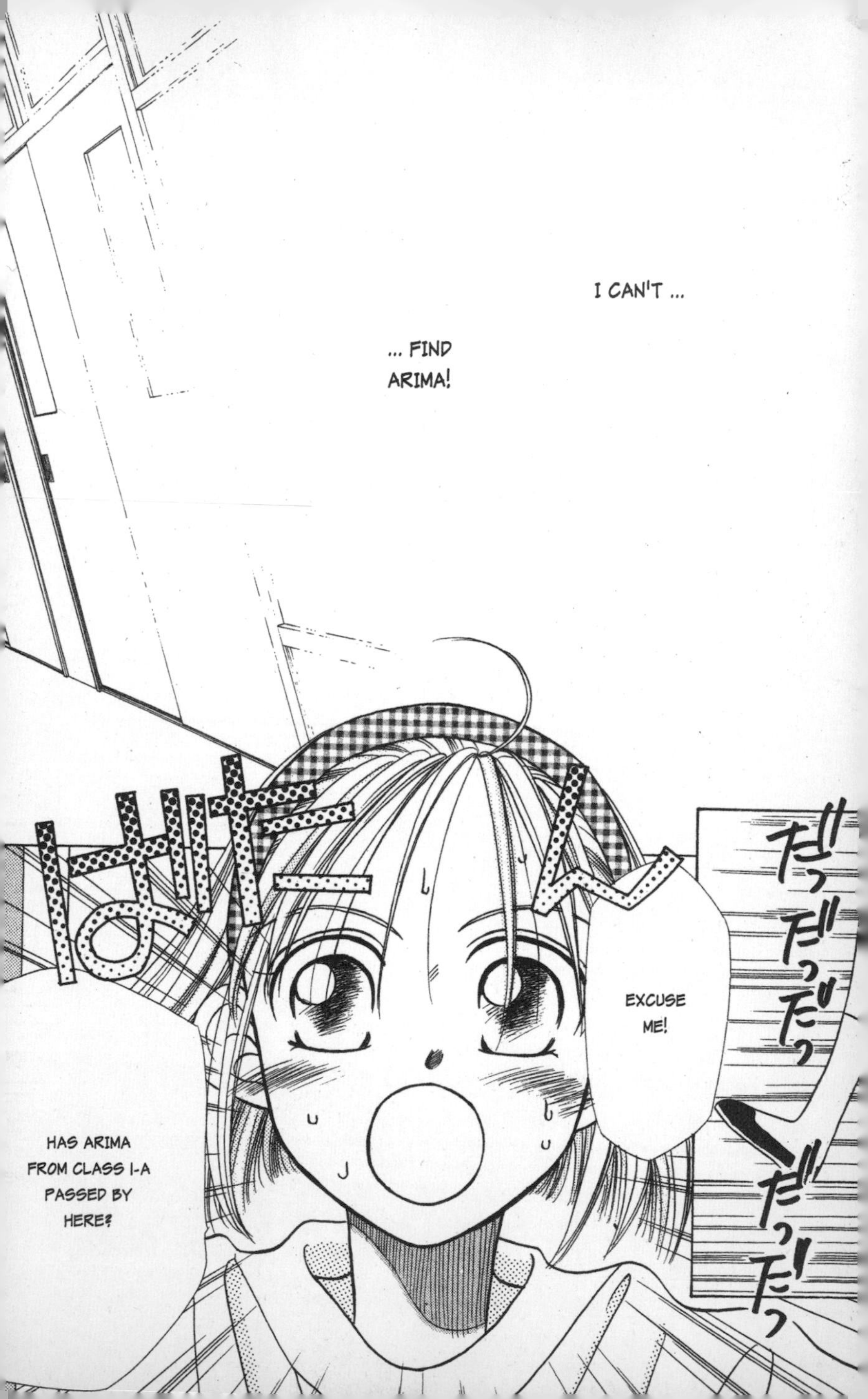

I CAN'T ...
... FIND ARIMA!
だっだっだっ
だっだっだっ
EXCUSE ME!
HAS ARIMA FROM CLASS 1-A PASSED BY HERE?

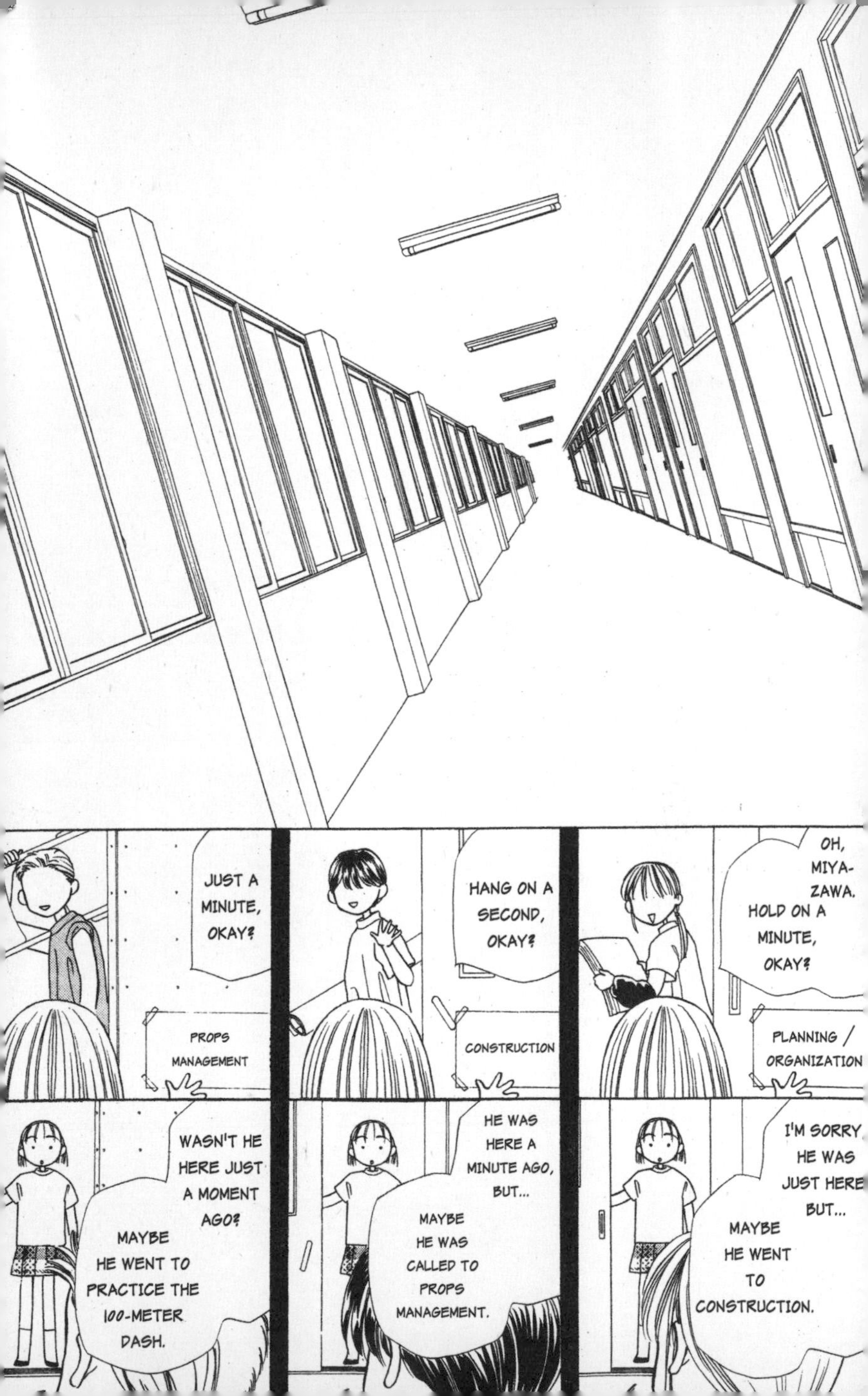
OH, MIYA-ZAWA. HOLD ON A MINUTE, OKAY?
PLANNING / ORGANIZATION
HANG ON A SECOND, OKAY?
CONSTRUCTION
JUST A MINUTE, OKAY?
PROPS MANAGEMENT
I'M SORRY HE WAS JUST HERE BUT...
MAYBE HE WENT TO CONSTRUCTION.
HE WAS HERE A MINUTE AGO, BUT...
MAYBE HE WAS CALLED TO PROPS MANAGEMENT.
WASN'T HE HERE JUST A MOMENT AGO?
MAYBE HE WENT TO PRACTICE THE 100-METER DASH.

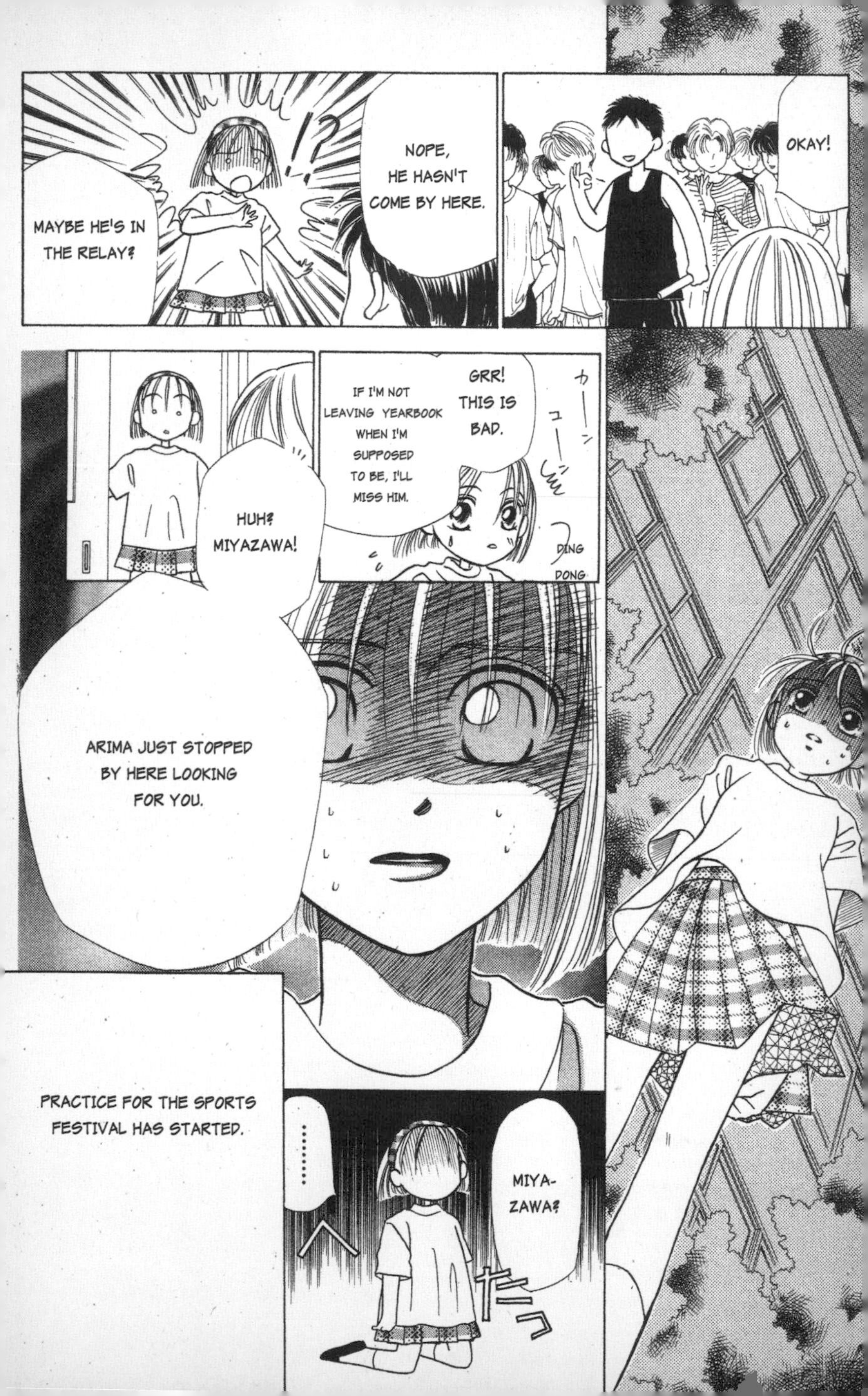
OKAY!
NOPE, HE HASN'T COME BY HERE.
MAYBE HE'S IN THE RELAY?
GRR! THIS IS BAD.
IF I'M NOT LEAVING YEARBOOK WHEN I'M SUPPOSED TO BE, I'LL MISS HIM.
カーン
コーン
DING DONG
HUH? MIYAZAWA!
ARIMA JUST STOPPED BY HERE LOOKING FOR YOU.
MIYA-ZAWA?
......
PRACTICE FOR THE SPORTS FESTIVAL HAS STARTED.

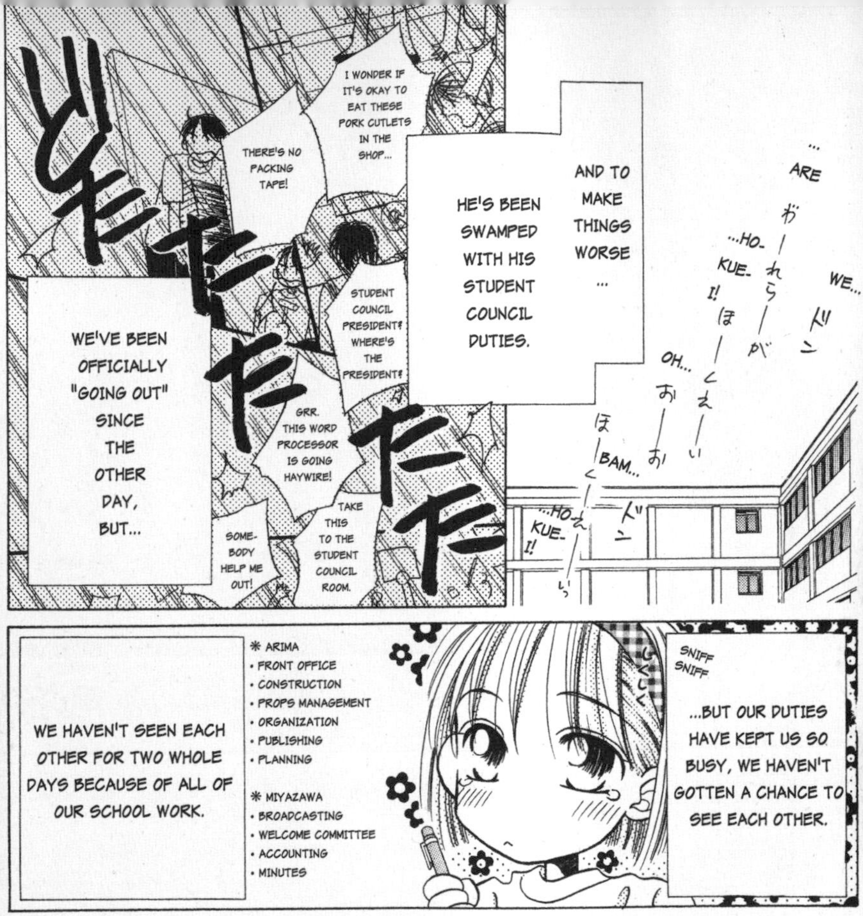
...ARE
WE...
...HO-KUE-I!
OH...
BAM...
...HO-KUE-I!
AND TO MAKE THINGS WORSE...
HE'S BEEN SWAMPED WITH HIS STUDENT COUNCIL DUTIES.
I WONDER IF IT'S OKAY TO EAT THESE PORK CUTLETS IN THE SHOP...
THERE'S NO PACKING TAPE!
STUDENT COUNCIL PRESIDENT? WHERE'S THE PRESIDENT?
GRR. THIS WORD PROCESSOR IS GOING HAYWIRE!
TAKE THIS TO THE STUDENT COUNCIL ROOM.
SOME-BODY HELP ME OUT!
WE'VE BEEN OFFICIALLY "GOING OUT" SINCE THE OTHER DAY, BUT...
SNIFF SNIFF
...BUT OUR DUTIES HAVE KEPT US SO BUSY, WE HAVEN'T GOTTEN A CHANCE TO SEE EACH OTHER.
❋ ARIMA
• FRONT OFFICE
• CONSTRUCTION
• PROPS MANAGEMENT
• ORGANIZATION
• PUBLISHING
• PLANNING
❋ MIYAZAWA
• BROADCASTING
• WELCOME COMMITTEE
• ACCOUNTING
• MINUTES
WE HAVEN'T SEEN EACH OTHER FOR TWO WHOLE DAYS BECAUSE OF ALL OF OUR SCHOOL WORK.
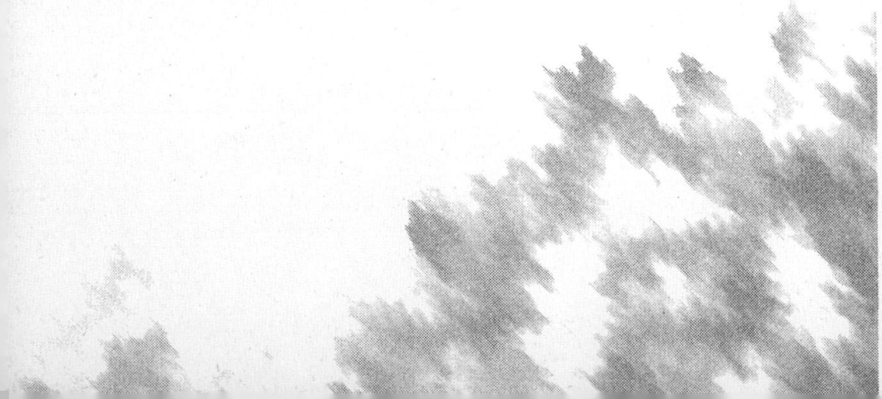

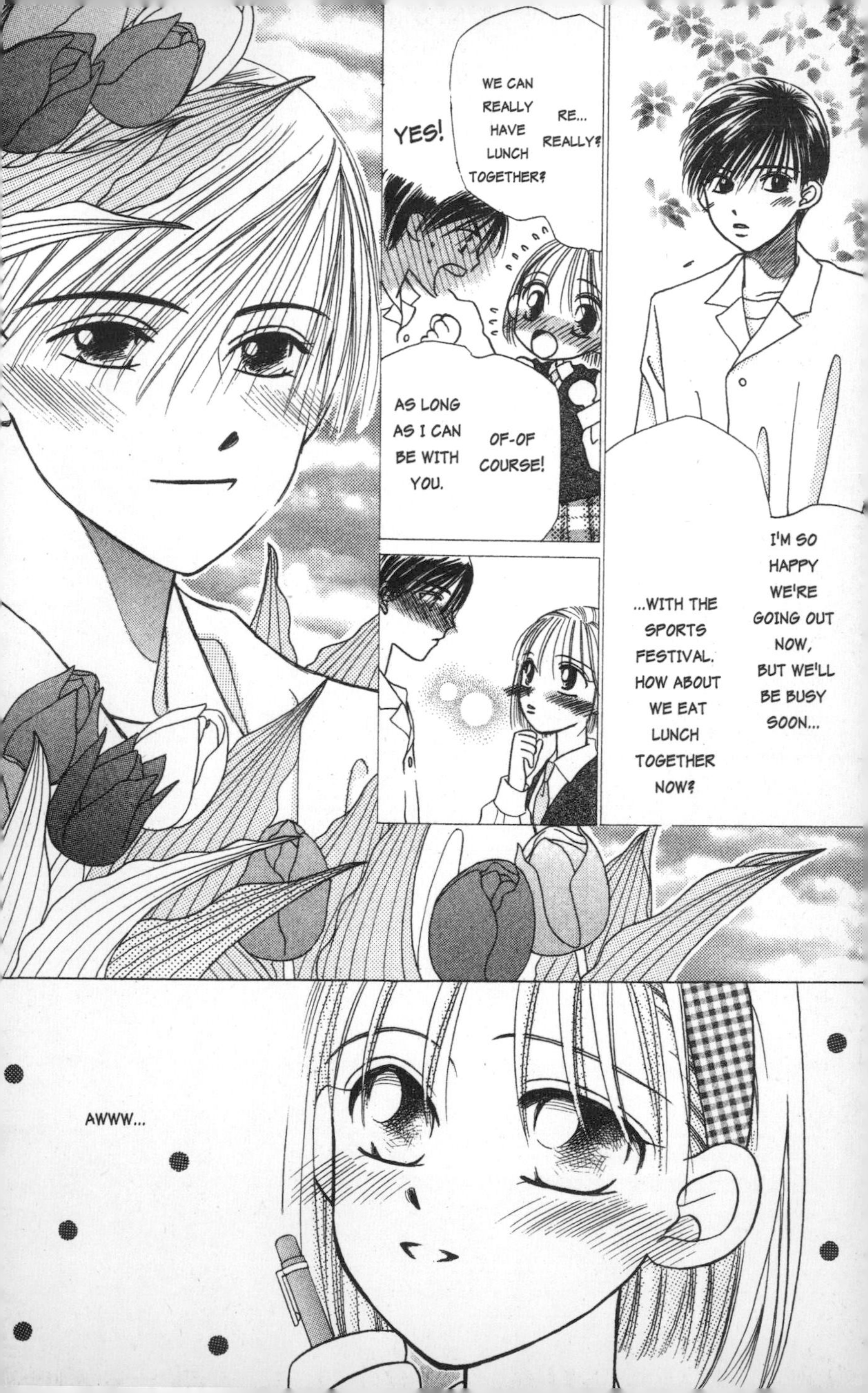

I'M SO HAPPY WE'RE GOING OUT NOW, BUT WE'LL BE BUSY SOON...
...WITH THE SPORTS FESTIVAL. HOW ABOUT WE EAT LUNCH TOGETHER NOW?
RE... REALLY?
WE CAN REALLY HAVE LUNCH TOGETHER?
YES!
OF-OF COURSE!
AS LONG AS I CAN BE WITH YOU.
AWWW...

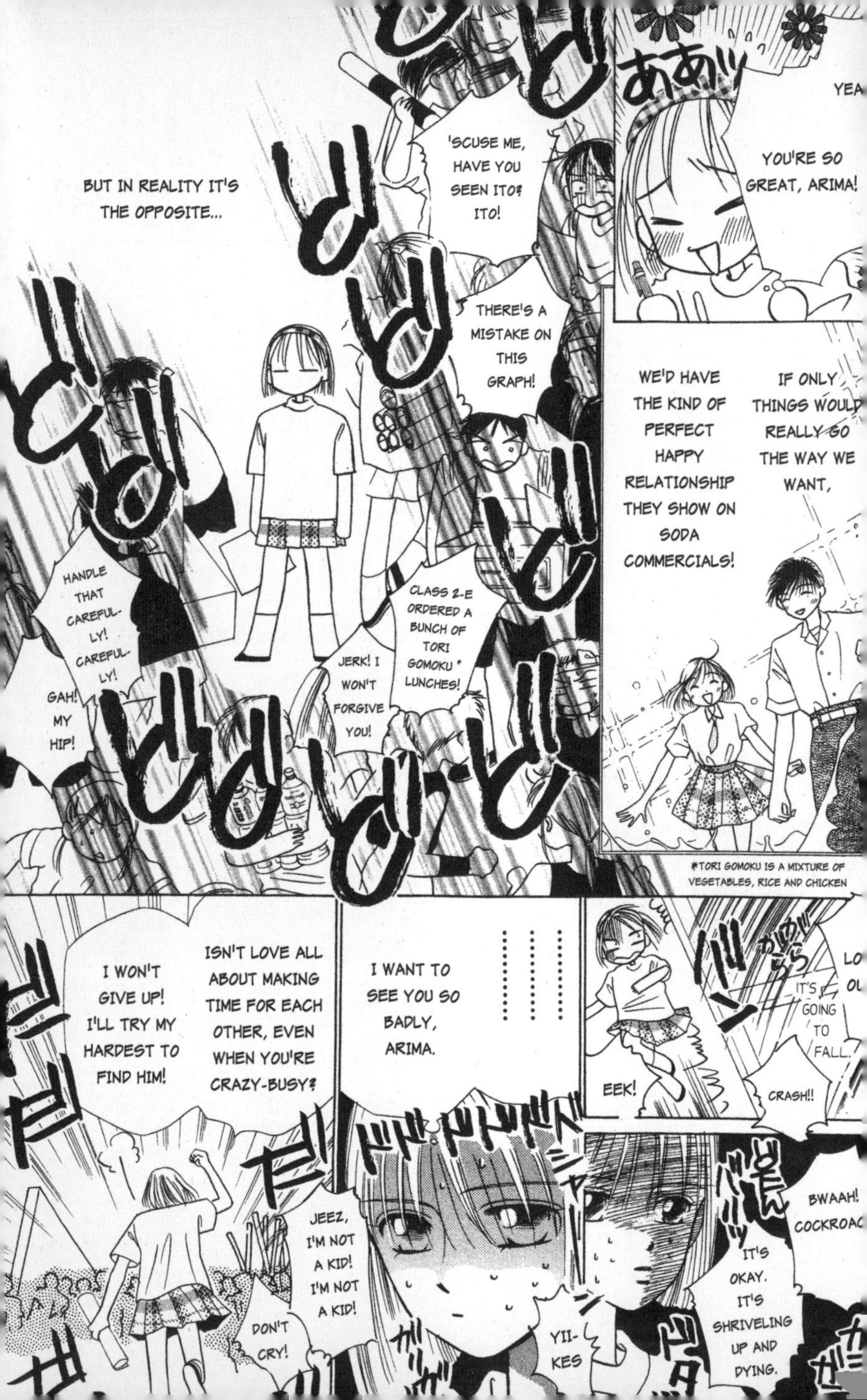
あああッ
YEA
YOU'RE SO GREAT, ARIMA!
IF ONLY THINGS WOULD REALLY GO THE WAY WE WANT,
WE'D HAVE THE KIND OF PERFECT HAPPY RELATIONSHIP THEY SHOW ON SODA COMMERCIALS!
'SCUSE ME, HAVE YOU SEEN ITO? ITO!
BUT IN REALITY IT'S THE OPPOSITE...
THERE'S A MISTAKE ON THIS GRAPH!
CLASS 2-E ORDERED A BUNCH OF TORI GOMOKU* LUNCHES!
JERK! I WON'T FORGIVE YOU!
HANDLE THAT CAREFUL-LY! CAREFUL-LY!
GAH! MY HIP!
LO OU
IT'S GOING TO FALL.
CRASH!!
EEK!
....
I WANT TO SEE YOU SO BADLY, ARIMA.
ISN'T LOVE ALL ABOUT MAKING TIME FOR EACH OTHER, EVEN WHEN YOU'RE CRAZY-BUSY?
I WON'T GIVE UP! I'LL TRY MY HARDEST TO FIND HIM!
BWAAH! COCKROAC
IT'S OKAY. IT'S SHRIVELING UP AND DYING.
YII-KES
JEEZ, I'M NOT A KID! I'M NOT A KID!
DON'T CRY!

*TORI GOMOKU IS A MIXTURE OF VEGETABLES, RICE AND CHICKEN

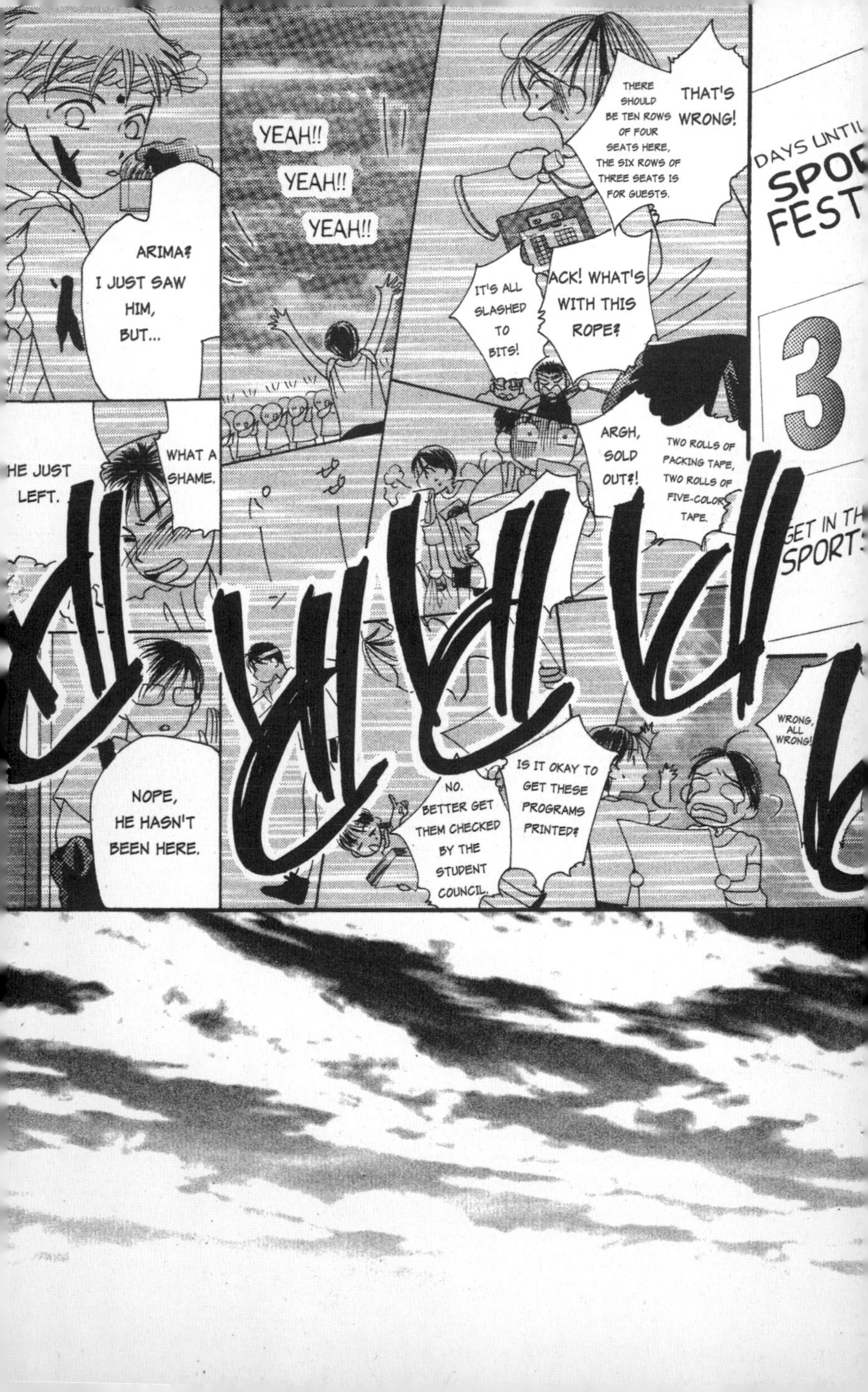
DAYS UNTIL
SPO
FEST
3
GET IN TH
SPORT
THAT'S WRONG!
THERE SHOULD BE TEN ROWS OF FOUR SEATS HERE, THE SIX ROWS OF THREE SEATS IS FOR GUESTS.
ACK! WHAT'S WITH THIS ROPE?
IT'S ALL SLASHED TO BITS!
TWO ROLLS OF PACKING TAPE, TWO ROLLS OF FIVE-COLOR TAPE.
ARGH, SOLD OUT?!
YEAH!!
YEAH!!
YEAH!!
ARIMA? I JUST SAW HIM, BUT...
WHAT A SHAME.
HE JUST LEFT.
WRONG, ALL WRONG!
IS IT OKAY TO GET THESE PROGRAMS PRINTED?
NO. BETTER GET THEM CHECKED BY THE STUDENT COUNCIL.
NOPE, HE HASN'T BEEN HERE.

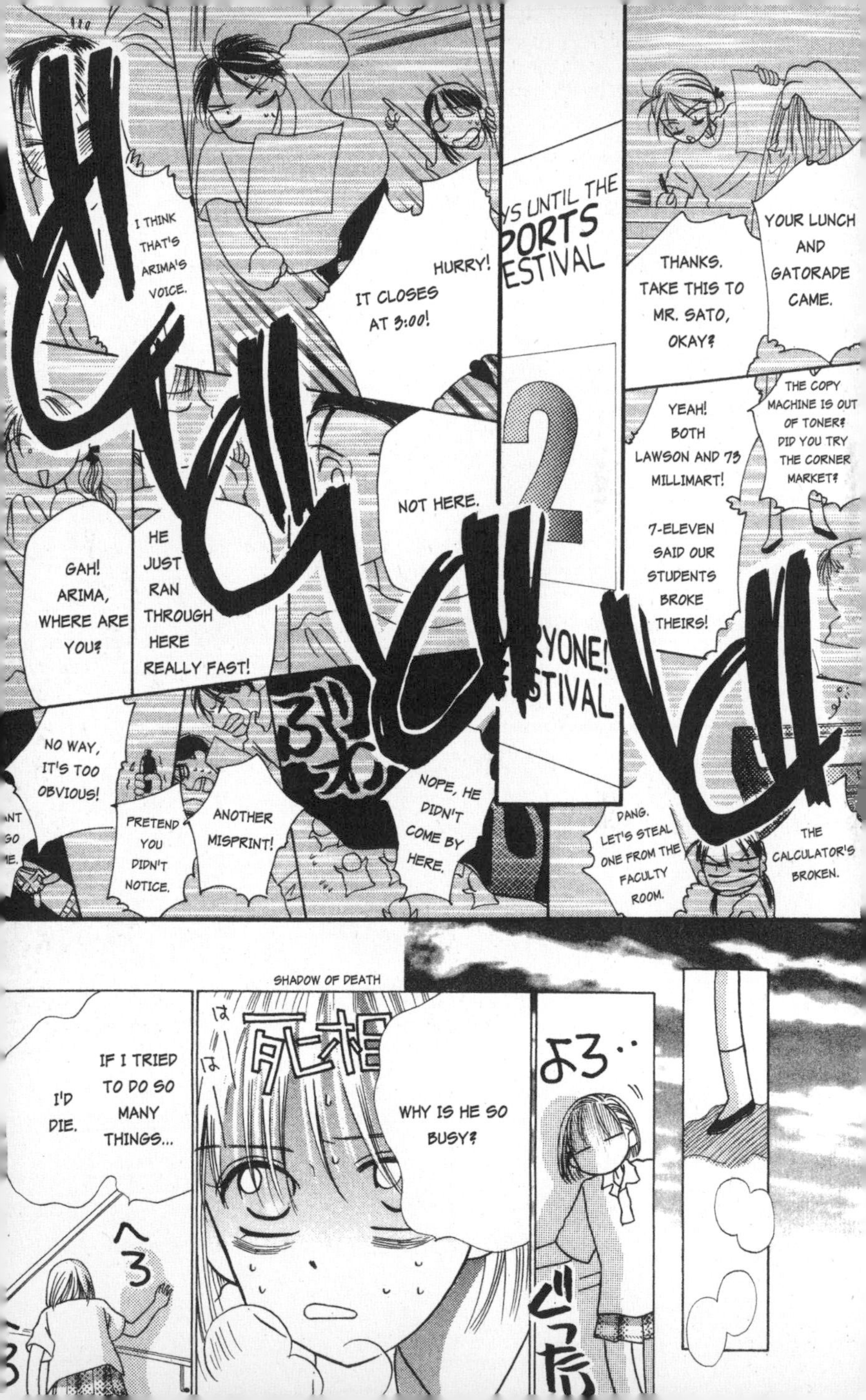

YOUR LUNCH AND GATORADE CAME.
THANKS. TAKE THIS TO MR. SATO, OKAY?
YS UNTIL THE
PORTS
ESTIVAL
2
HURRY!
IT CLOSES AT 3:00!
I THINK THAT'S ARIMA'S VOICE.
THE COPY MACHINE IS OUT OF TONER? DID YOU TRY THE CORNER MARKET?
YEAH! BOTH LAWSON AND 73 MILLIMART!
7-ELEVEN SAID OUR STUDENTS BROKE THEIRS!
RYONE!
STIVAL
NOT HERE.
HE JUST RAN THROUGH HERE REALLY FAST!
GAH! ARIMA, WHERE ARE YOU?
THE CALCULATOR'S BROKEN.
DANG. LET'S STEAL ONE FROM THE FACULTY ROOM.
NOPE, HE DIDN'T COME BY HERE.
ANOTHER MISPRINT!
PRETEND YOU DIDN'T NOTICE.
NO WAY, IT'S TOO OBVIOUS!
SHADOW OF DEATH
よろ‥
WHY IS HE SO BUSY?
はは
IF I TRIED TO DO SO MANY THINGS...
I'D DIE.
へろ

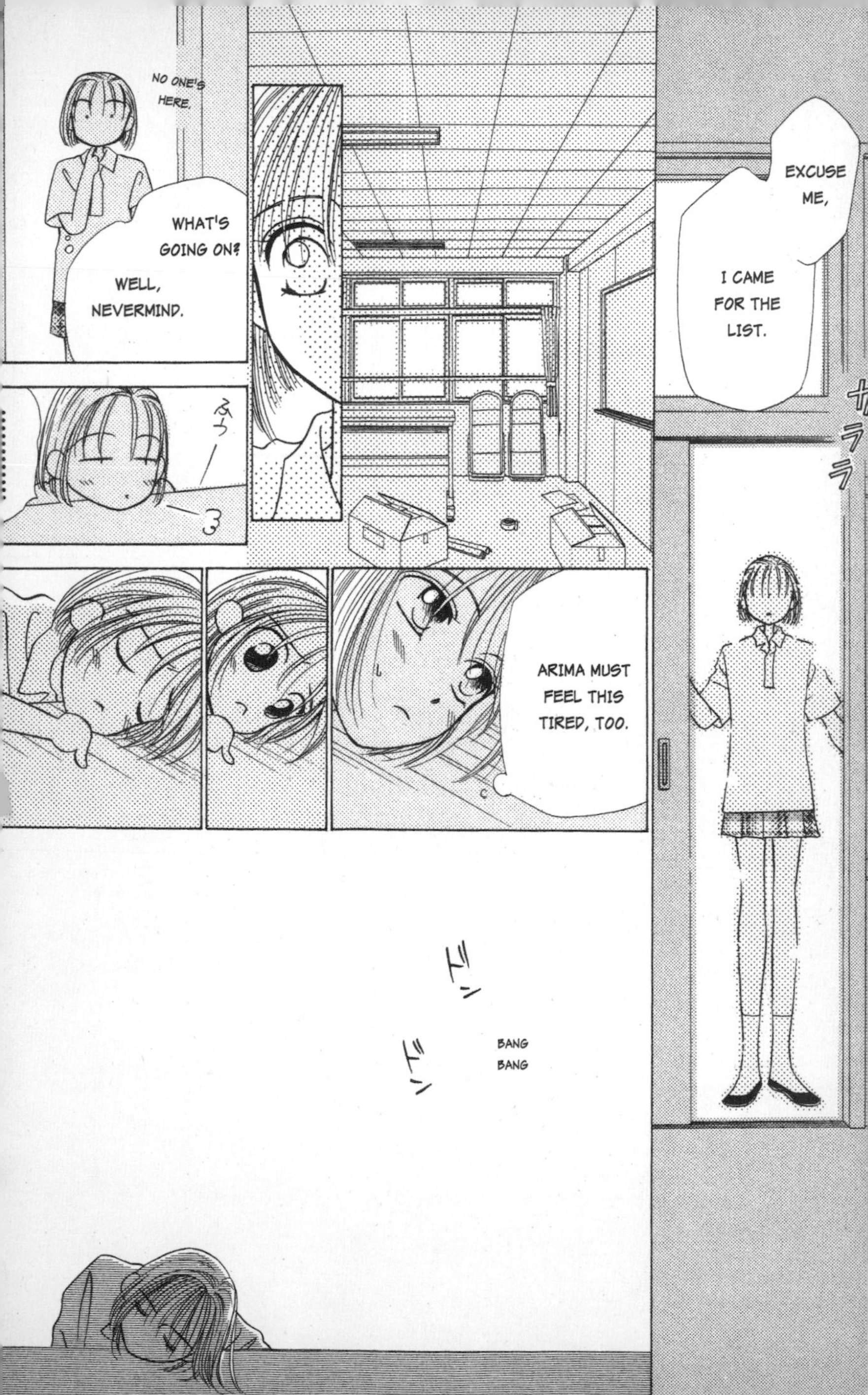
EXCUSE ME,
I CAME FOR THE LIST.
ガララ
NO ONE'S HERE.
WHAT'S GOING ON?
WELL, NEVERMIND.
ふう
ARIMA MUST FEEL THIS TIRED, TOO.
ドン
ドン
BANG
BANG

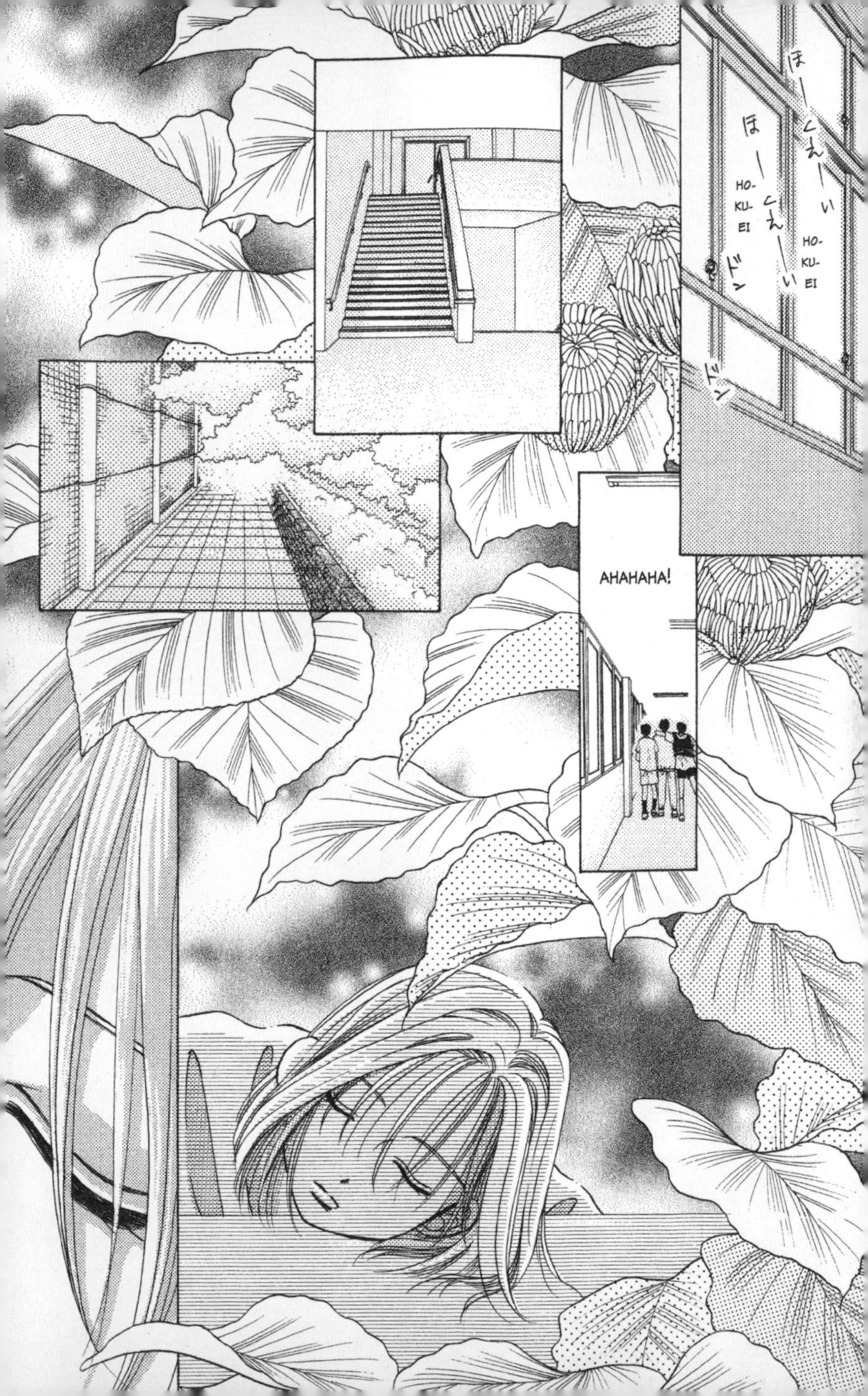
ほーくえーい
HO-KU-EI
ほーくえーい
HO-KU-EI
ドン
ドン
AHAHAHA!

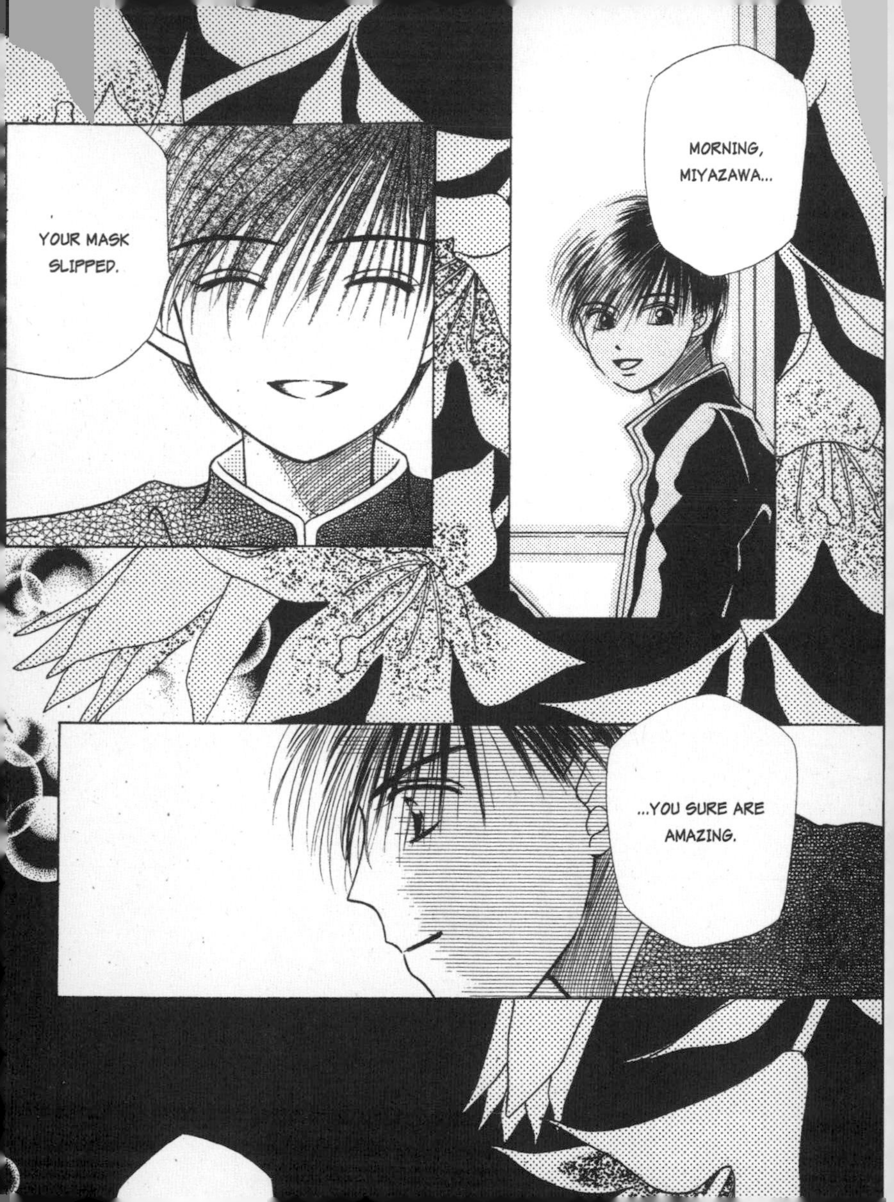
MORNING, MIYAZAWA...
YOUR MASK SLIPPED.
...YOU SURE ARE AMAZING.

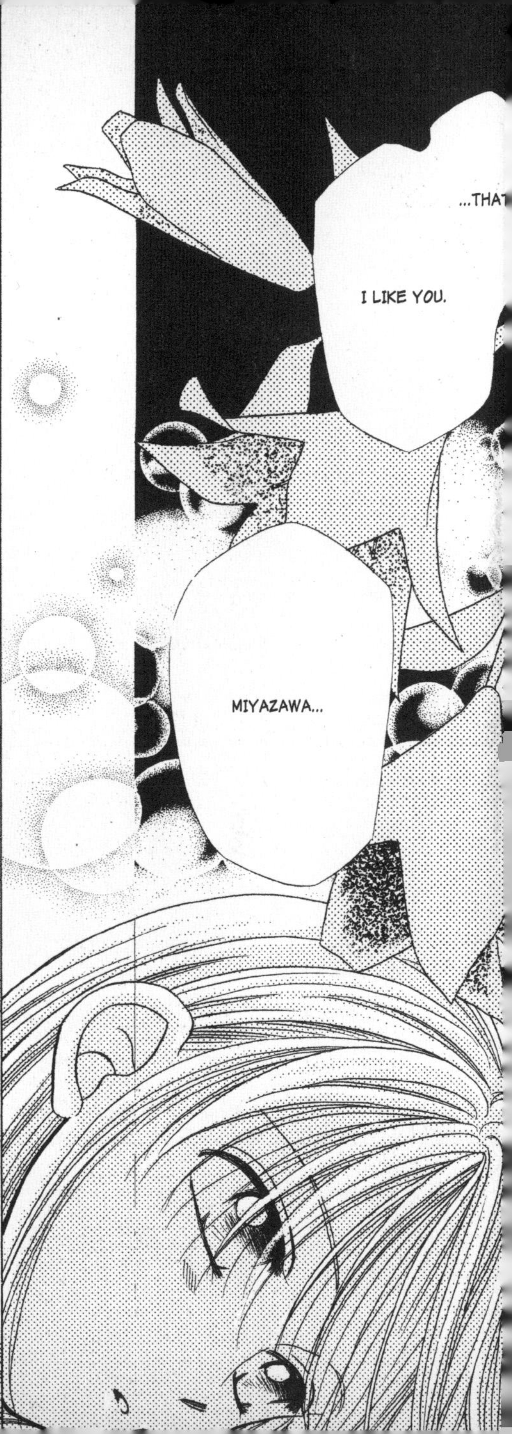
...THAT
I LIKE YOU.
MIYAZAWA...

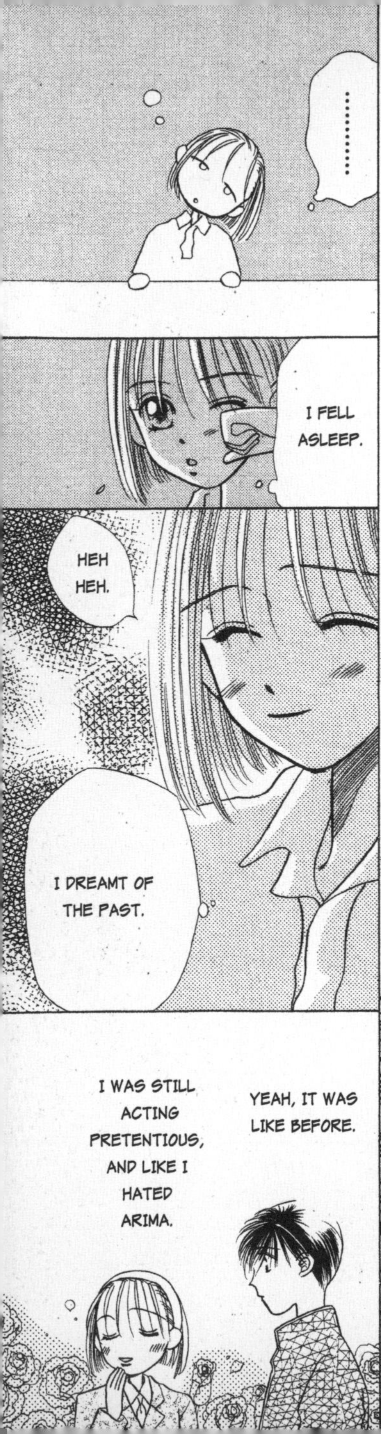
......
I FELL ASLEEP.
HEH HEH.
I DREAMT OF THE PAST.
YEAH, IT WAS LIKE BEFORE.
I WAS STILL ACTING PRETENTIOUS, AND LIKE I HATED ARIMA.

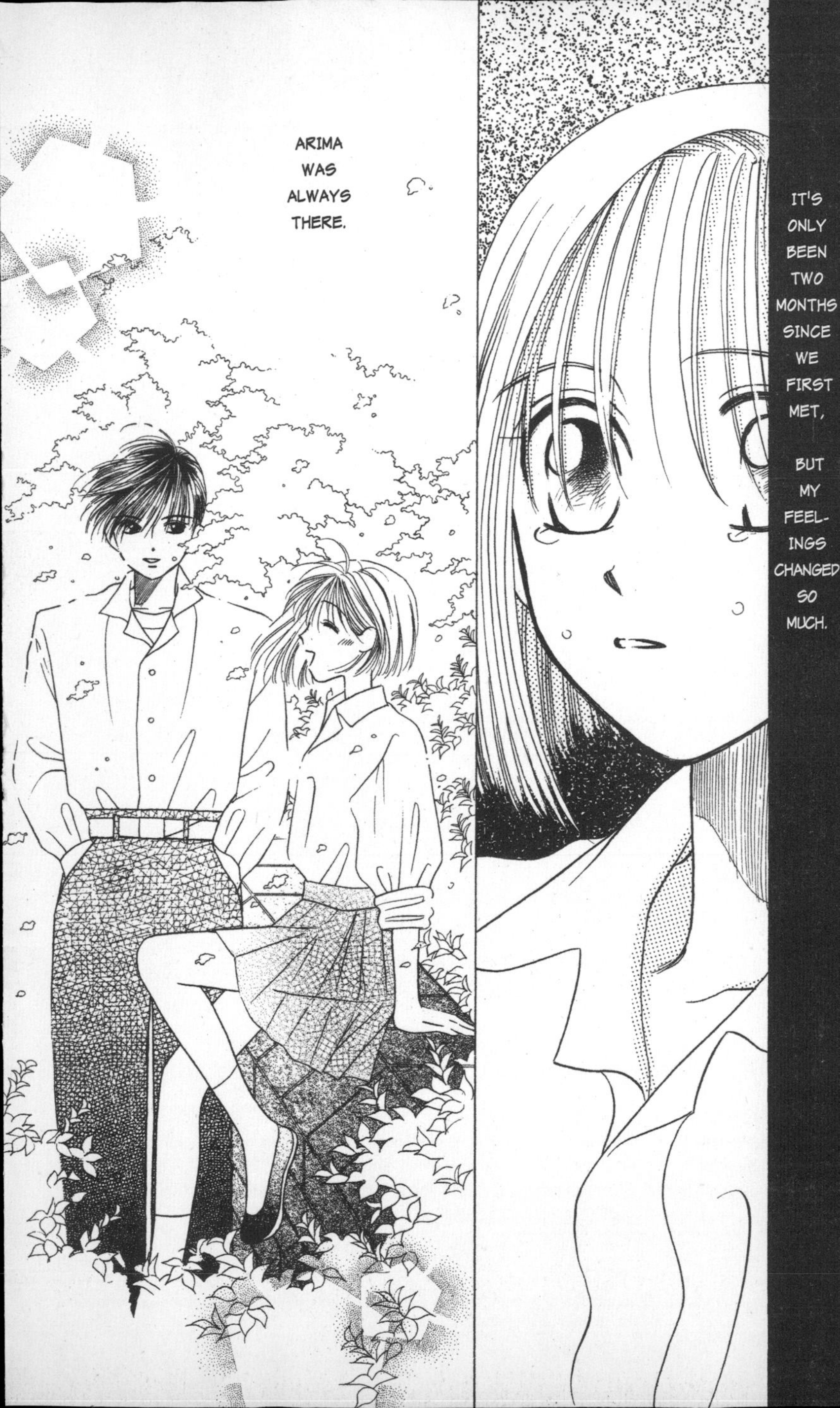
IT'S ONLY BEEN TWO MONTHS SINCE WE FIRST MET,
BUT MY FEEL-INGS CHANGED SO MUCH.
ARIMA WAS ALWAYS THERE.

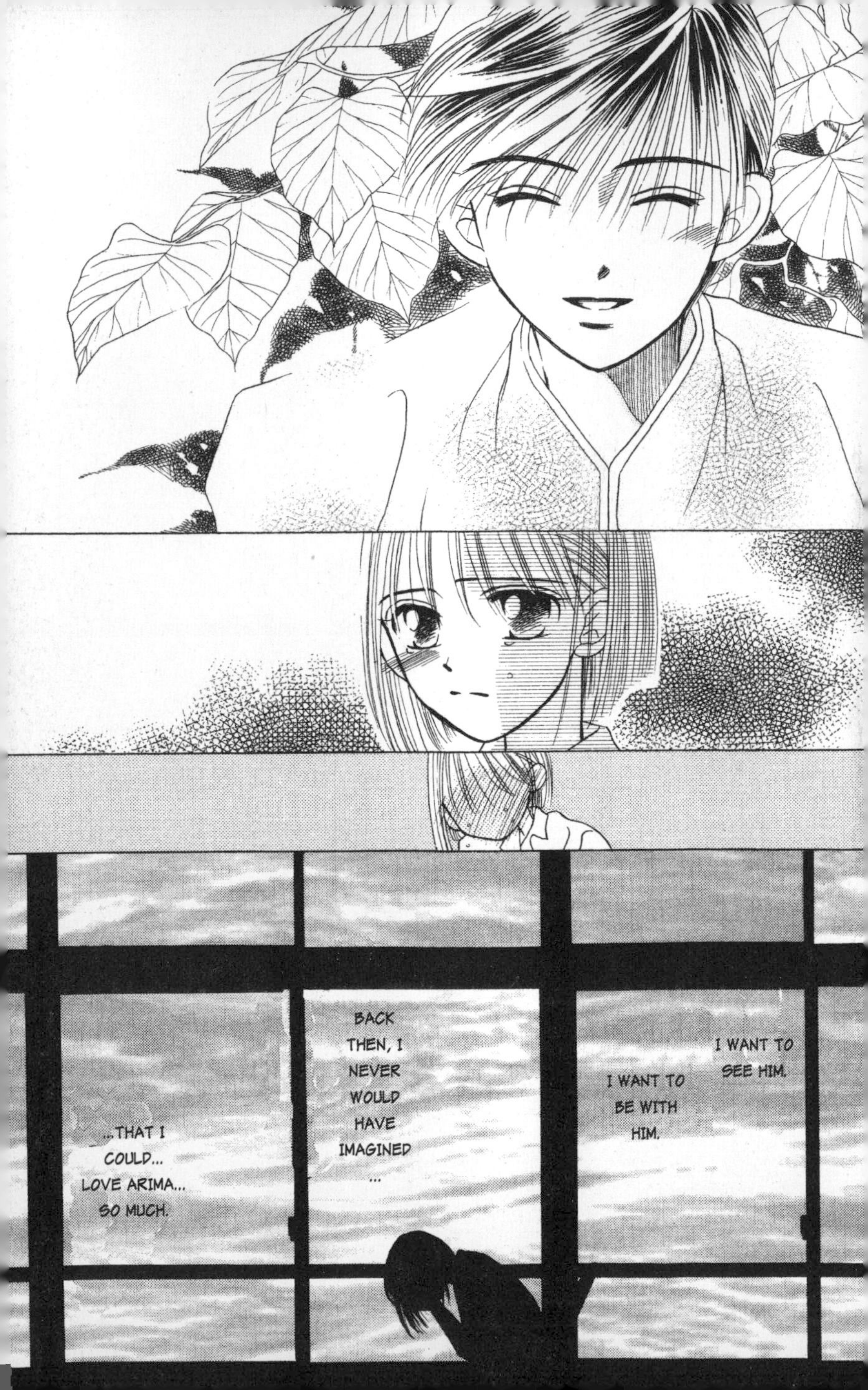
I WANT TO SEE HIM.
I WANT TO BE WITH HIM.
BACK THEN, I NEVER WOULD HAVE IMAGINED ...
...THAT I COULD... LOVE ARIMA... SO MUCH.

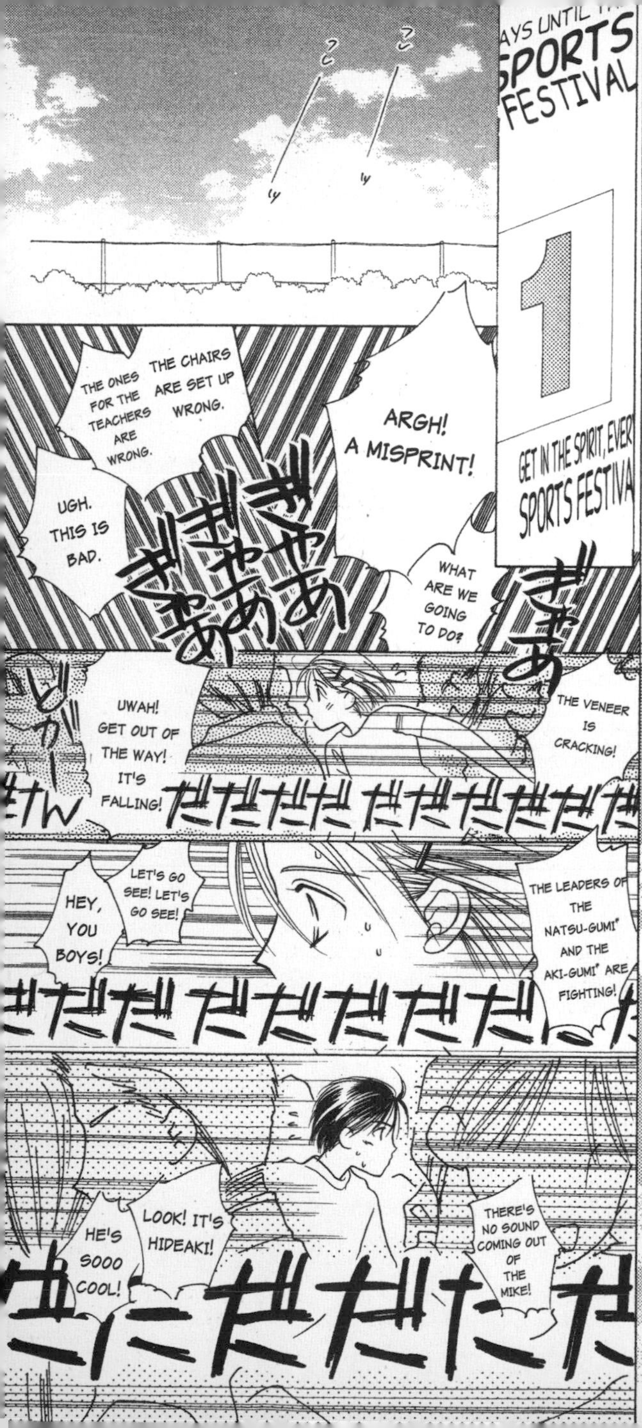
AYS UNTIL
SPORTS FESTIVAL
1
GET IN THE SPIRIT, EVER
SPORTS FESTIVA
ARGH! A MISPRINT!
WHAT ARE WE GOING TO DO?
ぎゃあぎゃあ
THE CHAIRS ARE SET UP WRONG.
THE ONES FOR THE TEACHERS ARE WRONG.
UGH. THIS IS BAD.
THE VENEER IS CRACKING!
UWAH! GET OUT OF THE WAY! IT'S FALLING!
だだだだだだだ
THE LEADERS OF THE NATSU-GUMI* AND THE AKI-GUMI* ARE FIGHTING!
LET'S GO SEE! LET'S GO SEE!
HEY, YOU BOYS!
THERE'S NO SOUND COMING OUT OF THE MIKE!
LOOK! IT'S HIDEAKI!
HE'S SOOO COOL!

* NATSU-GUMI - SUMMER GROUP
AKI-GUMI - FALL GROUP

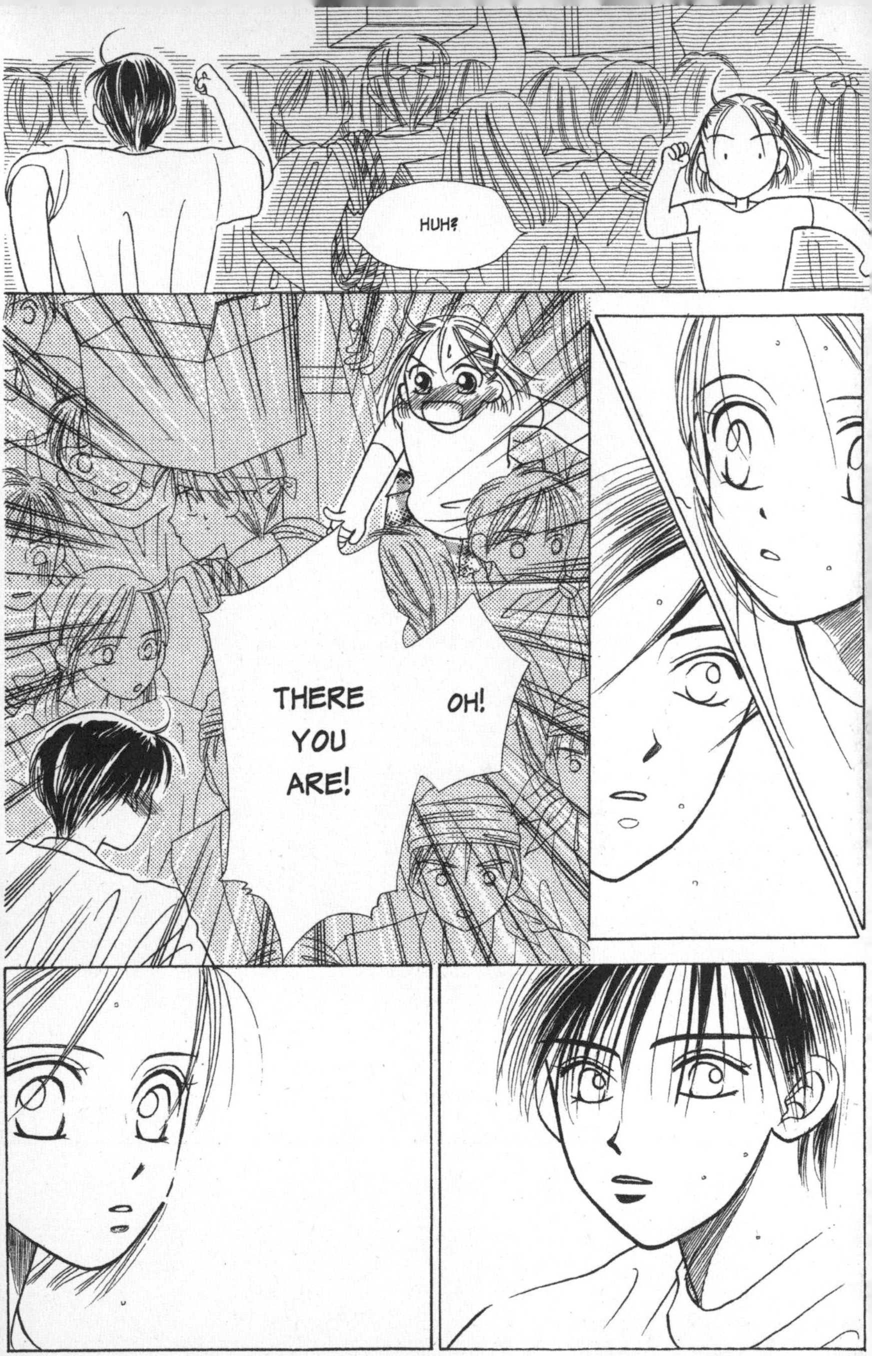
HUH?
OH!
THERE YOU ARE!

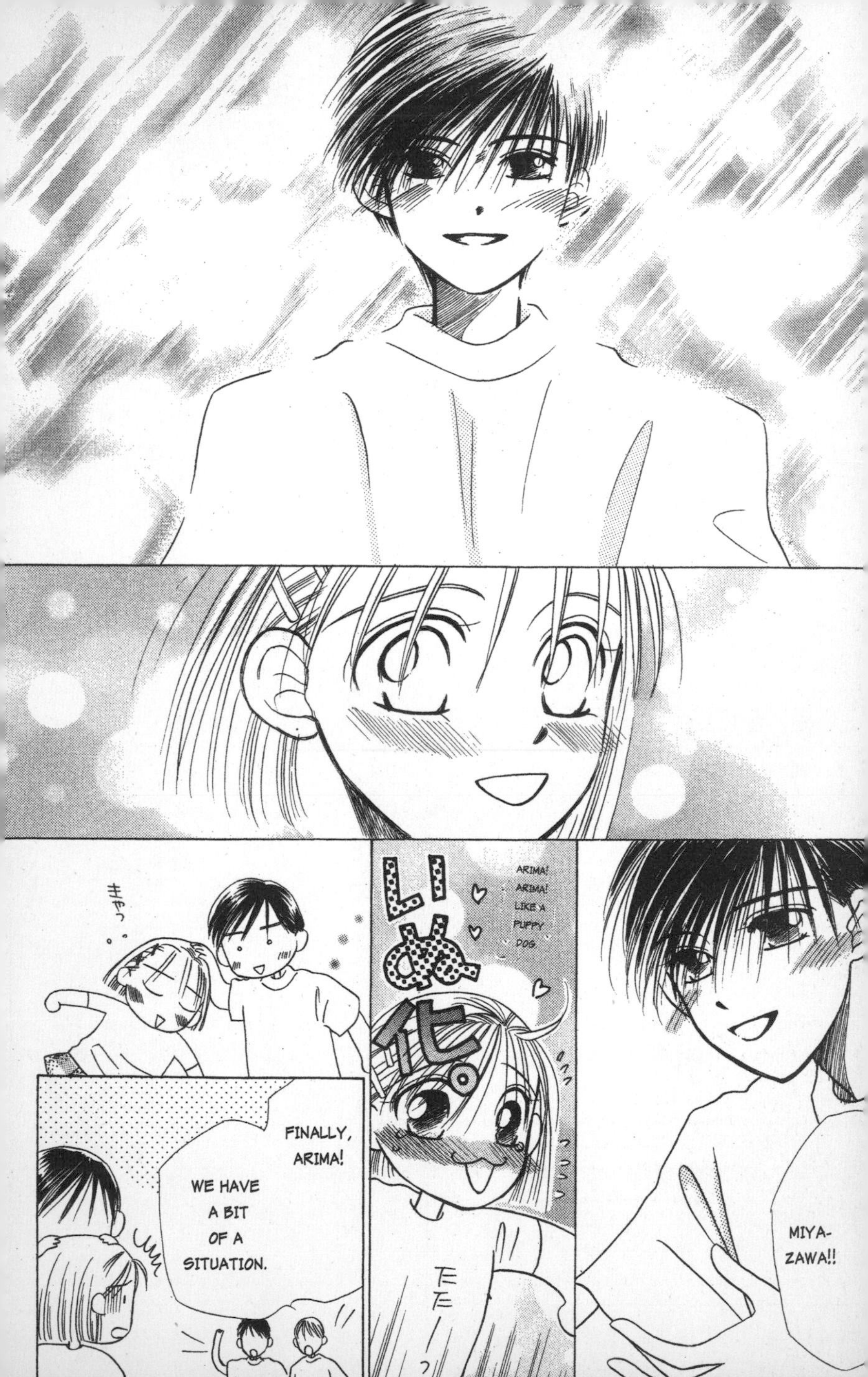
MIYA-ZAWA!!
いぬ化。
ARIMA! ARIMA! LIKE A PUPPY DOG.
FINALLY, ARIMA!
WE HAVE A BIT OF A SITUATION.

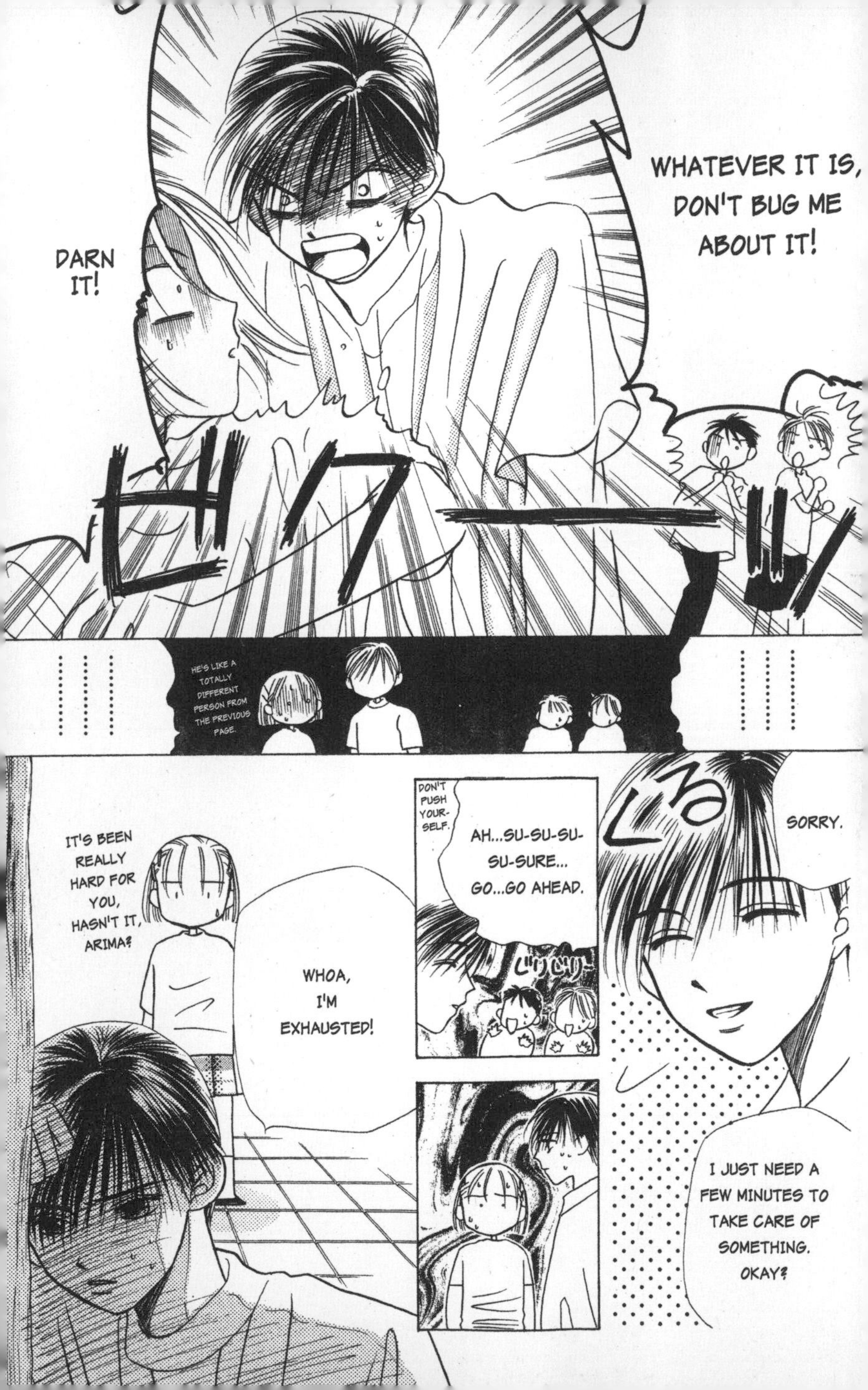
WHATEVER IT IS, DON'T BUG ME ABOUT IT!
DARN IT!
ビクーッ
......
HE'S LIKE A TOTALLY DIFFERENT PERSON FROM THE PREVIOUS PAGE.
......
SORRY.
I JUST NEED A FEW MINUTES TO TAKE CARE OF SOMETHING. OKAY?
AH...SU-SU-SU-SU-SURE... GO...GO AHEAD.
DON'T PUSH YOURSELF.
WHOA, I'M EXHAUSTED!
IT'S BEEN REALLY HARD FOR YOU, HASN'T IT, ARIMA?

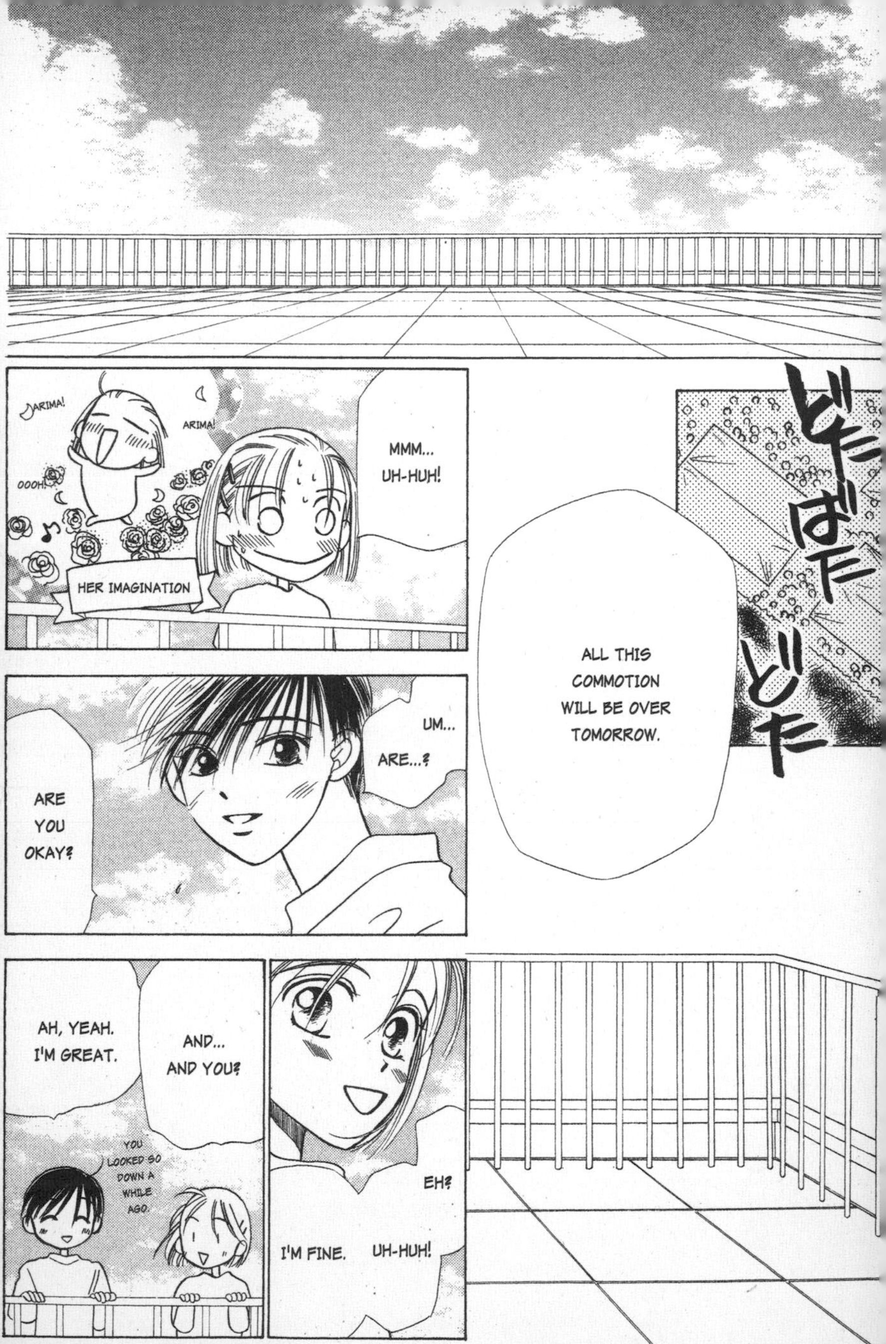

どたばたどた
ALL THIS COMMOTION WILL BE OVER TOMORROW.
MMM... UH-HUH!
ARIMA!
ARIMA!
OOOH!
HER IMAGINATION
UM... ARE...?
ARE YOU OKAY?
EH?
I'M FINE. UH-HUH!
AND... AND YOU?
AH, YEAH. I'M GREAT.
YOU LOOKED SO DOWN A WHILE AGO.

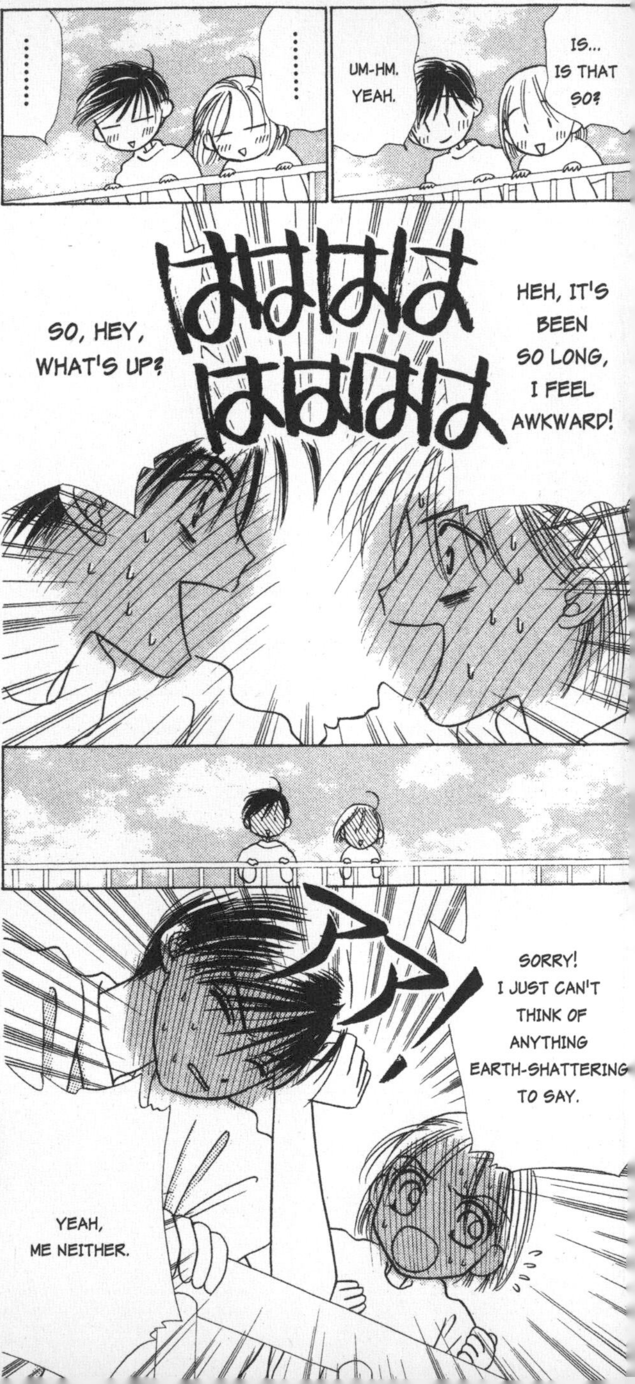
IS... IS THAT SO?
UM-HM. YEAH.
......
......
HEH, IT'S BEEN SO LONG, I FEEL AWKWARD!
はははは
ははは は
SO, HEY, WHAT'S UP?
アア!
SORRY! I JUST CAN'T THINK OF ANYTHING EARTH-SHATTERING TO SAY.
YEAH, ME NEITHER.

3

The Taiwanese edition of "Kare Kano" is called...

「男女会会板」といいます。

These are characters that aren't in Japanese.

I wonder what the literal translation is!

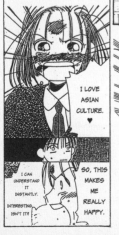

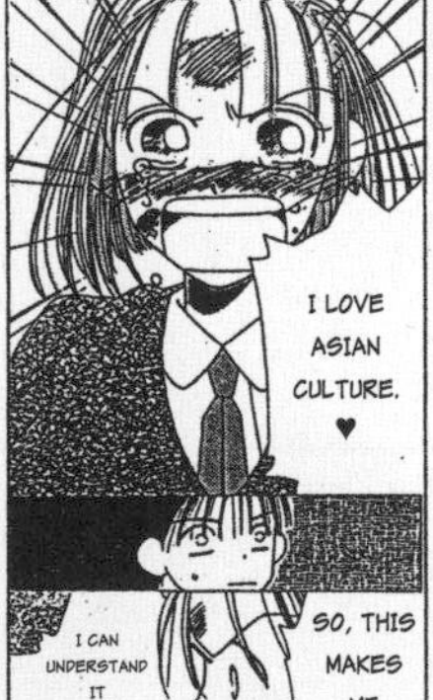
I LOVE ASIAN CULTURE. ♥
SO, THIS MAKES ME REALLY HAPPY.
I CAN UNDERSTAND IT INSTANTLY.
INTERESTING ISN'T IT?

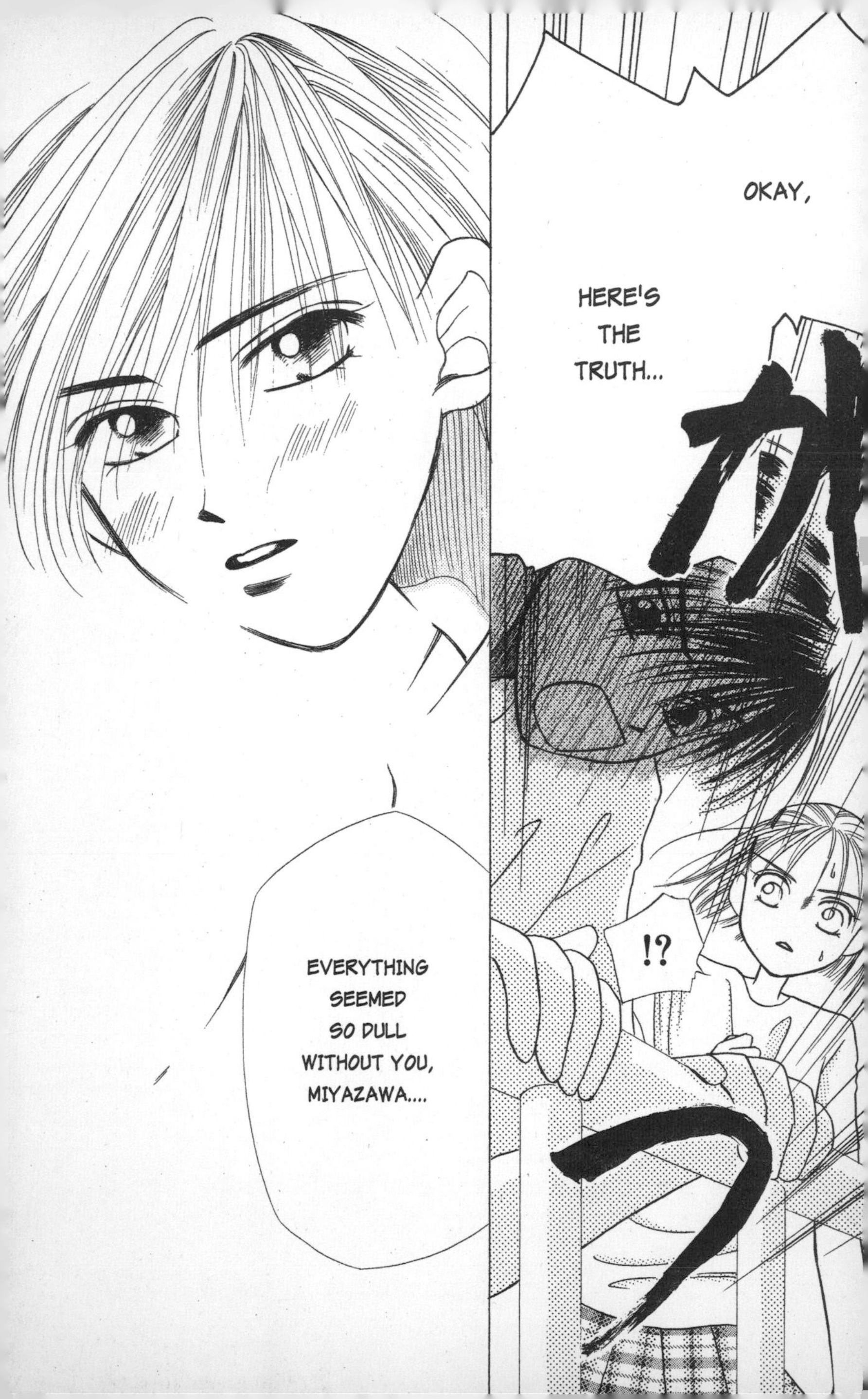
OKAY,
HERE'S THE TRUTH...
!?
EVERYTHING SEEMED SO DULL WITHOUT YOU, MIYAZAWA....

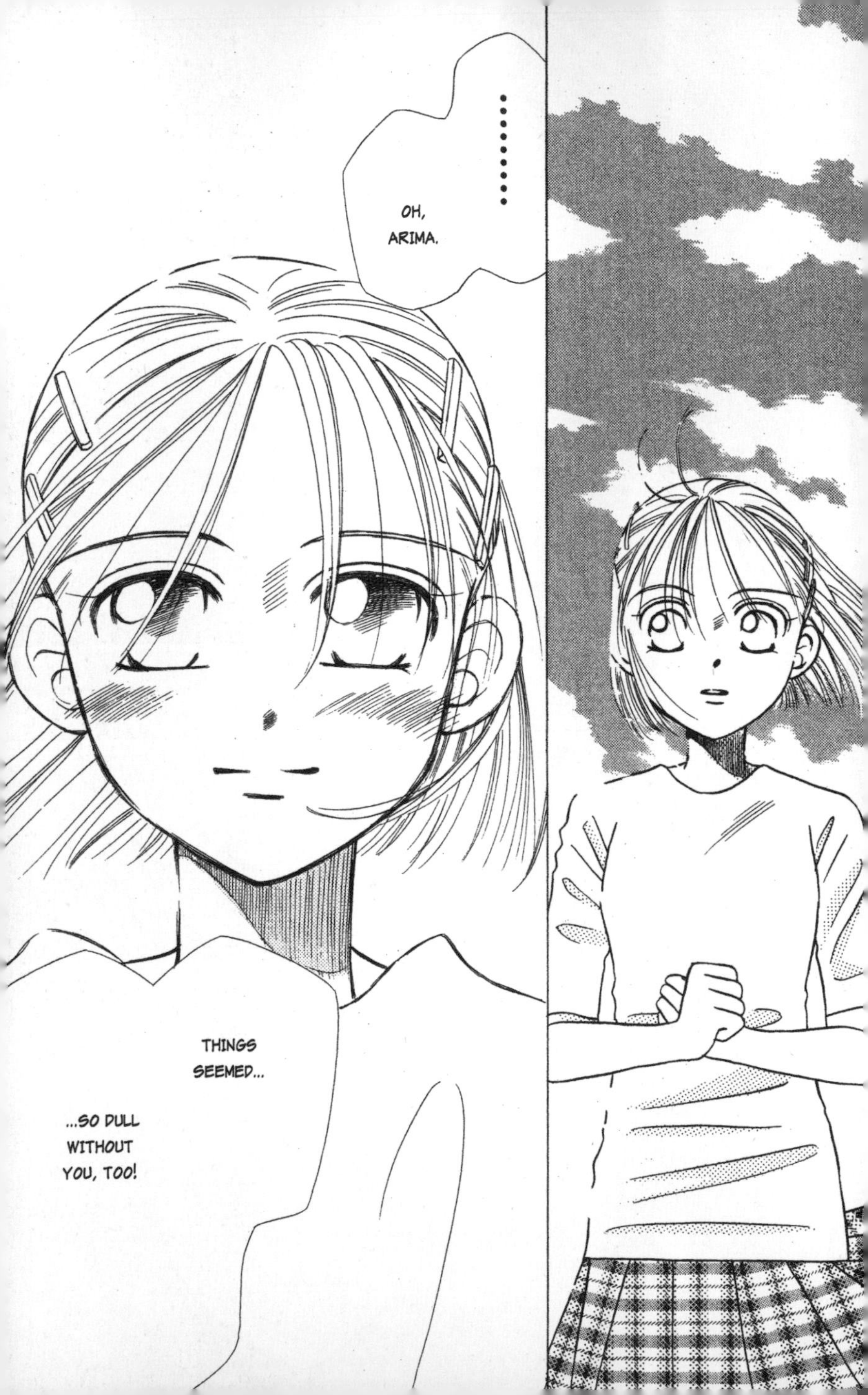

......
OH, ARIMA.
THINGS SEEMED...
...SO DULL WITHOUT YOU, TOO!

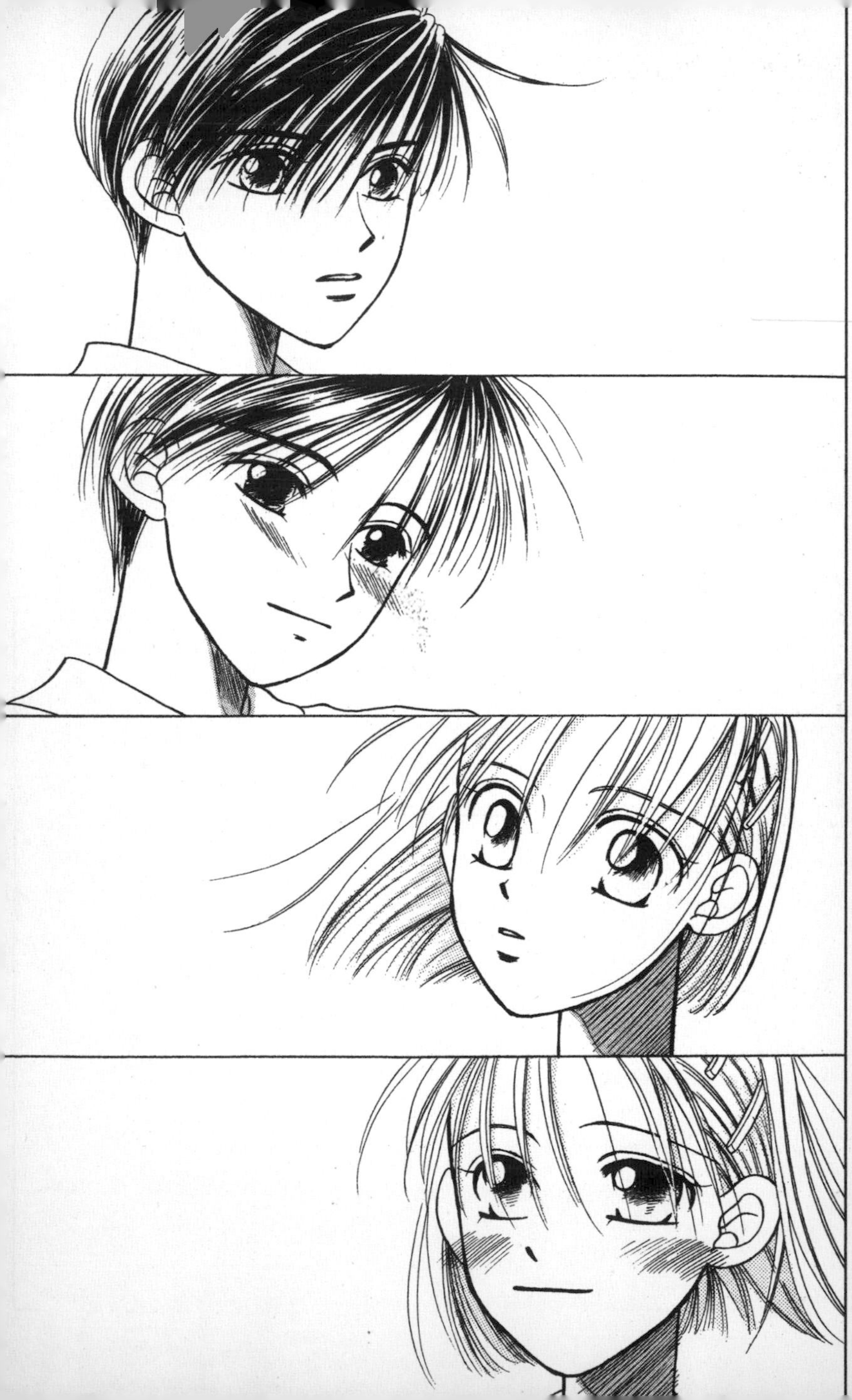

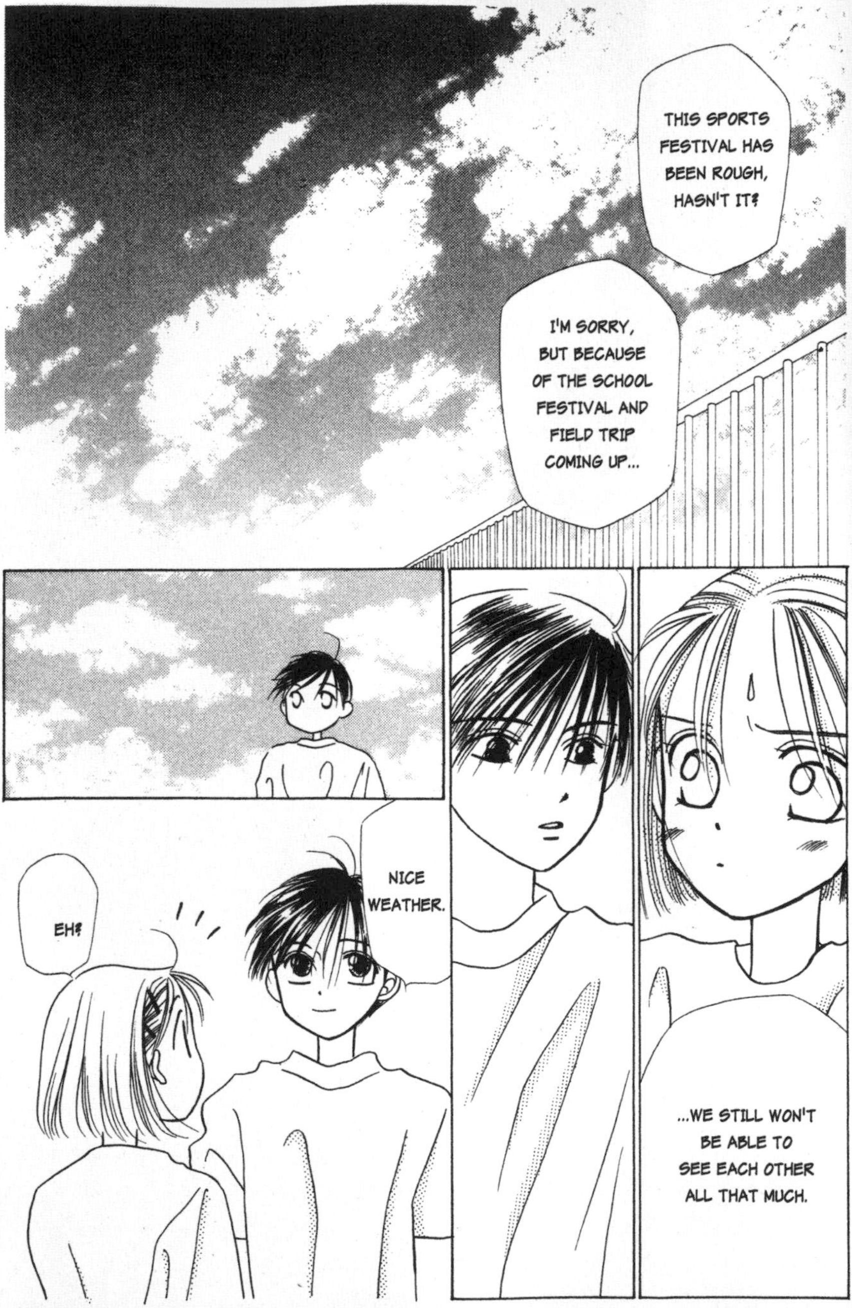
THIS SPORTS FESTIVAL HAS BEEN ROUGH, HASN'T IT?
I'M SORRY, BUT BECAUSE OF THE SCHOOL FESTIVAL AND FIELD TRIP COMING UP...
...WE STILL WON'T BE ABLE TO SEE EACH OTHER ALL THAT MUCH.
NICE WEATHER.
EH?

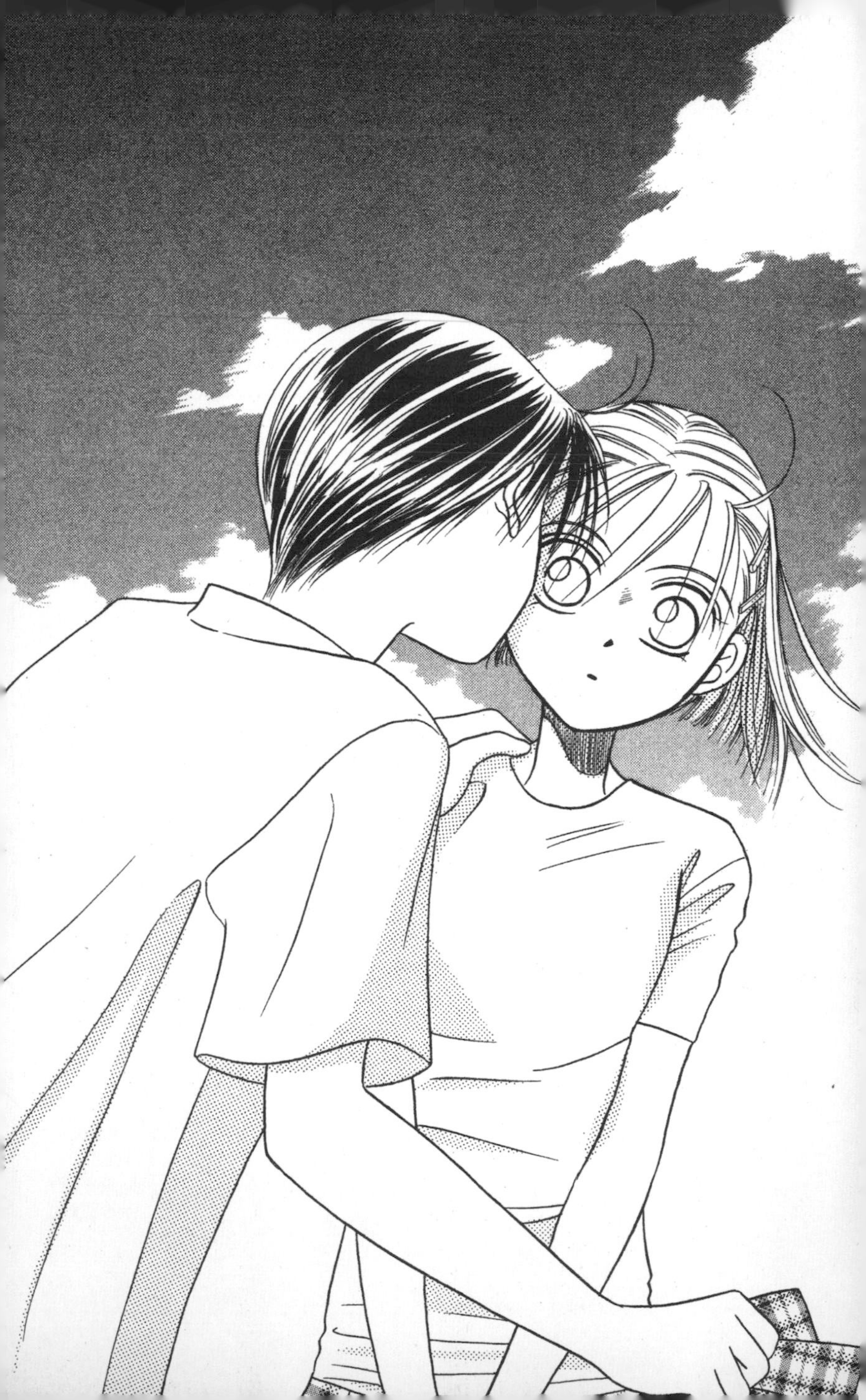

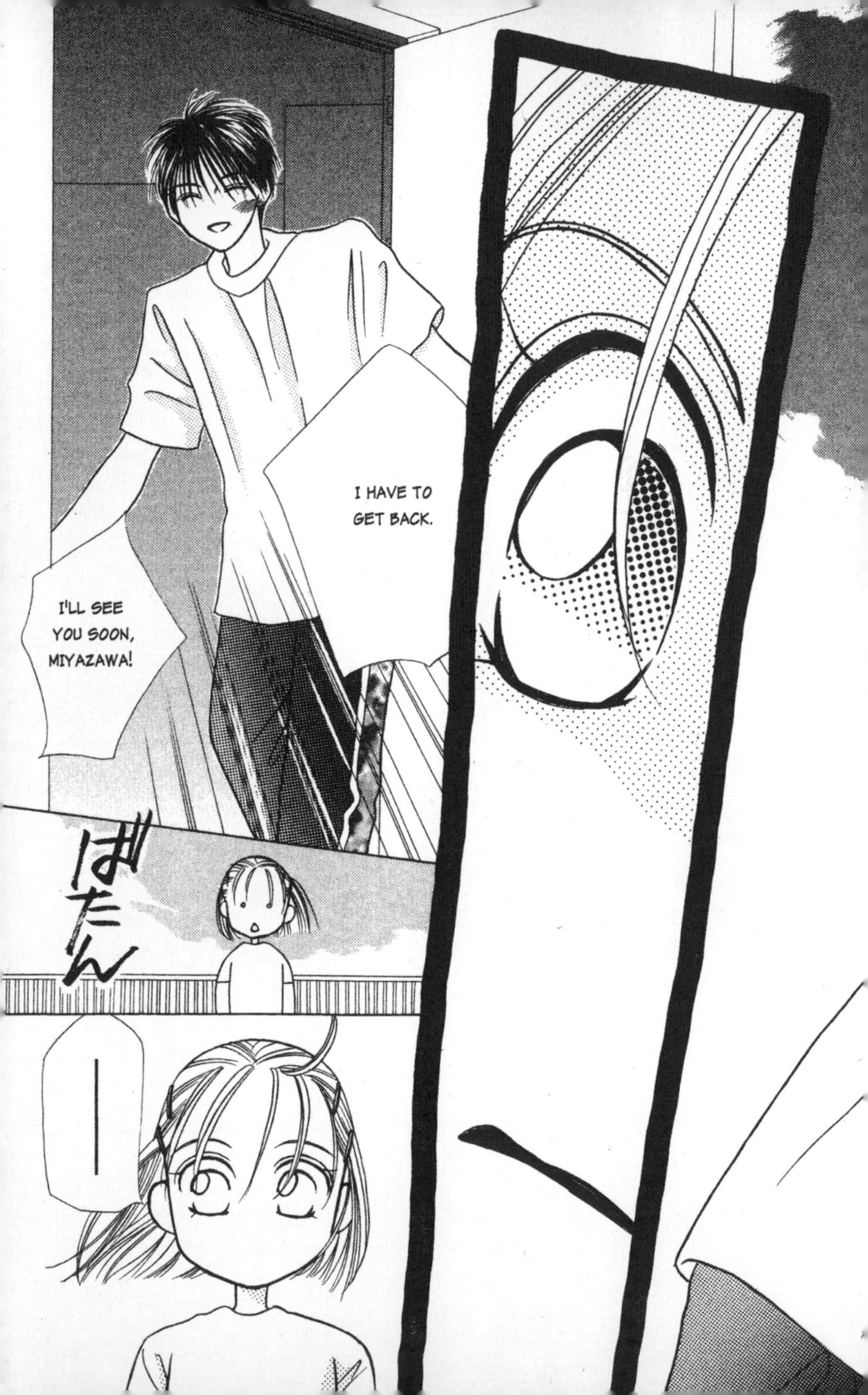
I HAVE TO GET BACK.
I'LL SEE YOU SOON, MIYAZAWA!
ばたん
―

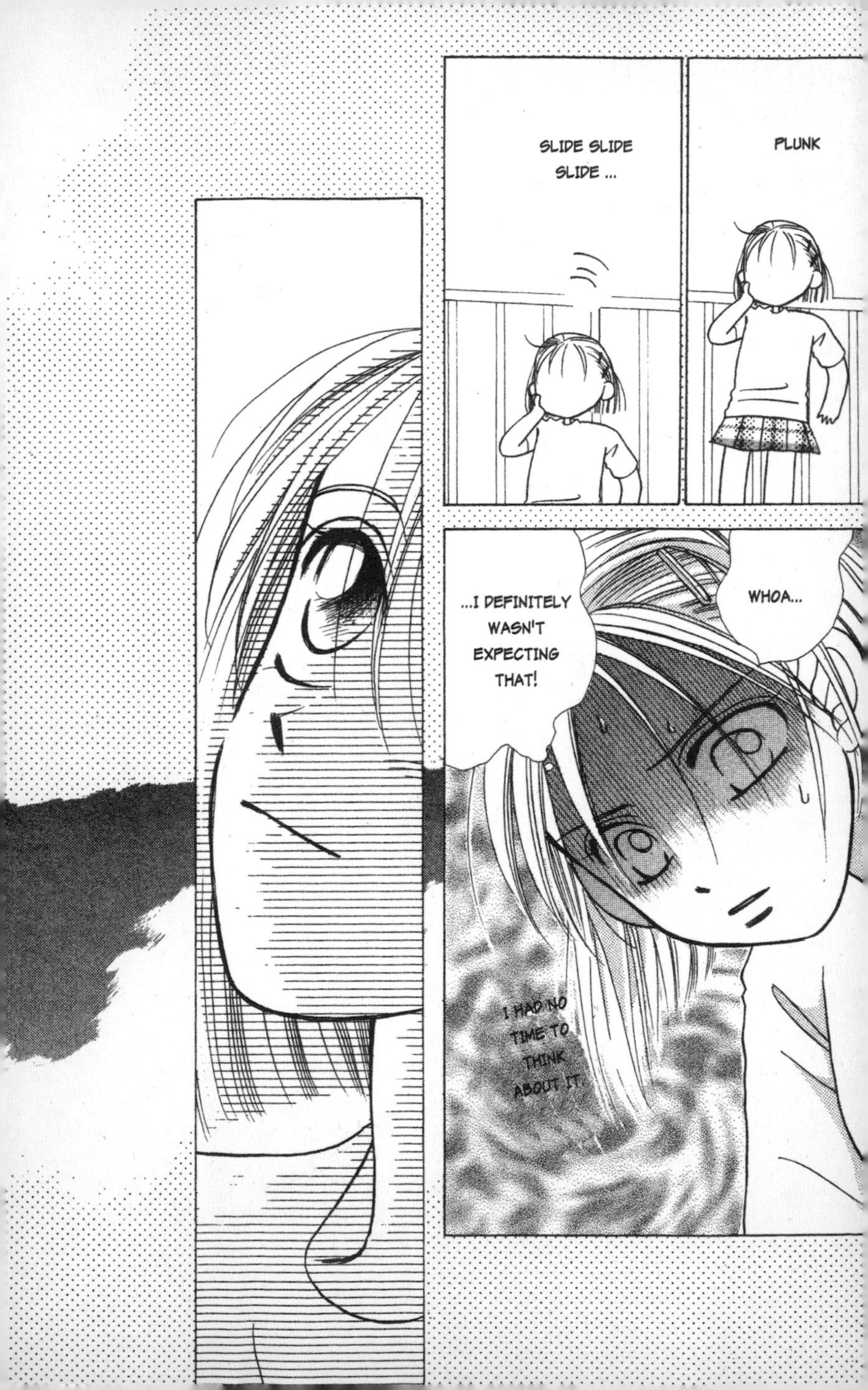
PLUNK
SLIDE SLIDE SLIDE ...
WHOA...
...I DEFINITELY WASN'T EXPECTING THAT!
I HAD NO TIME TO THINK ABOUT IT.

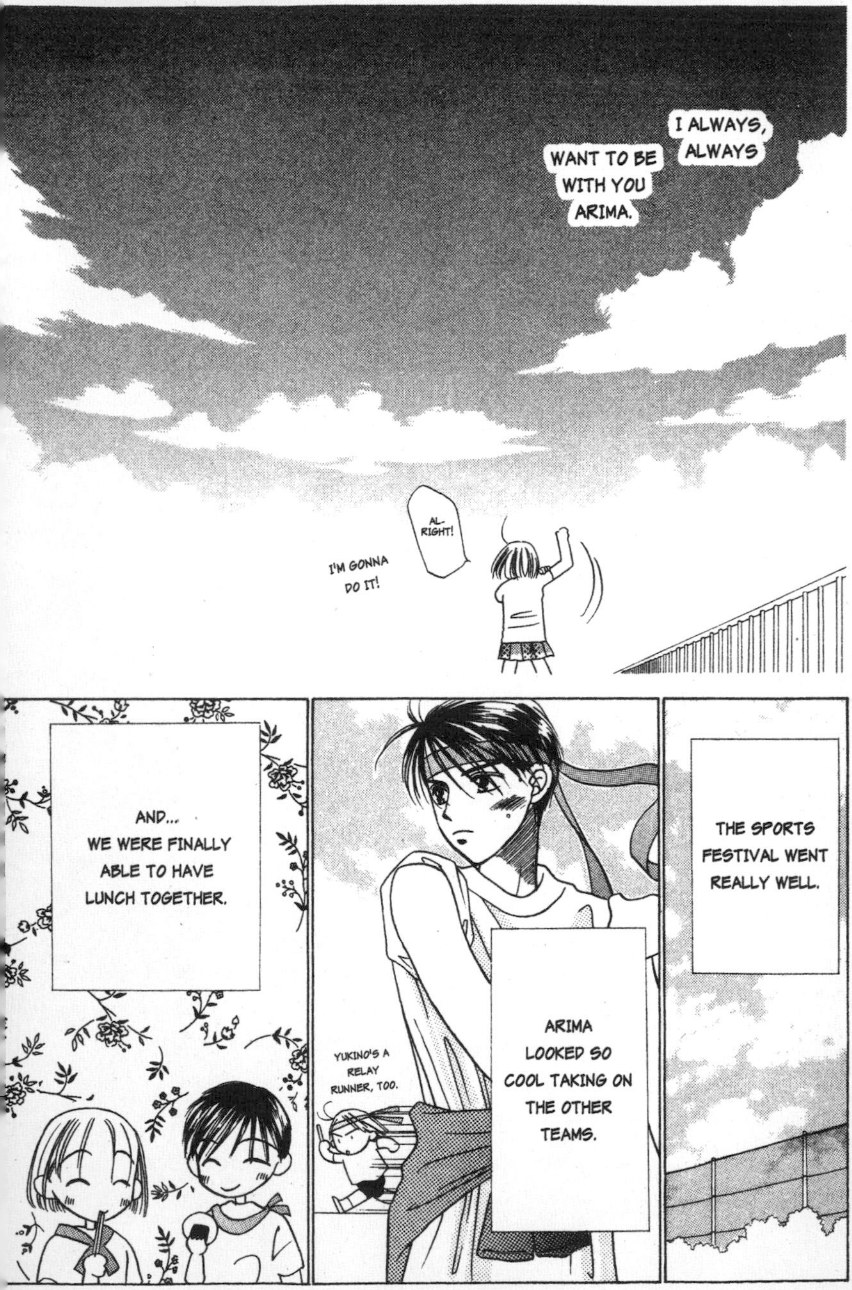
I ALWAYS, ALWAYS
WANT TO BE WITH YOU ARIMA.
AL-RIGHT!
I'M GONNA DO IT!
THE SPORTS FESTIVAL WENT REALLY WELL.
ARIMA LOOKED SO COOL TAKING ON THE OTHER TEAMS.
YUKINO'S A RELAY RUNNER, TOO.
AND... WE WERE FINALLY ABLE TO HAVE LUNCH TOGETHER.

ACT 5 ✱ SCHOOL MAZE - THE END

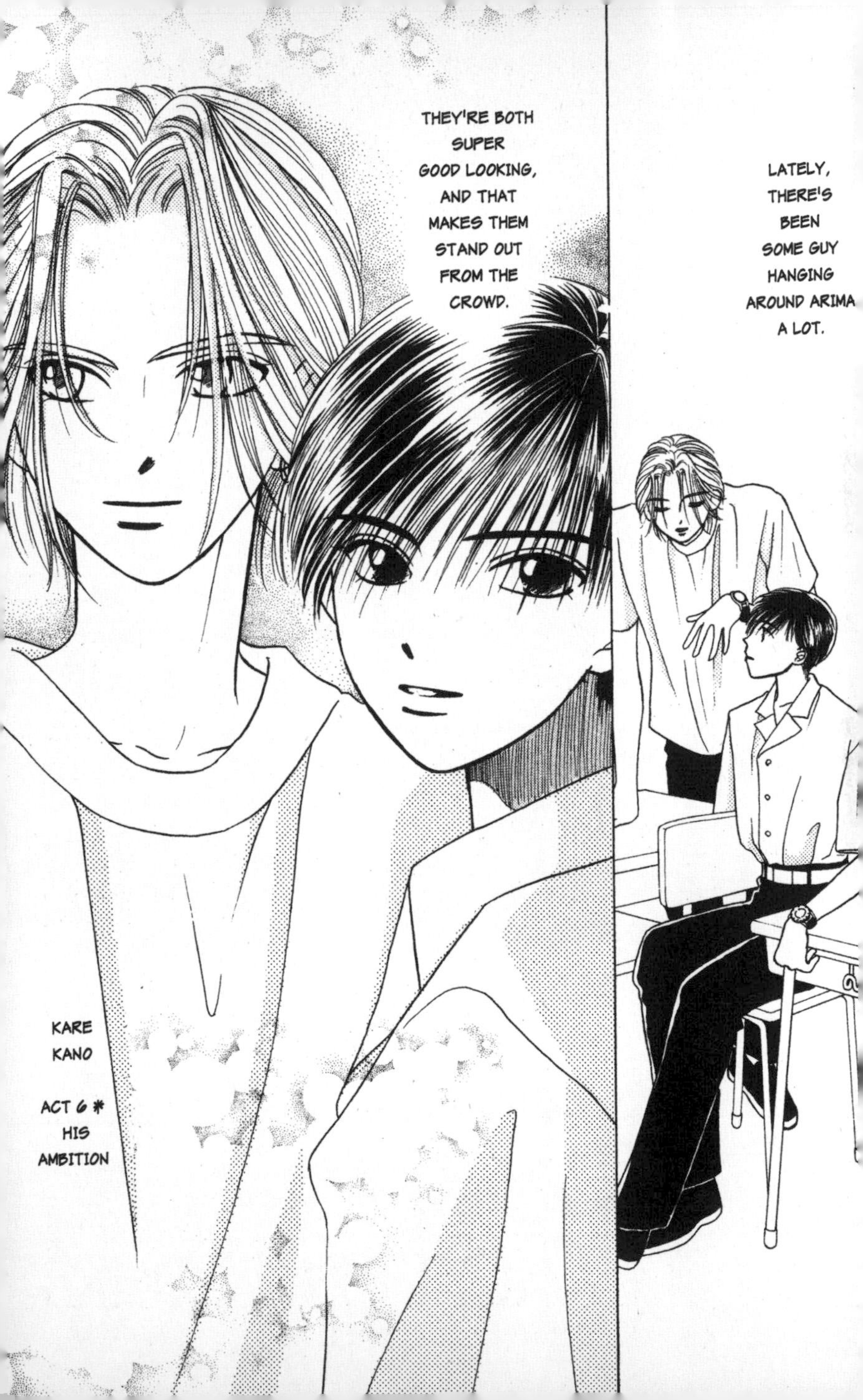
LATELY, THERE'S BEEN SOME GUY HANGING AROUND ARIMA A LOT.
THEY'RE BOTH SUPER GOOD LOOKING, AND THAT MAKES THEM STAND OUT FROM THE CROWD.
KARE KANO
ACT 6 * HIS AMBITION

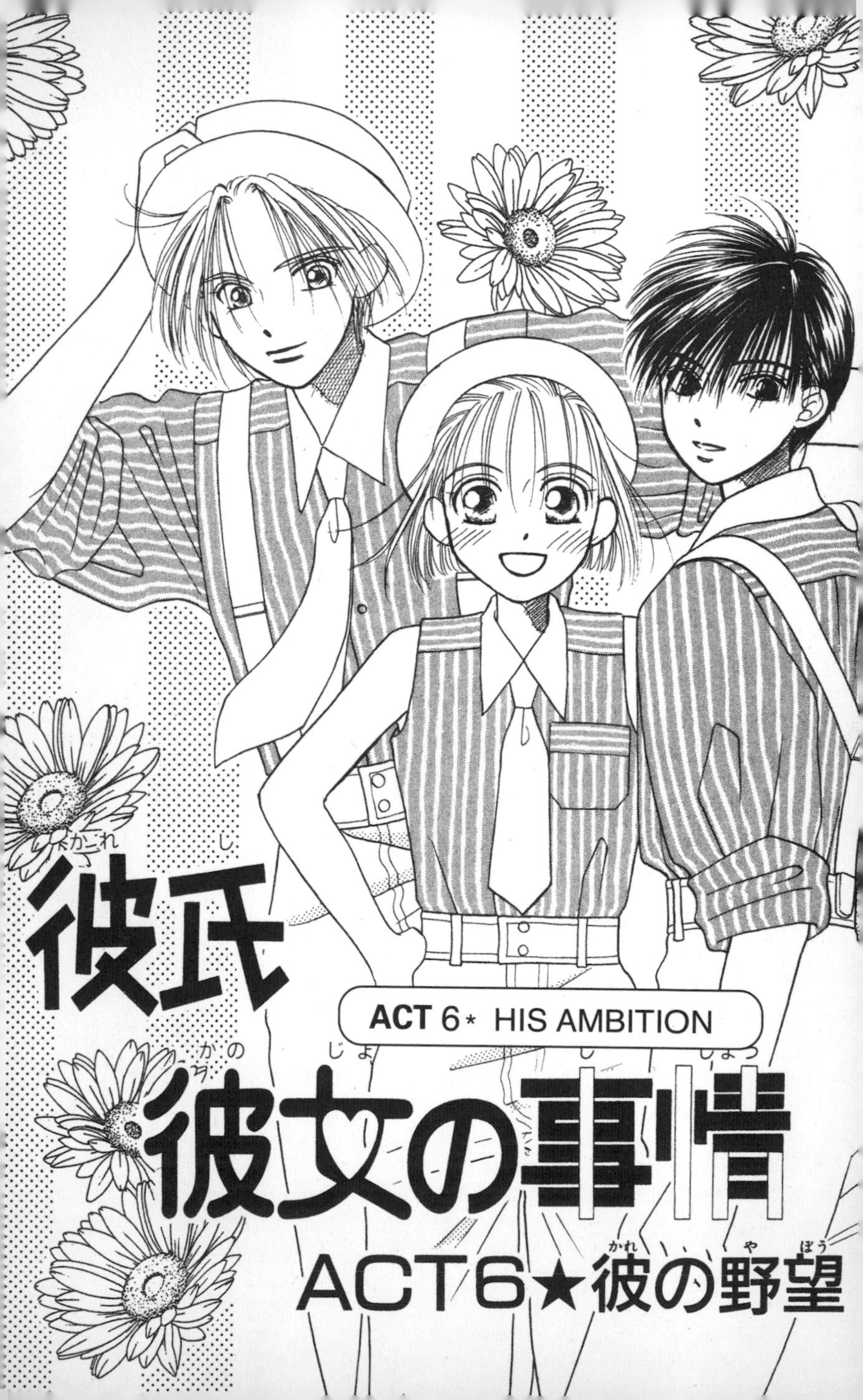
彼氏彼女の事情
ACT 6★ HIS AMBITION
ACT6★彼の野望

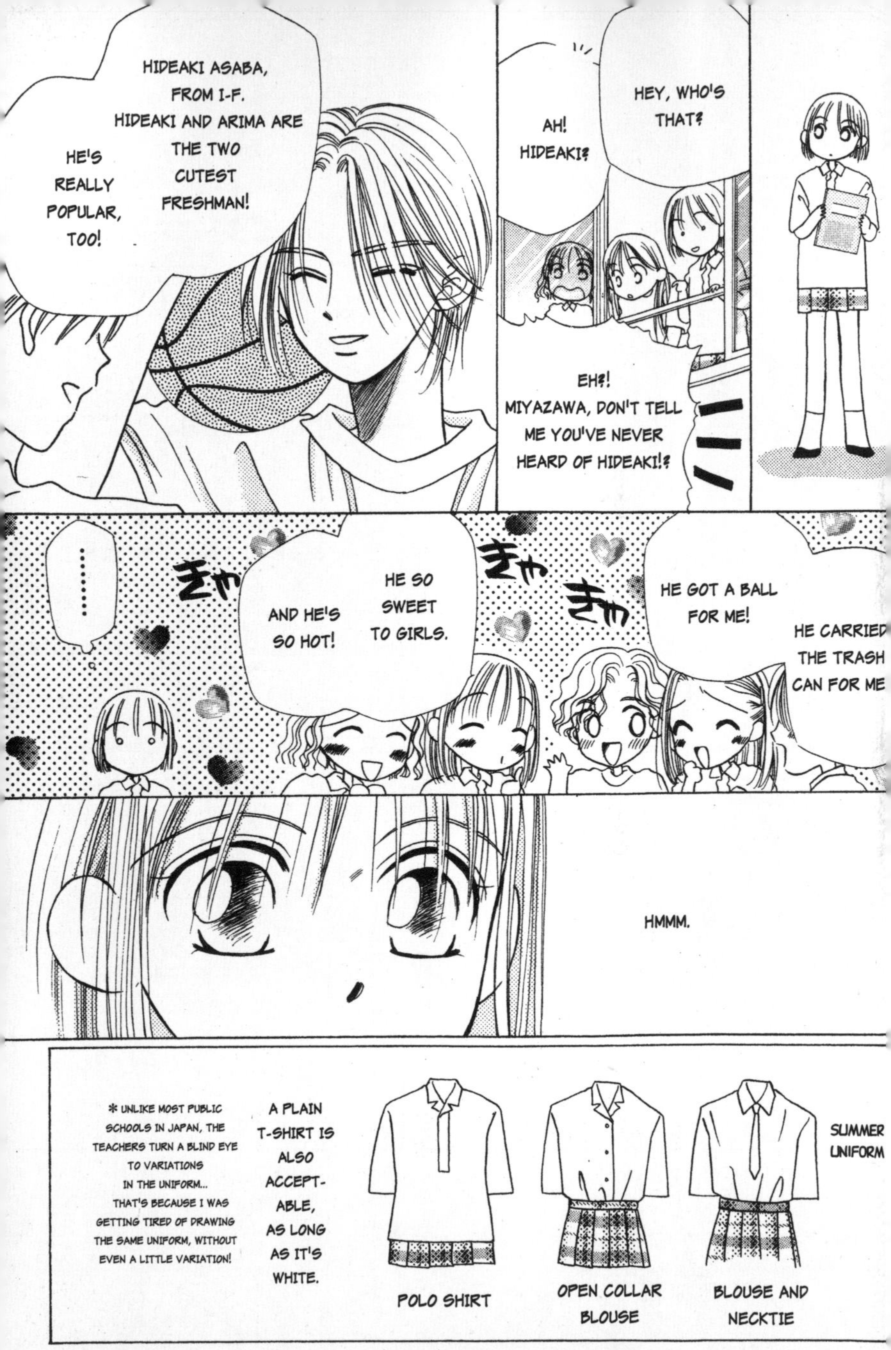
HEY, WHO'S THAT?
AH! HIDEAKI?
EH?! MIYAZAWA, DON'T TELL ME YOU'VE NEVER HEARD OF HIDEAKI!?
HIDEAKI ASABA, FROM I-F. HIDEAKI AND ARIMA ARE THE TWO CUTEST FRESHMAN!
HE'S REALLY POPULAR, TOO!
HE CARRIED THE TRASH CAN FOR ME
きゃ
きゃ
HE GOT A BALL FOR ME!
きゃ
HE SO SWEET TO GIRLS.
AND HE'S SO HOT!
きゃ
......
HMMM.
SUMMER UNIFORM
BLOUSE AND NECKTIE
OPEN COLLAR BLOUSE
POLO SHIRT
A PLAIN T-SHIRT IS ALSO ACCEPT-ABLE, AS LONG AS IT'S WHITE.
* UNLIKE MOST PUBLIC SCHOOLS IN JAPAN, THE TEACHERS TURN A BLIND EYE TO VARIATIONS IN THE UNIFORM... THAT'S BECAUSE I WAS GETTING TIRED OF DRAWING THE SAME UNIFORM, WITHOUT EVEN A LITTLE VARIATION!

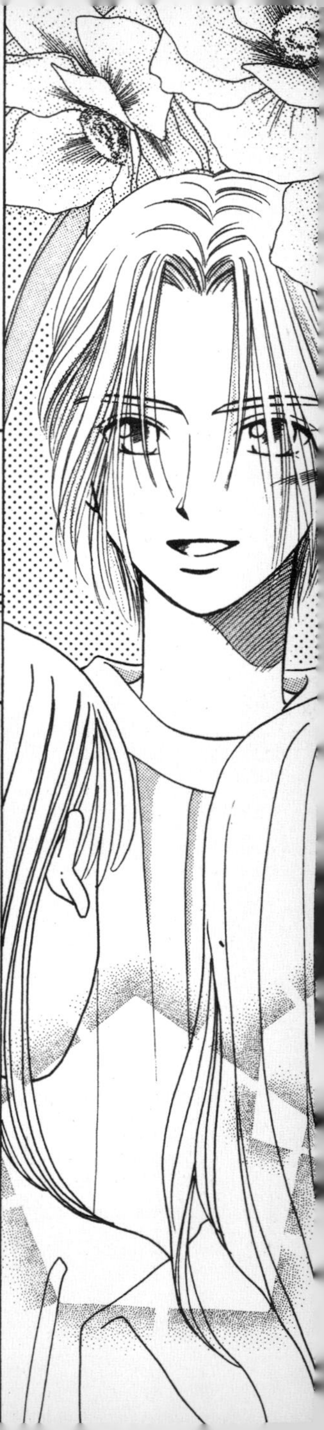

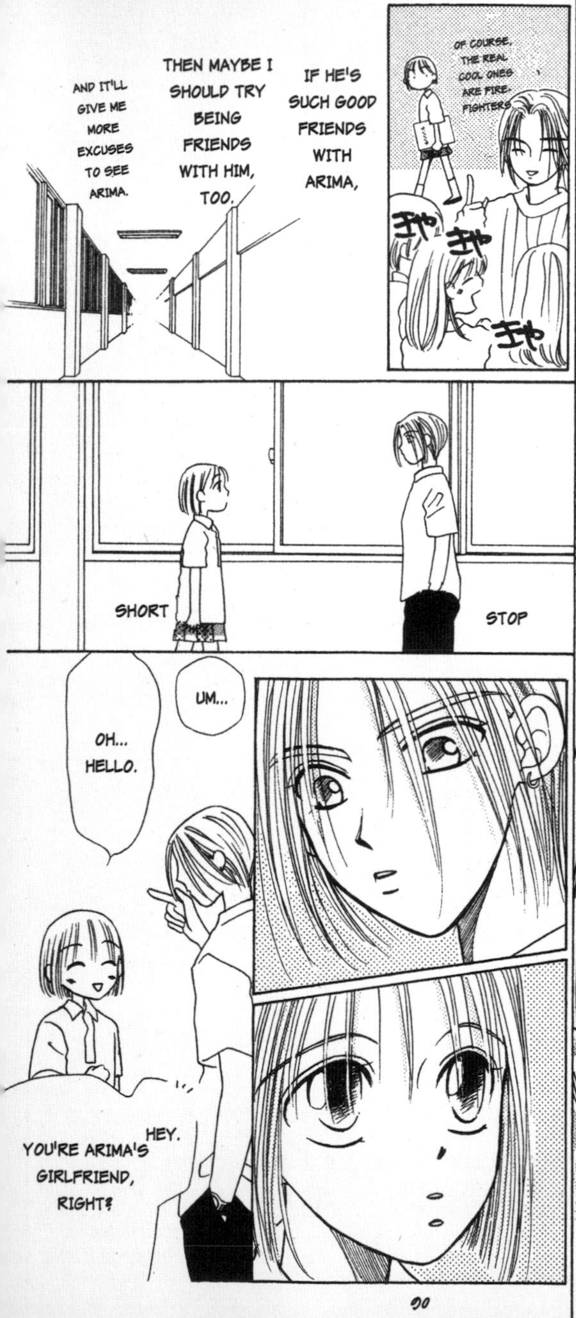
OF COURSE, THE REAL COOL ONES ARE FIRE-FIGHTERS
ぎゃ
ぎゃ
ぎゃ
IF HE'S SUCH GOOD FRIENDS WITH ARIMA,
THEN MAYBE I SHOULD TRY BEING FRIENDS WITH HIM, TOO.
AND IT'LL GIVE ME MORE EXCUSES TO SEE ARIMA.
STOP
SHORT
UM...
OH... HELLO.
HEY.
YOU'RE ARIMA'S GIRLFRIEND, RIGHT?

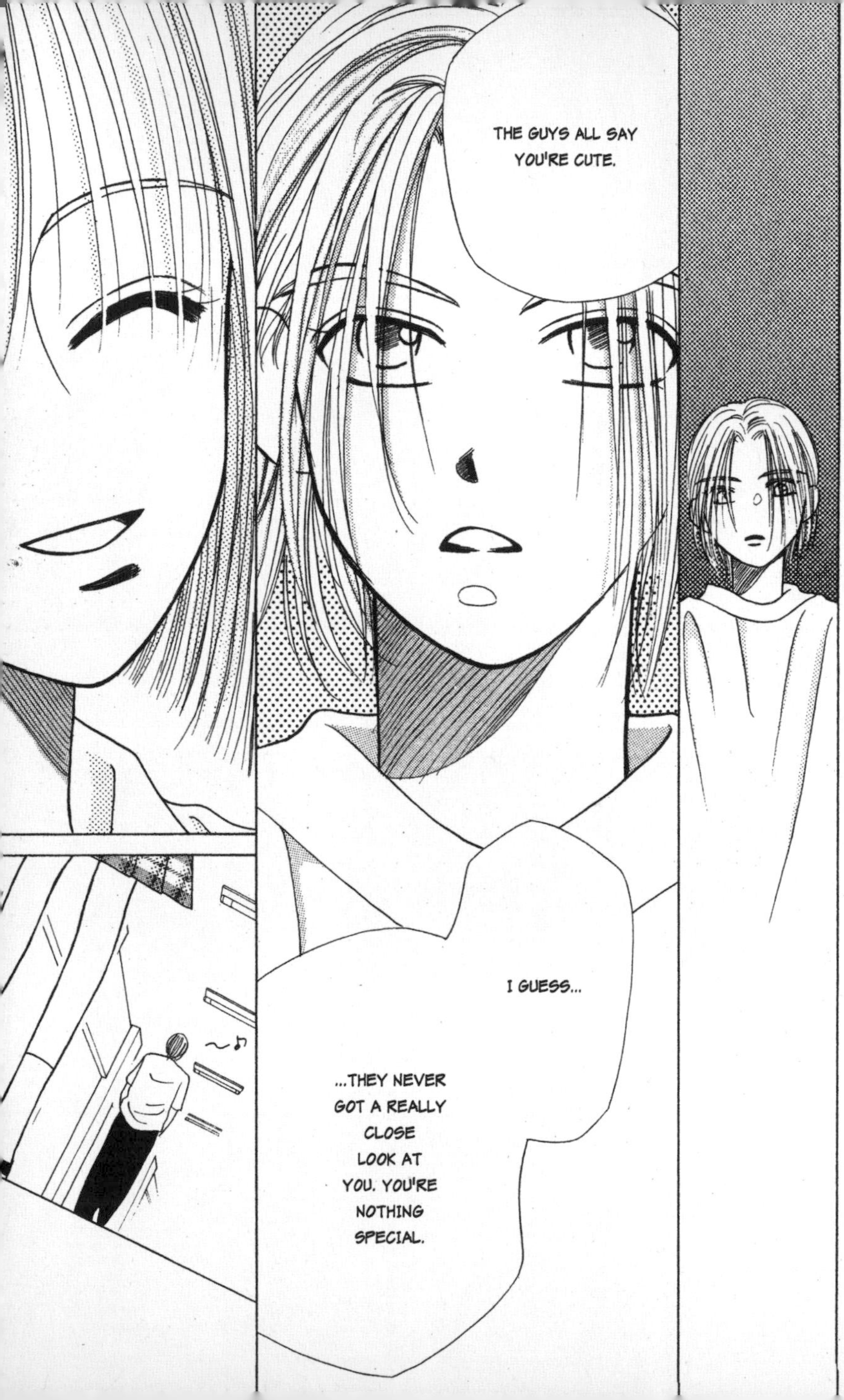
THE GUYS ALL SAY YOU'RE CUTE.
I GUESS...
...THEY NEVER GOT A REALLY CLOSE LOOK AT YOU. YOU'RE NOTHING SPECIAL.
~♪

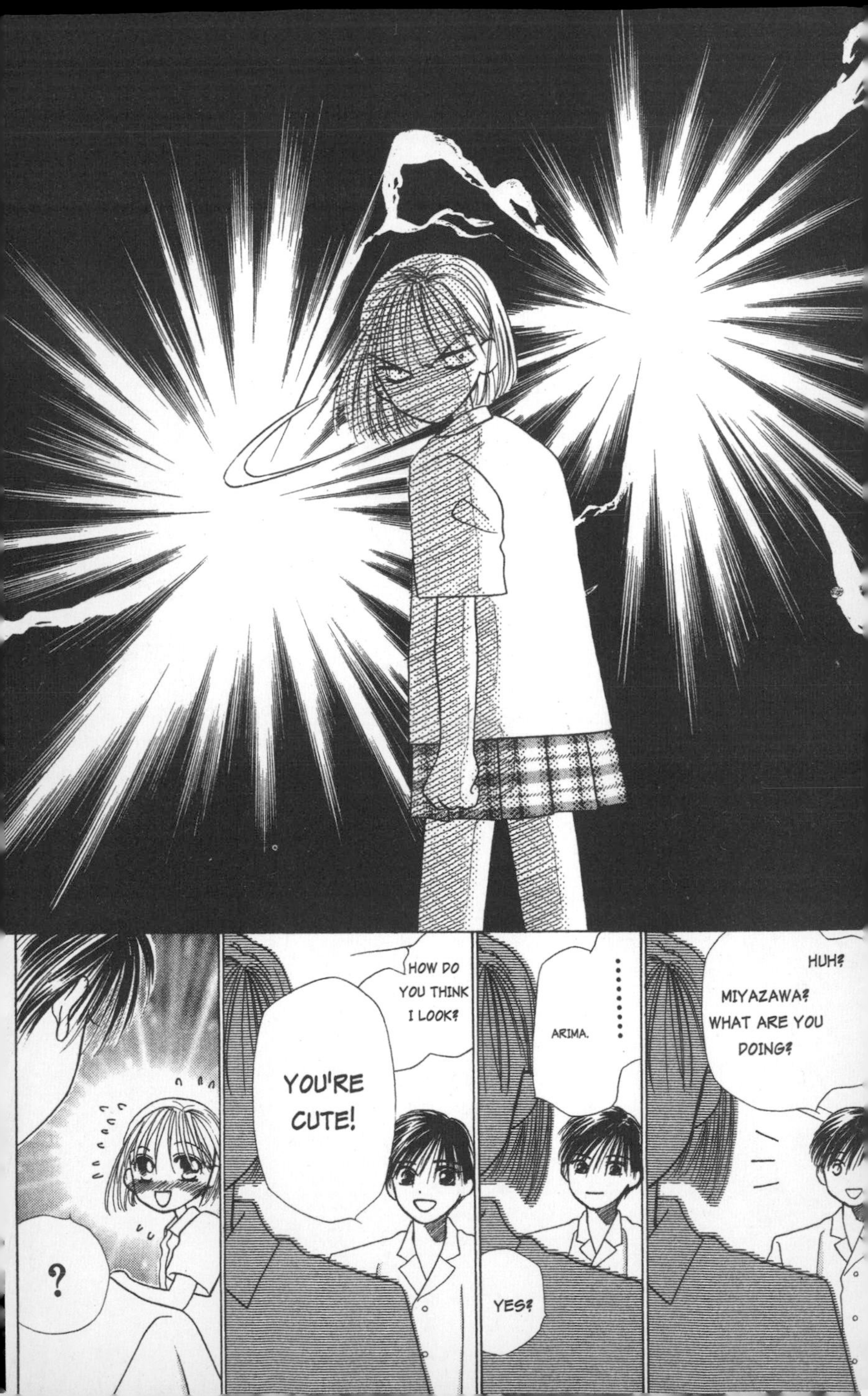
HUH?
MIYAZAWA? WHAT ARE YOU DOING?
....
ARIMA.
YES?
HOW DO YOU THINK I LOOK?
YOU'RE CUTE!
?

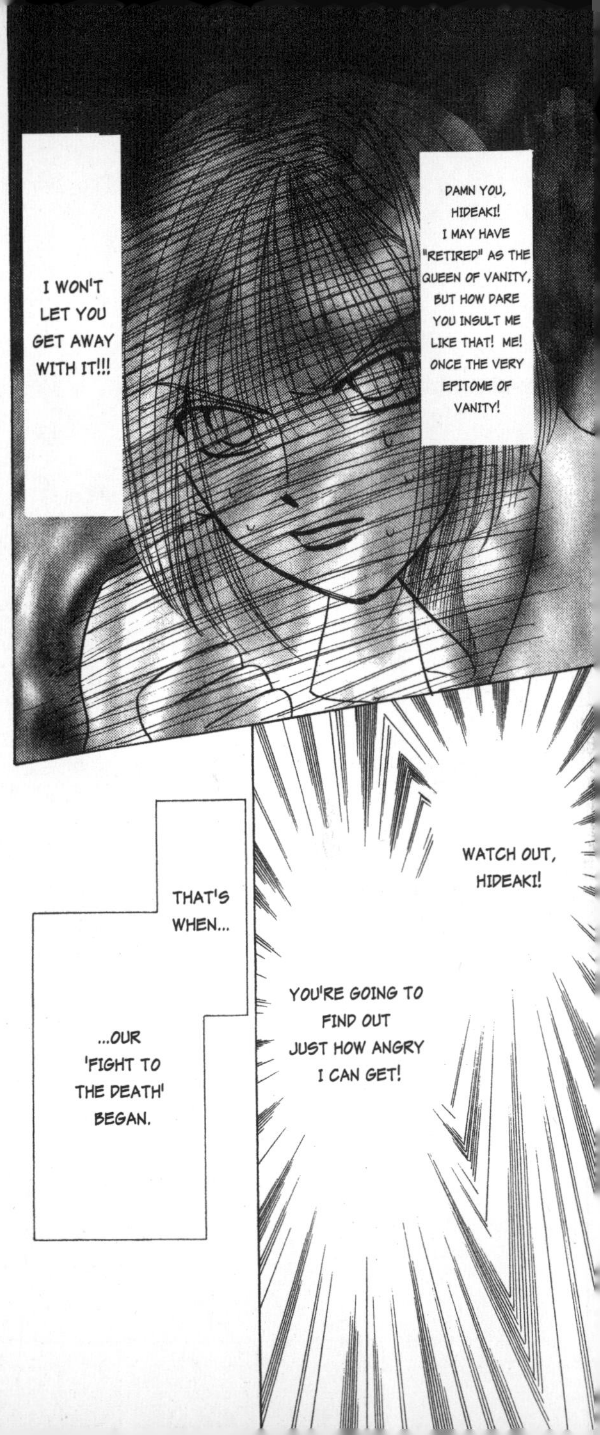
DAMN YOU, HIDEAKI! I MAY HAVE "RETIRED" AS THE QUEEN OF VANITY, BUT HOW DARE YOU INSULT ME LIKE THAT! ME! ONCE THE VERY EPITOME OF VANITY!
I WON'T LET YOU GET AWAY WITH IT!!!
WATCH OUT, HIDEAKI!
YOU'RE GOING TO FIND OUT JUST HOW ANGRY I CAN GET!
THAT'S WHEN...
...OUR 'FIGHT TO THE DEATH' BEGAN.

4

I love annindofu.*

Its strange-tasting syrup is so... ♥

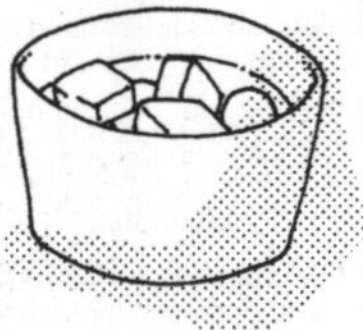

I wonder why whenever I'm eating it, people tell me things like, "That looks so good!" and "You look so happy eating that!"

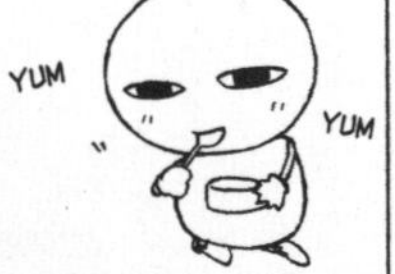
YUM
YUM

"Annindofu" is a kind of tofu dished out with fruit and milk.

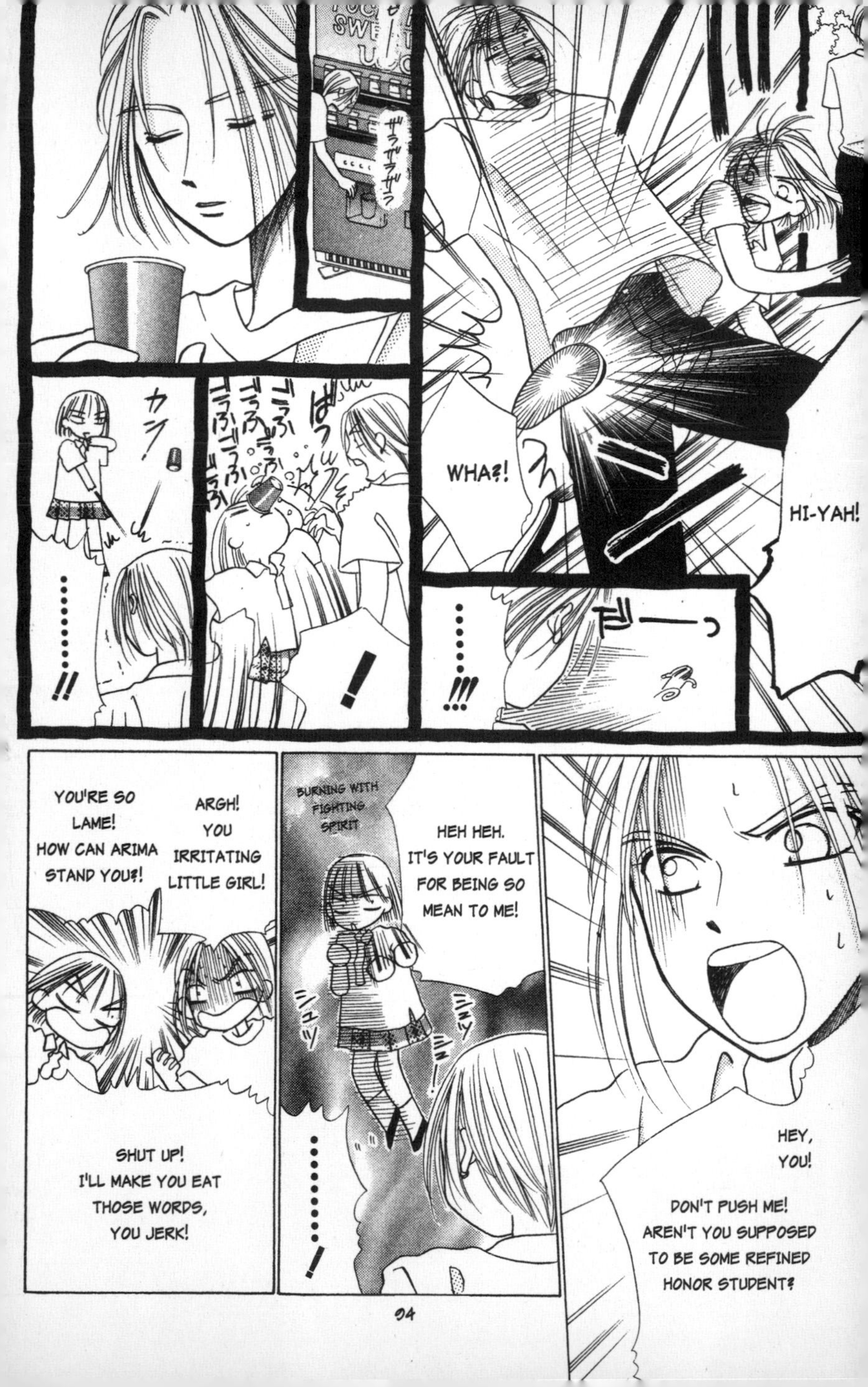
HI-YAH!
WHA?!
……!!!
……!!
!
HEY, YOU!
DON'T PUSH ME! AREN'T YOU SUPPOSED TO BE SOME REFINED HONOR STUDENT?
BURNING WITH FIGHTING SPIRIT
HEH HEH. IT'S YOUR FAULT FOR BEING SO MEAN TO ME!
……!
ARGH! YOU IRRITATING LITTLE GIRL!
YOU'RE SO LAME! HOW CAN ARIMA STAND YOU?!
SHUT UP! I'LL MAKE YOU EAT THOSE WORDS, YOU JERK!

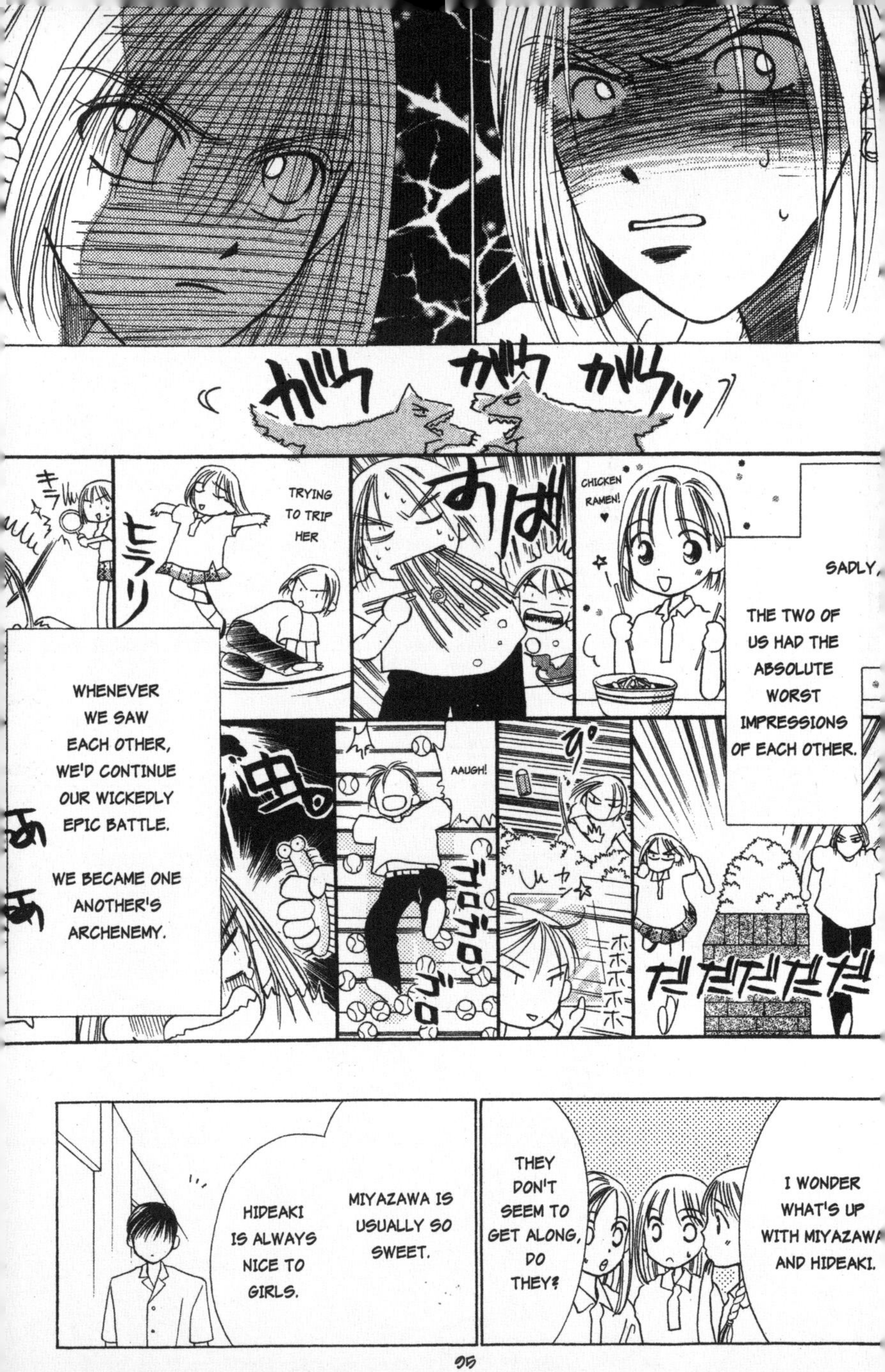
SADLY,
THE TWO OF US HAD THE ABSOLUTE WORST IMPRESSIONS OF EACH OTHER.
CHICKEN RAMEN!
TRYING TO TRIP HER
ヒラリ
だだだだだ
ホホホホホ
AAUGH!
ゴロゴロ
ゴロ
WHENEVER WE SAW EACH OTHER, WE'D CONTINUE OUR WICKEDLY EPIC BATTLE.
WE BECAME ONE ANOTHER'S ARCHENEMY.
I WONDER WHAT'S UP WITH MIYAZAWA AND HIDEAKI.
THEY DON'T SEEM TO GET ALONG, DO THEY?
MIYAZAWA IS USUALLY SO SWEET.
HIDEAKI IS ALWAYS NICE TO GIRLS.

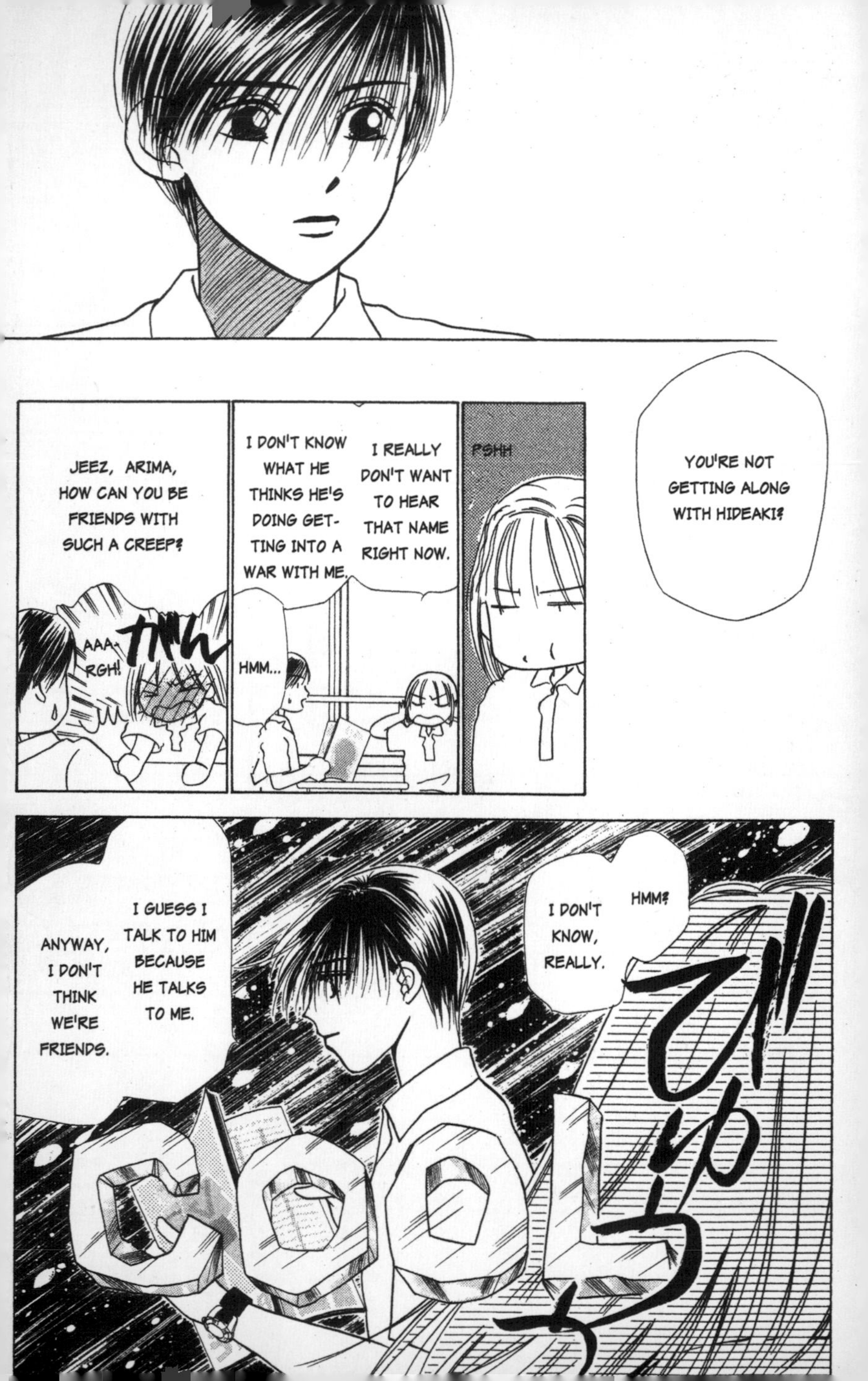
YOU'RE NOT GETTING ALONG WITH HIDEAKI?
PSHH
I REALLY DON'T WANT TO HEAR THAT NAME RIGHT NOW.
I DON'T KNOW WHAT HE THINKS HE'S DOING GETTING INTO A WAR WITH ME.
HMM...
JEEZ, ARIMA, HOW CAN YOU BE FRIENDS WITH SUCH A CREEP?
AAA-RGH!
HMM?
I DON'T KNOW, REALLY.
I GUESS I TALK TO HIM BECAUSE HE TALKS TO ME.
ANYWAY, I DON'T THINK WE'RE FRIENDS.
COOL

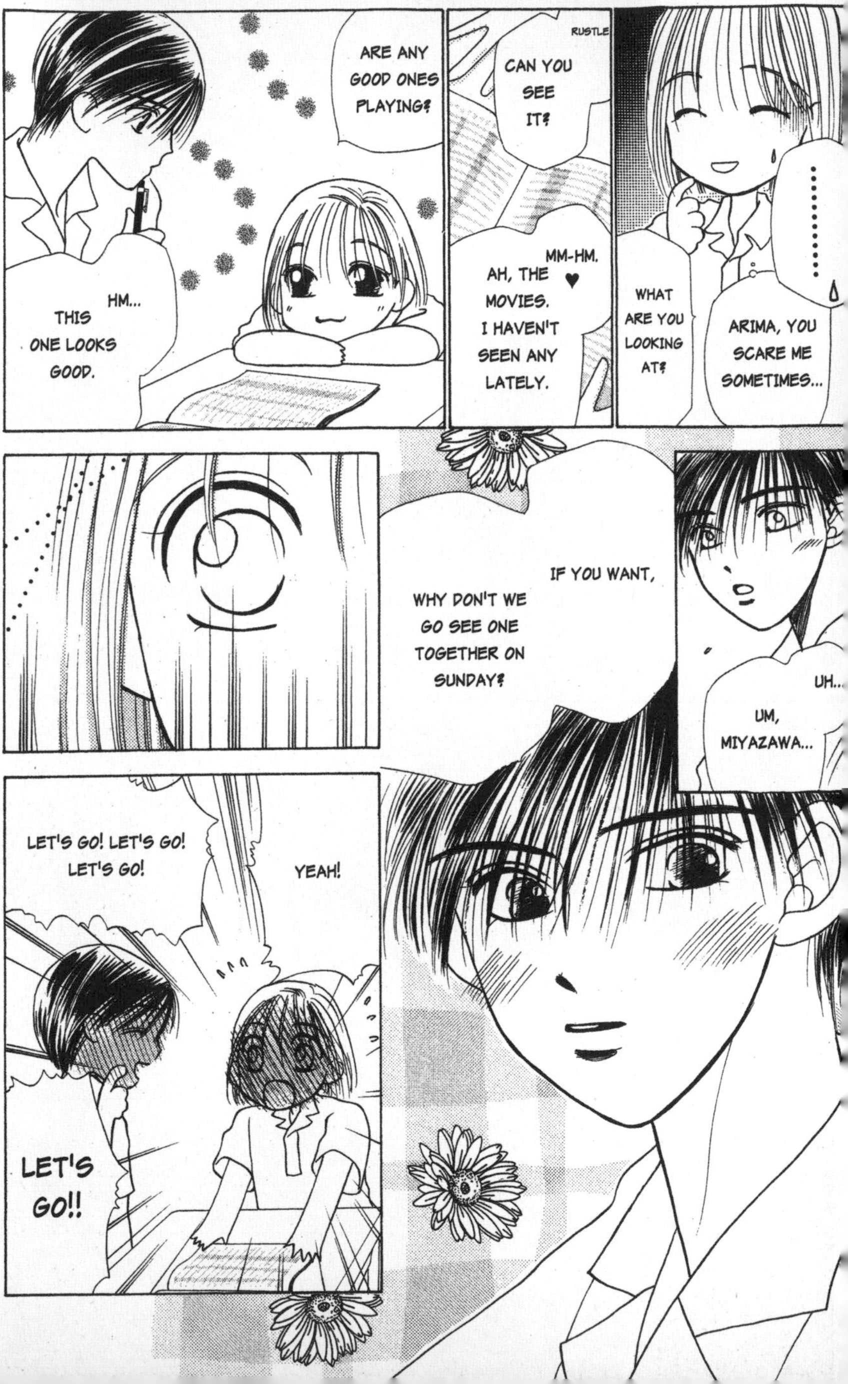
......
ARIMA, YOU SCARE ME SOMETIMES...
WHAT ARE YOU LOOKING AT?
RUSTLE
CAN YOU SEE IT?
MM-HM. ♥
AH, THE MOVIES. I HAVEN'T SEEN ANY LATELY.
ARE ANY GOOD ONES PLAYING?
HM... THIS ONE LOOKS GOOD.
UH... UM, MIYAZAWA...
IF YOU WANT,
WHY DON'T WE GO SEE ONE TOGETHER ON SUNDAY?
YEAH!
LET'S GO! LET'S GO! LET'S GO!
LET'S GO!!

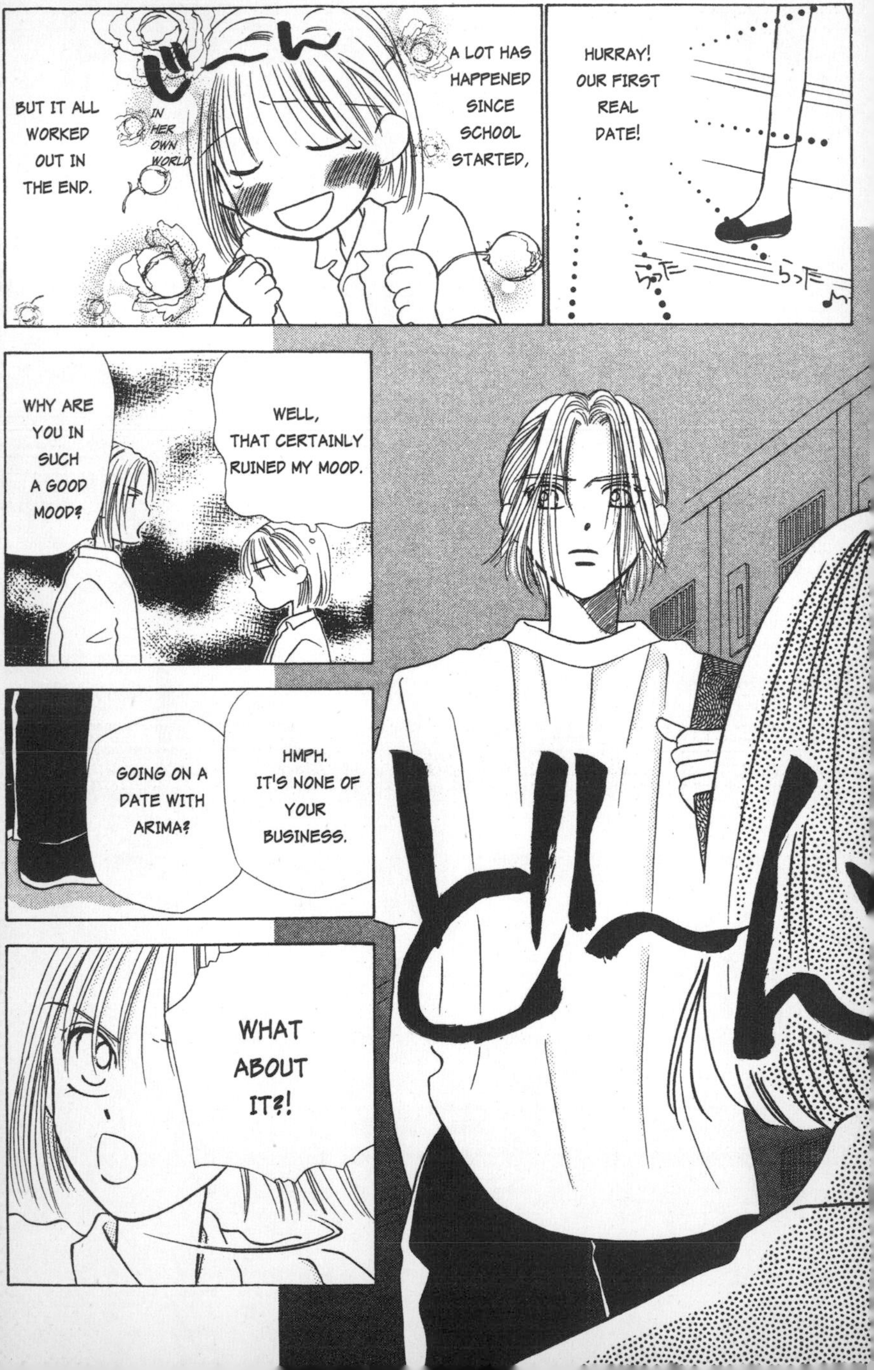
HURRAY! OUR FIRST REAL DATE!
A LOT HAS HAPPENED SINCE SCHOOL STARTED,
じ〜ん
IN HER OWN WORLD
BUT IT ALL WORKED OUT IN THE END.
WELL, THAT CERTAINLY RUINED MY MOOD.
WHY ARE YOU IN SUCH A GOOD MOOD?
HMPH. IT'S NONE OF YOUR BUSINESS.
GOING ON A DATE WITH ARIMA?
WHAT ABOUT IT?!

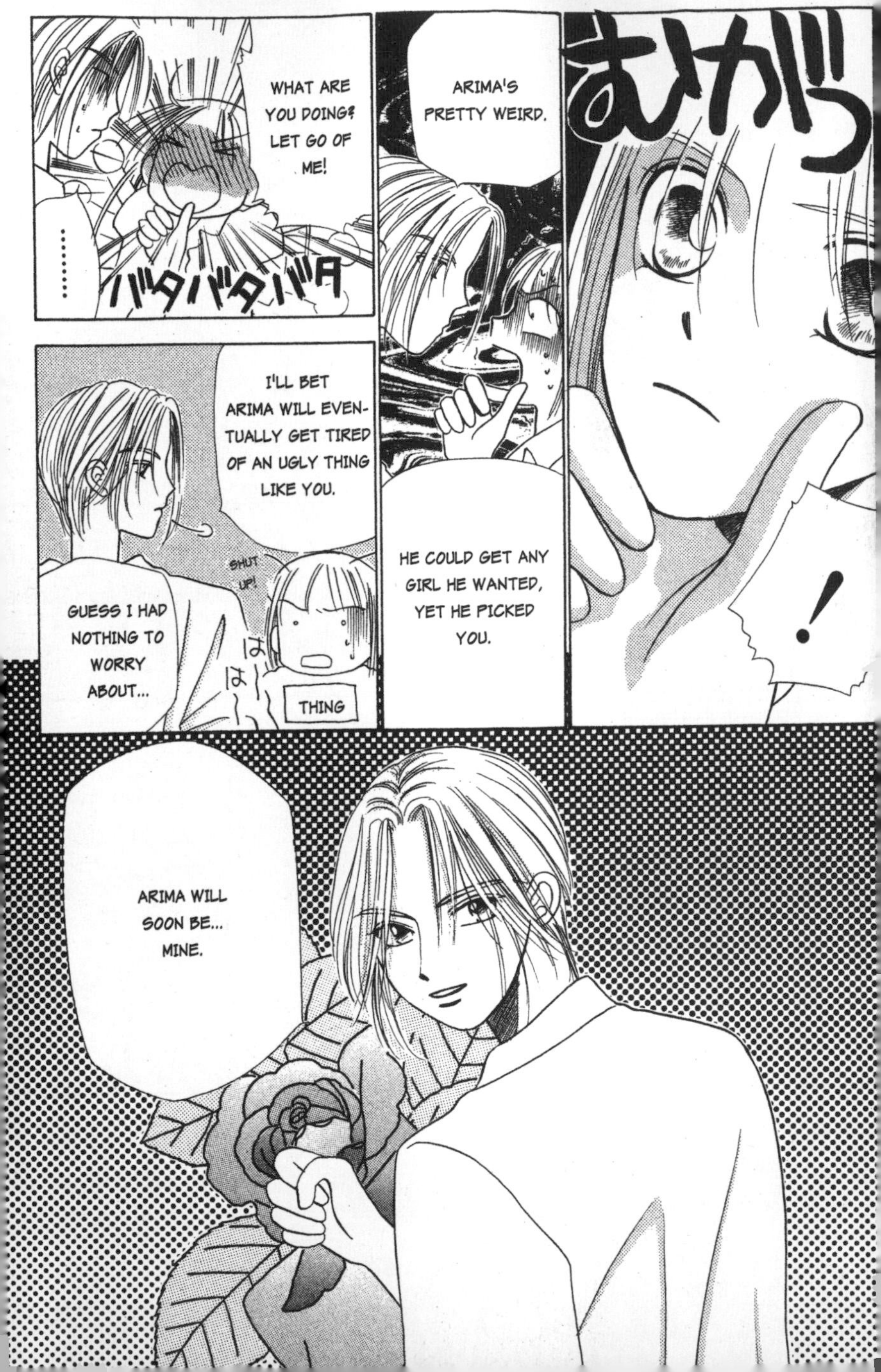

むかっ
!
ARIMA'S PRETTY WEIRD.
HE COULD GET ANY GIRL HE WANTED, YET HE PICKED YOU.
WHAT ARE YOU DOING? LET GO OF ME!
……
バタバタバタ
I'LL BET ARIMA WILL EVEN-TUALLY GET TIRED OF AN UGLY THING LIKE YOU.
SHUT UP!
はは~
THING
GUESS I HAD NOTHING TO WORRY ABOUT...
ARIMA WILL SOON BE... MINE.

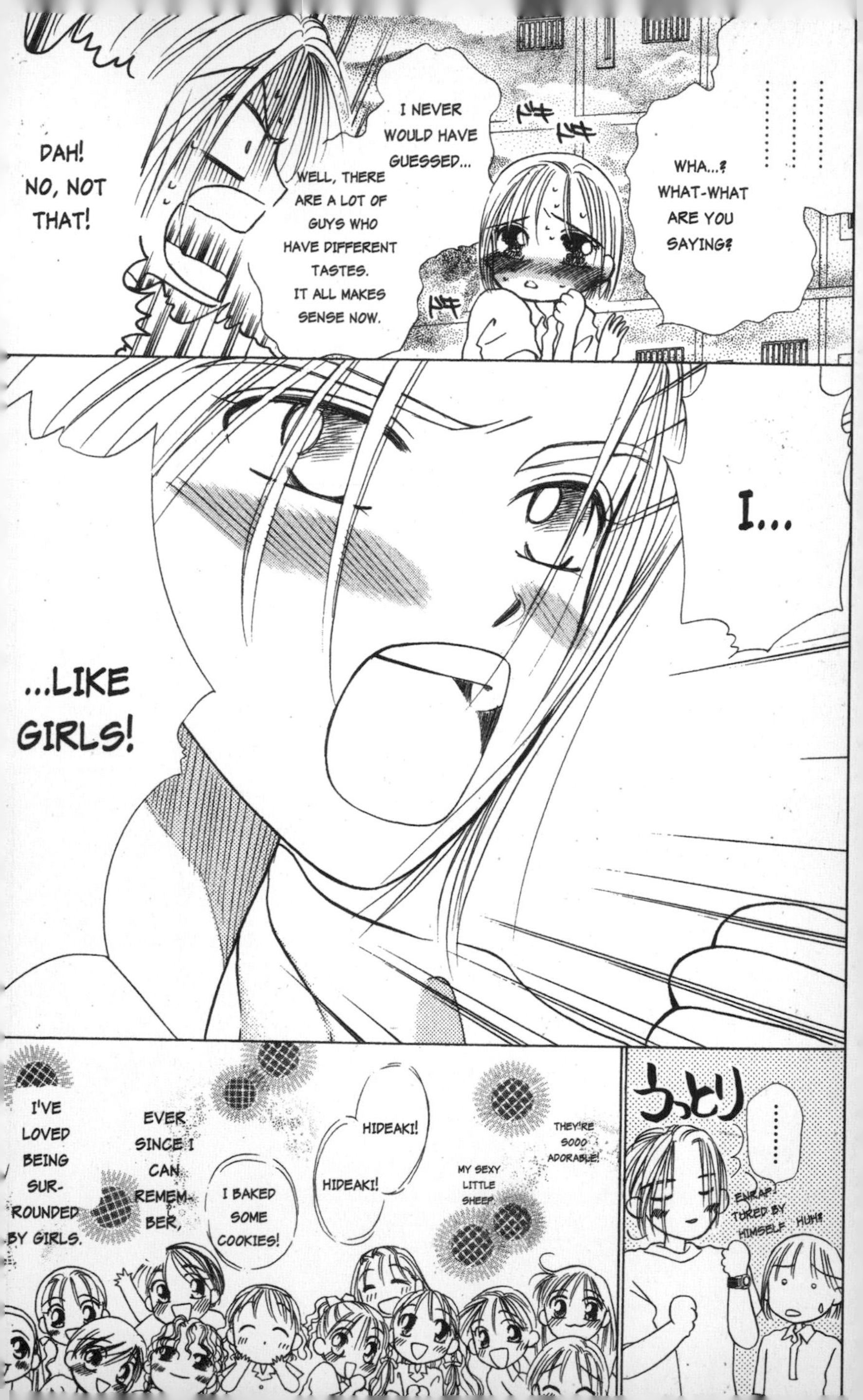
WHA...? WHAT-WHAT ARE YOU SAYING?
ドキ
ドキ
I NEVER WOULD HAVE GUESSED...
WELL, THERE ARE A LOT OF GUYS WHO HAVE DIFFERENT TASTES. IT ALL MAKES SENSE NOW.
ドキ
DAH! NO, NOT THAT!
I...
...LIKE GIRLS!
うっとり
......
ENRAPTURED BY HIMSELF HUH?
THEY'RE SOOO ADORABLE!
HIDEAKI!
MY SEXY LITTLE SHEEP.
HIDEAKI!
I BAKED SOME COOKIES!
EVER SINCE I CAN REMEMBER,
I'VE LOVED BEING SURROUNDED BY GIRLS.

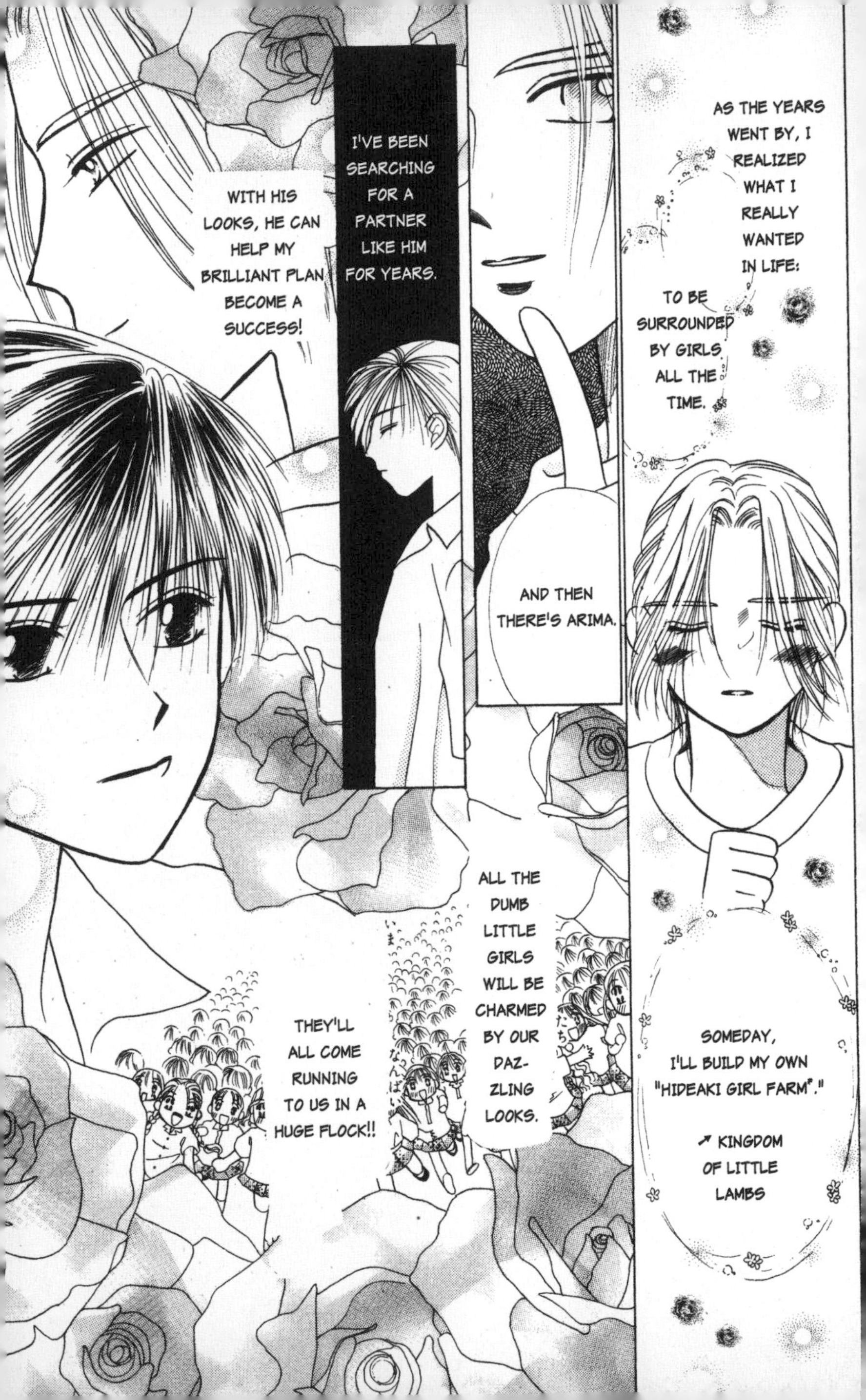
AS THE YEARS WENT BY, I REALIZED WHAT I REALLY WANTED IN LIFE:
TO BE SURROUNDED BY GIRLS ALL THE TIME.
SOMEDAY, I'LL BUILD MY OWN "HIDEAKI GIRL FARM"."
KINGDOM OF LITTLE LAMBS
AND THEN THERE'S ARIMA.
I'VE BEEN SEARCHING FOR A PARTNER LIKE HIM FOR YEARS.
WITH HIS LOOKS, HE CAN HELP MY BRILLIANT PLAN BECOME A SUCCESS!
ALL THE DUMB LITTLE GIRLS WILL BE CHARMED BY OUR DAZ-ZLING LOOKS.
THEY'LL ALL COME RUNNING TO US IN A HUGE FLOCK!!

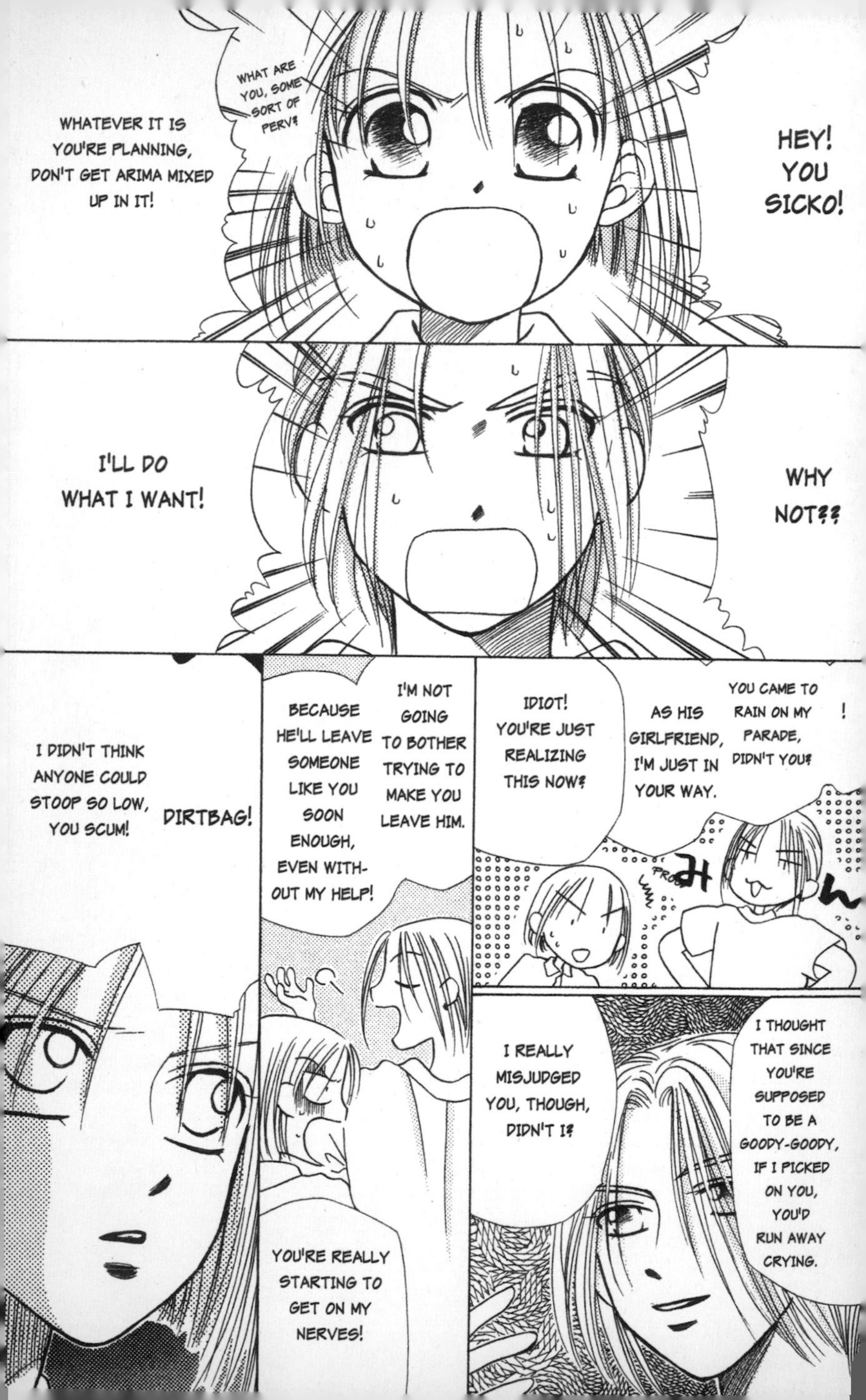
HEY! YOU SICKO!
WHAT ARE YOU, SOME SORT OF PERV?
WHATEVER IT IS YOU'RE PLANNING, DON'T GET ARIMA MIXED UP IN IT!
WHY NOT??
I'LL DO WHAT I WANT!
YOU CAME TO RAIN ON MY PARADE, DIDN'T YOU?
!
AS HIS GIRLFRIEND, I'M JUST IN YOUR WAY.
IDIOT! YOU'RE JUST REALIZING THIS NOW?
PROD
I THOUGHT THAT SINCE YOU'RE SUPPOSED TO BE A GOODY-GOODY, IF I PICKED ON YOU, YOU'D RUN AWAY CRYING.
I REALLY MISJUDGED YOU, THOUGH, DIDN'T I?
I'M NOT GOING TO BOTHER TRYING TO MAKE YOU LEAVE HIM.
BECAUSE HE'LL LEAVE SOMEONE LIKE YOU SOON ENOUGH, EVEN WITHOUT MY HELP!
YOU'RE REALLY STARTING TO GET ON MY NERVES!
DIRTBAG!
I DIDN'T THINK ANYONE COULD STOOP SO LOW, YOU SCUM!

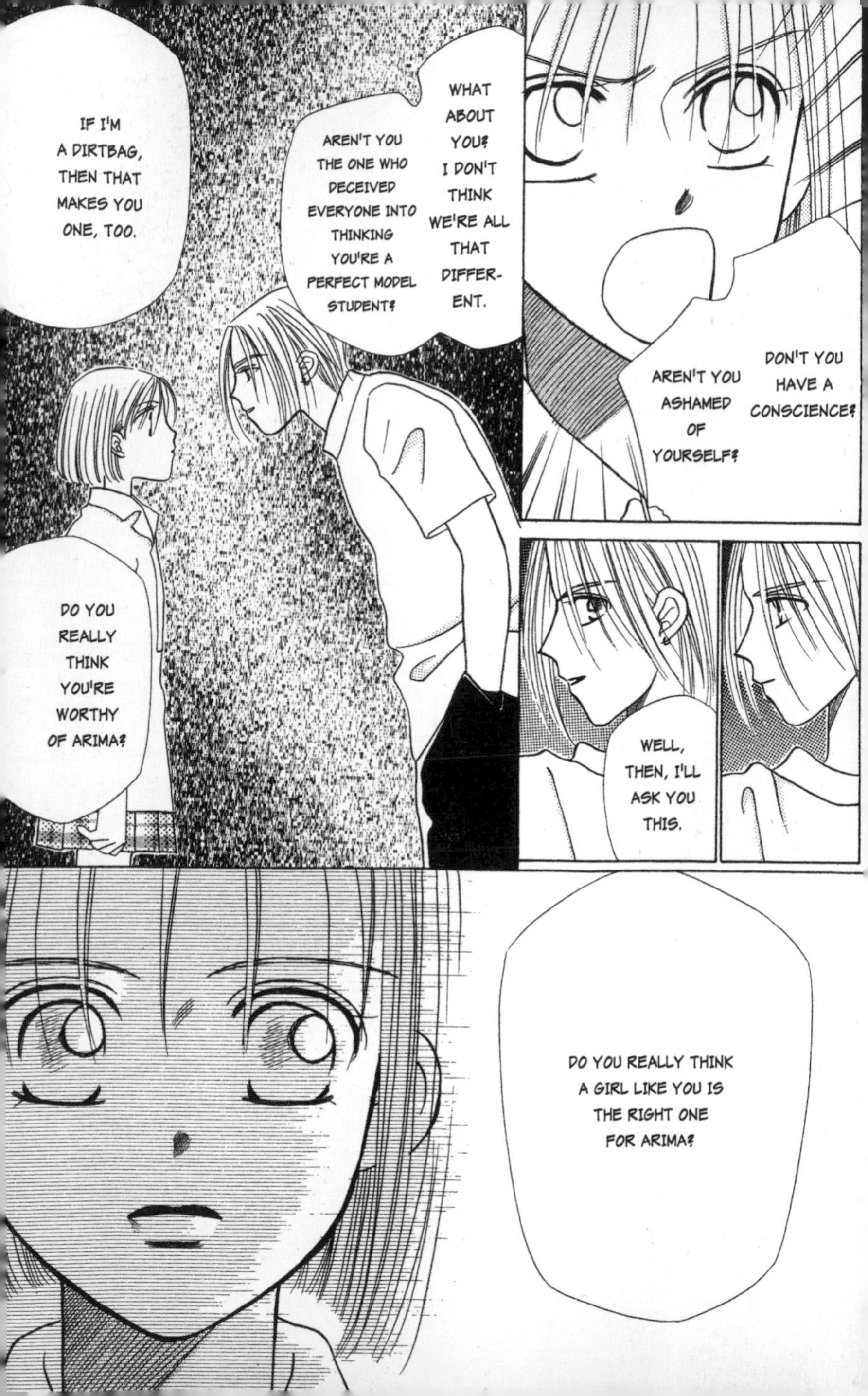
DON'T YOU HAVE A CONSCIENCE?
AREN'T YOU ASHAMED OF YOURSELF?
WELL, THEN, I'LL ASK YOU THIS.
WHAT ABOUT YOU? I DON'T THINK WE'RE ALL THAT DIFFER-ENT.
AREN'T YOU THE ONE WHO DECEIVED EVERYONE INTO THINKING YOU'RE A PERFECT MODEL STUDENT?
IF I'M A DIRTBAG, THEN THAT MAKES YOU ONE, TOO.
DO YOU REALLY THINK YOU'RE WORTHY OF ARIMA?
DO YOU REALLY THINK A GIRL LIKE YOU IS THE RIGHT ONE FOR ARIMA?

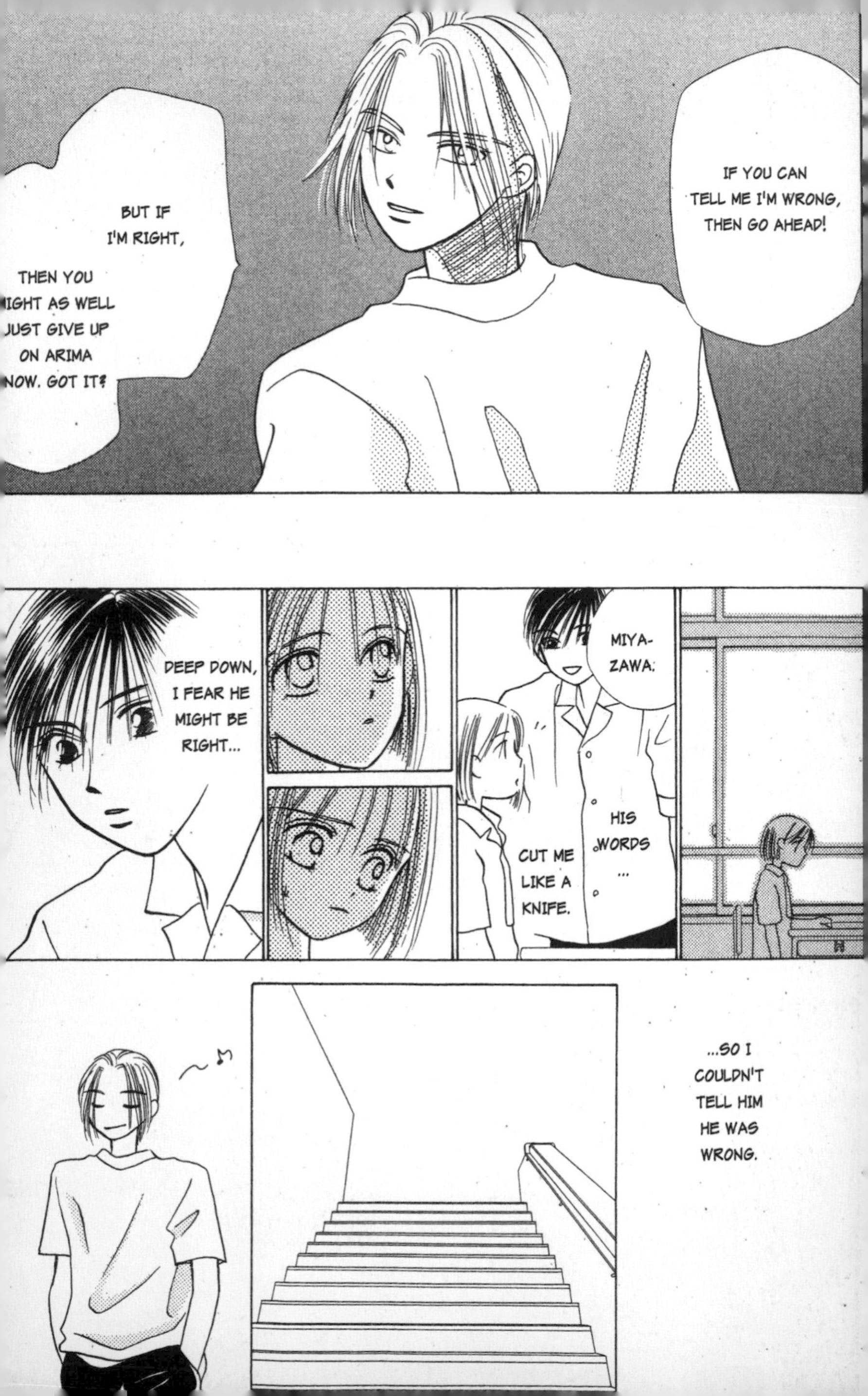
IF YOU CAN TELL ME I'M WRONG, THEN GO AHEAD!
BUT IF I'M RIGHT,
THEN YOU IGHT AS WELL JUST GIVE UP ON ARIMA NOW. GOT IT?
MIYA-ZAWA.
HIS WORDS ...
CUT ME LIKE A KNIFE.
DEEP DOWN, I FEAR HE MIGHT BE RIGHT...
...SO I COULDN'T TELL HIM HE WAS WRONG.
~♪

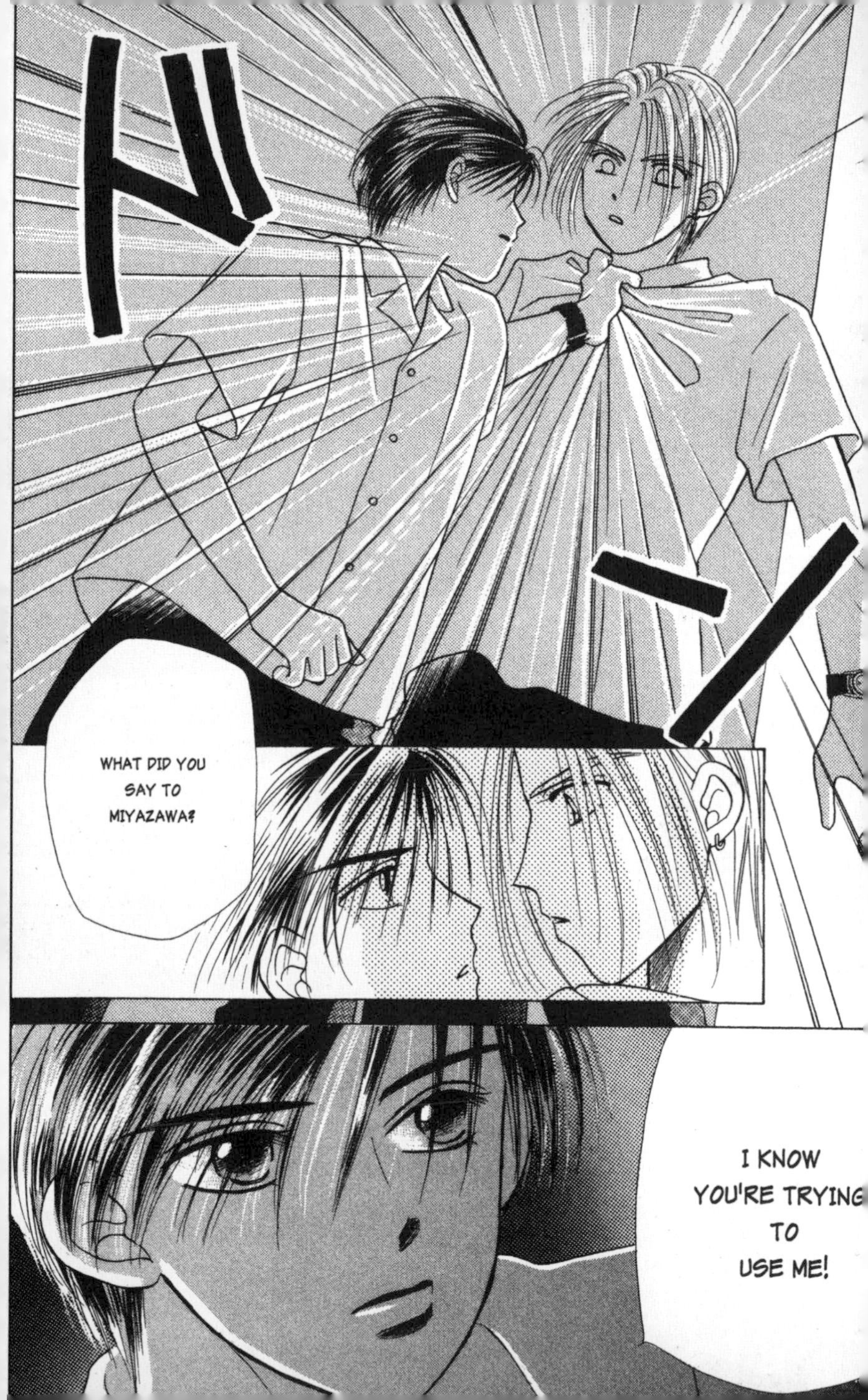
WHAT DID YOU SAY TO MIYAZAWA?
I KNOW YOU'RE TRYING TO USE ME!

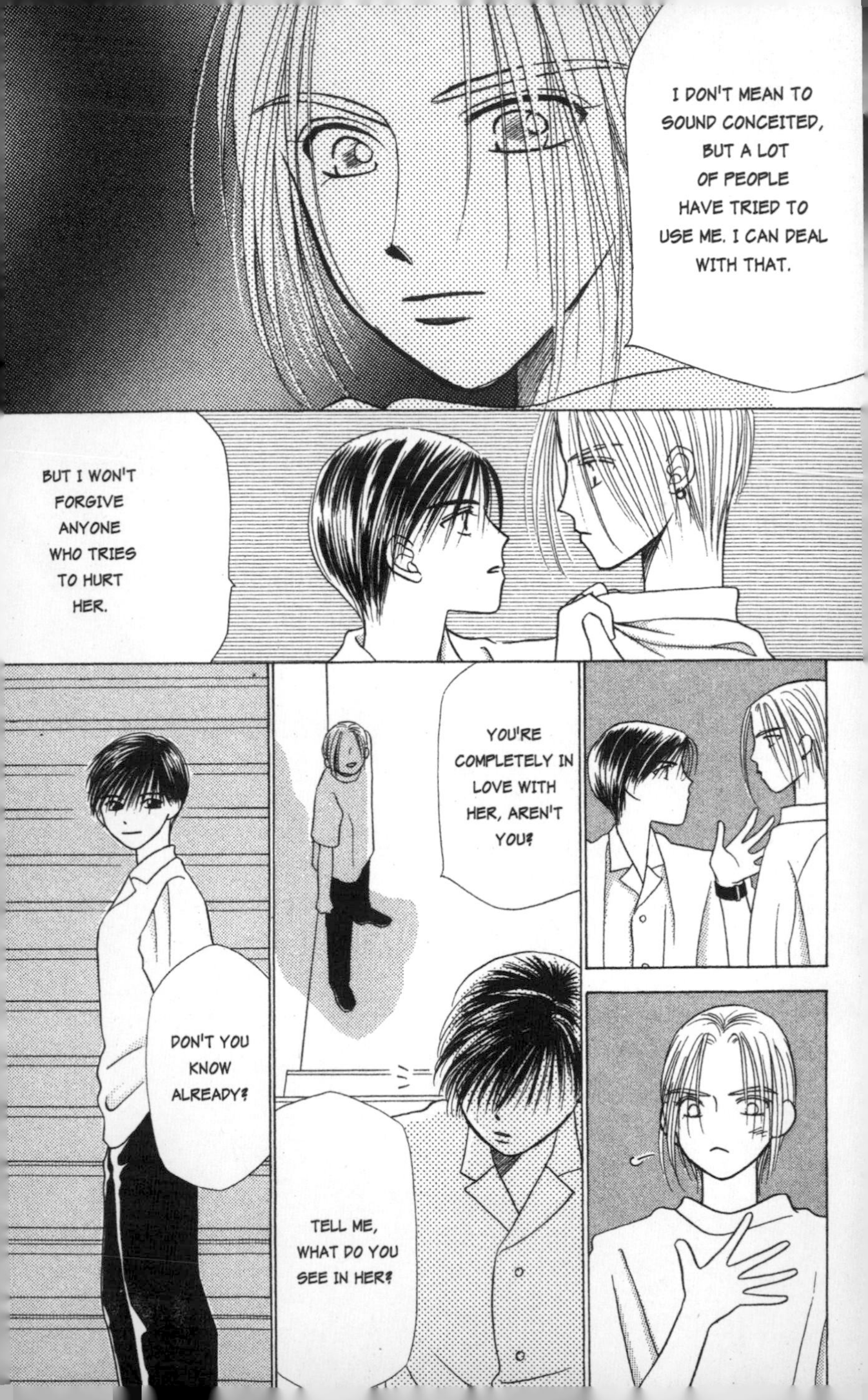
I DON'T MEAN TO SOUND CONCEITED, BUT A LOT OF PEOPLE HAVE TRIED TO USE ME. I CAN DEAL WITH THAT.
BUT I WON'T FORGIVE ANYONE WHO TRIES TO HURT HER.
YOU'RE COMPLETELY IN LOVE WITH HER, AREN'T YOU?
TELL ME, WHAT DO YOU SEE IN HER?
DON'T YOU KNOW ALREADY?

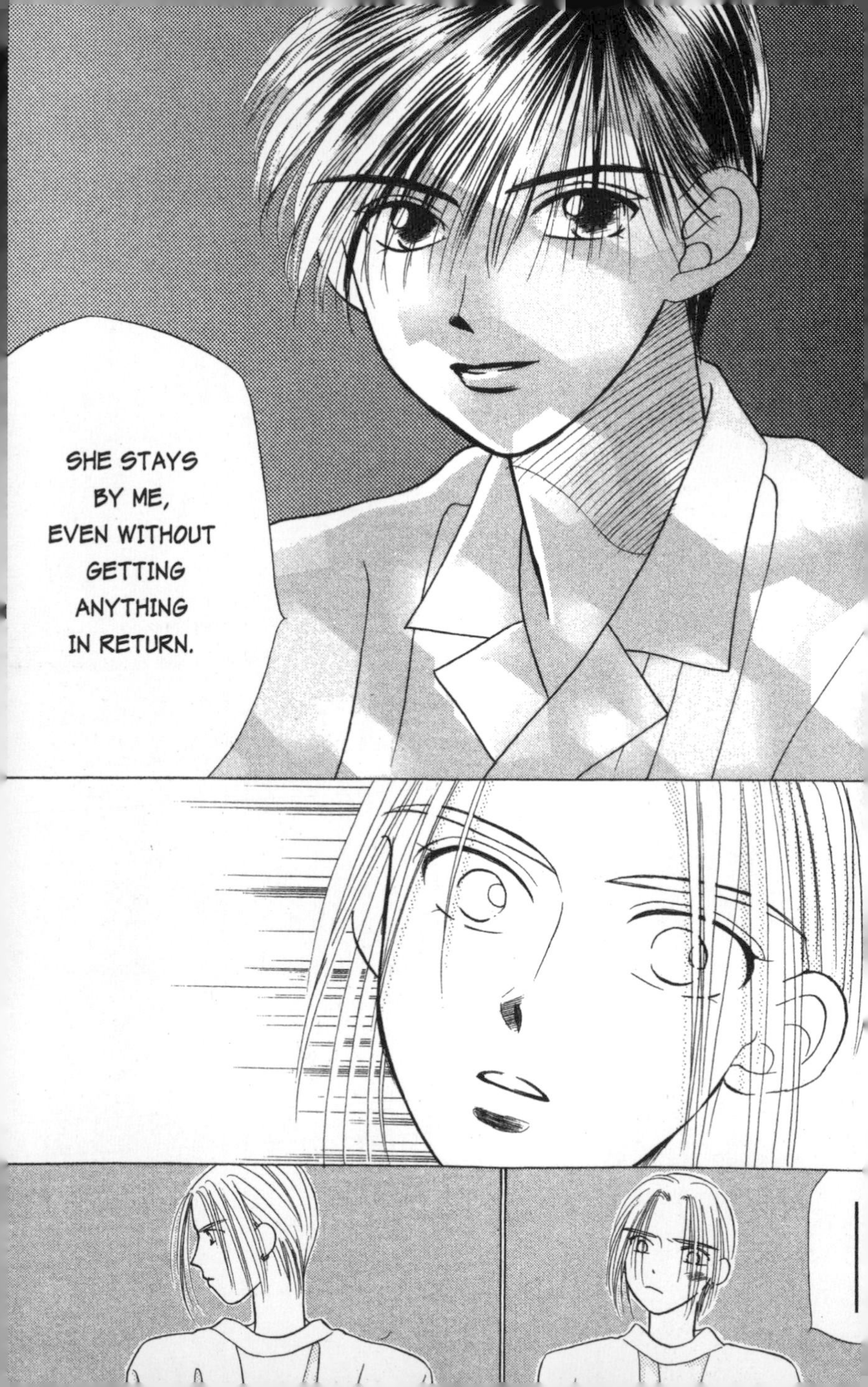
SHE STAYS BY ME, EVEN WITHOUT GETTING ANYTHING IN RETURN.

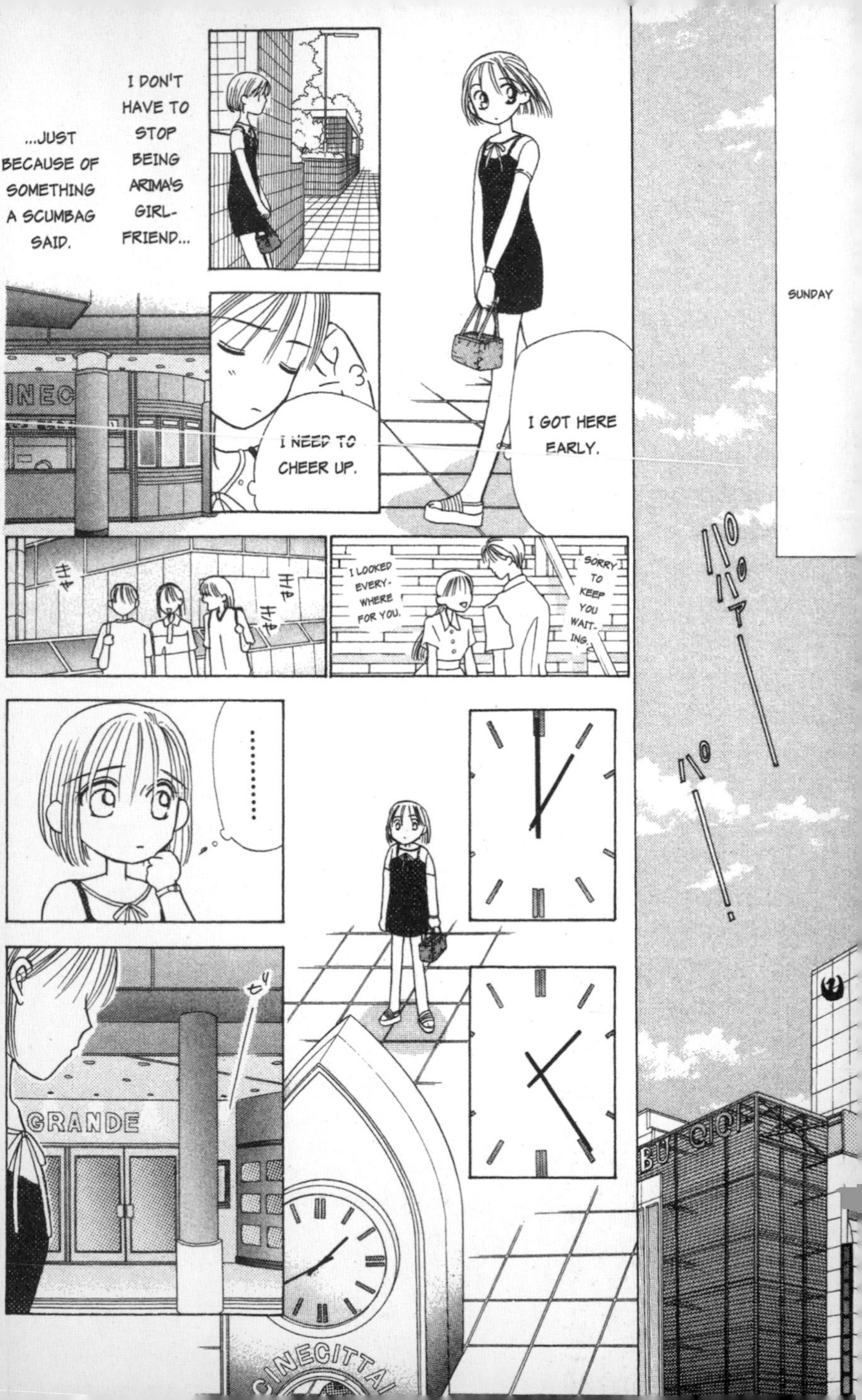
SUNDAY
パパーー
パーー!
I GOT HERE EARLY.
I DON'T HAVE TO STOP BEING ARIMA'S GIRL-FRIEND...
...JUST BECAUSE OF SOMETHING A SCUMBAG SAID.
I NEED TO CHEER UP.
SORRY TO KEEP YOU WAIT-ING.
I LOOKED EVERY-WHERE FOR YOU.
キャ
キャ
キャ
....
GRANDE
CINECITTA

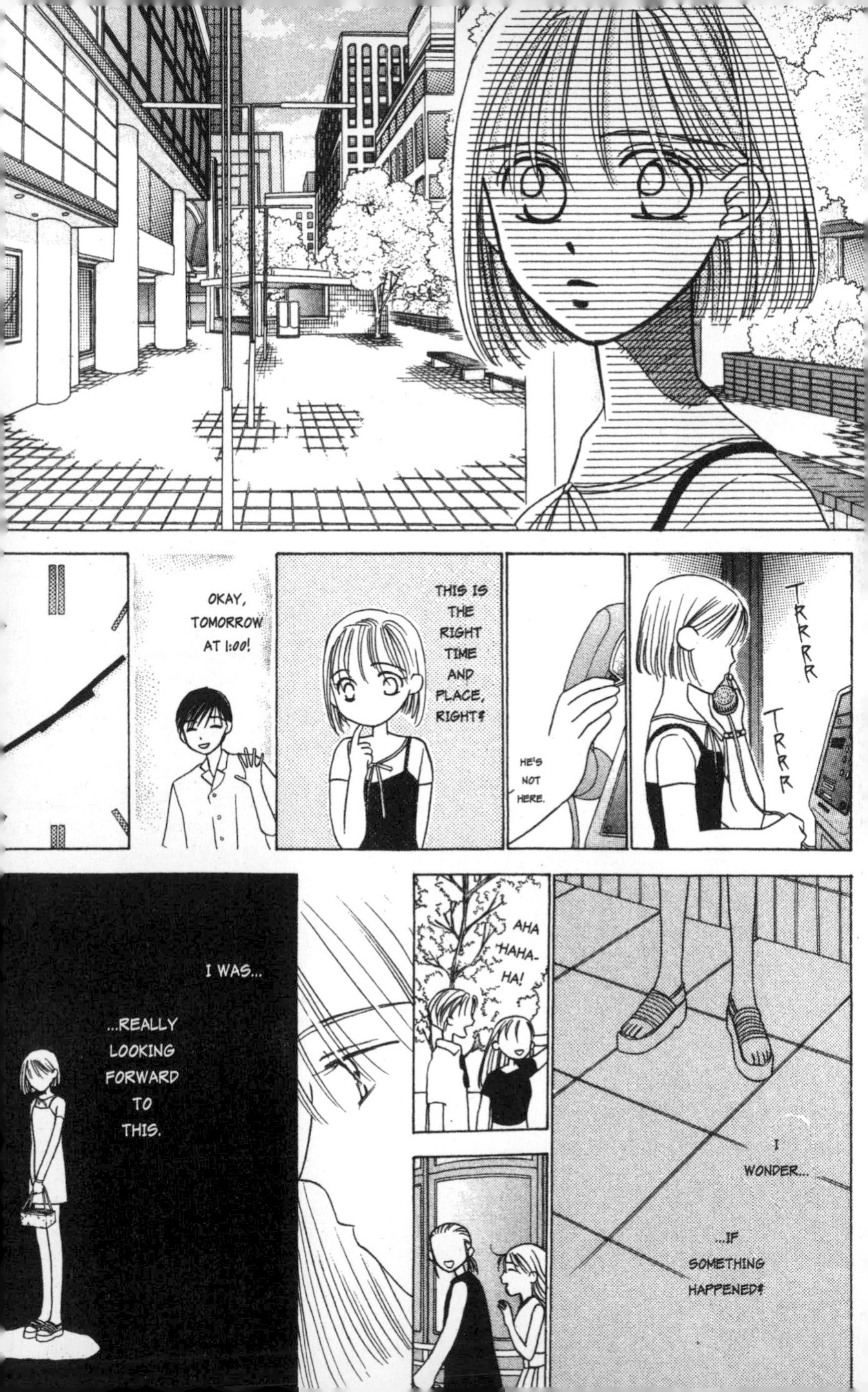

TRRRR
TRRR
HE'S NOT HERE.
THIS IS THE RIGHT TIME AND PLACE, RIGHT?
OKAY, TOMORROW AT 1:00!
I WONDER...
...IF SOMETHING HAPPENED?
AHA HAHAHA-HA!
I WAS...
...REALLY LOOKING FORWARD TO THIS.

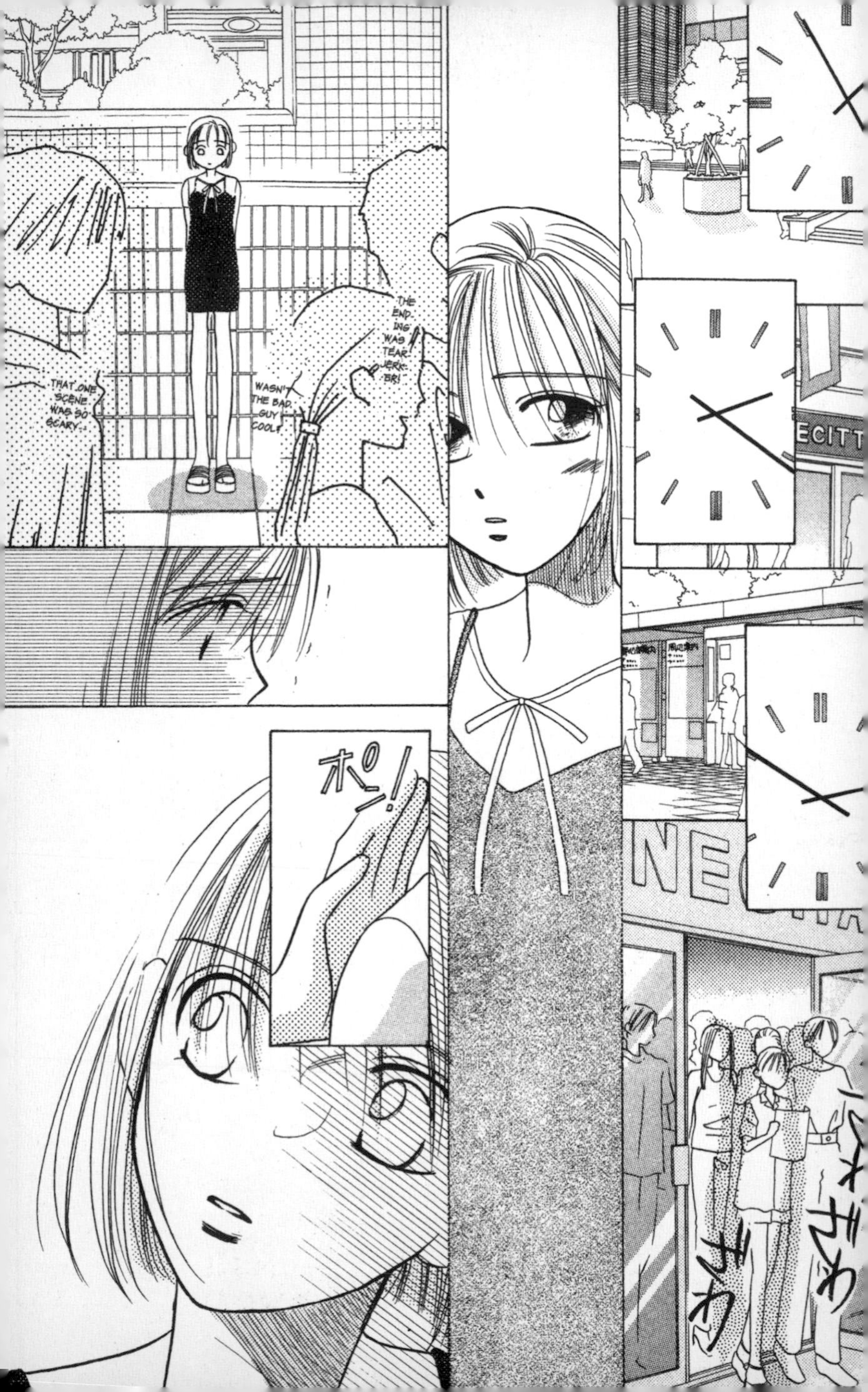
ECITT
NE
ざわざわ
THE ENDING WAS TEARJERKER!
WASN'T THE BAD GUY COOL?
THAT ONE SCENE WAS SO SCARY...
ポン!

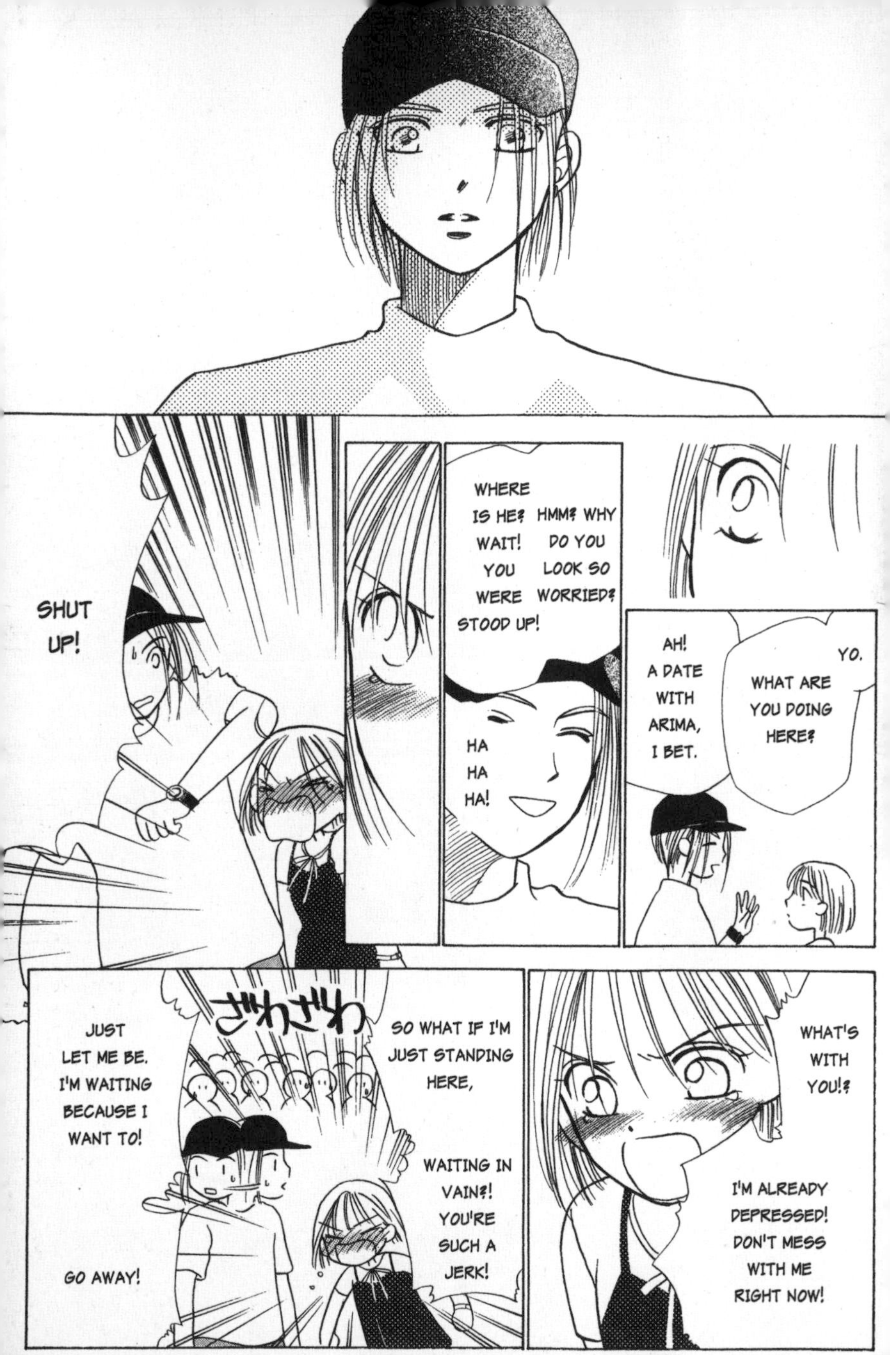
YO. WHAT ARE YOU DOING HERE?
AH! A DATE WITH ARIMA, I BET.
HMM? WHY DO YOU LOOK SO WORRIED?
WHERE IS HE? WAIT! YOU WERE STOOD UP!
HA HA HA!
SHUT UP!
WHAT'S WITH YOU!?
I'M ALREADY DEPRESSED! DON'T MESS WITH ME RIGHT NOW!
SO WHAT IF I'M JUST STANDING HERE,
WAITING IN VAIN?! YOU'RE SUCH A JERK!
ざわざわ
JUST LET ME BE. I'M WAITING BECAUSE I WANT TO!
GO AWAY!

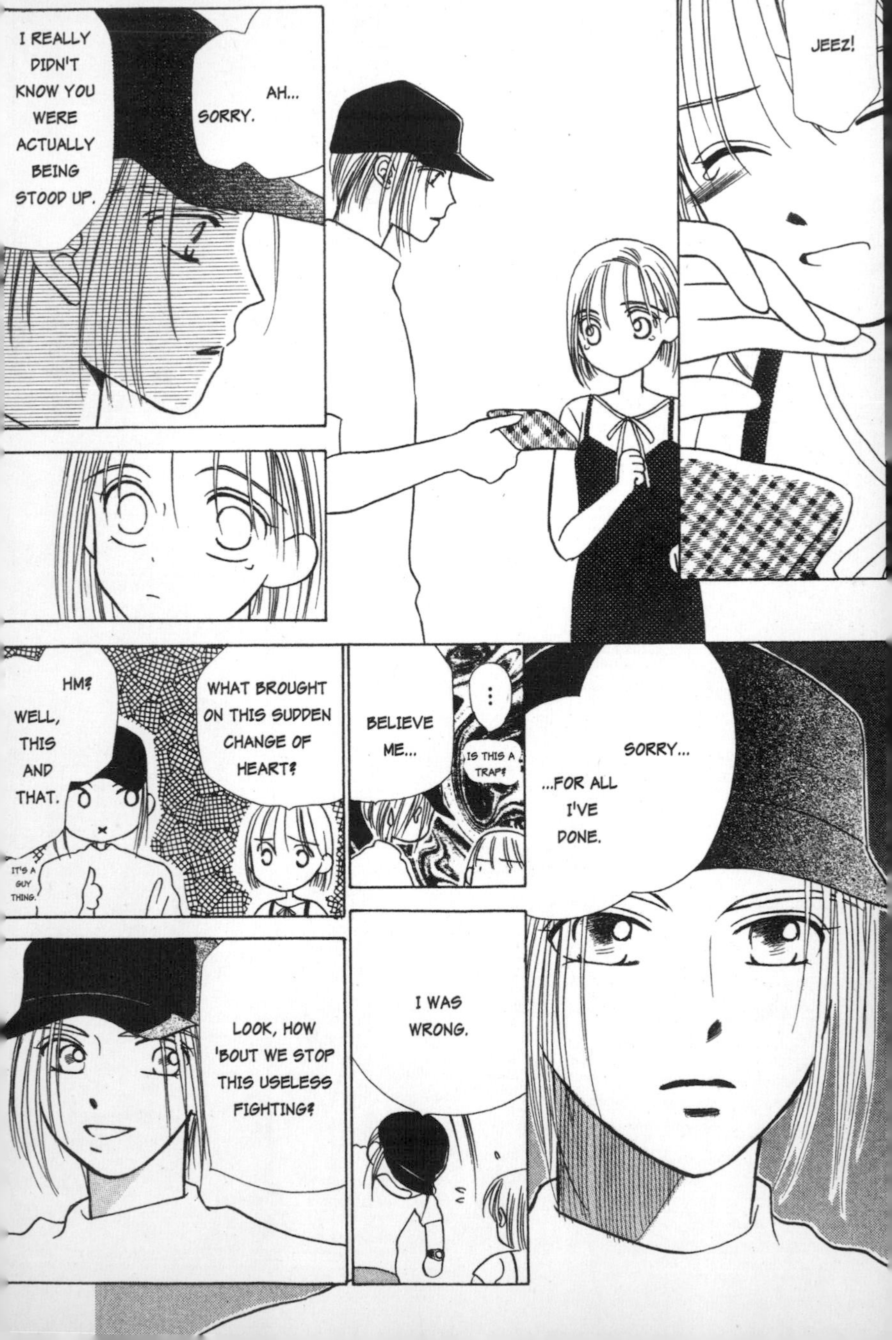
JEEZ!
AH... SORRY.
I REALLY DIDN'T KNOW YOU WERE ACTUALLY BEING STOOD UP.
SORRY... ...FOR ALL I'VE DONE.
...
BELIEVE ME...
IS THIS A TRAP?
WHAT BROUGHT ON THIS SUDDEN CHANGE OF HEART?
HM? WELL, THIS AND THAT.
IT'S A GUY THING.
I WAS WRONG.
LOOK, HOW 'BOUT WE STOP THIS USELESS FIGHTING?

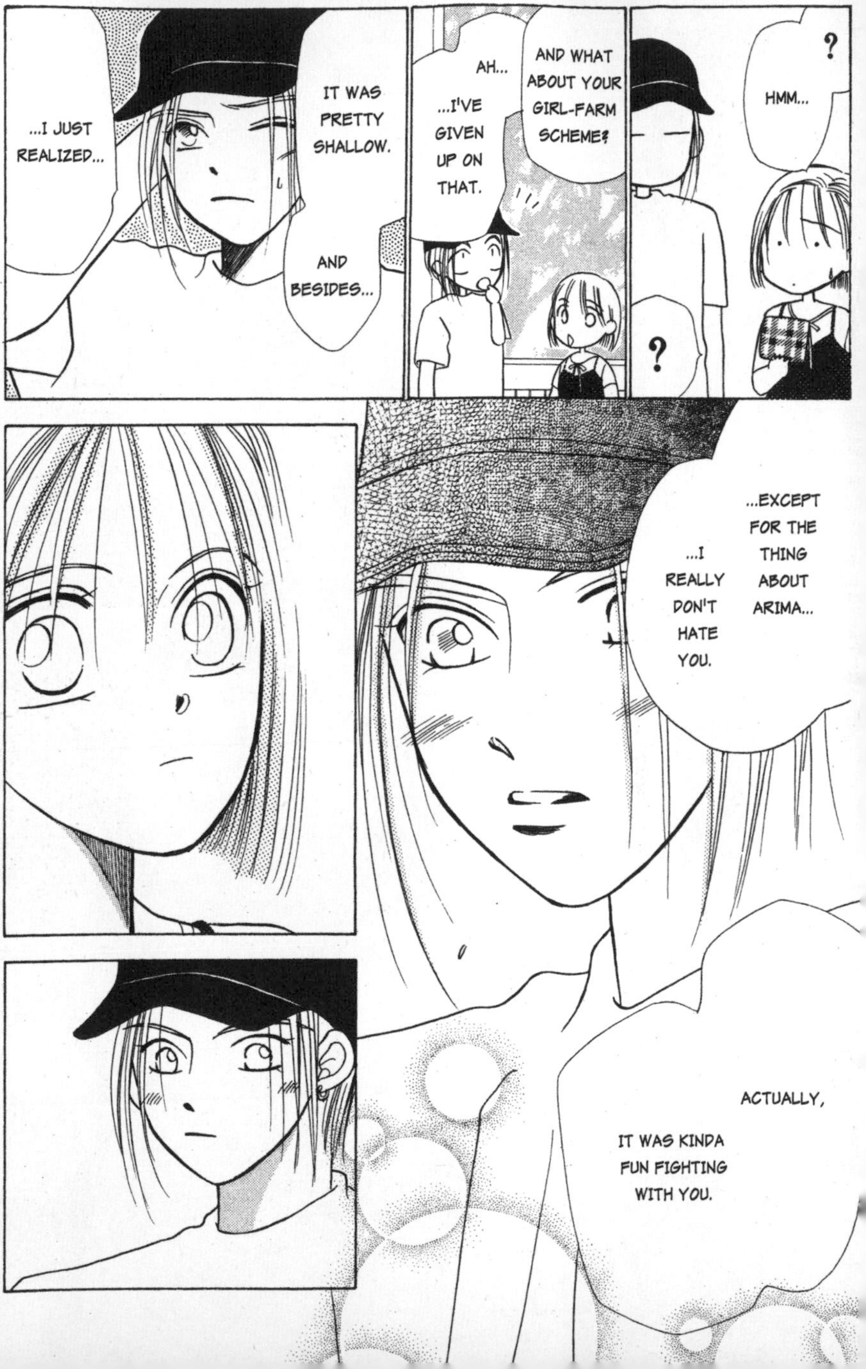
?
HMM...
?
AND WHAT ABOUT YOUR GIRL-FARM SCHEME?
AH...
...I'VE GIVEN UP ON THAT.
IT WAS PRETTY SHALLOW.
...I JUST REALIZED...
AND BESIDES...
...EXCEPT FOR THE THING ABOUT ARIMA...
...I REALLY DON'T HATE YOU.
ACTUALLY,
IT WAS KINDA FUN FIGHTING WITH YOU.

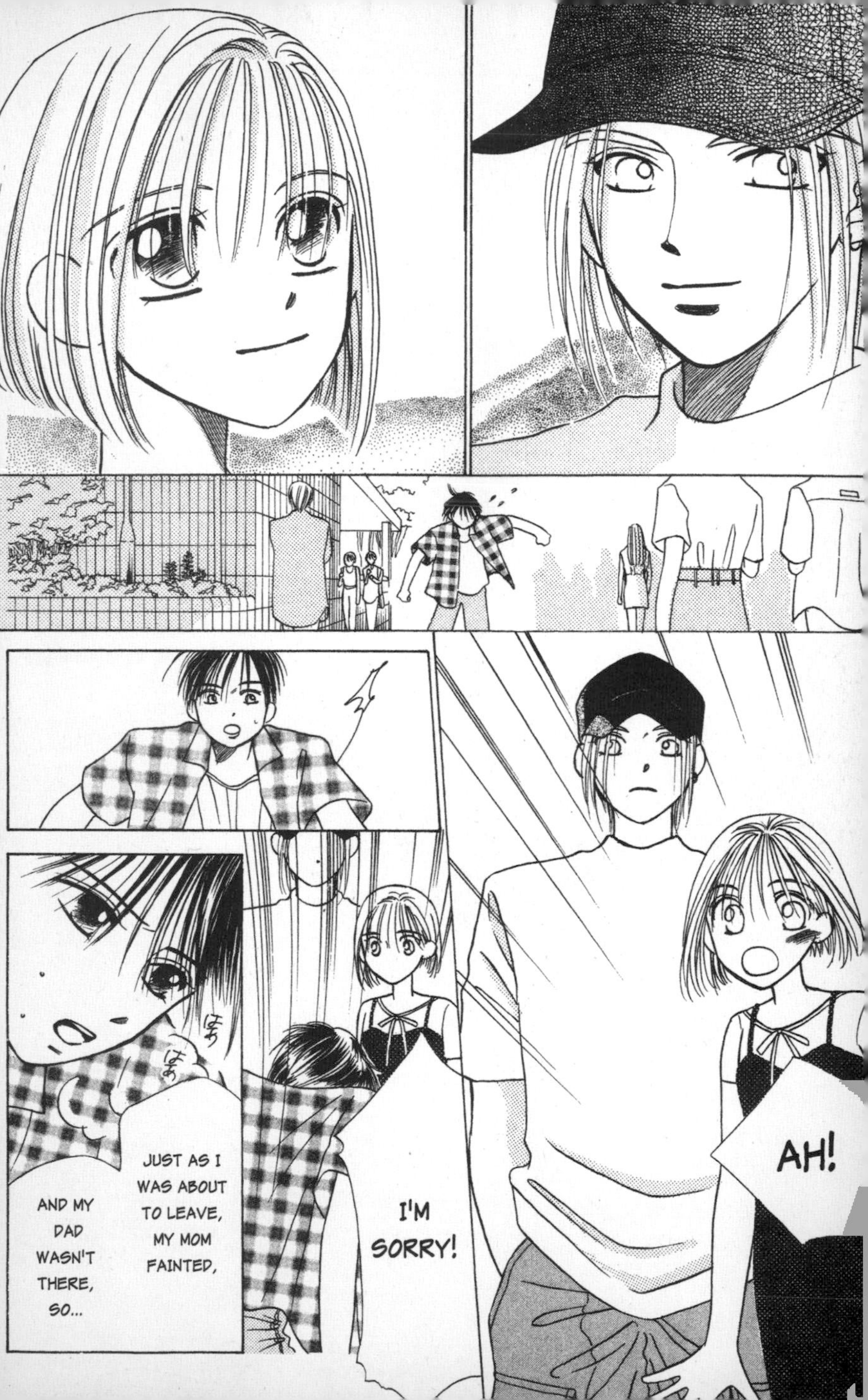
AH!
I'M SORRY!
はぁ はぁ
JUST AS I WAS ABOUT TO LEAVE, MY MOM FAINTED,
AND MY DAD WASN'T THERE, SO...

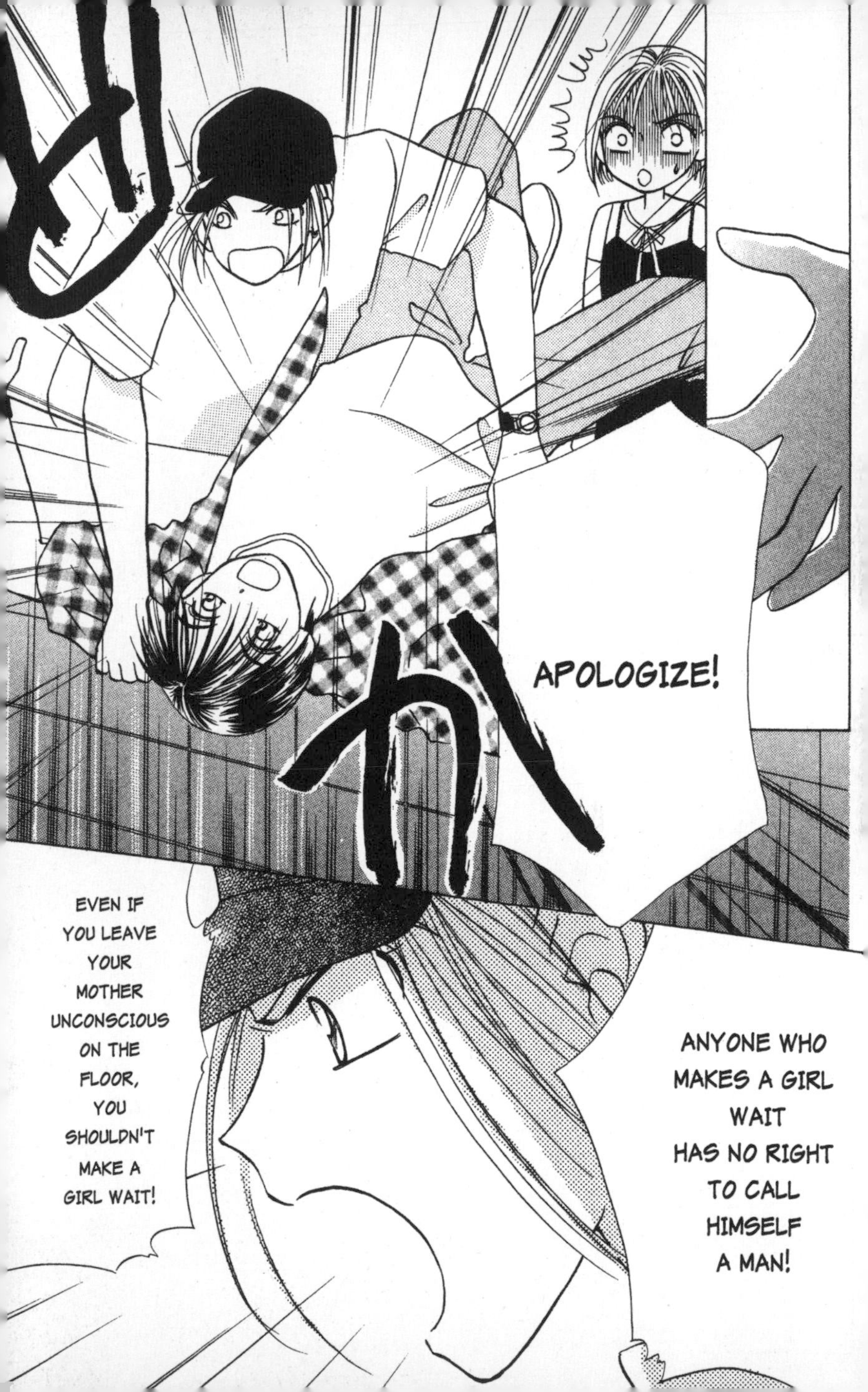
APOLOGIZE!
ANYONE WHO MAKES A GIRL WAIT HAS NO RIGHT TO CALL HIMSELF A MAN!
EVEN IF YOU LEAVE YOUR MOTHER UNCONSCIOUS ON THE FLOOR, YOU SHOULDN'T MAKE A GIRL WAIT!

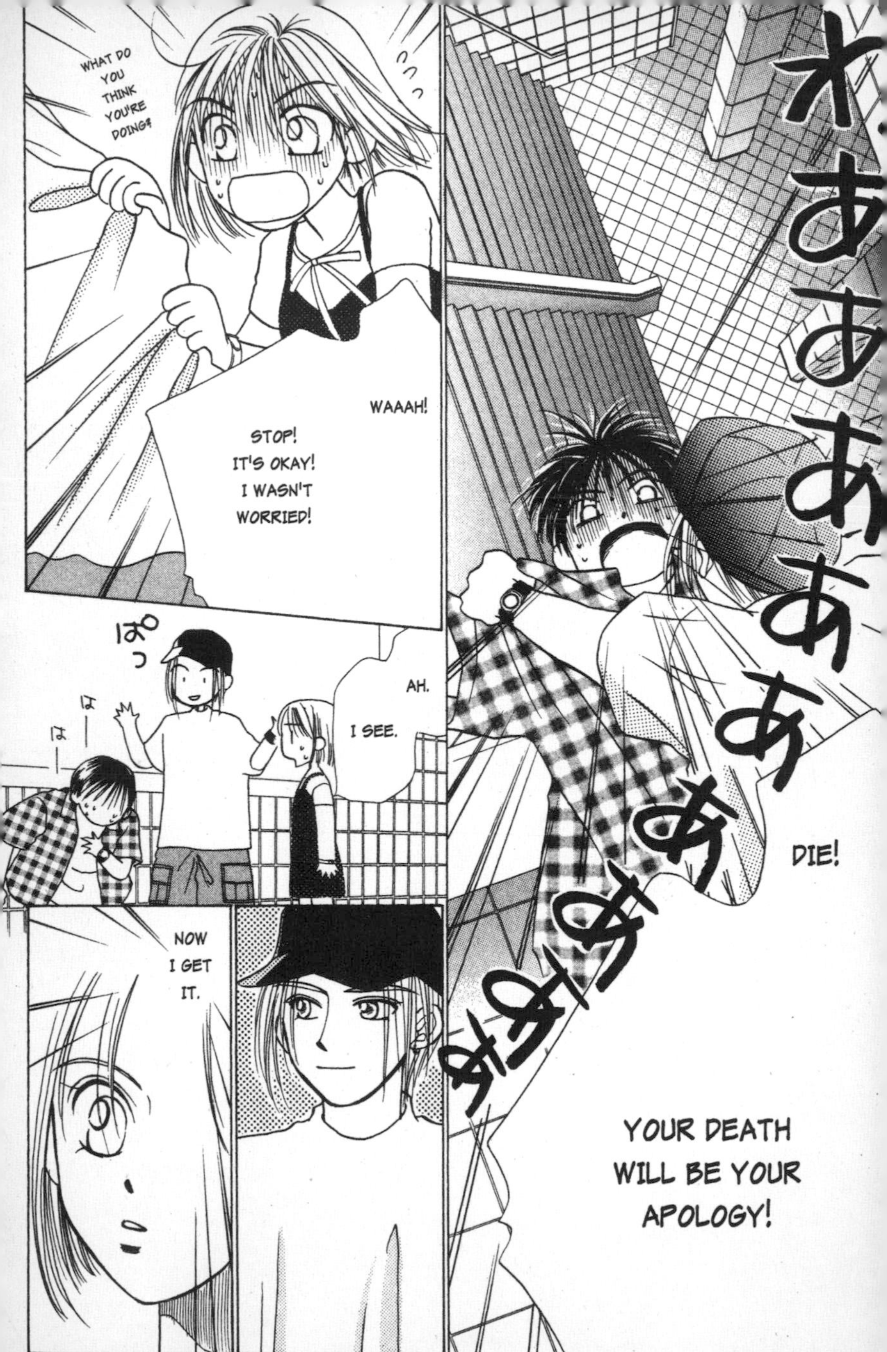
おあああああああ
DIE!
YOUR DEATH WILL BE YOUR APOLOGY!
WHAT DO YOU THINK YOU'RE DOING?
WAAAH!
STOP! IT'S OKAY! I WASN'T WORRIED!
ぱっ
AH.
I SEE.
はーはー
NOW I GET IT.

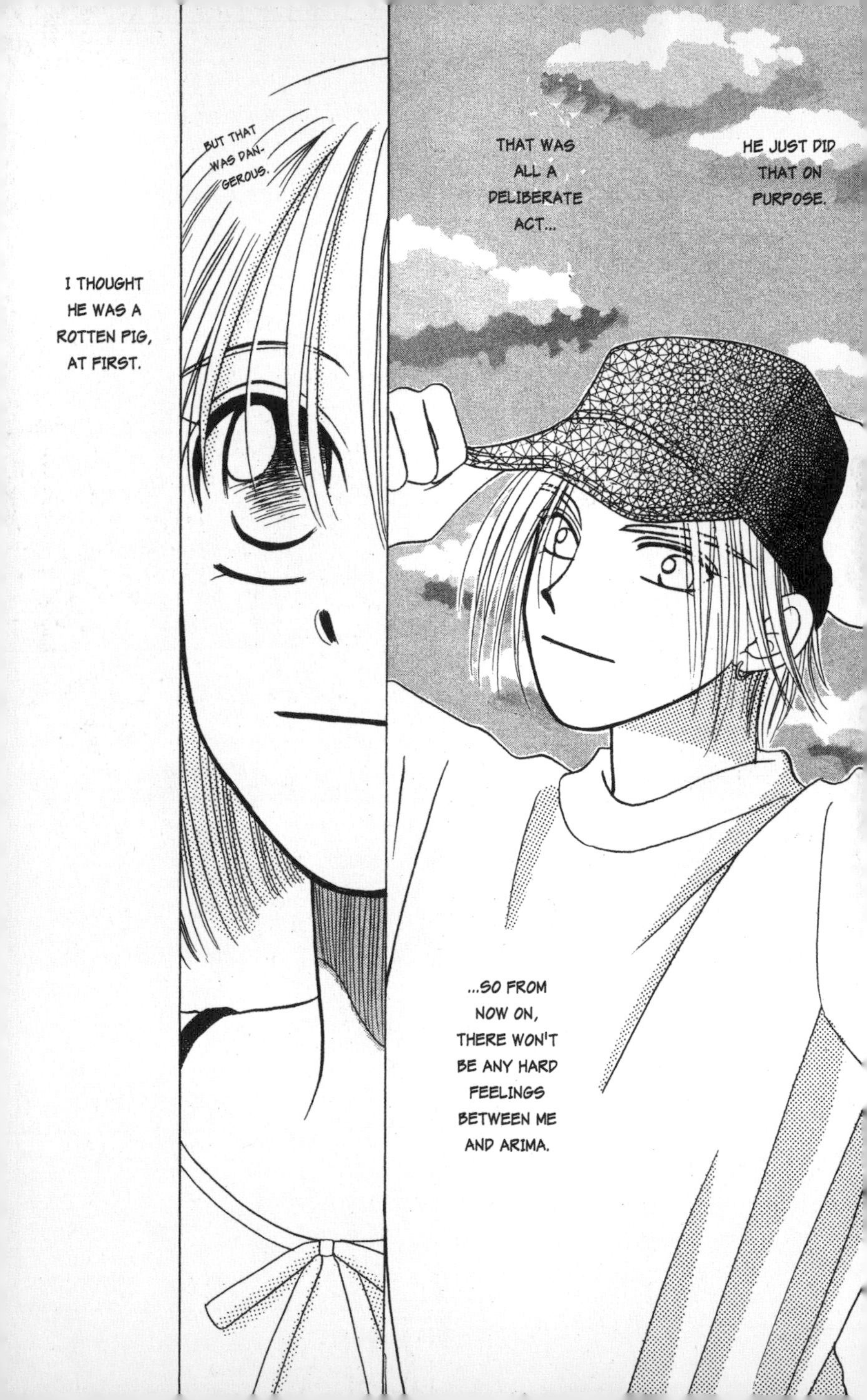
HE JUST DID THAT ON PURPOSE.
THAT WAS ALL A DELIBERATE ACT...
...SO FROM NOW ON, THERE WON'T BE ANY HARD FEELINGS BETWEEN ME AND ARIMA.
BUT THAT WAS DAN-GEROUS.
I THOUGHT HE WAS A ROTTEN PIG, AT FIRST.

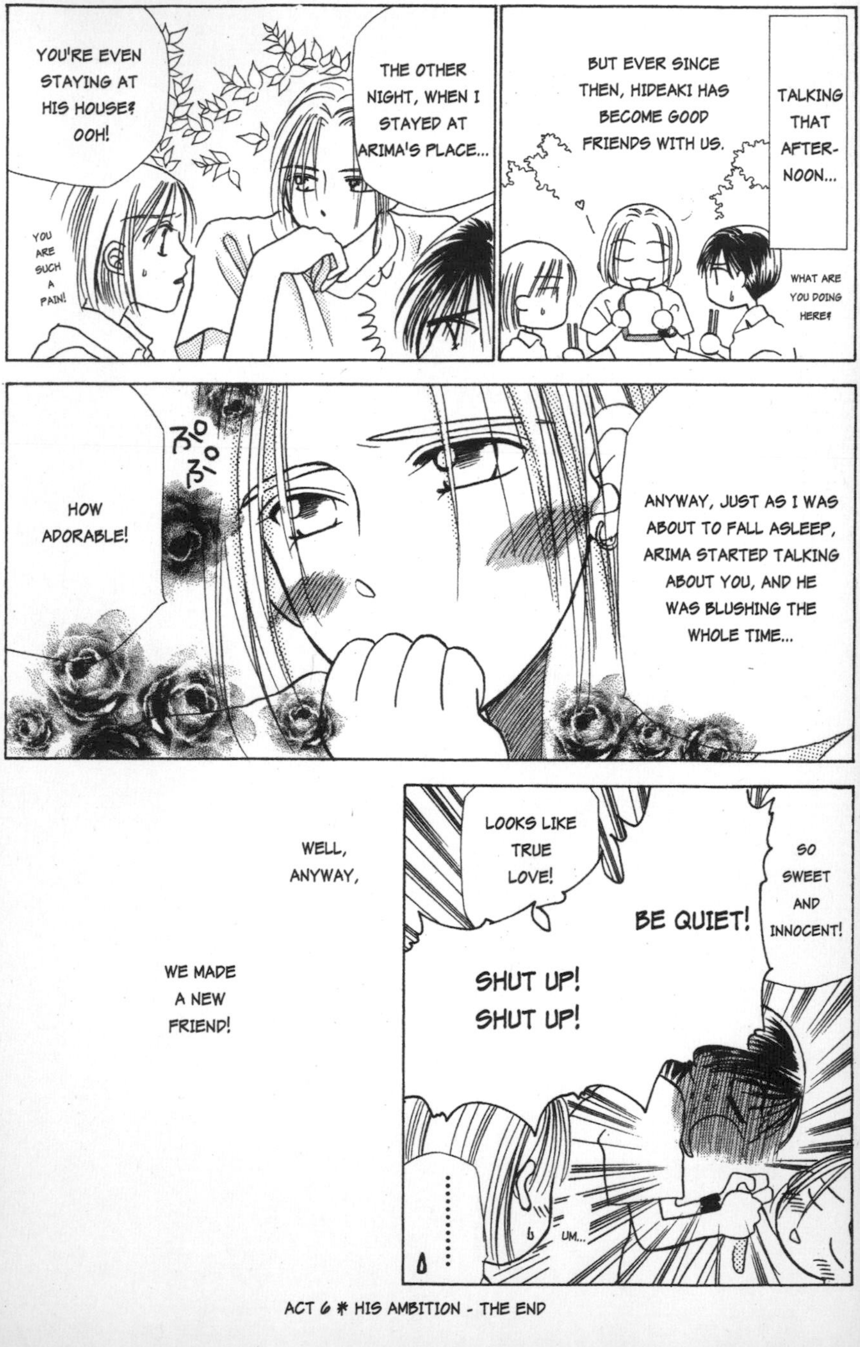
TALKING THAT AFTERNOON...
BUT EVER SINCE THEN, HIDEAKI HAS BECOME GOOD FRIENDS WITH US.
WHAT ARE YOU DOING HERE?
THE OTHER NIGHT, WHEN I STAYED AT ARIMA'S PLACE...
YOU'RE EVEN STAYING AT HIS HOUSE? OOH!
YOU ARE SUCH A PAIN!
ANYWAY, JUST AS I WAS ABOUT TO FALL ASLEEP, ARIMA STARTED TALKING ABOUT YOU, AND HE WAS BLUSHING THE WHOLE TIME...
HOW ADORABLE!
SO SWEET AND INNOCENT!
BE QUIET!
LOOKS LIKE TRUE LOVE!
SHUT UP! SHUT UP!
UM...
......
WELL, ANYWAY,
WE MADE A NEW FRIEND!

ACT 6 * HIS AMBITION - THE END

彼氏彼女の事情

ACT7★クレイジー・フォー・ユー

HE IS "PERFECT."

BUT HE'S STRUGGLED
TO ACHIEVE THAT PERFECTION.

EVEN THE PEOPLE AROUND HIM
CANNOT DENY THAT.

ASIDE FROM HIS ACADEMIC
ACHIEVEMENT,

ASIDE FROM HIS PERSONALITY
AND CHARACTER,

PERFECTION
HAS BECOME A PART
OF HIM.

BUT THAT WAS ALL BEFORE
HE DISCOVERED WHAT LOVE IS.

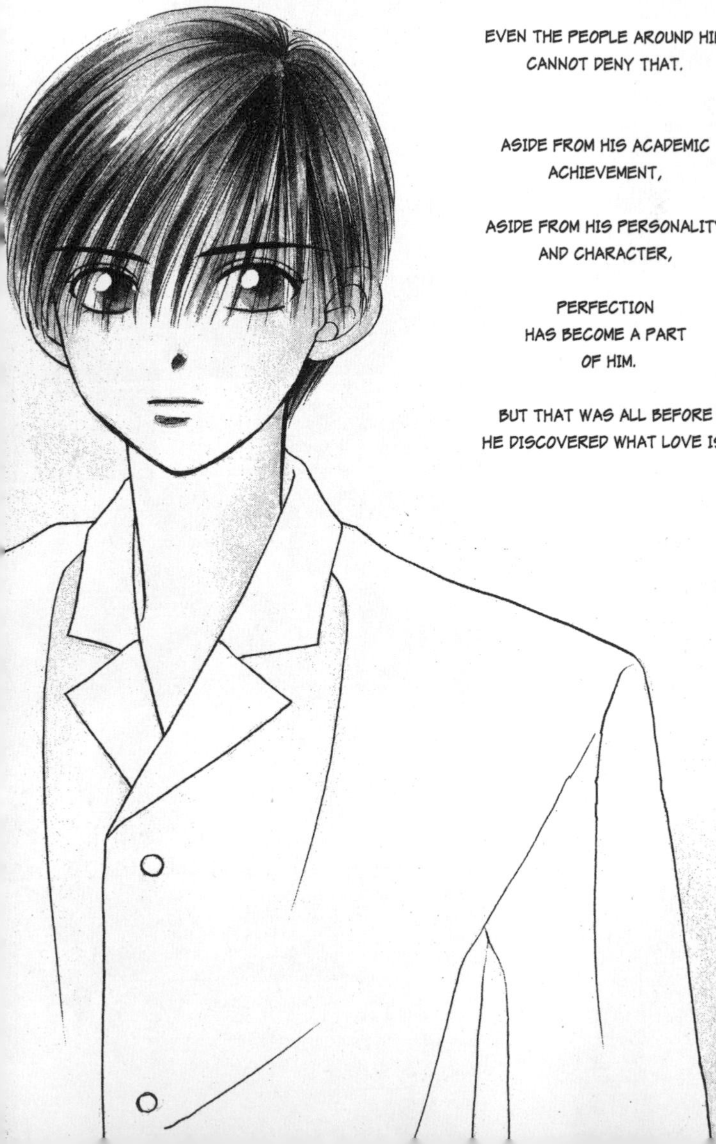

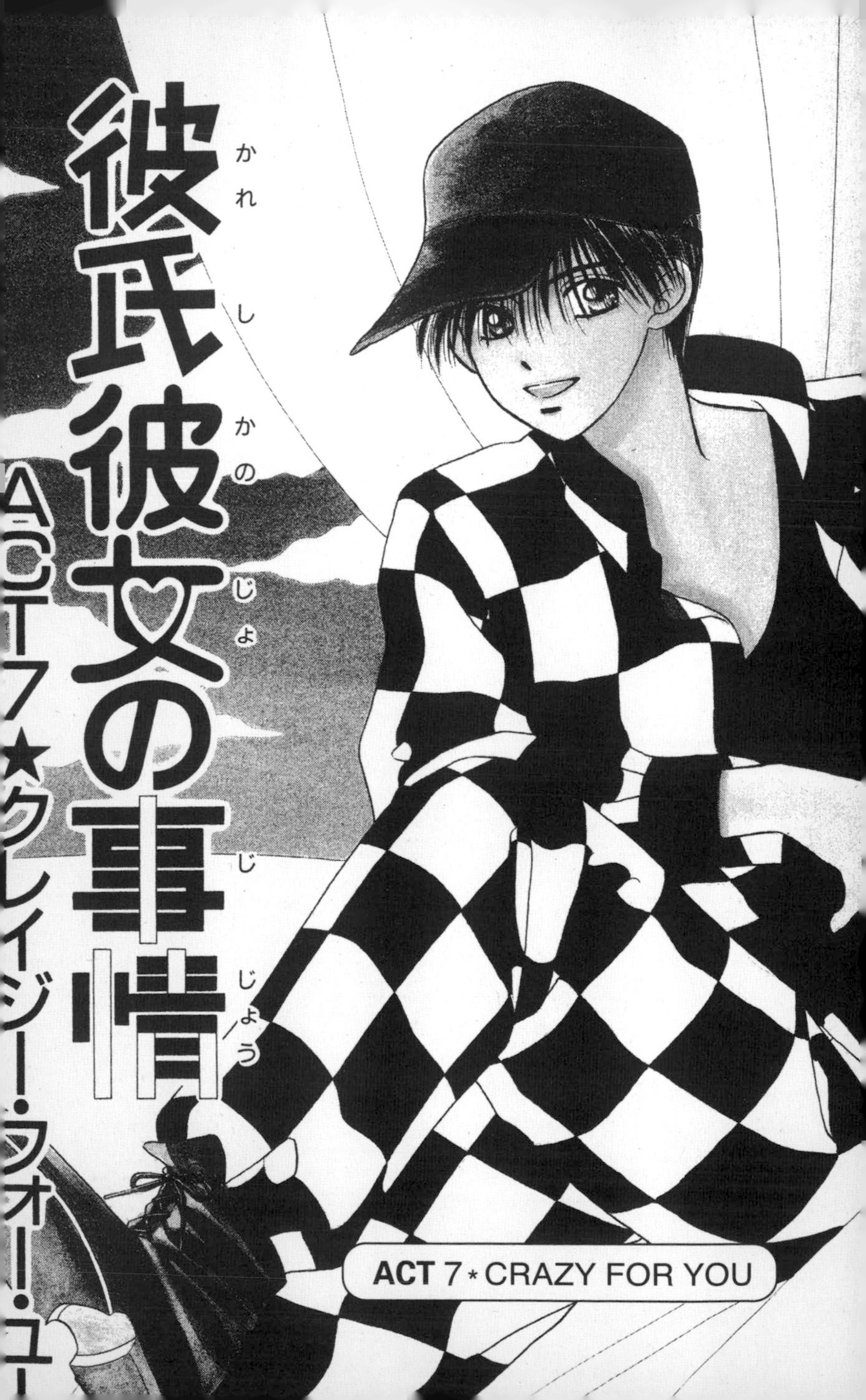
彼氏彼女の事情（かれしかのじょのじじょう）
ACT7★クレイジー・フォー・ユー
ACT 7 * CRAZY FOR YOU

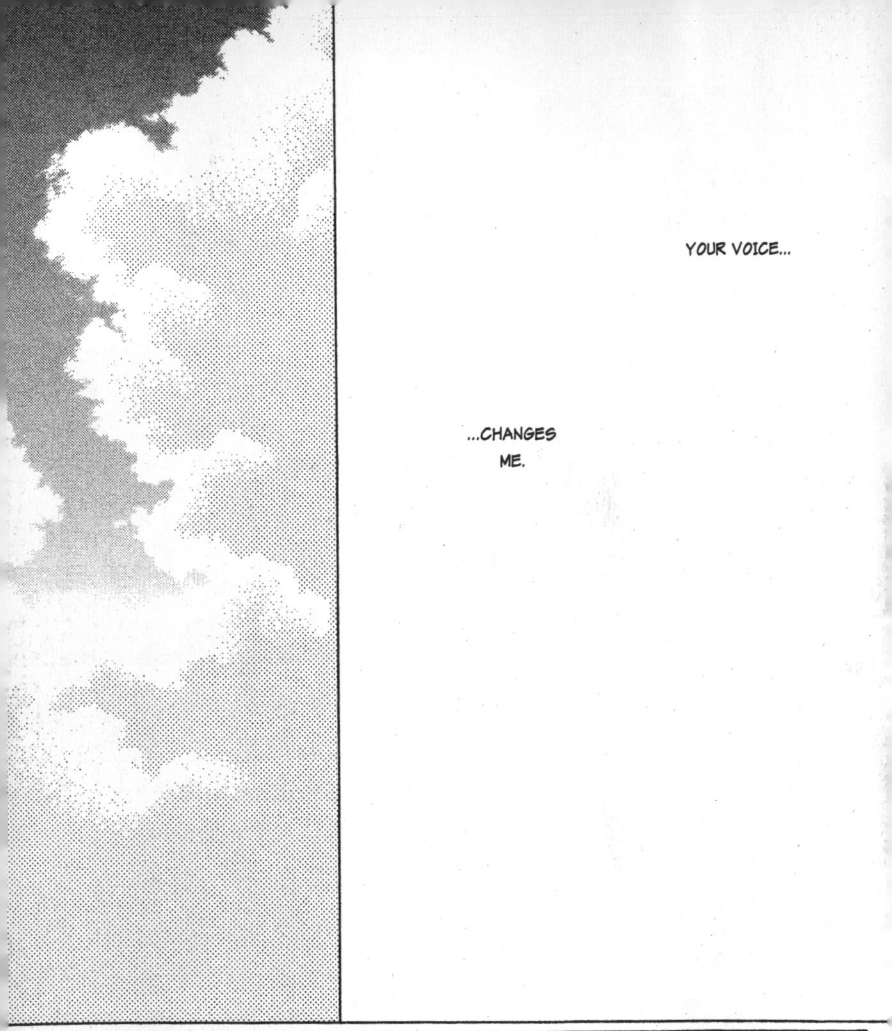
YOUR VOICE...
...CHANGES ME.

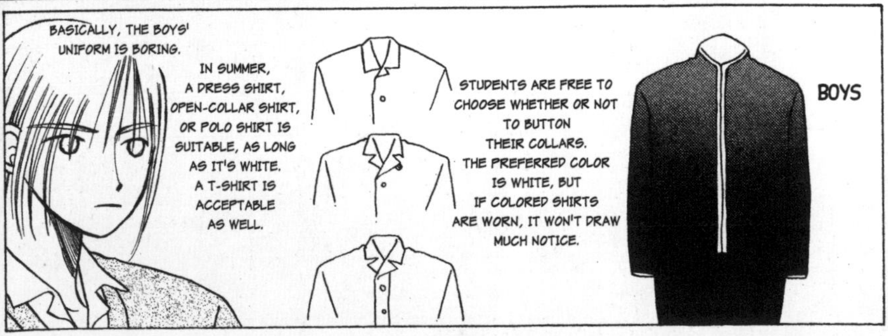
BOYS
STUDENTS ARE FREE TO CHOOSE WHETHER OR NOT TO BUTTON THEIR COLLARS. THE PREFERRED COLOR IS WHITE, BUT IF COLORED SHIRTS ARE WORN, IT WON'T DRAW MUCH NOTICE.
BASICALLY, THE BOYS' UNIFORM IS BORING.
IN SUMMER, A DRESS SHIRT, OPEN-COLLAR SHIRT, OR POLO SHIRT IS SUITABLE, AS LONG AS IT'S WHITE. A T-SHIRT IS ACCEPTABLE AS WELL.

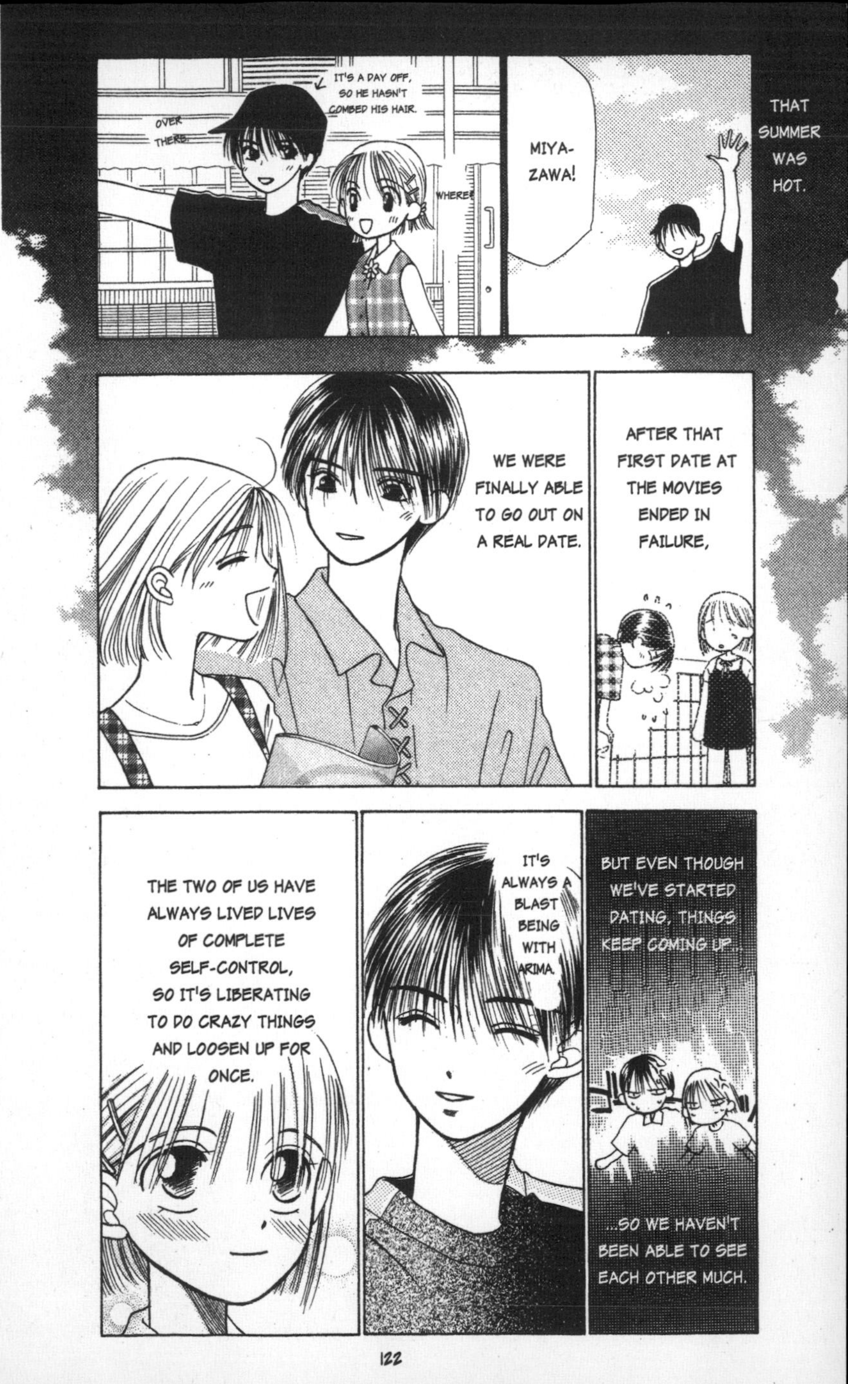
THAT SUMMER WAS HOT.
MIYA-ZAWA!
IT'S A DAY OFF, SO HE HASN'T COMBED HIS HAIR.
OVER THERE.
WHERE?
AFTER THAT FIRST DATE AT THE MOVIES ENDED IN FAILURE,
WE WERE FINALLY ABLE TO GO OUT ON A REAL DATE.
BUT EVEN THOUGH WE'VE STARTED DATING, THINGS KEEP COMING UP...
...SO WE HAVEN'T BEEN ABLE TO SEE EACH OTHER MUCH.
IT'S ALWAYS A BLAST BEING WITH ARIMA.
THE TWO OF US HAVE ALWAYS LIVED LIVES OF COMPLETE SELF-CONTROL, SO IT'S LIBERATING TO DO CRAZY THINGS AND LOOSEN UP FOR ONCE.

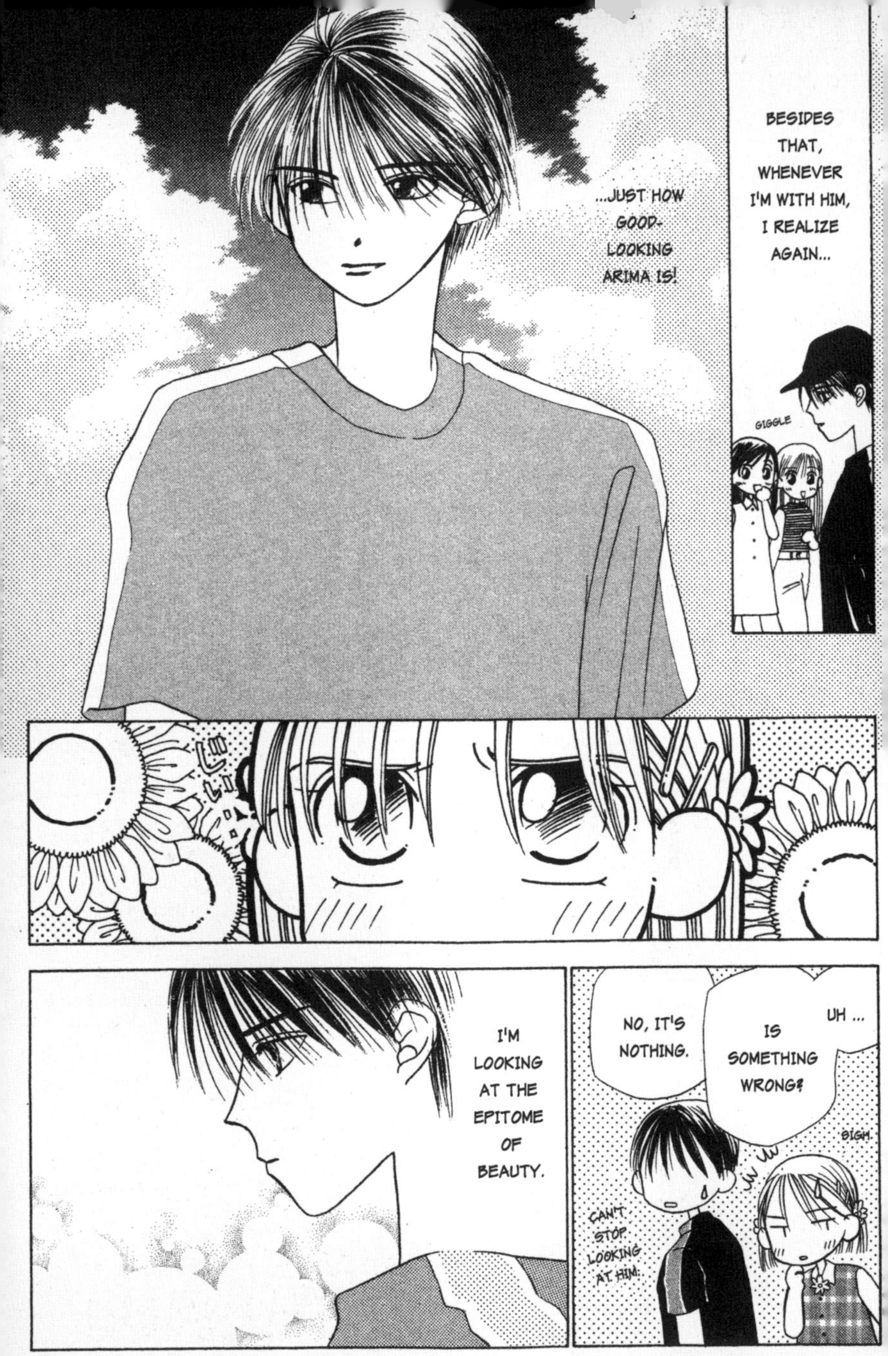
BESIDES THAT, WHENEVER I'M WITH HIM, I REALIZE AGAIN...
GIGGLE
...JUST HOW GOOD-LOOKING ARIMA IS!
UH ...
IS SOMETHING WRONG?
NO, IT'S NOTHING.
SIGH.
CAN'T STOP LOOKING AT HIM.
I'M LOOKING AT THE EPITOME OF BEAUTY.

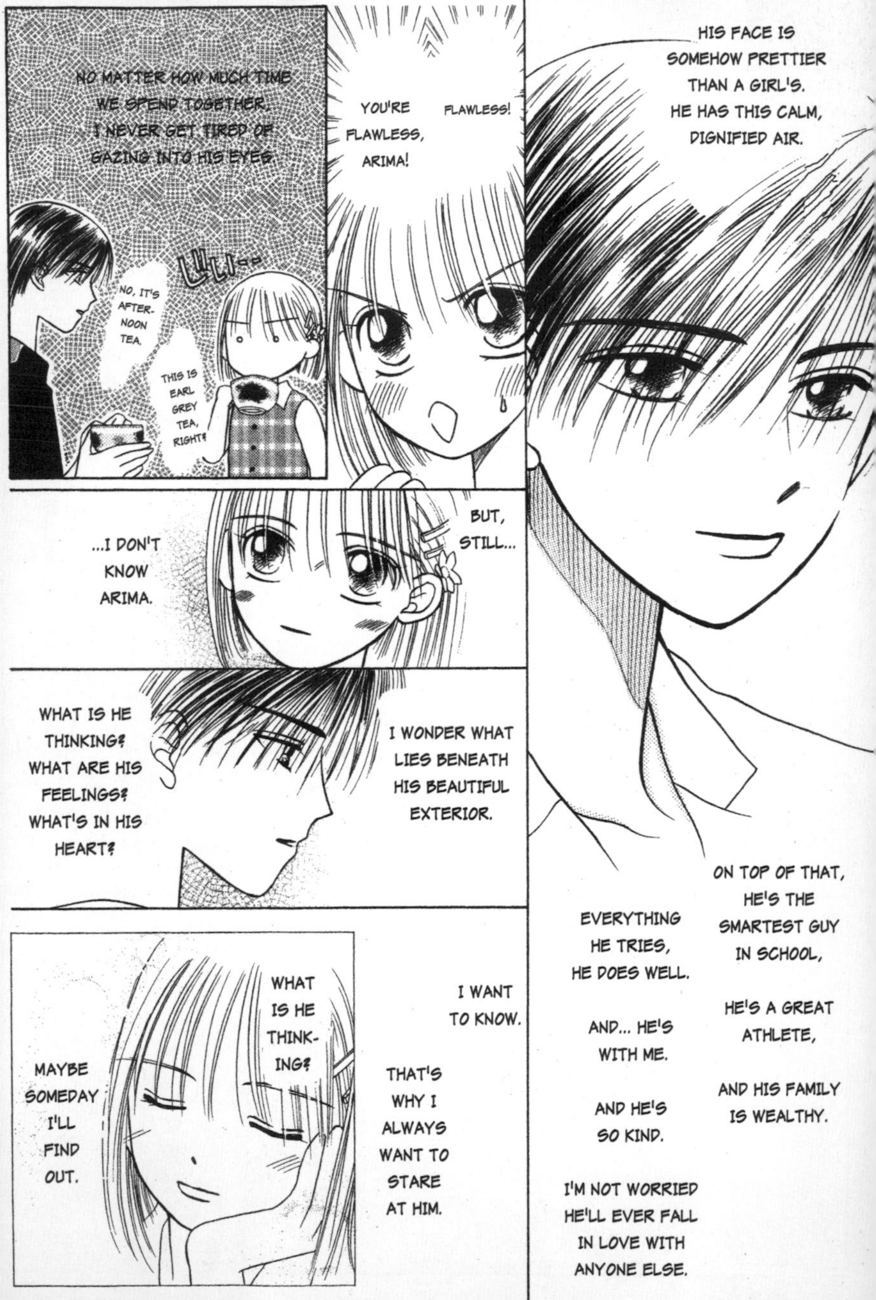
HIS FACE IS SOMEHOW PRETTIER THAN A GIRL'S. HE HAS THIS CALM, DIGNIFIED AIR.
ON TOP OF THAT, HE'S THE SMARTEST GUY IN SCHOOL,
HE'S A GREAT ATHLETE,
AND HIS FAMILY IS WEALTHY.
EVERYTHING HE TRIES, HE DOES WELL.
AND... HE'S WITH ME.
AND HE'S SO KIND.
I'M NOT WORRIED HE'LL EVER FALL IN LOVE WITH ANYONE ELSE.
FLAWLESS!
YOU'RE FLAWLESS, ARIMA!
NO MATTER HOW MUCH TIME WE SPEND TOGETHER, I NEVER GET TIRED OF GAZING INTO HIS EYES.
THIS IS EARL GREY TEA, RIGHT?
NO, IT'S AFTER-NOON TEA.
BUT, STILL...
...I DON'T KNOW ARIMA.
I WONDER WHAT LIES BENEATH HIS BEAUTIFUL EXTERIOR.
WHAT IS HE THINKING? WHAT ARE HIS FEELINGS? WHAT'S IN HIS HEART?
I WANT TO KNOW.
THAT'S WHY I ALWAYS WANT TO STARE AT HIM.
WHAT IS HE THINK-ING?
MAYBE SOMEDAY I'LL FIND OUT.

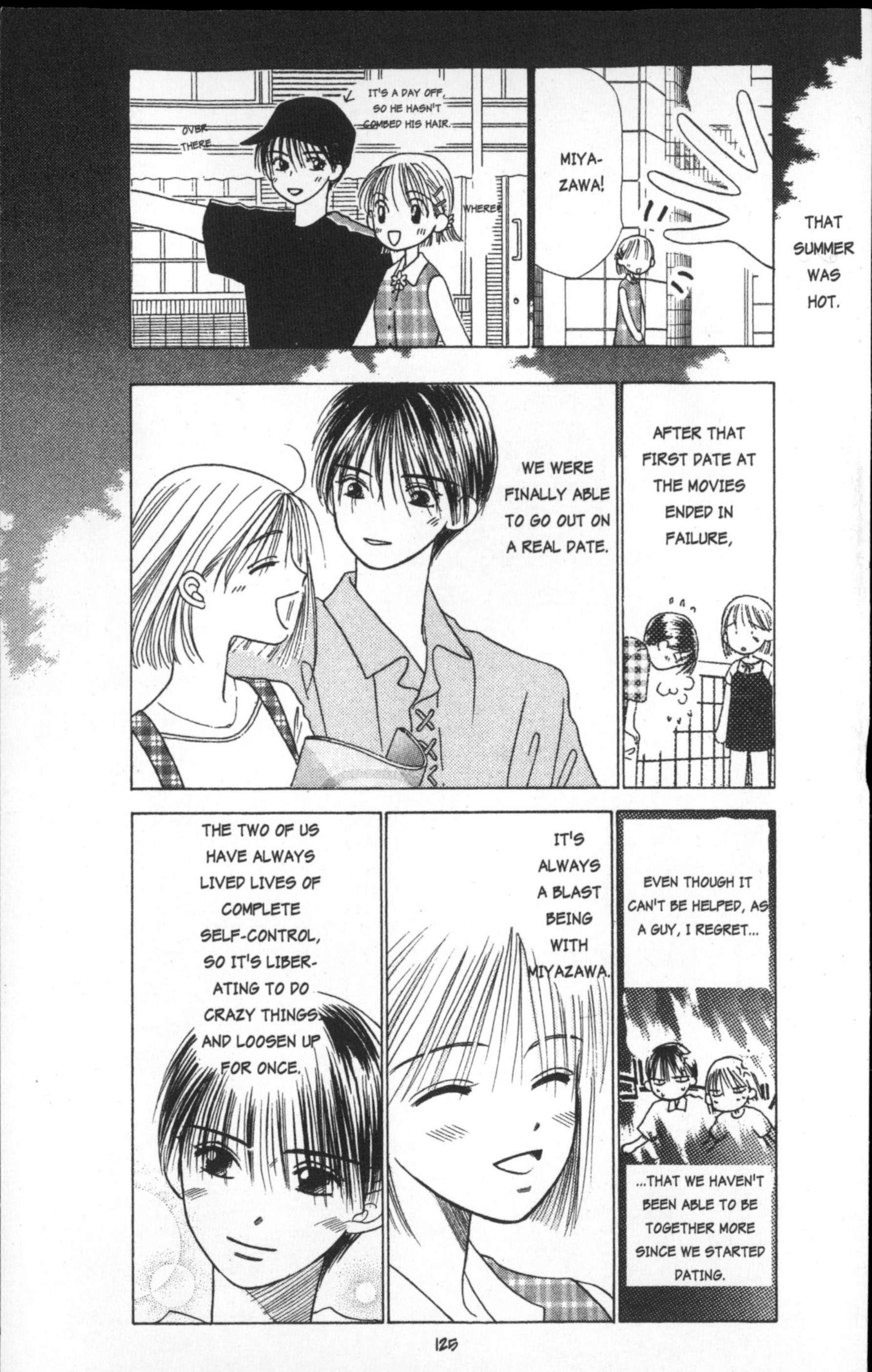
THAT SUMMER WAS HOT.
MIYA-ZAWA!
IT'S A DAY OFF, SO HE HASN'T COMBED HIS HAIR.
OVER THERE.
WHERE?
AFTER THAT FIRST DATE AT THE MOVIES ENDED IN FAILURE,
WE WERE FINALLY ABLE TO GO OUT ON A REAL DATE.
EVEN THOUGH IT CAN'T BE HELPED, AS A GUY, I REGRET...
...THAT WE HAVEN'T BEEN ABLE TO BE TOGETHER MORE SINCE WE STARTED DATING.
IT'S ALWAYS A BLAST BEING WITH MIYAZAWA.
THE TWO OF US HAVE ALWAYS LIVED LIVES OF COMPLETE SELF-CONTROL, SO IT'S LIBER-ATING TO DO CRAZY THINGS AND LOOSEN UP FOR ONCE.

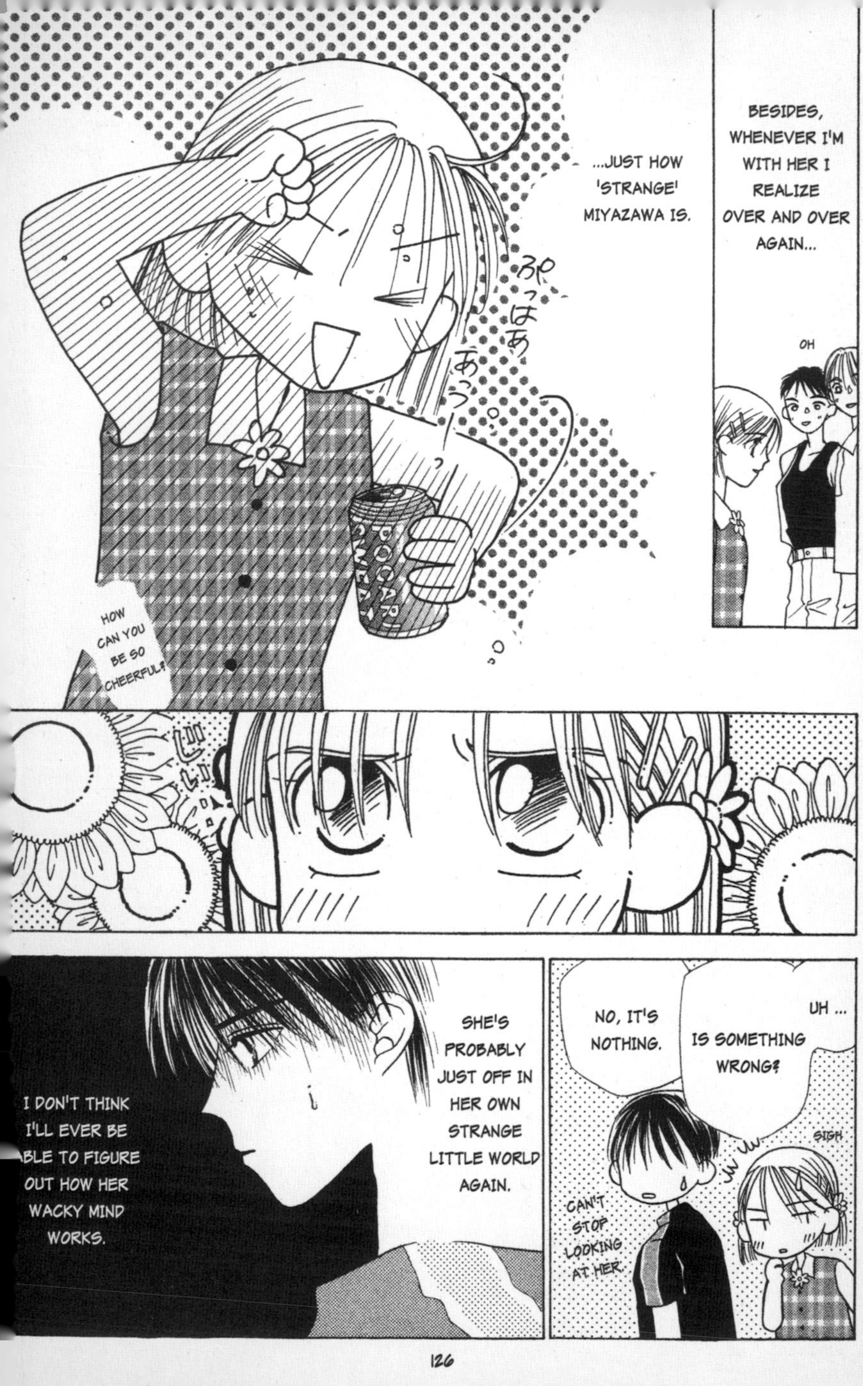
BESIDES, WHENEVER I'M WITH HER I REALIZE OVER AND OVER AGAIN...
OH
...JUST HOW 'STRANGE' MIYAZAWA IS.
ぷっはあ
あうー
HOW CAN YOU BE SO CHEERFUL?
UH ... IS SOMETHING WRONG?
NO, IT'S NOTHING.
SIGH
CAN'T STOP LOOKING AT HER
SHE'S PROBABLY JUST OFF IN HER OWN STRANGE LITTLE WORLD AGAIN.
I DON'T THINK I'LL EVER BE ABLE TO FIGURE OUT HOW HER WACKY MIND WORKS.

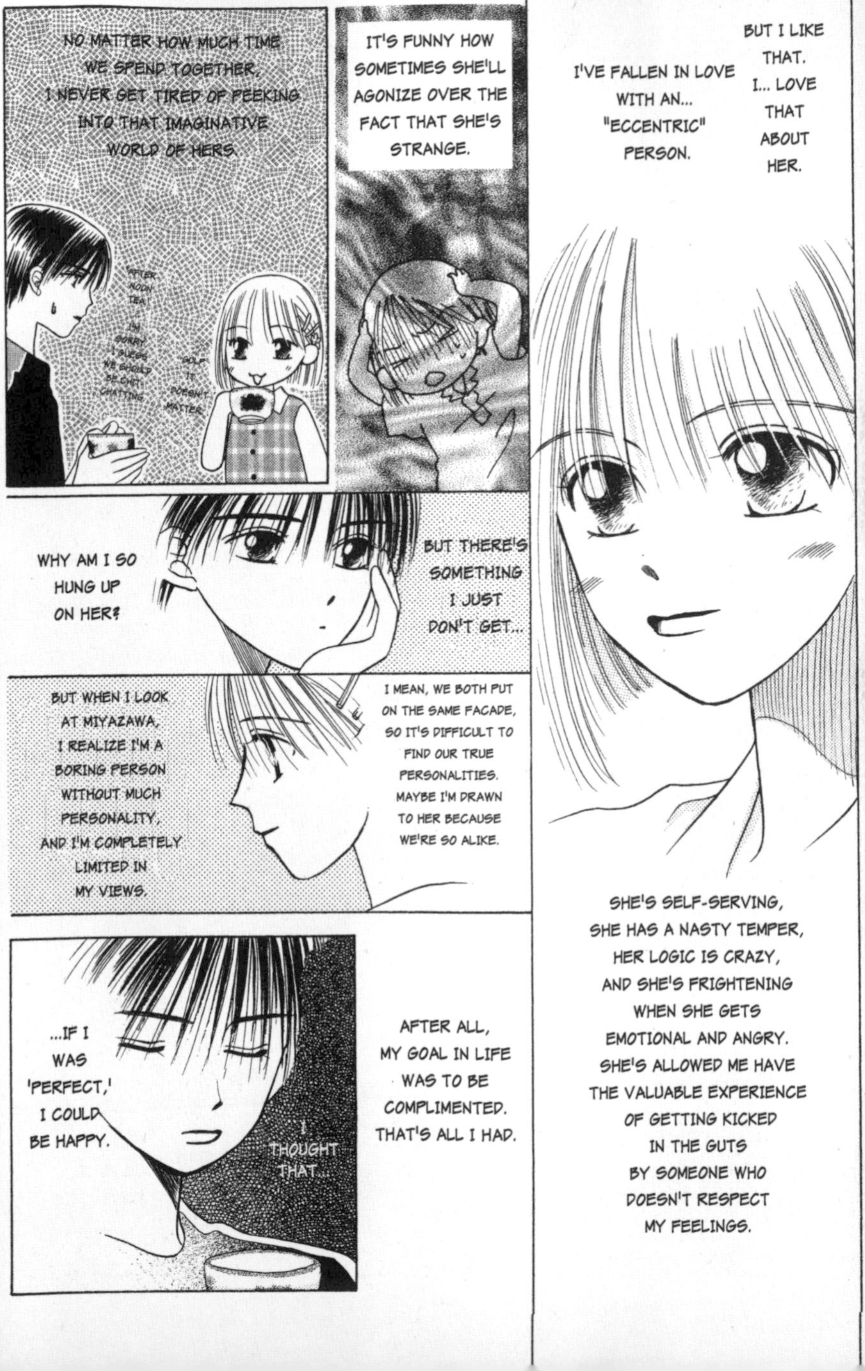
BUT I LIKE THAT. I... LOVE THAT ABOUT HER.
I'VE FALLEN IN LOVE WITH AN... "ECCENTRIC" PERSON.
SHE'S SELF-SERVING, SHE HAS A NASTY TEMPER, HER LOGIC IS CRAZY, AND SHE'S FRIGHTENING WHEN SHE GETS EMOTIONAL AND ANGRY. SHE'S ALLOWED ME HAVE THE VALUABLE EXPERIENCE OF GETTING KICKED IN THE GUTS BY SOMEONE WHO DOESN'T RESPECT MY FEELINGS.
IT'S FUNNY HOW SOMETIMES SHE'LL AGONIZE OVER THE FACT THAT SHE'S STRANGE.
NO MATTER HOW MUCH TIME WE SPEND TOGETHER, I NEVER GET TIRED OF PEEKING INTO THAT IMAGINATIVE WORLD OF HERS.
AFTERNOON TEA!
GOLF IT DOESN'T MATTER.
I'M SORRY I GUESS WE SHOULD BE CHIT-CHATTING
BUT THERE'S SOMETHING I JUST DON'T GET...
WHY AM I SO HUNG UP ON HER?
I MEAN, WE BOTH PUT ON THE SAME FACADE, SO IT'S DIFFICULT TO FIND OUR TRUE PERSONALITIES. MAYBE I'M DRAWN TO HER BECAUSE WE'RE SO ALIKE.
BUT WHEN I LOOK AT MIYAZAWA, I REALIZE I'M A BORING PERSON WITHOUT MUCH PERSONALITY, AND I'M COMPLETELY LIMITED IN MY VIEWS.
AFTER ALL, MY GOAL IN LIFE WAS TO BE COMPLIMENTED. THAT'S ALL I HAD.
I THOUGHT THAT...
...IF I WAS 'PERFECT,' I COULD BE HAPPY.

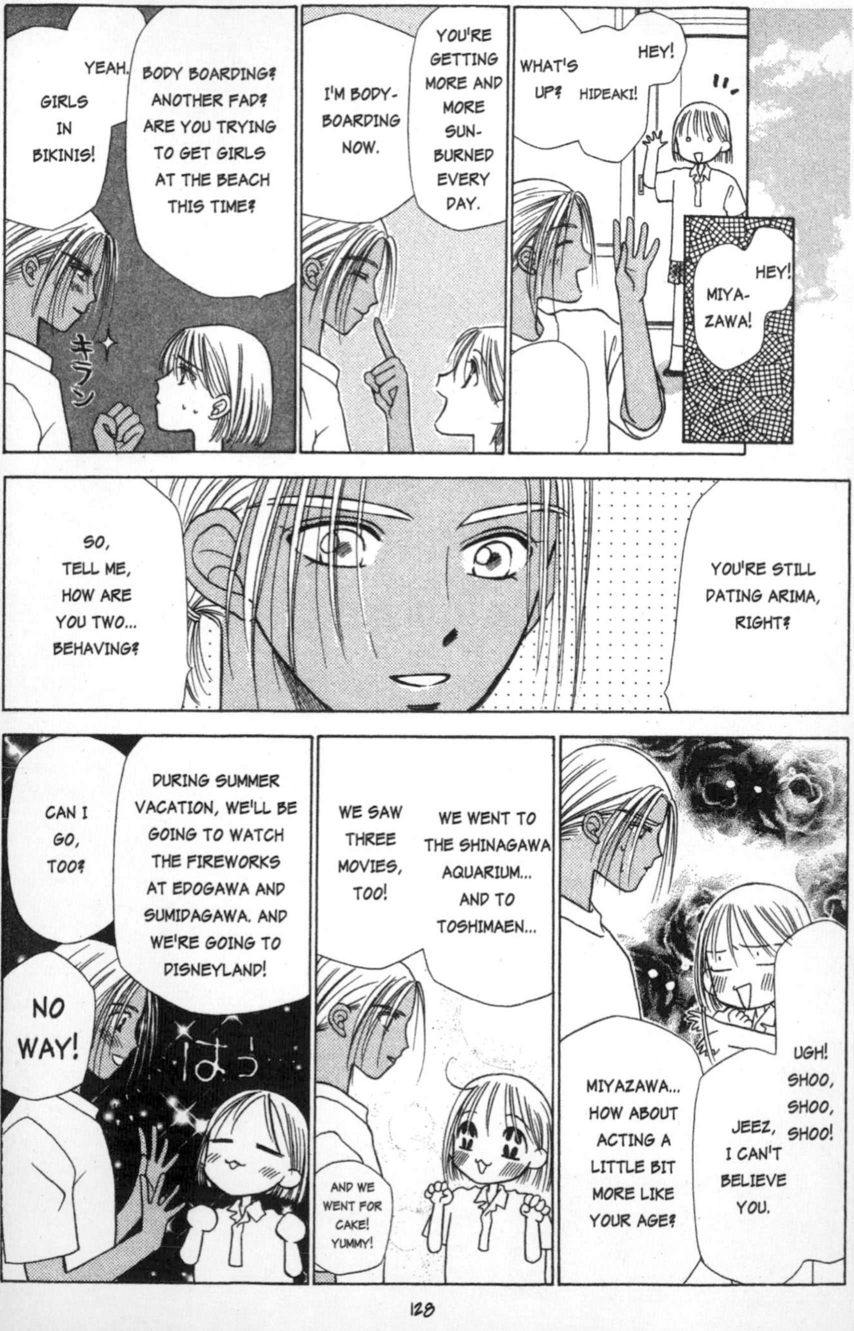
HEY! HIDEAKI!
WHAT'S UP?
HEY! MIYA-ZAWA!
YOU'RE GETTING MORE AND MORE SUN-BURNED EVERY DAY.
I'M BODY-BOARDING NOW.
BODY BOARDING? ANOTHER FAD? ARE YOU TRYING TO GET GIRLS AT THE BEACH THIS TIME?
YEAH. GIRLS IN BIKINIS!
キラン
YOU'RE STILL DATING ARIMA, RIGHT?
SO, TELL ME, HOW ARE YOU TWO... BEHAVING?
MIYAZAWA... HOW ABOUT ACTING A LITTLE BIT MORE LIKE YOUR AGE?
JEEZ, I CAN'T BELIEVE YOU.
UGH! SHOO, SHOO, SHOO!
WE WENT TO THE SHINAGAWA AQUARIUM... AND TO TOSHIMAEN...
WE SAW THREE MOVIES, TOO!
AND WE WENT FOR CAKE! YUMMY!
DURING SUMMER VACATION, WE'LL BE GOING TO WATCH THE FIREWORKS AT EDOGAWA AND SUMIDAGAWA. AND WE'RE GOING TO DISNEYLAND!
CAN I GO, TOO?
NO WAY!
はっ

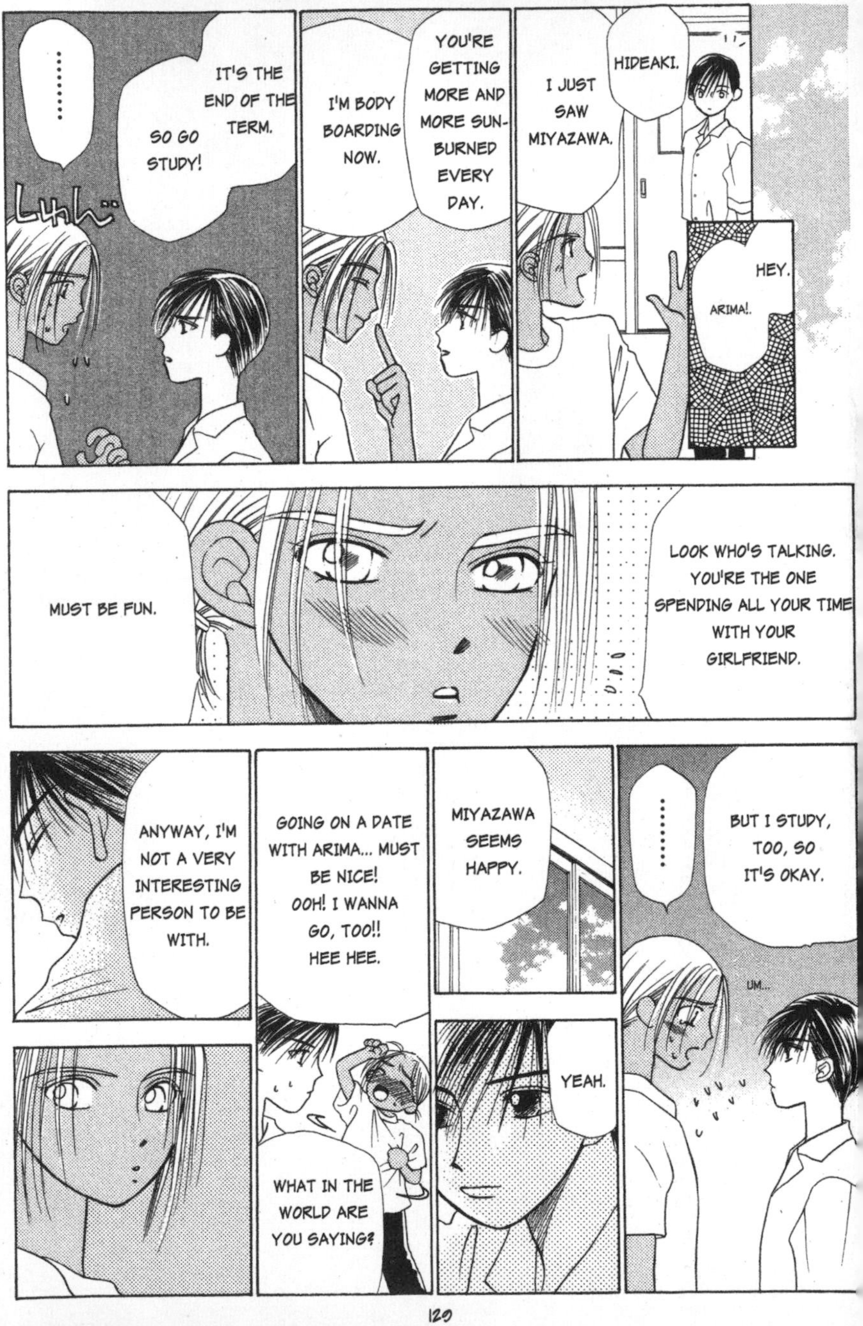
HIDEAKI.
I JUST SAW MIYAZAWA.
HEY.
ARIMA!.
YOU'RE GETTING MORE AND MORE SUN-BURNED EVERY DAY.
I'M BODY BOARDING NOW.
IT'S THE END OF THE TERM.
SO GO STUDY!
......
しゅん
LOOK WHO'S TALKING. YOU'RE THE ONE SPENDING ALL YOUR TIME WITH YOUR GIRLFRIEND.
MUST BE FUN.
BUT I STUDY, TOO, SO IT'S OKAY.
......
UM...
MIYAZAWA SEEMS HAPPY.
YEAH.
GOING ON A DATE WITH ARIMA... MUST BE NICE! OOH! I WANNA GO, TOO!! HEE HEE.
WHAT IN THE WORLD ARE YOU SAYING?
ANYWAY, I'M NOT A VERY INTERESTING PERSON TO BE WITH.

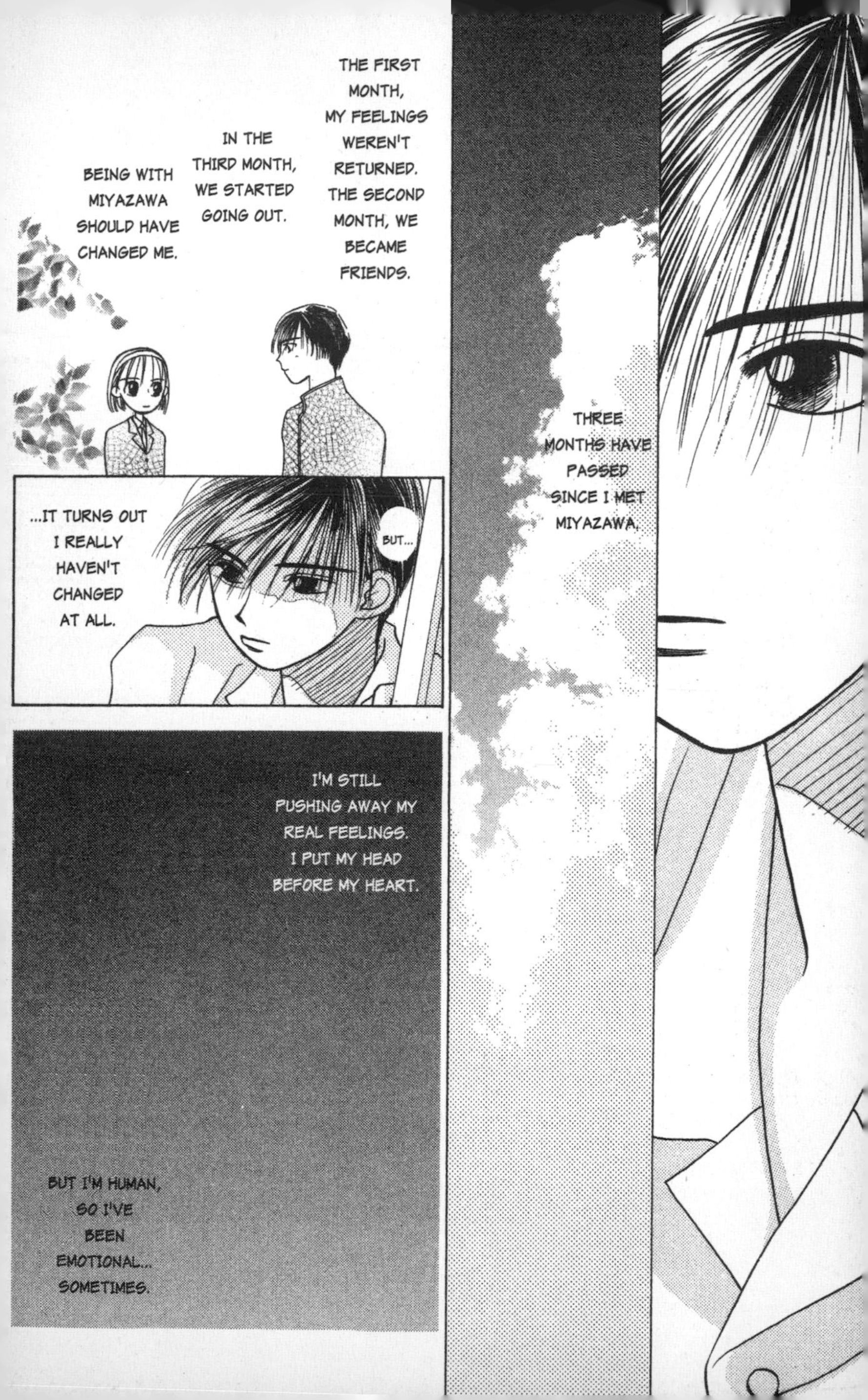
THREE MONTHS HAVE PASSED SINCE I MET MIYAZAWA.
THE FIRST MONTH, MY FEELINGS WEREN'T RETURNED. THE SECOND MONTH, WE BECAME FRIENDS.
IN THE THIRD MONTH, WE STARTED GOING OUT.
BEING WITH MIYAZAWA SHOULD HAVE CHANGED ME.
BUT...
...IT TURNS OUT I REALLY HAVEN'T CHANGED AT ALL.
I'M STILL PUSHING AWAY MY REAL FEELINGS. I PUT MY HEAD BEFORE MY HEART.
BUT I'M HUMAN, SO I'VE BEEN EMOTIONAL... SOMETIMES.

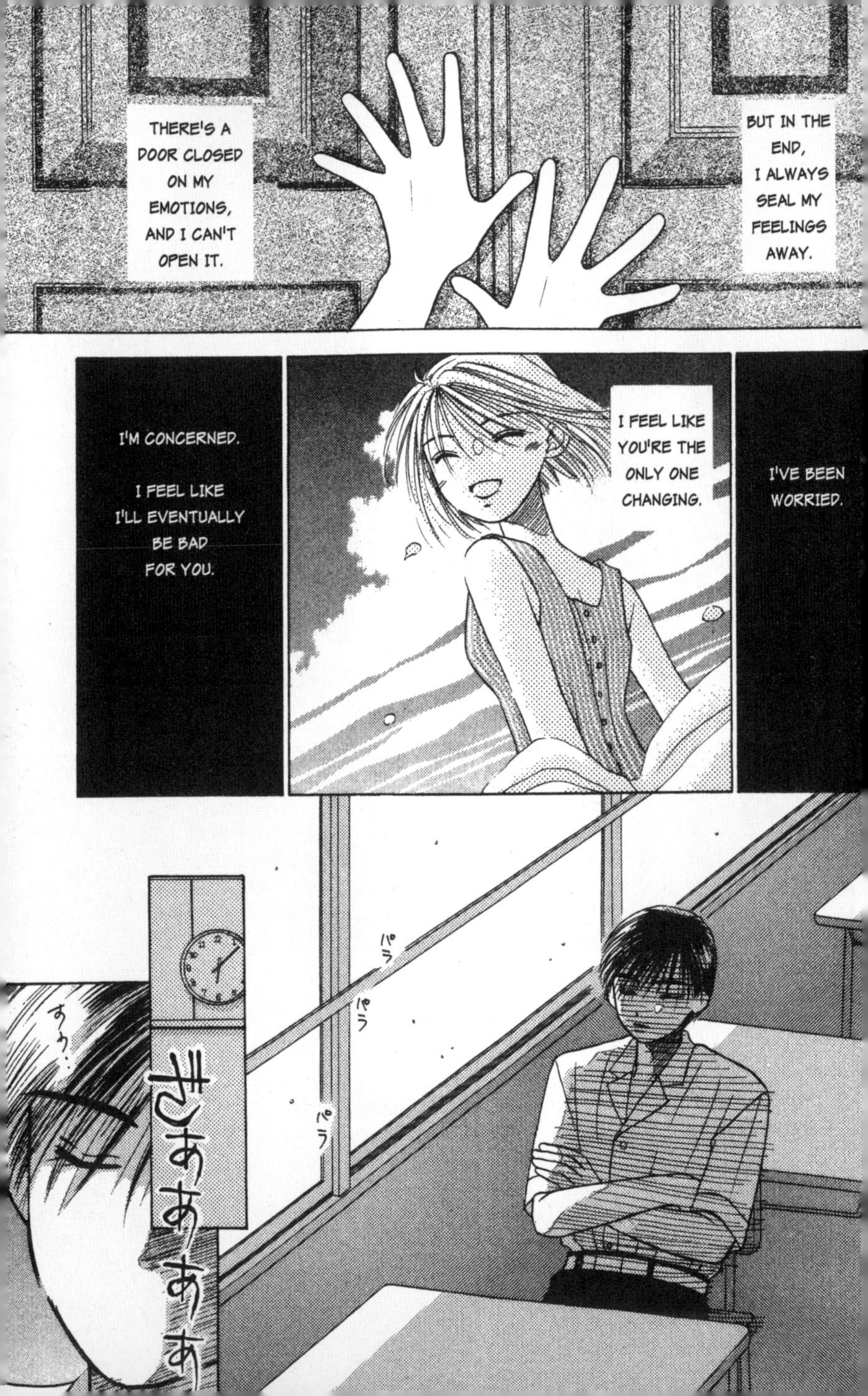
BUT IN THE END, I ALWAYS SEAL MY FEELINGS AWAY.
THERE'S A DOOR CLOSED ON MY EMOTIONS, AND I CAN'T OPEN IT.
I'VE BEEN WORRIED.
I FEEL LIKE YOU'RE THE ONLY ONE CHANGING.
I'M CONCERNED.
I FEEL LIKE I'LL EVENTUALLY BE BAD FOR YOU.
パラ
パラ
パラ
ざあああ
すう…

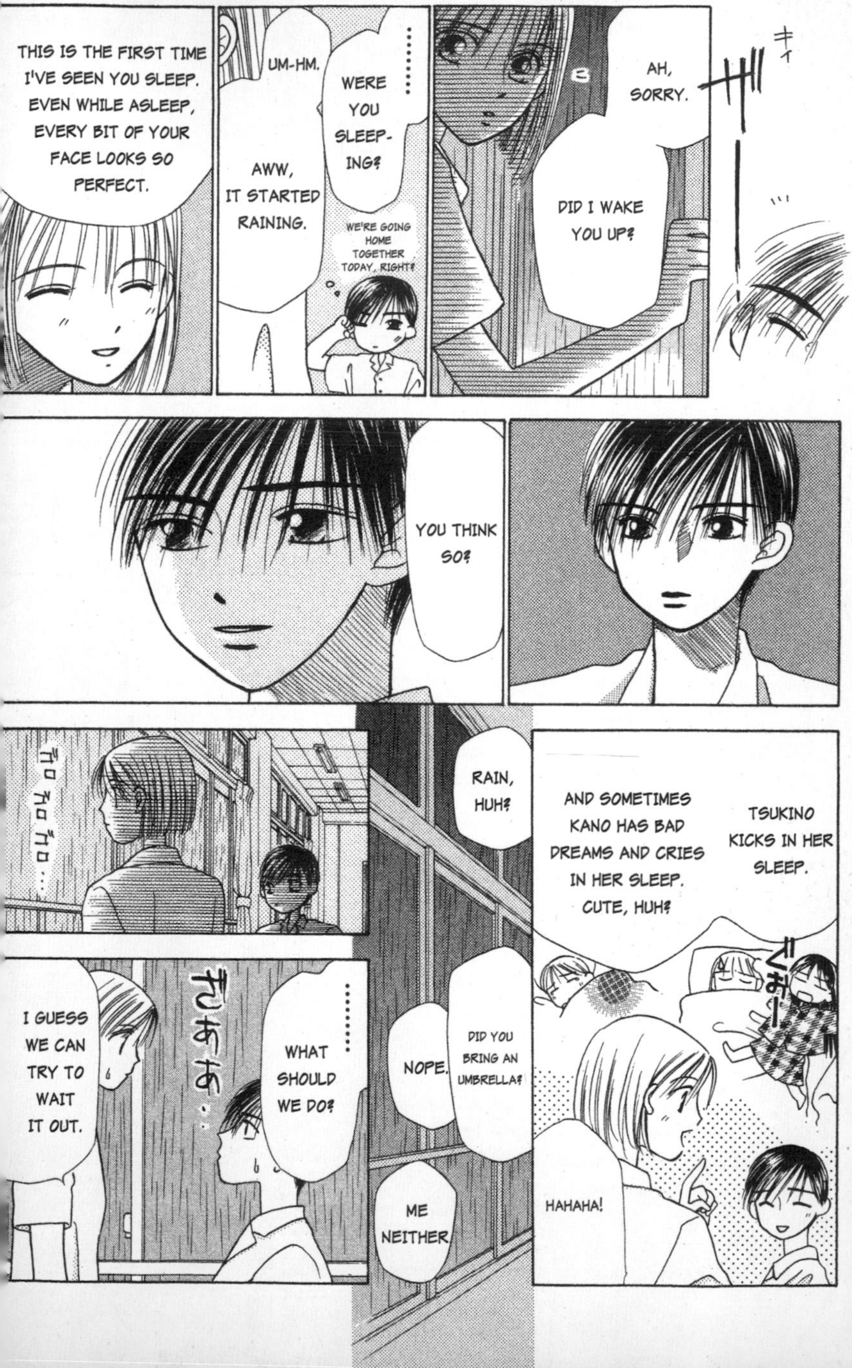
キィ
AH, SORRY.
DID I WAKE YOU UP?
......
WERE YOU SLEEPING?
UM-HM.
AWW, IT STARTED RAINING.
WE'RE GOING HOME TOGETHER TODAY, RIGHT?
THIS IS THE FIRST TIME I'VE SEEN YOU SLEEP. EVEN WHILE ASLEEP, EVERY BIT OF YOUR FACE LOOKS SO PERFECT.
YOU THINK SO?
TSUKINO KICKS IN HER SLEEP.
AND SOMETIMES KANO HAS BAD DREAMS AND CRIES IN HER SLEEP. CUTE, HUH?
ぐぉー
HAHAHA!
RAIN, HUH?
DID YOU BRING AN UMBRELLA?
NOPE.
ME NEITHER
ガロガロガロ...
......
WHAT SHOULD WE DO?
ざあぁ...
I GUESS WE CAN TRY TO WAIT IT OUT.

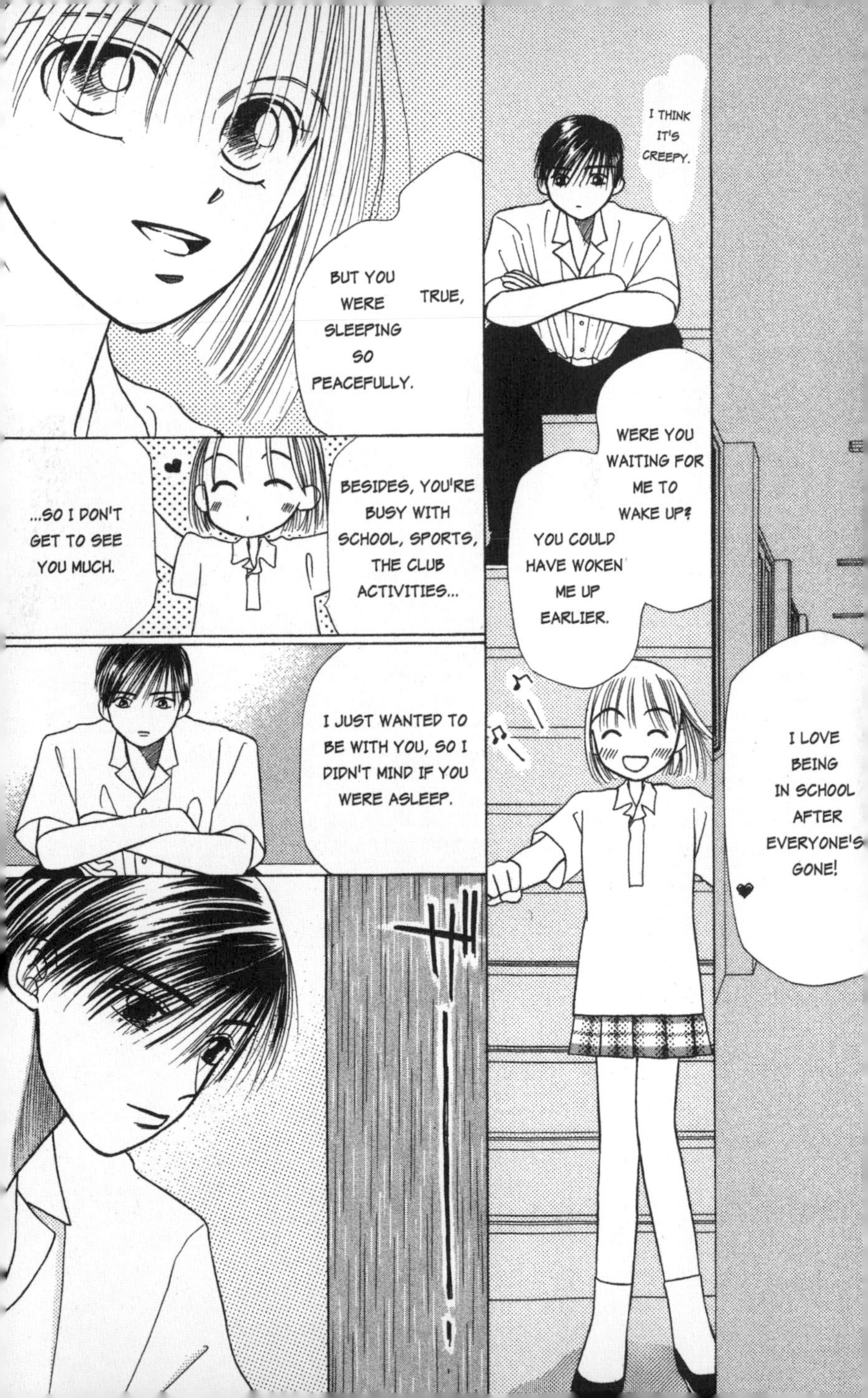
I THINK IT'S CREEPY.
WERE YOU WAITING FOR ME TO WAKE UP?
YOU COULD HAVE WOKEN ME UP EARLIER.
I LOVE BEING IN SCHOOL AFTER EVERYONE'S GONE!
TRUE,
BUT YOU WERE SLEEPING SO PEACEFULLY.
BESIDES, YOU'RE BUSY WITH SCHOOL, SPORTS, THE CLUB ACTIVITIES...
...SO I DON'T GET TO SEE YOU MUCH.
I JUST WANTED TO BE WITH YOU, SO I DIDN'T MIND IF YOU WERE ASLEEP.

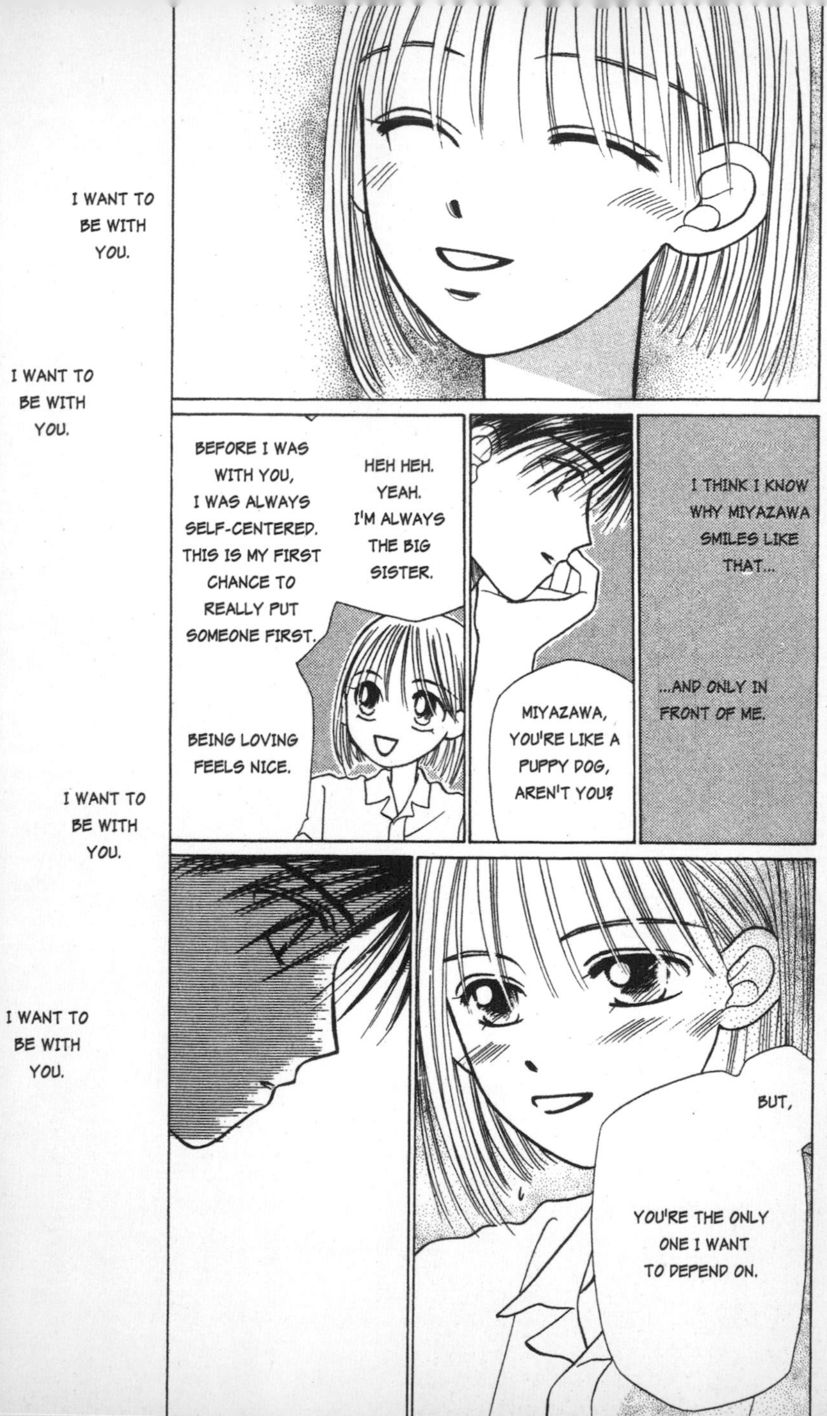
I WANT TO BE WITH YOU.
I WANT TO BE WITH YOU.
I THINK I KNOW WHY MIYAZAWA SMILES LIKE THAT...
...AND ONLY IN FRONT OF ME.
MIYAZAWA, YOU'RE LIKE A PUPPY DOG, AREN'T YOU?
HEH HEH. YEAH. I'M ALWAYS THE BIG SISTER.
BEFORE I WAS WITH YOU, I WAS ALWAYS SELF-CENTERED. THIS IS MY FIRST CHANCE TO REALLY PUT SOMEONE FIRST.
BEING LOVING FEELS NICE.
I WANT TO BE WITH YOU.
I WANT TO BE WITH YOU.
BUT,
YOU'RE THE ONLY ONE I WANT TO DEPEND ON.

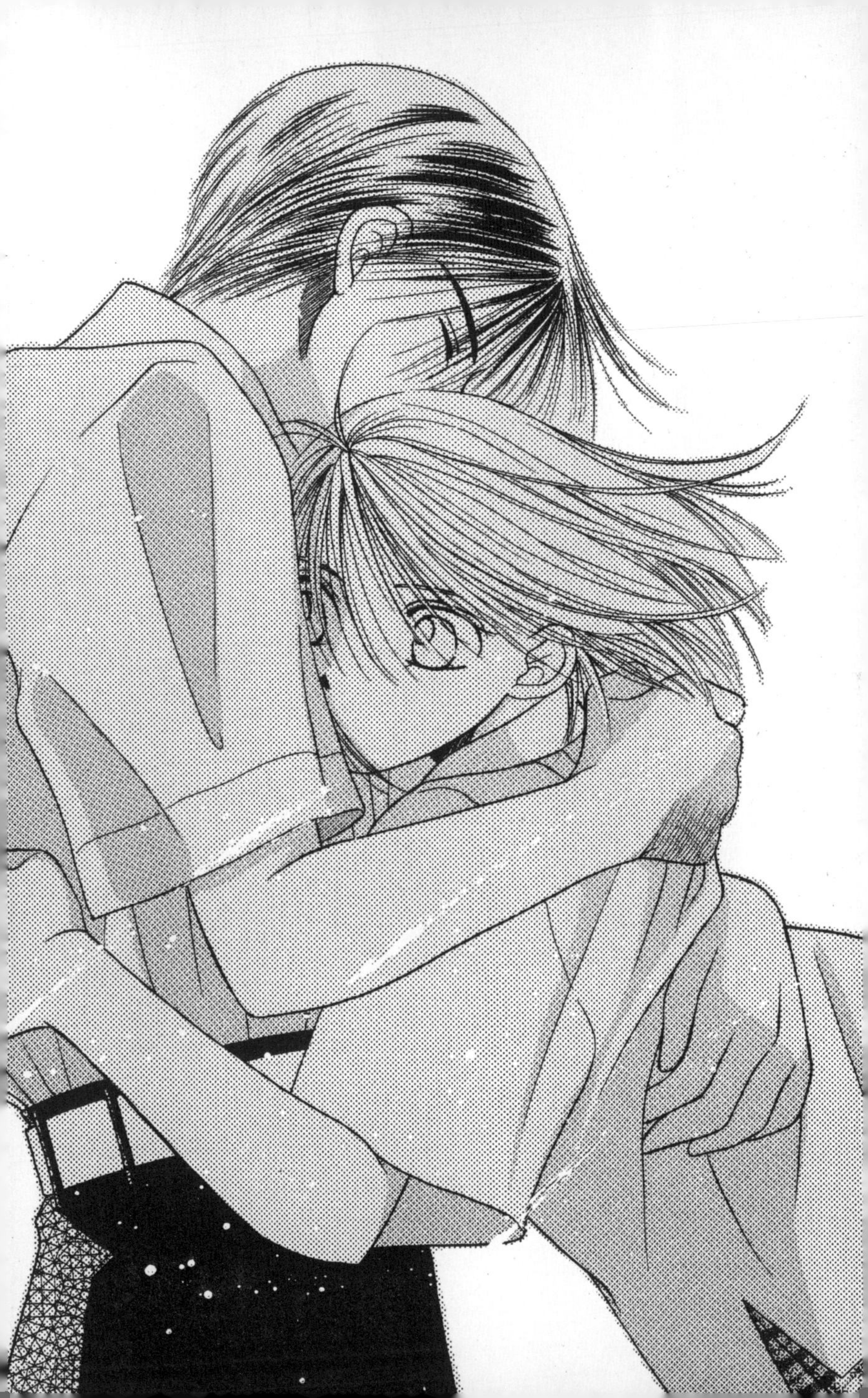

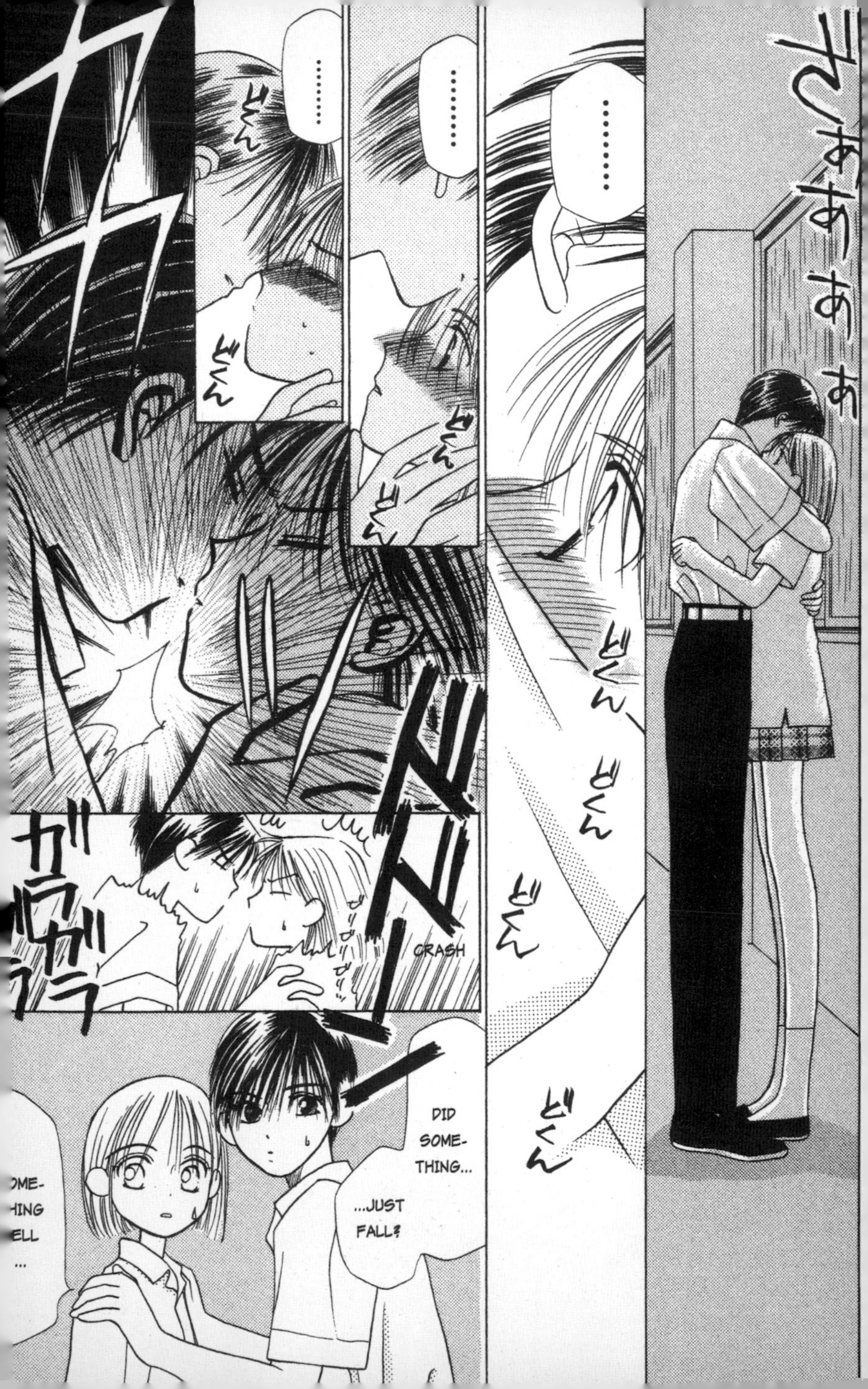
さあああああ
……
どくん
……
どくん
……
どくん
どくん
どくん
どくん
どくん
どくん
どくん
どくん
ガラガラ
CRASH
DID SOME-THING...
...JUST FALL?
OME-HING ELL ...

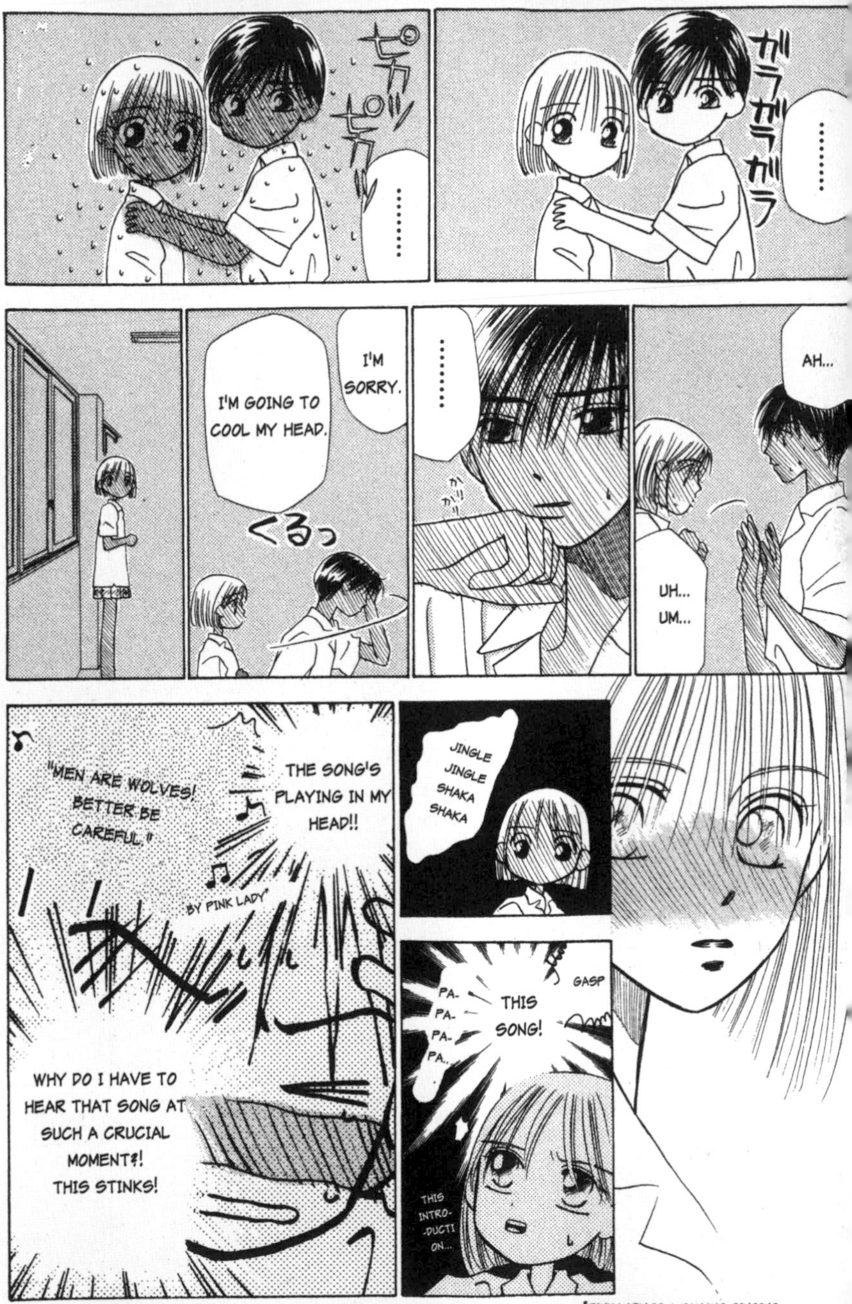
ガラガラガラ
......
ピカッ ピカ
......
AH...
UH... UM...
....
かりかり
I'M SORRY.
I'M GOING TO COOL MY HEAD.
くるっ
JINGLE JINGLE SHAKA SHAKA
GASP
THIS SONG!
PA-PA-PA-PA..
THIS INTRO-DUCTION...
THE SONG'S PLAYING IN MY HEAD!!
"MEN ARE WOLVES! BETTER BE CAREFUL."
BY PINK LADY*
WHY DO I HAVE TO HEAR THAT SONG AT SUCH A CRUCIAL MOMENT?! THIS STINKS!

DO YOU KNOW PINK LADY?

*PINK LADY IS A FAMOUS SINGING DUO IN JAPAN.

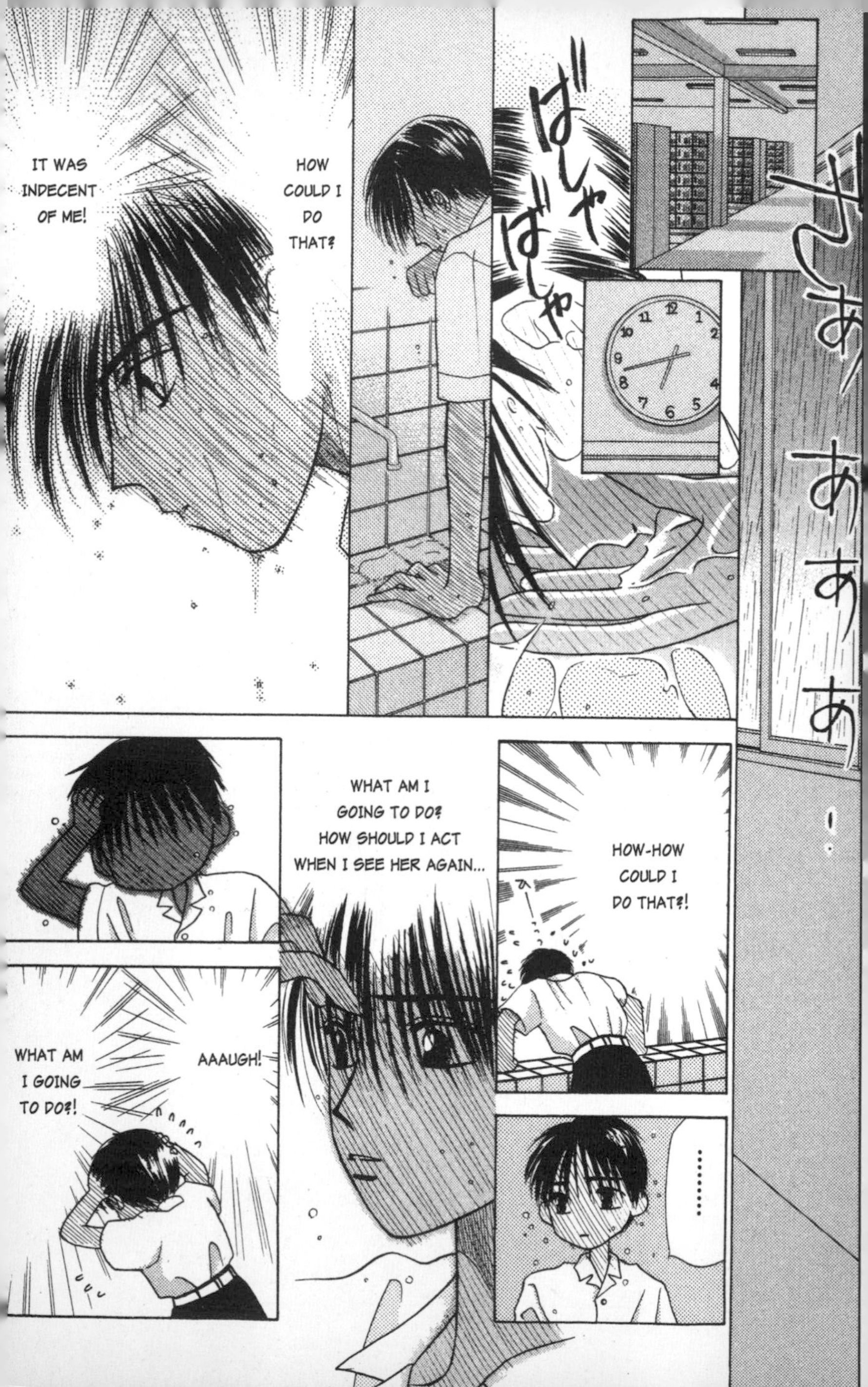
ざあああ
ばしゃばしゃ
HOW COULD I DO THAT?
IT WAS INDECENT OF ME!
HOW-HOW COULD I DO THAT?!
ひー
......
WHAT AM I GOING TO DO? HOW SHOULD I ACT WHEN I SEE HER AGAIN...
AAAUGH!
WHAT AM I GOING TO DO?!

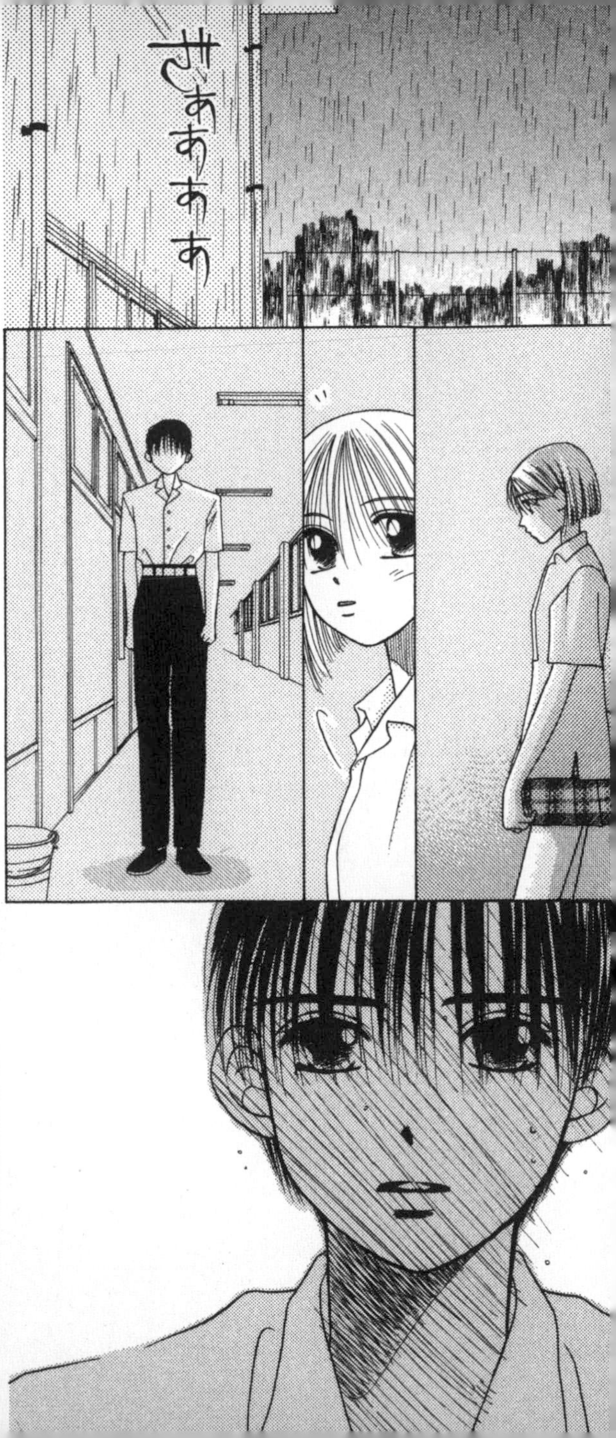
ざああああ

5

As I was writing in Act 7 that Soichiro's height is 5'5", there was a voice in my head that sounded kind of worried.

Ohohohoho!

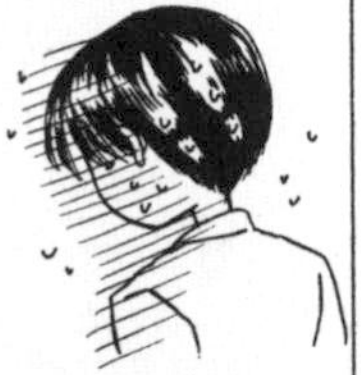

But he's still just in his first semester in high school, isn't he? (Ha!) I wanted Soichiro's body type (although I don't draw it well) to be that of a young boy. I thought he'd look elegant being on the verge of that final boyhood growth spurt. That's why he's that height.

Hideaki is nearing the end of junior high, so from now on he won't grow much.

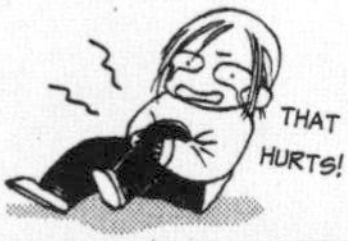
THAT HURTS!

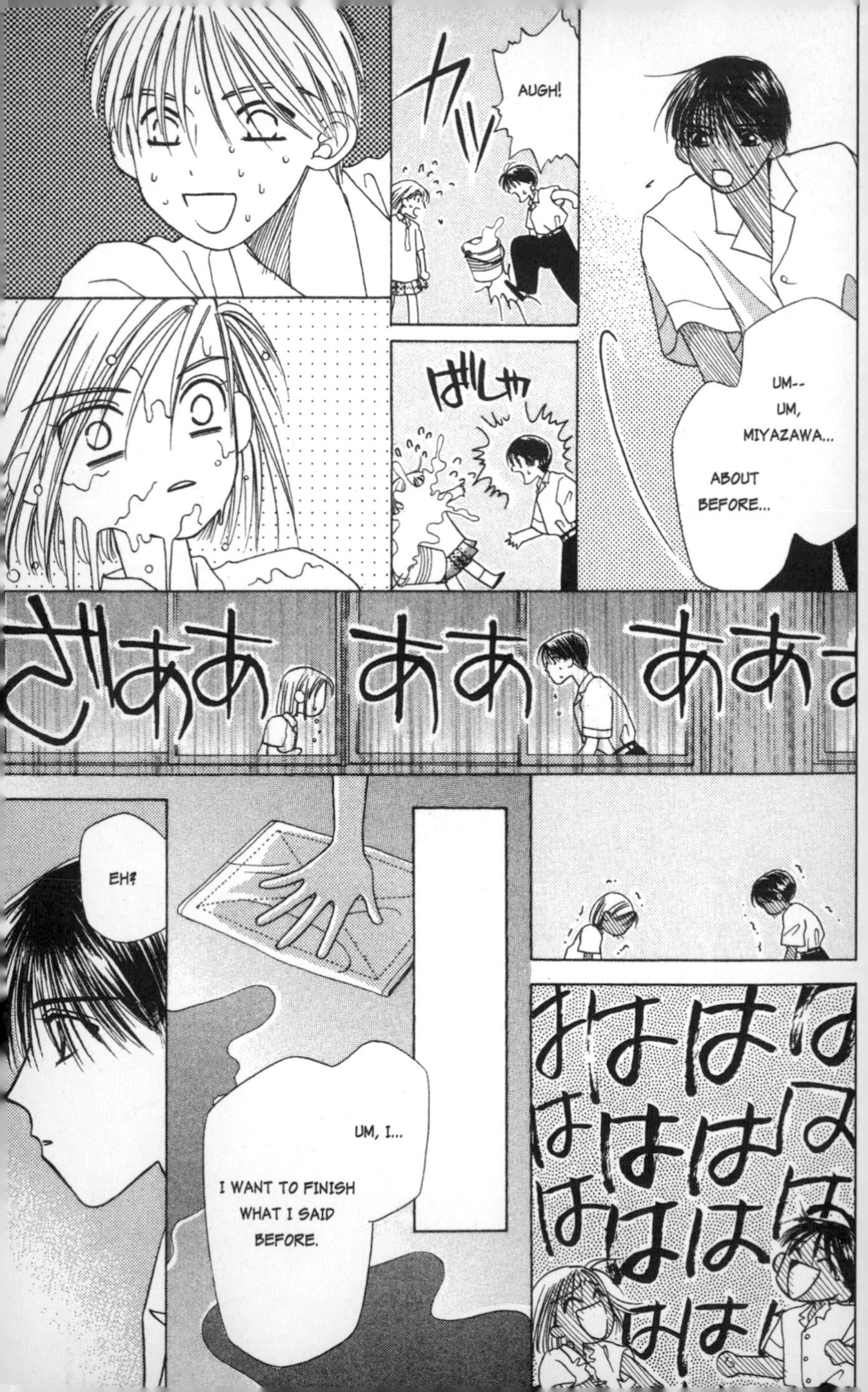
UM-- UM, MIYAZAWA...
ABOUT BEFORE...
カッ
AUGH!
ばしゃ
さあああああああ
おははははははははははは!
UM, I...
I WANT TO FINISH WHAT I SAID BEFORE.
EH?

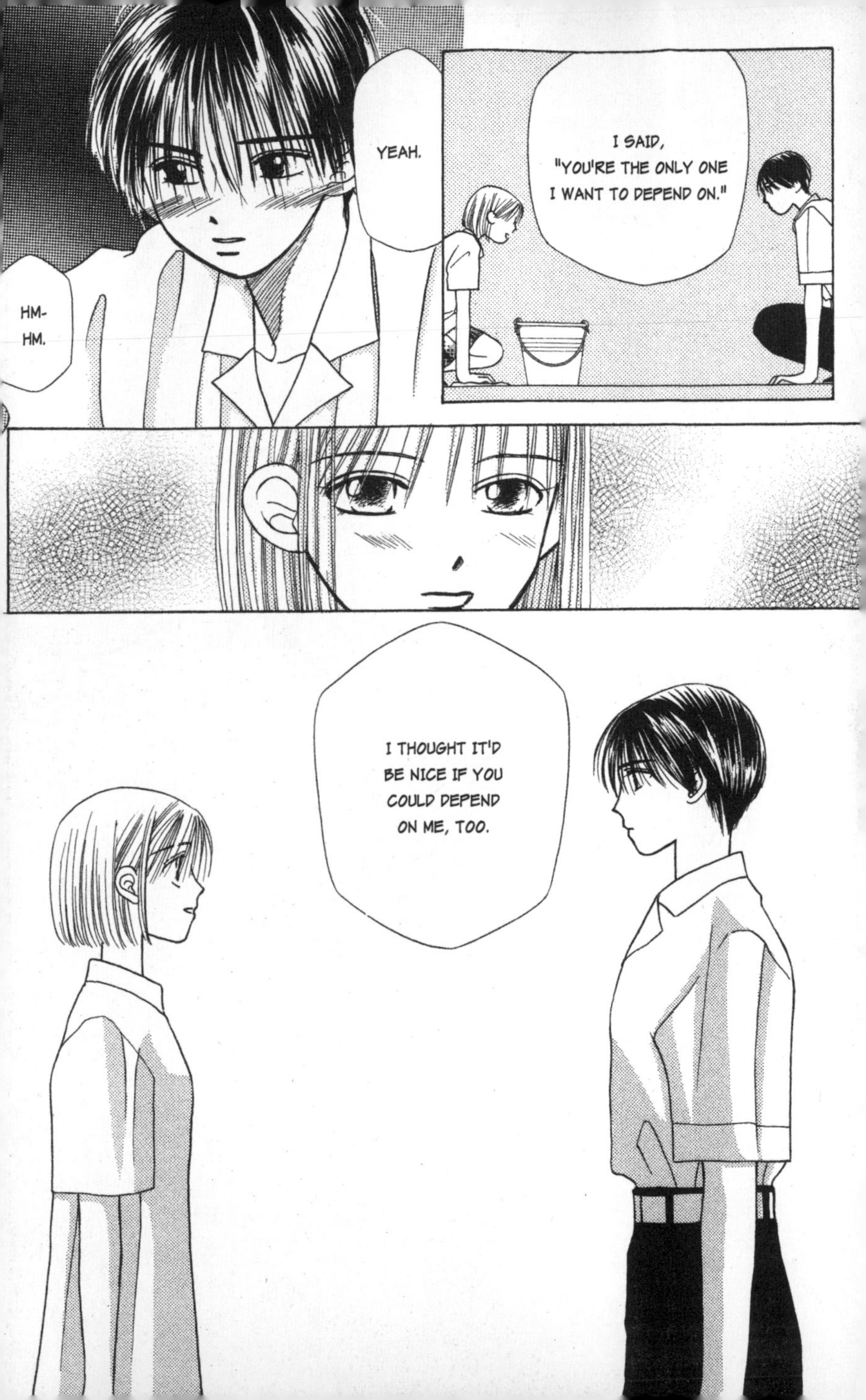
I SAID, "YOU'RE THE ONLY ONE I WANT TO DEPEND ON."
YEAH.
HM-HM.
I THOUGHT IT'D BE NICE IF YOU COULD DEPEND ON ME, TOO.

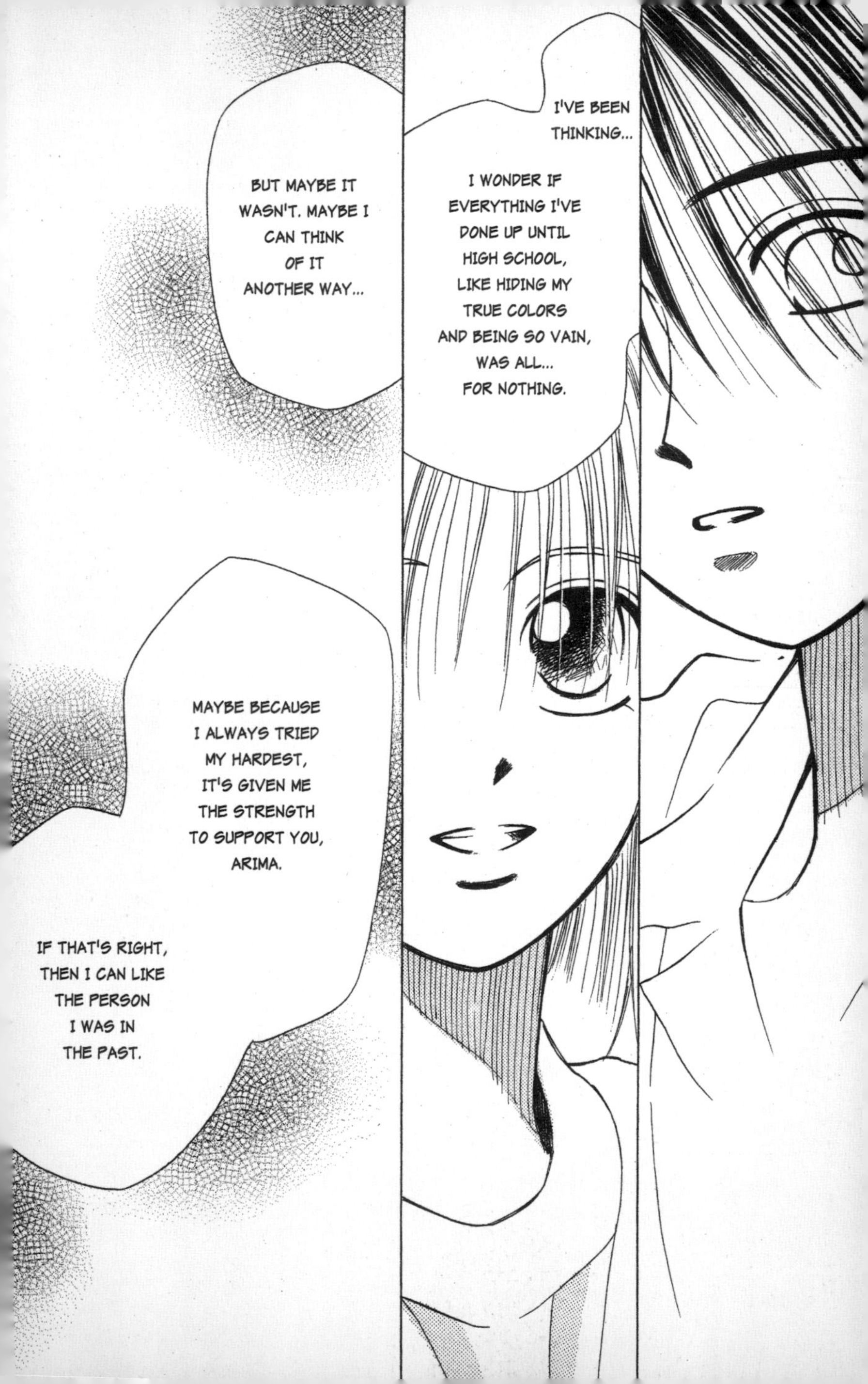
I'VE BEEN THINKING...
I WONDER IF EVERYTHING I'VE DONE UP UNTIL HIGH SCHOOL, LIKE HIDING MY TRUE COLORS AND BEING SO VAIN, WAS ALL... FOR NOTHING.
BUT MAYBE IT WASN'T. MAYBE I CAN THINK OF IT ANOTHER WAY...
MAYBE BECAUSE I ALWAYS TRIED MY HARDEST, IT'S GIVEN ME THE STRENGTH TO SUPPORT YOU, ARIMA.
IF THAT'S RIGHT, THEN I CAN LIKE THE PERSON I WAS IN THE PAST.

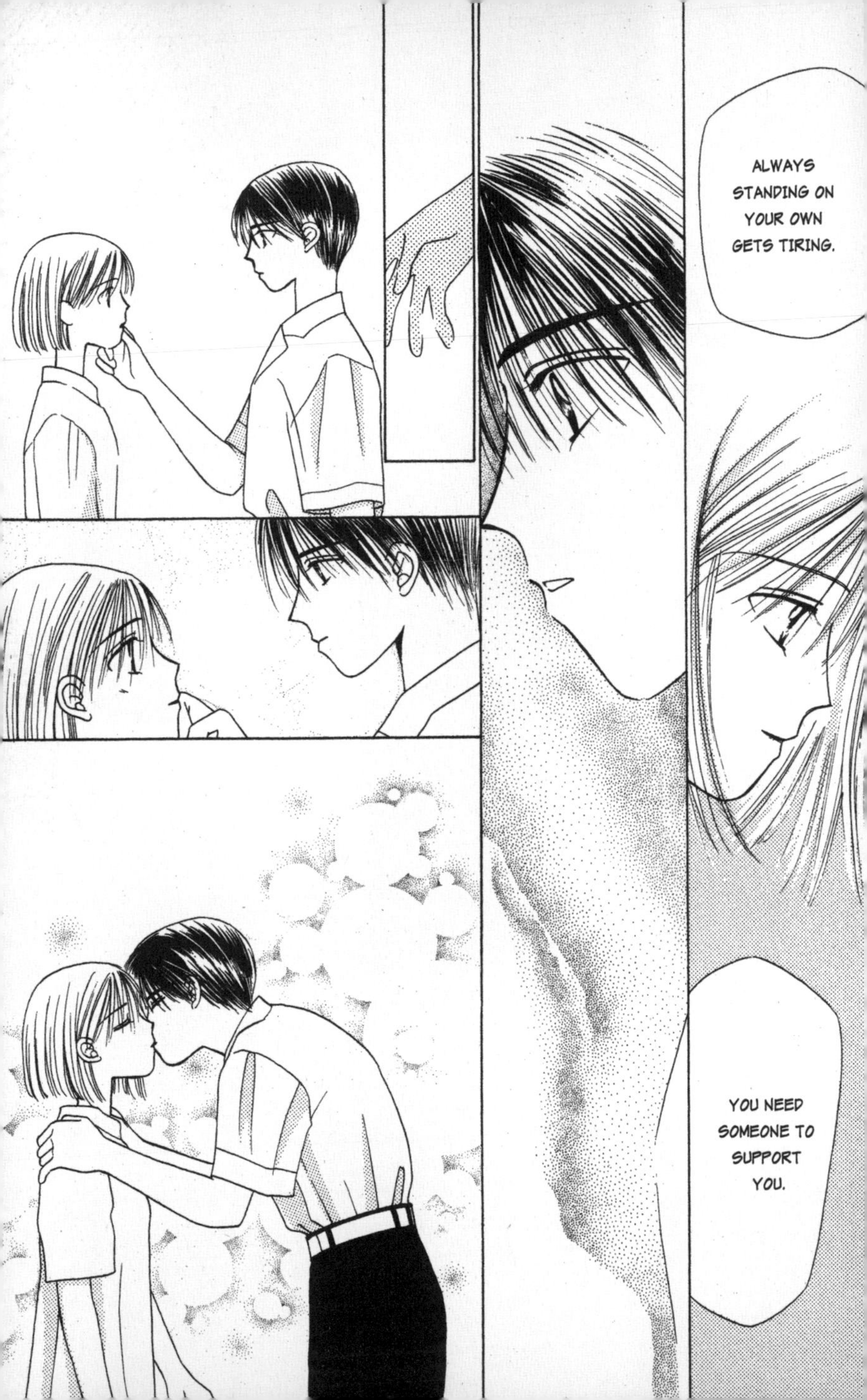
ALWAYS STANDING ON YOUR OWN GETS TIRING.
YOU NEED SOMEONE TO SUPPORT YOU.

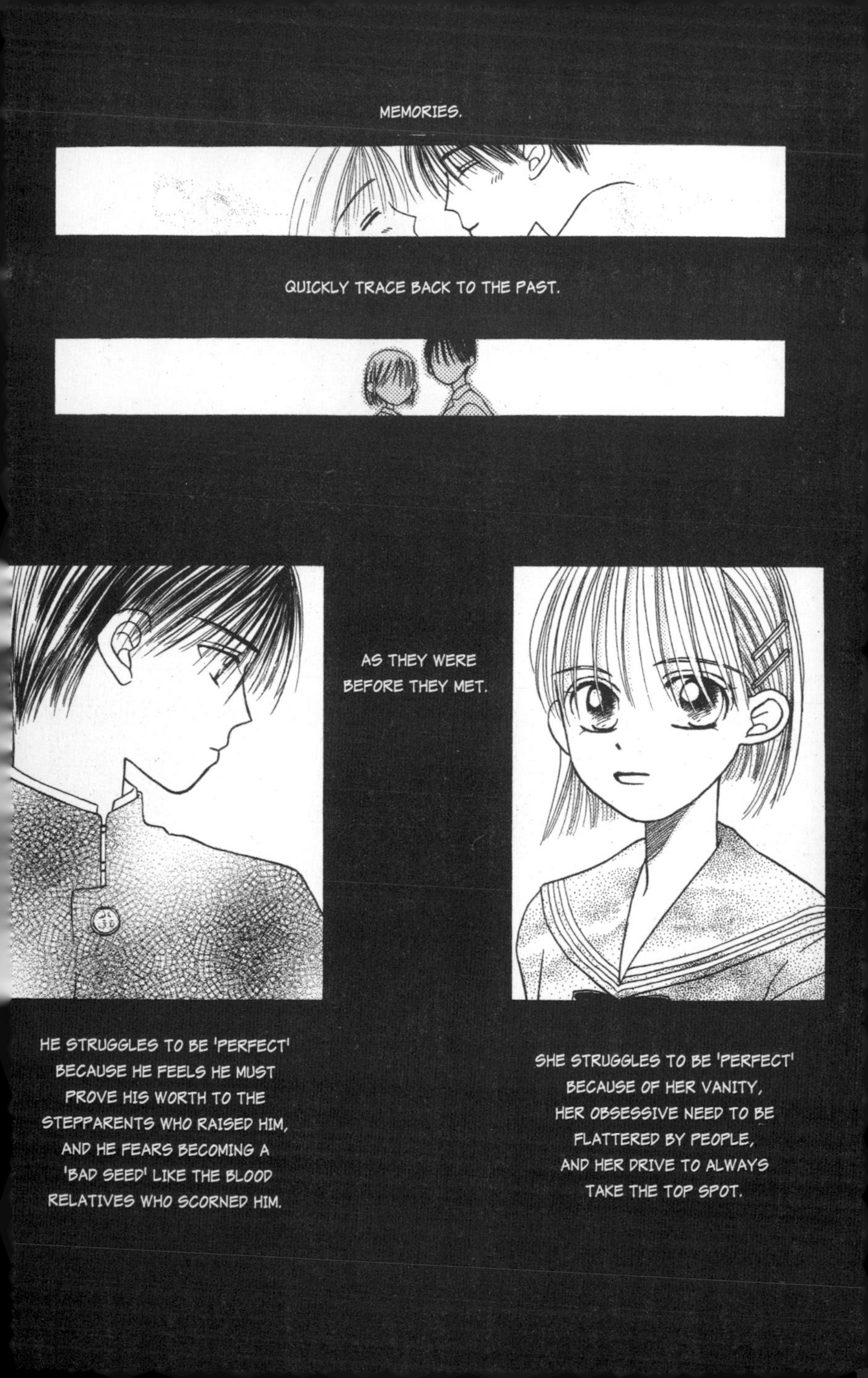
MEMORIES.
QUICKLY TRACE BACK TO THE PAST.
AS THEY WERE BEFORE THEY MET.
SHE STRUGGLES TO BE 'PERFECT' BECAUSE OF HER VANITY, HER OBSESSIVE NEED TO BE FLATTERED BY PEOPLE, AND HER DRIVE TO ALWAYS TAKE THE TOP SPOT.
HE STRUGGLES TO BE 'PERFECT' BECAUSE HE FEELS HE MUST PROVE HIS WORTH TO THE STEPPARENTS WHO RAISED HIM, AND HE FEARS BECOMING A 'BAD SEED' LIKE THE BLOOD RELATIVES WHO SCORNED HIM.

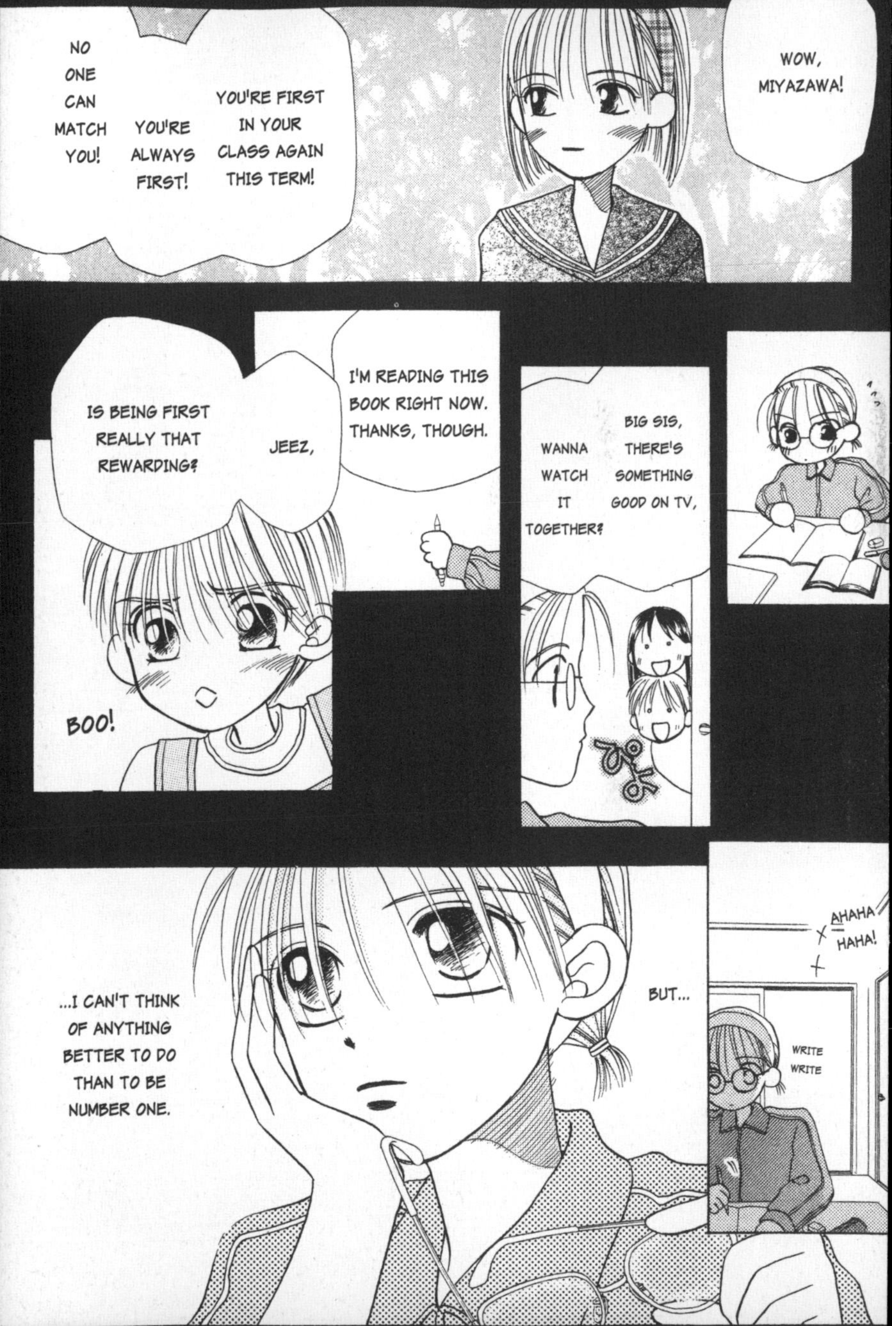
WOW, MIYAZAWA!
YOU'RE FIRST IN YOUR CLASS AGAIN THIS TERM!
YOU'RE ALWAYS FIRST!
NO ONE CAN MATCH YOU!
BIG SIS, THERE'S SOMETHING GOOD ON TV,
WANNA WATCH IT TOGETHER?
ぴょ
I'M READING THIS BOOK RIGHT NOW. THANKS, THOUGH.
JEEZ,
IS BEING FIRST REALLY THAT REWARDING?
BOO!
AHAHA HAHA!
WRITE WRITE
BUT...
...I CAN'T THINK OF ANYTHING BETTER TO DO THAN TO BE NUMBER ONE.

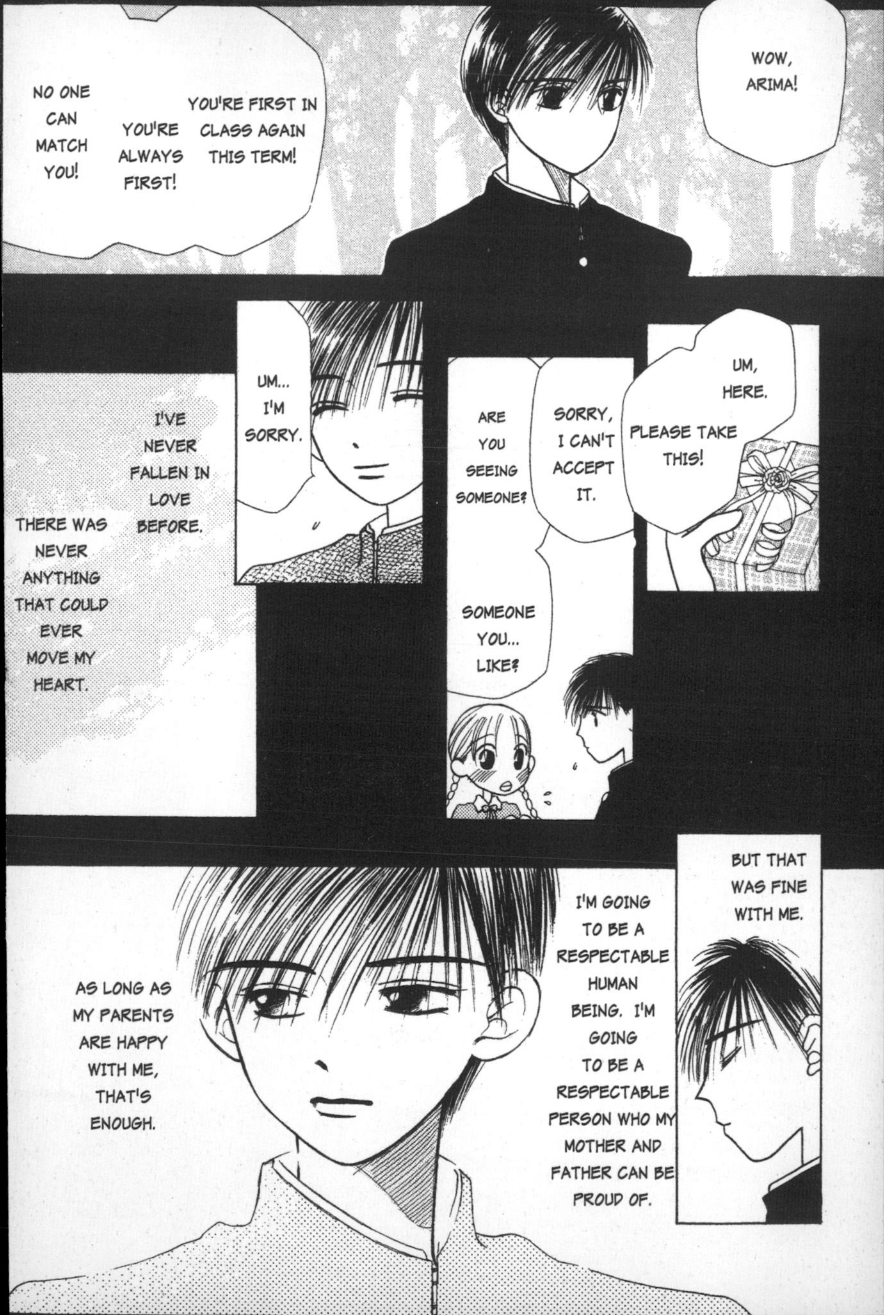
WOW, ARIMA!
YOU'RE FIRST IN CLASS AGAIN THIS TERM!
YOU'RE ALWAYS FIRST!
NO ONE CAN MATCH YOU!
UM, HERE.
PLEASE TAKE THIS!
SORRY, I CAN'T ACCEPT IT.
ARE YOU SEEING SOMEONE?
SOMEONE YOU... LIKE?
UM... I'M SORRY.
I'VE NEVER FALLEN IN LOVE BEFORE.
THERE WAS NEVER ANYTHING THAT COULD EVER MOVE MY HEART.
BUT THAT WAS FINE WITH ME.
I'M GOING TO BE A RESPECTABLE HUMAN BEING. I'M GOING TO BE A RESPECTABLE PERSON WHO MY MOTHER AND FATHER CAN BE PROUD OF.
AS LONG AS MY PARENTS ARE HAPPY WITH ME, THAT'S ENOUGH.

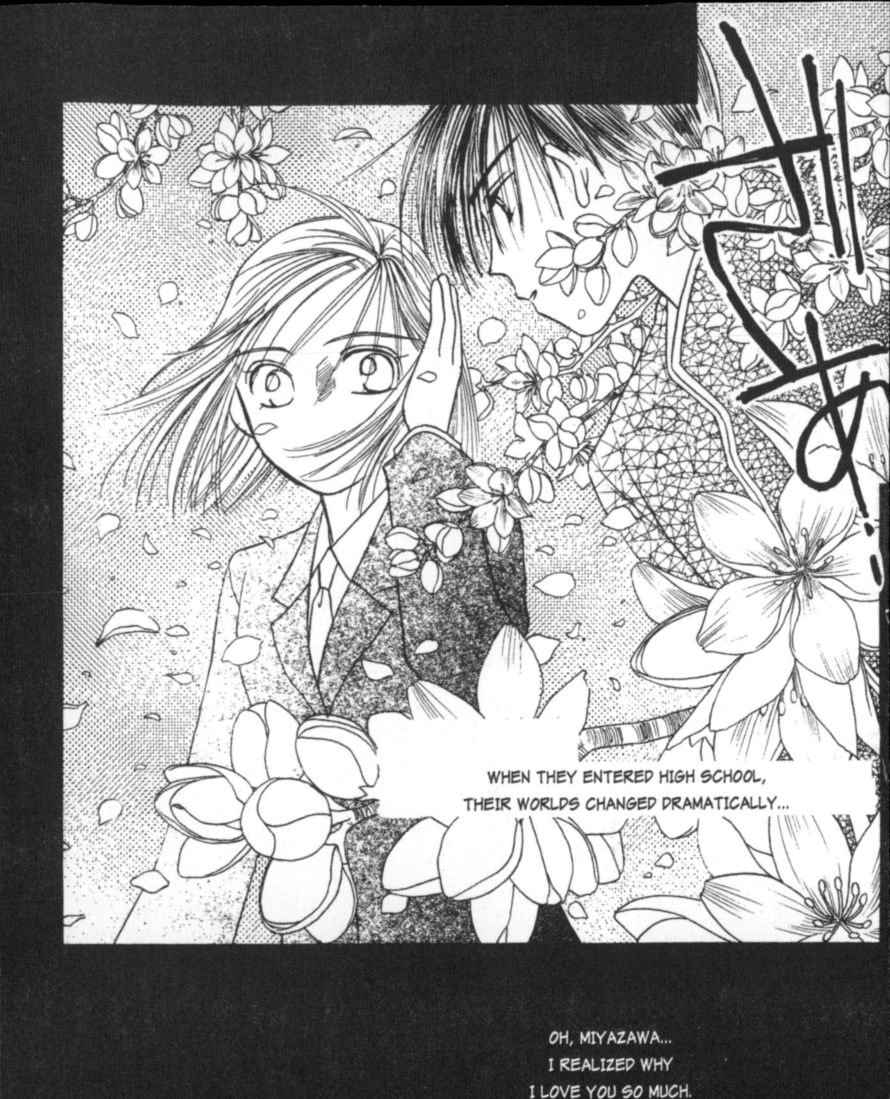
WHEN THEY ENTERED HIGH SCHOOL, THEIR WORLDS CHANGED DRAMATICALLY...
OH, MIYAZAWA... I REALIZED WHY I LOVE YOU SO MUCH.

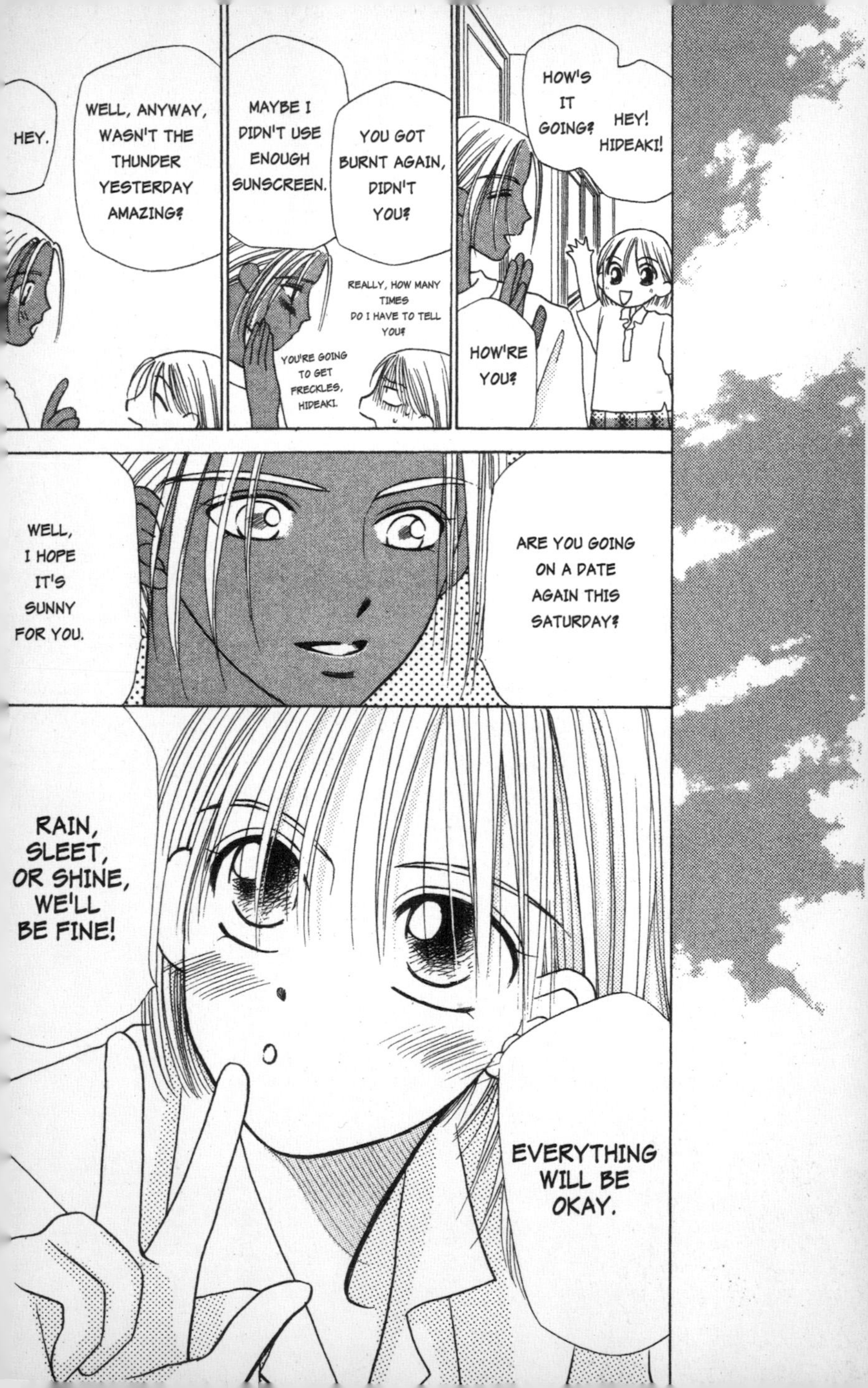
HEY! HIDEAKI!
HOW'S IT GOING?
HOW'RE YOU?
YOU GOT BURNT AGAIN, DIDN'T YOU?
MAYBE I DIDN'T USE ENOUGH SUNSCREEN.
REALLY, HOW MANY TIMES DO I HAVE TO TELL YOU?
YOU'RE GOING TO GET FRECKLES, HIDEAKI.
WELL, ANYWAY, WASN'T THE THUNDER YESTERDAY AMAZING?
HEY.
ARE YOU GOING ON A DATE AGAIN THIS SATURDAY?
WELL, I HOPE IT'S SUNNY FOR YOU.
RAIN, SLEET, OR SHINE, WE'LL BE FINE!
EVERYTHING WILL BE OKAY.

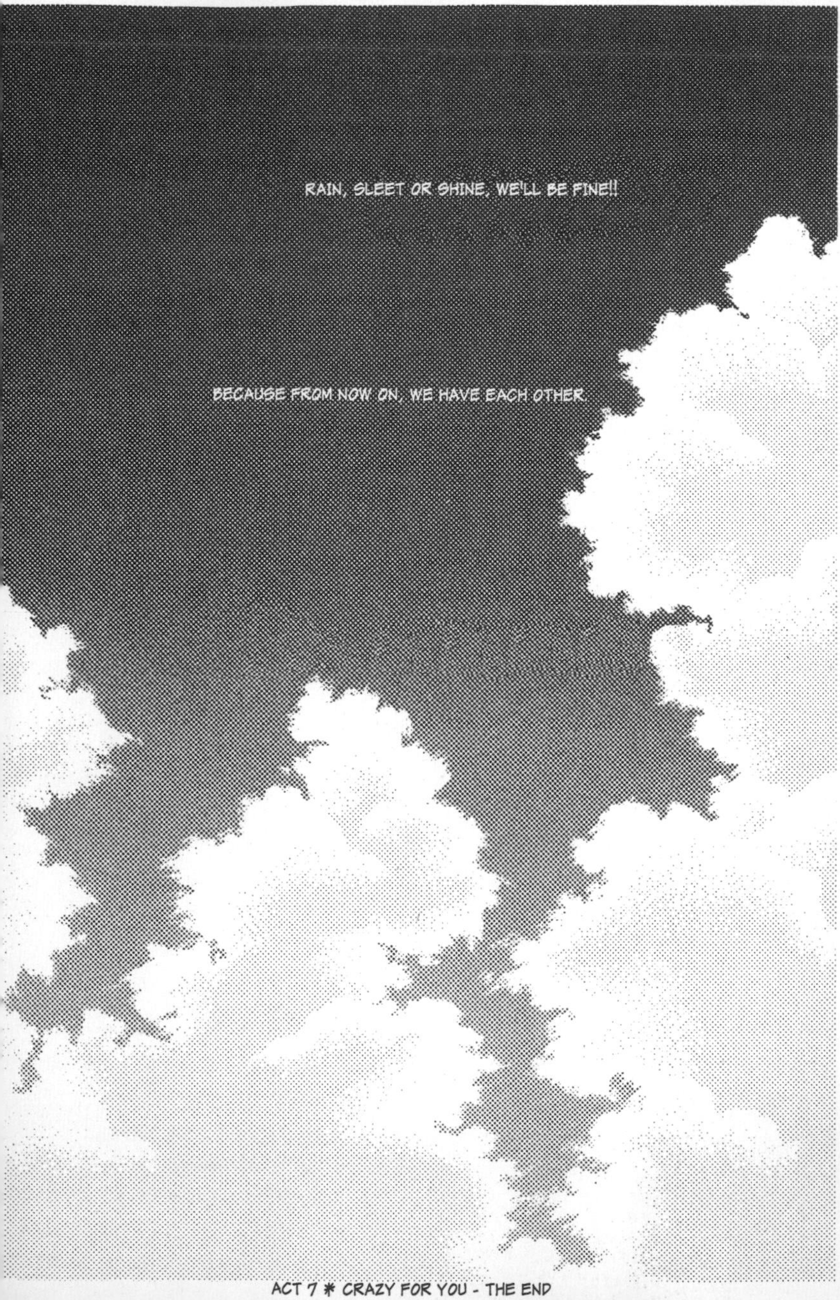
RAIN, SLEET OR SHINE, WE'LL BE FINE!!
BECAUSE FROM NOW ON, WE HAVE EACH OTHER.

ACT 7 * CRAZY FOR YOU - THE END

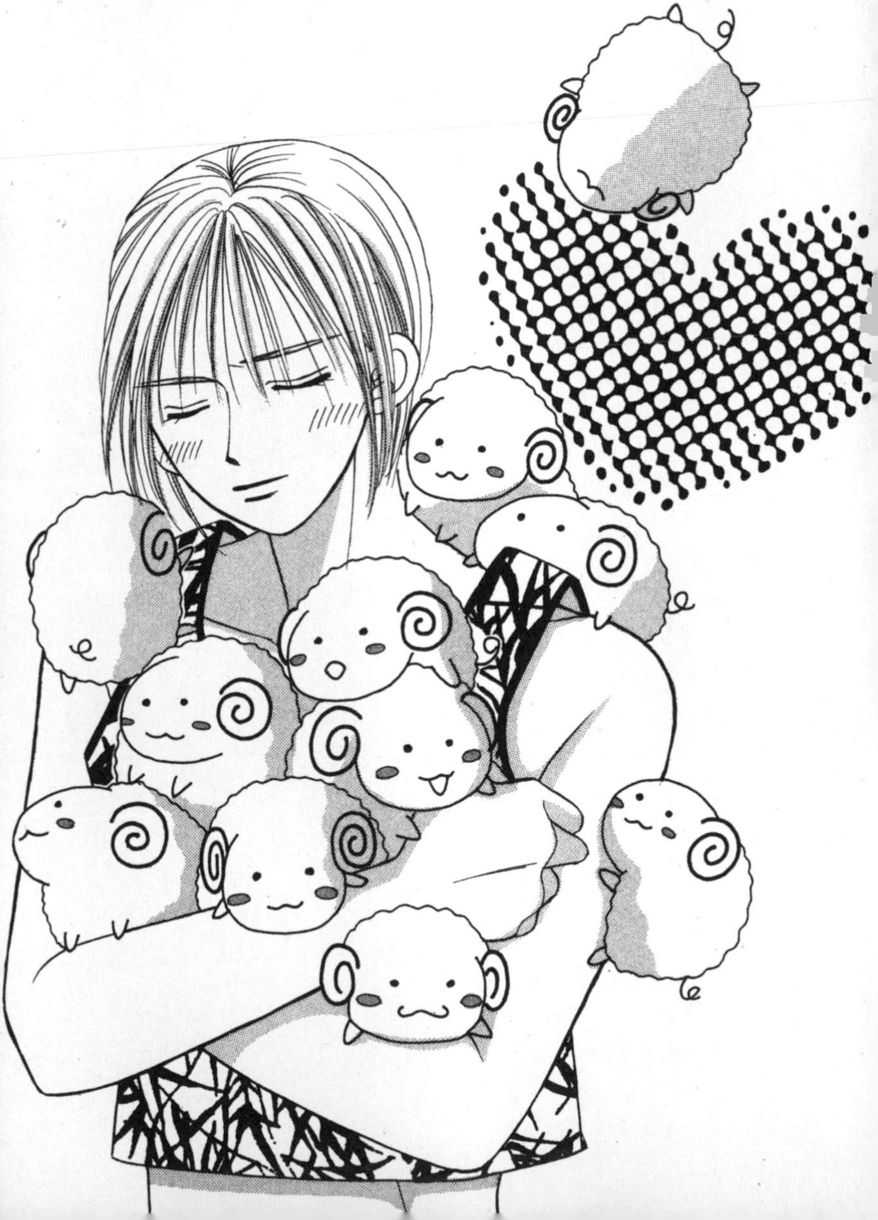

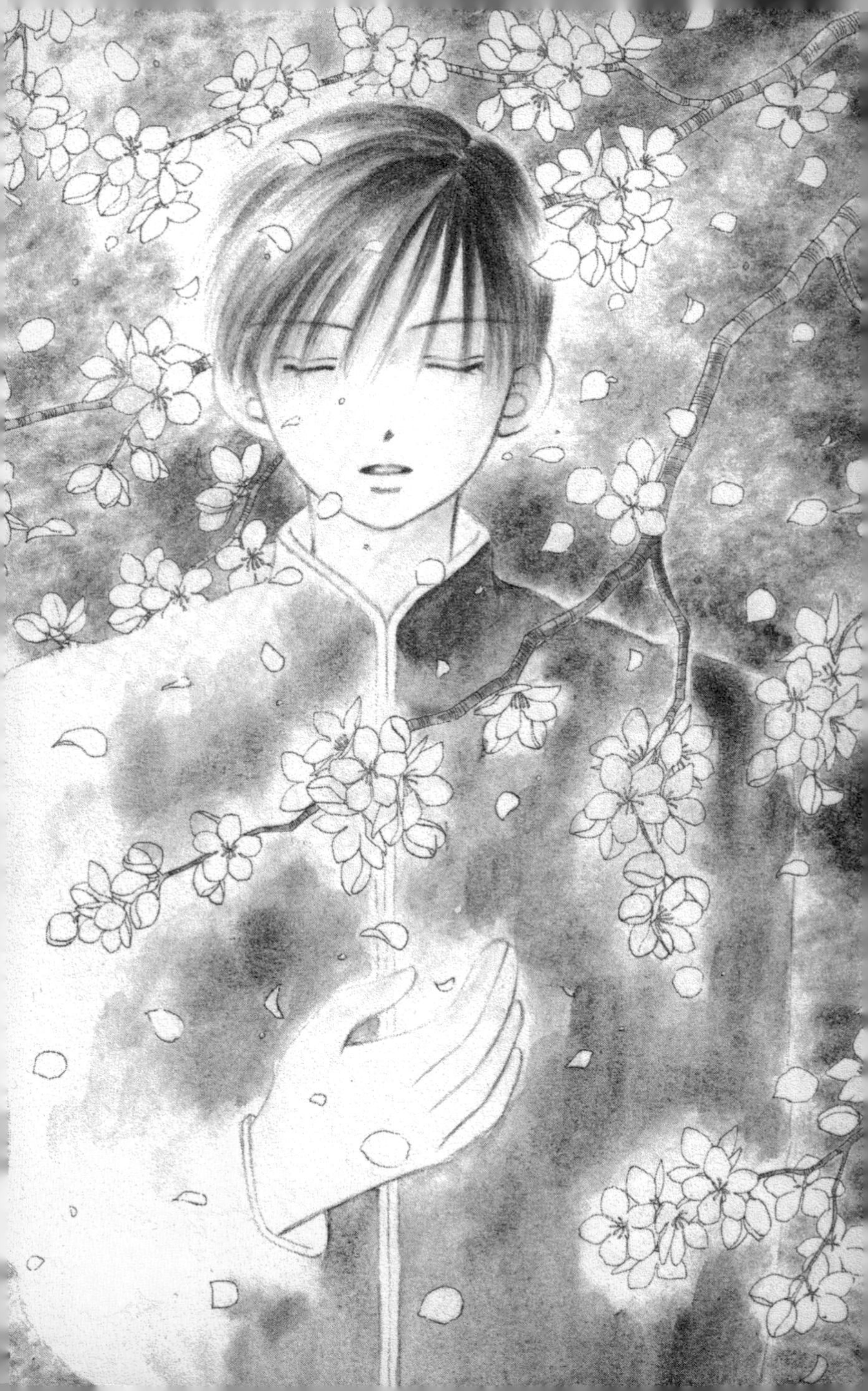

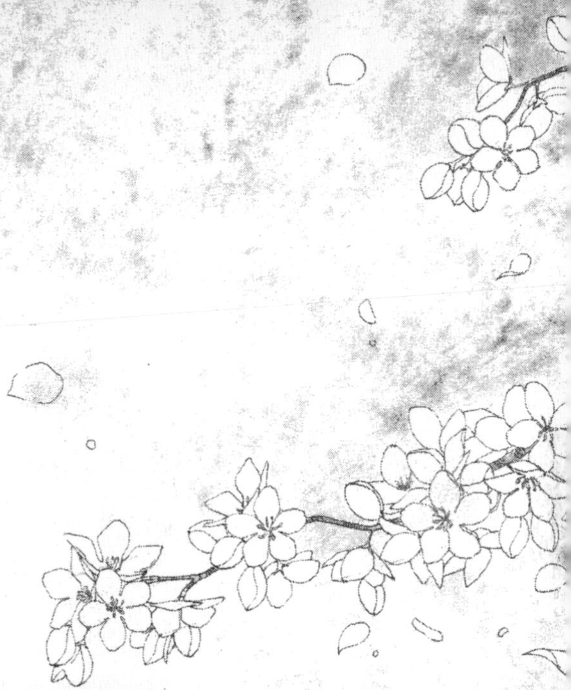

彼氏
かれ　し

彼女の事情
かの　じょ　　　じ　じょう

番外編★桜の林の満開の下
ばん　がい　へん　　さくら　　はやし　　まん　かい　　した

EXTRA * UNDER THE CHERRY TREES

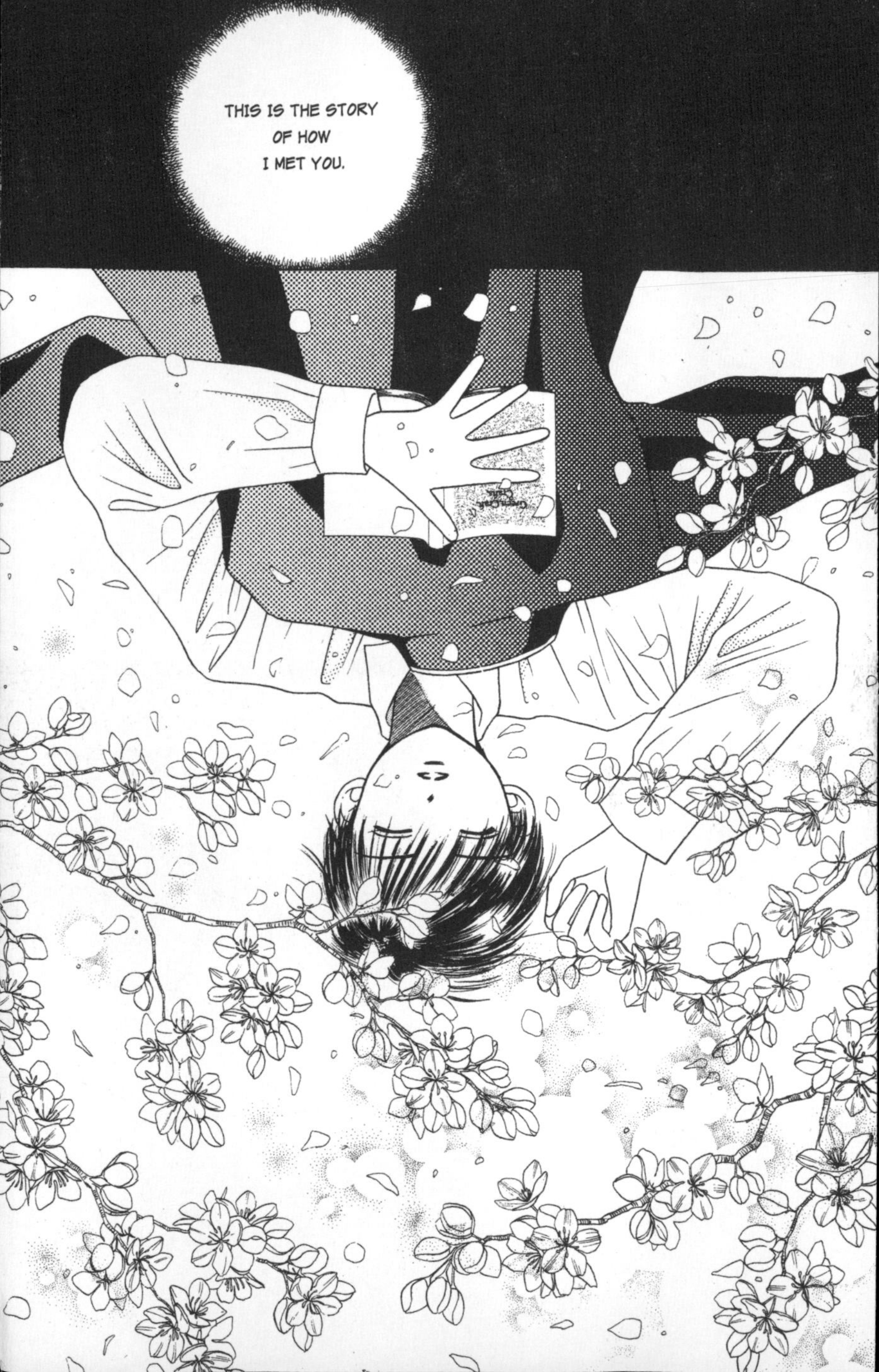
THIS IS THE STORY OF HOW I MET YOU.

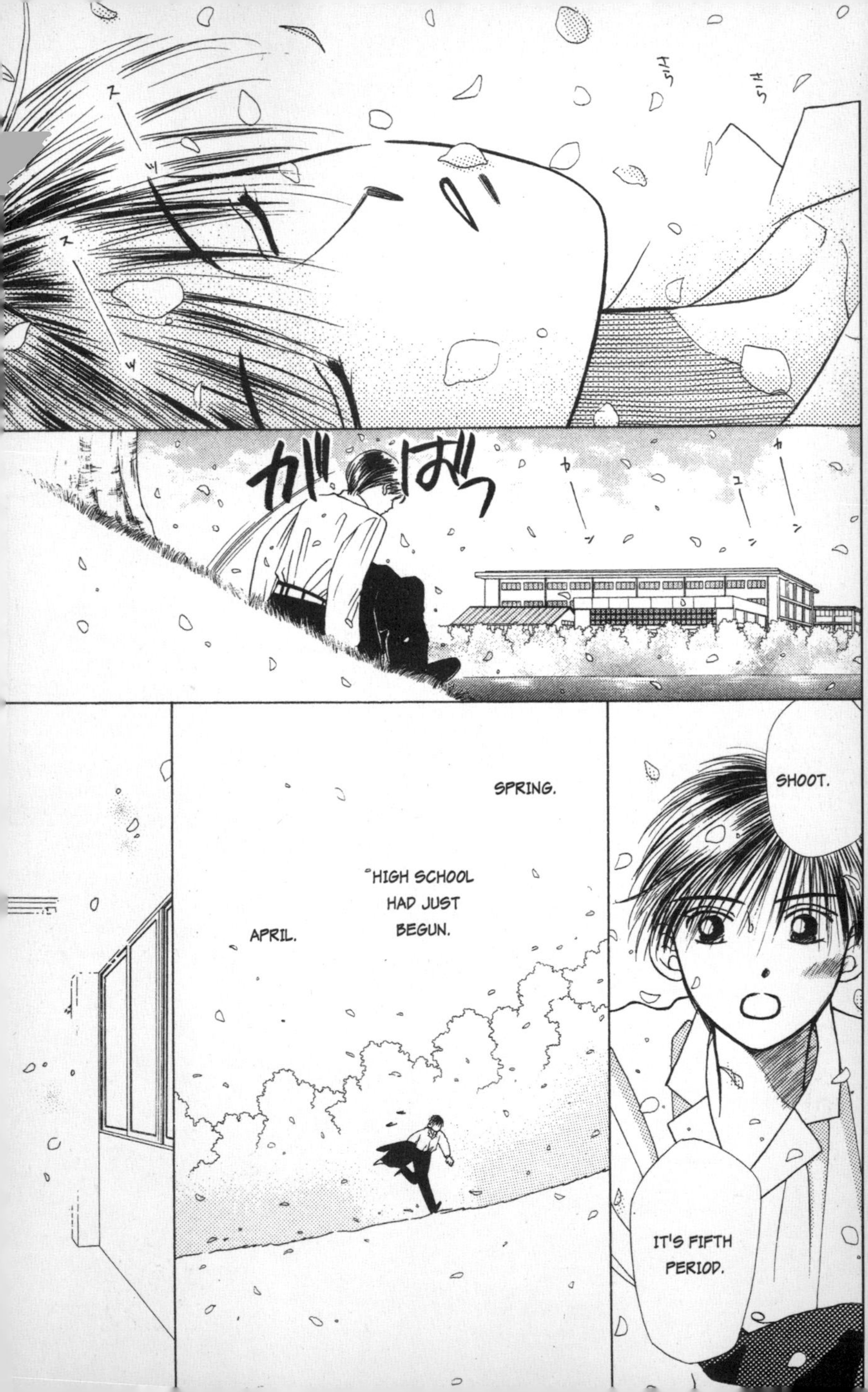
がばっ
SHOOT.
IT'S FIFTH PERIOD.
SPRING.
HIGH SCHOOL HAD JUST BEGUN.
APRIL.

I WAS STILL ALONE.

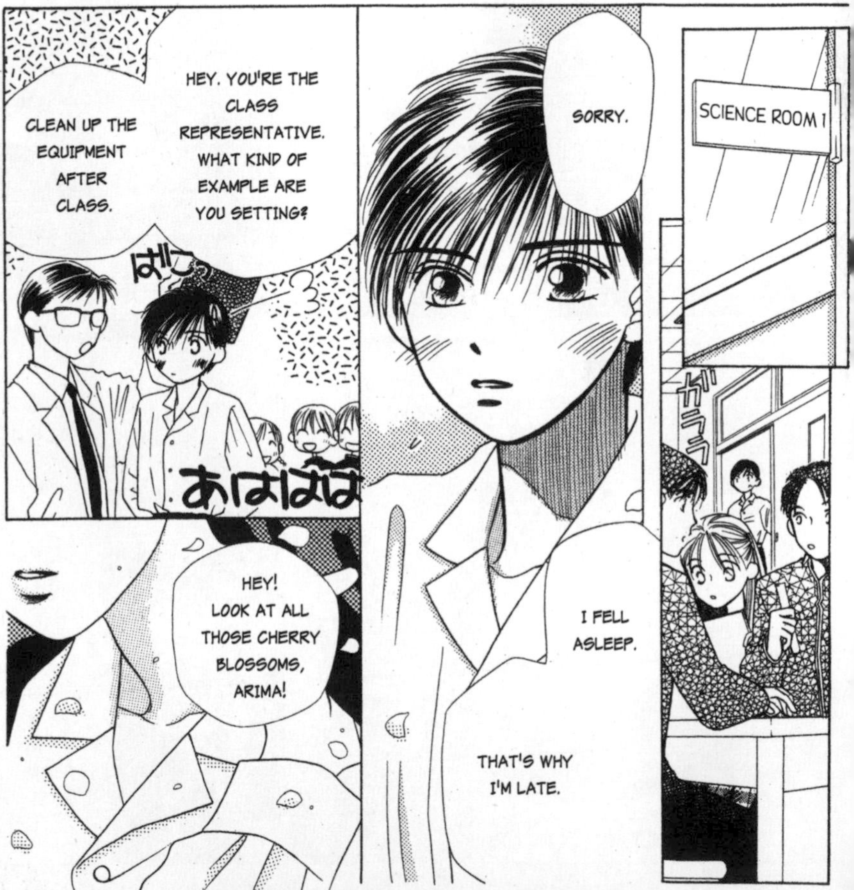
SCIENCE ROOM 1
ガラッ
SORRY.
I FELL ASLEEP.
THAT'S WHY I'M LATE.
HEY. YOU'RE THE CLASS REPRESENTATIVE. WHAT KIND OF EXAMPLE ARE YOU SETTING?
CLEAN UP THE EQUIPMENT AFTER CLASS.
ぱこっ
あははは
HEY! LOOK AT ALL THOSE CHERRY BLOSSOMS, ARIMA!

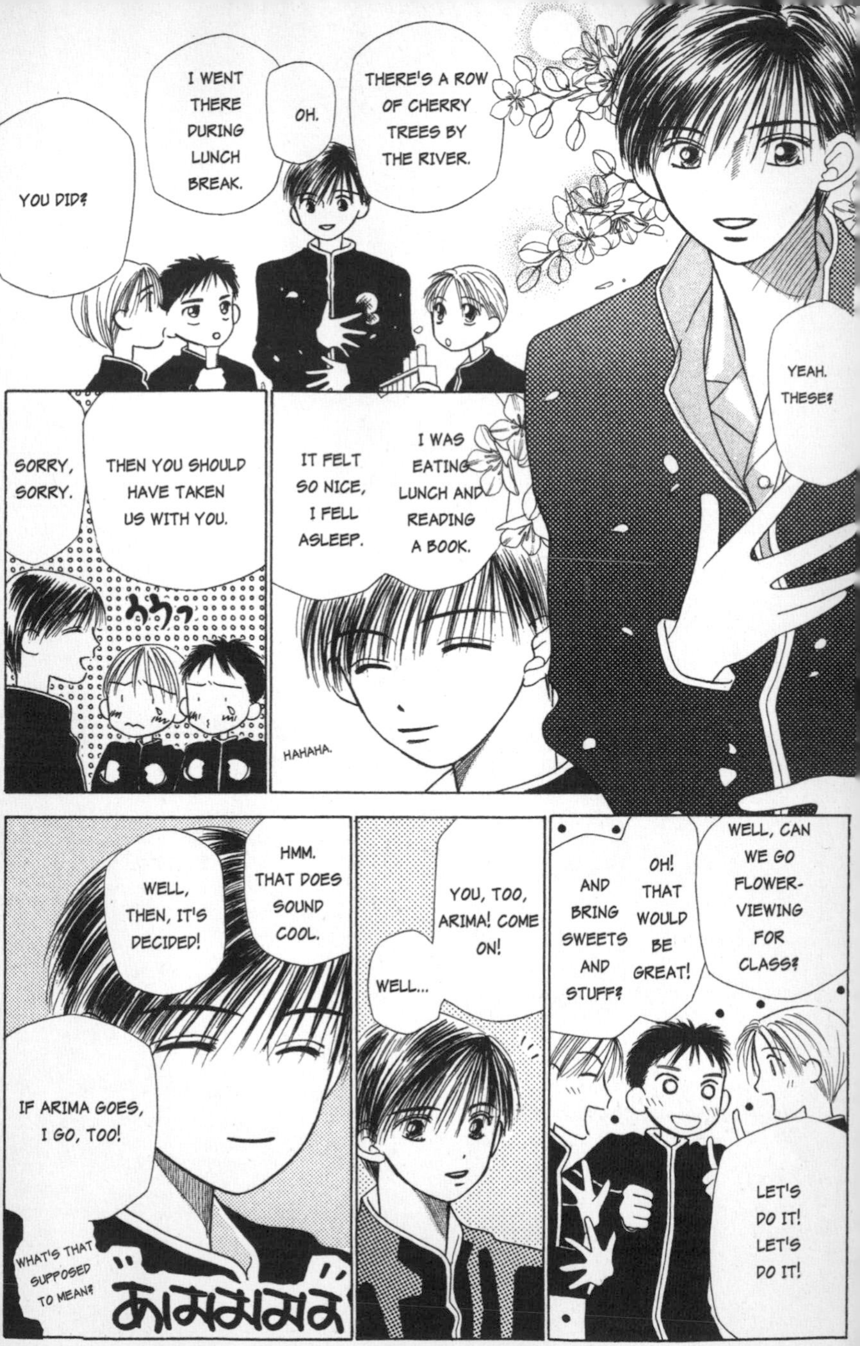
YEAH. THESE?
THERE'S A ROW OF CHERRY TREES BY THE RIVER.
OH.
I WENT THERE DURING LUNCH BREAK.
YOU DID?
I WAS EATING LUNCH AND READING A BOOK.
IT FELT SO NICE, I FELL ASLEEP.
HAHAHA.
THEN YOU SHOULD HAVE TAKEN US WITH YOU.
SORRY, SORRY.
ううっ
WELL, CAN WE GO FLOWER-VIEWING FOR CLASS?
OH! THAT WOULD BE GREAT!
AND BRING SWEETS AND STUFF?
LET'S DO IT! LET'S DO IT!
YOU, TOO, ARIMA! COME ON!
WELL...
HMM. THAT DOES SOUND COOL.
WELL, THEN, IT'S DECIDED!
IF ARIMA GOES, I GO, TOO!
WHAT'S THAT SUPPOSED TO MEAN?
あははははは

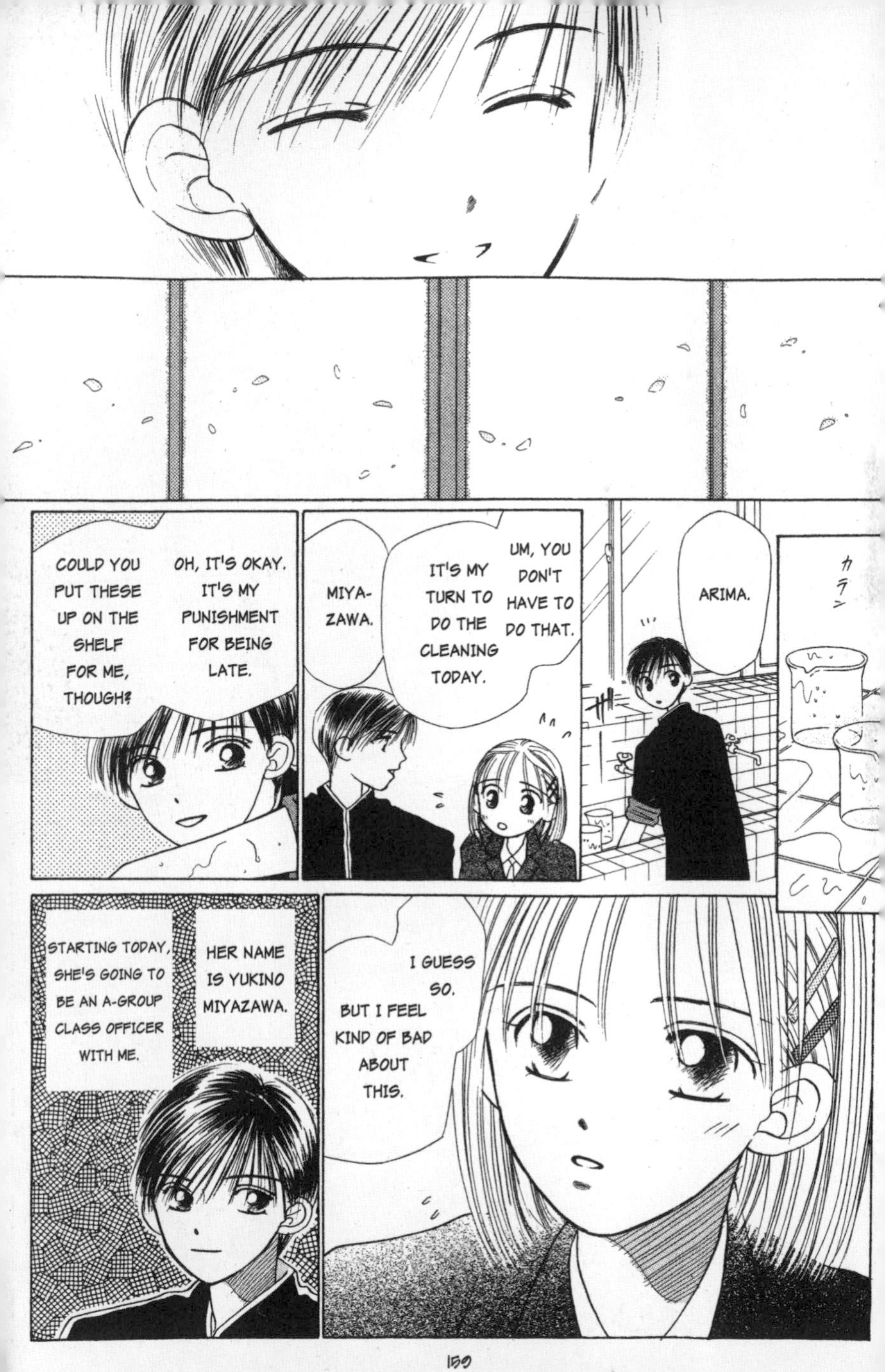
カラン
ARIMA.
UM, YOU DON'T HAVE TO DO THAT.
IT'S MY TURN TO DO THE CLEANING TODAY.
MIYA-ZAWA.
OH, IT'S OKAY. IT'S MY PUNISHMENT FOR BEING LATE.
COULD YOU PUT THESE UP ON THE SHELF FOR ME, THOUGH?
I GUESS SO.
BUT I FEEL KIND OF BAD ABOUT THIS.
HER NAME IS YUKINO MIYAZAWA.
STARTING TODAY, SHE'S GOING TO BE AN A-GROUP CLASS OFFICER WITH ME.

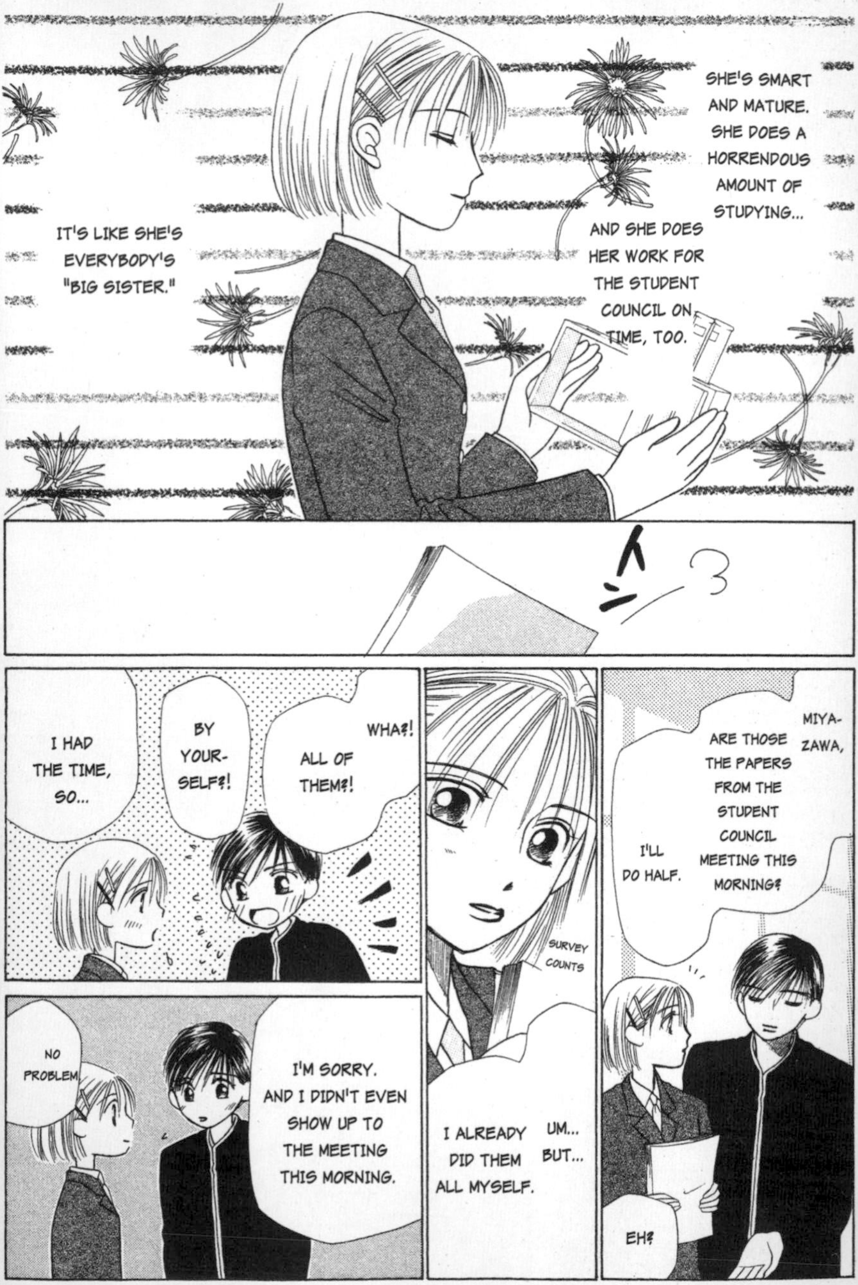
SHE'S SMART AND MATURE. SHE DOES A HORRENDOUS AMOUNT OF STUDYING...
AND SHE DOES HER WORK FOR THE STUDENT COUNCIL ON TIME, TOO.
IT'S LIKE SHE'S EVERYBODY'S "BIG SISTER."
MIYA-ZAWA,
ARE THOSE THE PAPERS FROM THE STUDENT COUNCIL MEETING THIS MORNING?
I'LL DO HALF.
EH?
SURVEY COUNTS
UM... BUT...
I ALREADY DID THEM ALL MYSELF.
WHA?!
ALL OF THEM?!
BY YOURSELF?!
I HAD THE TIME, SO...
I'M SORRY. AND I DIDN'T EVEN SHOW UP TO THE MEETING THIS MORNING.
NO PROBLEM.

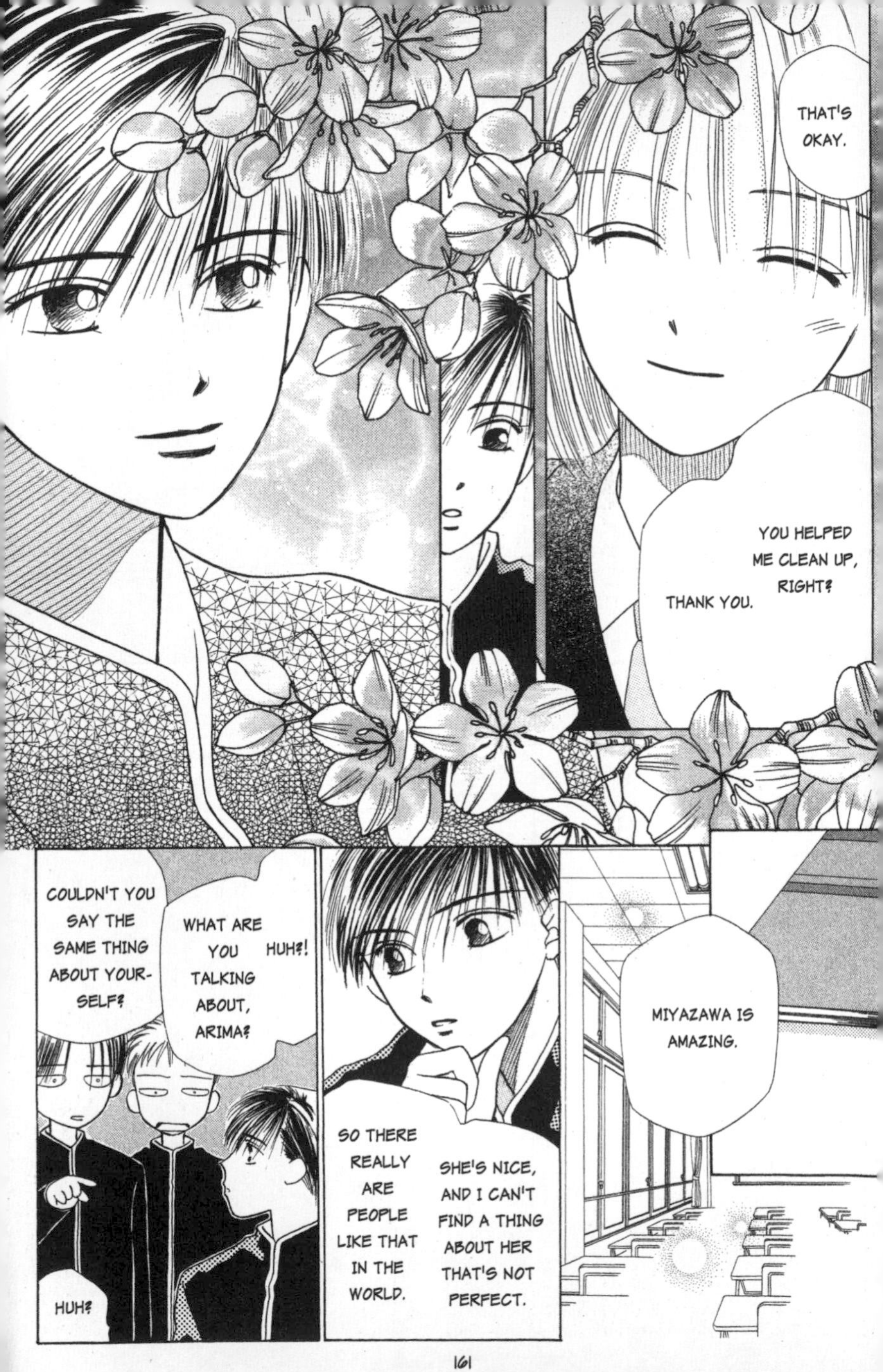
THAT'S OKAY.
YOU HELPED ME CLEAN UP, RIGHT?
THANK YOU.
MIYAZAWA IS AMAZING.
SHE'S NICE, AND I CAN'T FIND A THING ABOUT HER THAT'S NOT PERFECT.
SO THERE REALLY ARE PEOPLE LIKE THAT IN THE WORLD.
HUH?!
WHAT ARE YOU TALKING ABOUT, ARIMA?
COULDN'T YOU SAY THE SAME THING ABOUT YOUR-SELF?
HUH?

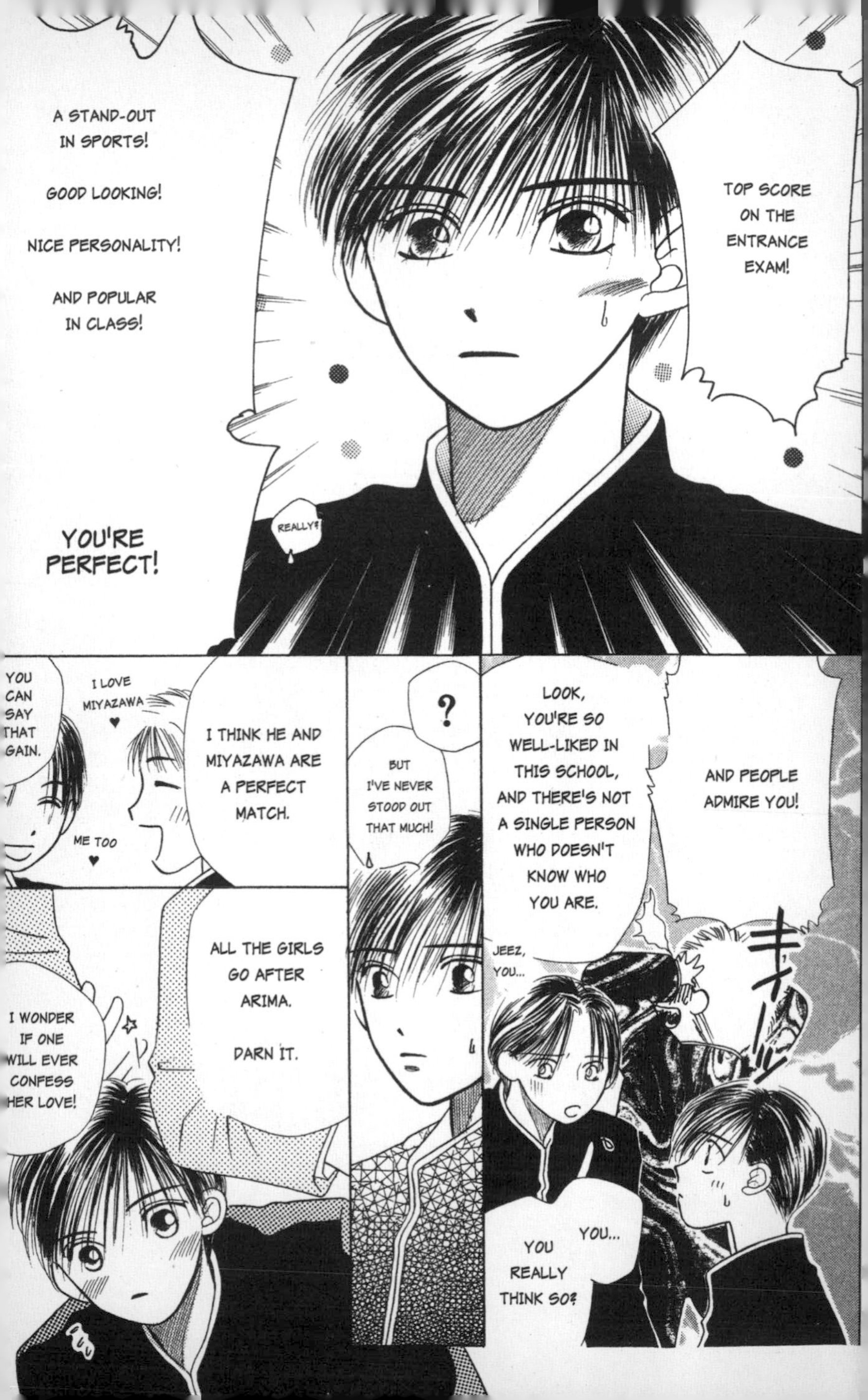
TOP SCORE ON THE ENTRANCE EXAM!
A STAND-OUT IN SPORTS!
GOOD LOOKING!
NICE PERSONALITY!
AND POPULAR IN CLASS!
REALLY?
YOU'RE PERFECT!
AND PEOPLE ADMIRE YOU!
LOOK, YOU'RE SO WELL-LIKED IN THIS SCHOOL, AND THERE'S NOT A SINGLE PERSON WHO DOESN'T KNOW WHO YOU ARE.
JEEZ, YOU...
YOU...
YOU REALLY THINK SO?
?
BUT I'VE NEVER STOOD OUT THAT MUCH!
I THINK HE AND MIYAZAWA ARE A PERFECT MATCH.
I LOVE MIYAZAWA ♥
ME TOO ♥
YOU CAN SAY THAT GAIN.
ALL THE GIRLS GO AFTER ARIMA.
DARN IT.
I WONDER IF ONE WILL EVER CONFESS HER LOVE!

DON'T GET THE WRONG IDEA, BUT FROM ONE GUY TO ANOTHER, I CAN'T SEE ANYTHING BAD ABOUT YOU. I THINK YOU'RE AMAZING.

AARGH DAMNIT!

YOU'RE SO PERFECT, IT ALMOST MAKES ME SICK!

YET IT'S IMPOSSIBLE FOR PEOPLE NOT TO LIKE YOU!

AH,

IT'S A BEAUTIFUL WORLD.

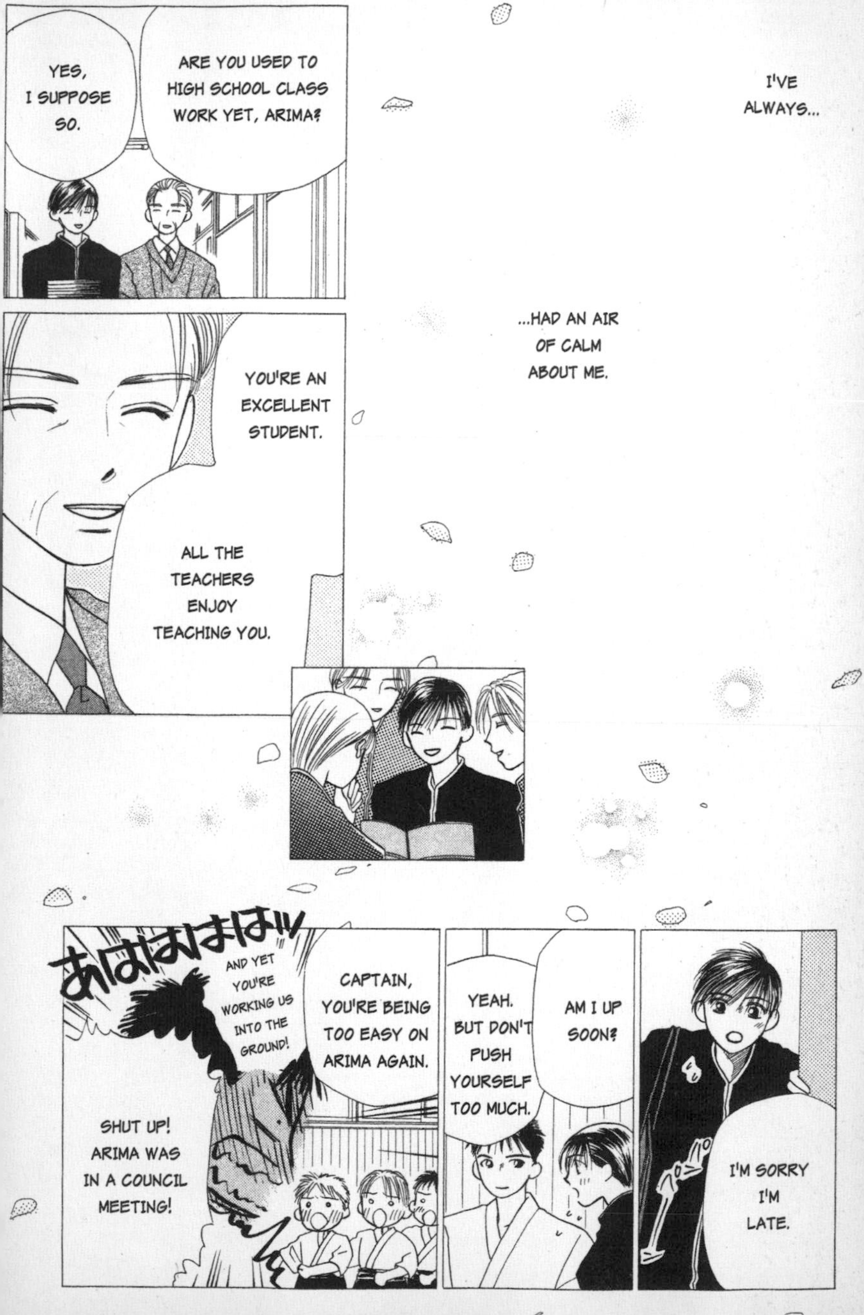
I'VE ALWAYS...
ARE YOU USED TO HIGH SCHOOL CLASS WORK YET, ARIMA?
YES, I SUPPOSE SO.
...HAD AN AIR OF CALM ABOUT ME.
YOU'RE AN EXCELLENT STUDENT.
ALL THE TEACHERS ENJOY TEACHING YOU.
I'M SORRY I'M LATE.
AM I UP SOON?
YEAH. BUT DON'T PUSH YOURSELF TOO MUCH.
CAPTAIN, YOU'RE BEING TOO EASY ON ARIMA AGAIN.
AND YET YOU'RE WORKING US INTO THE GROUND!
あはははは!!
SHUT UP! ARIMA WAS IN A COUNCIL MEETING!

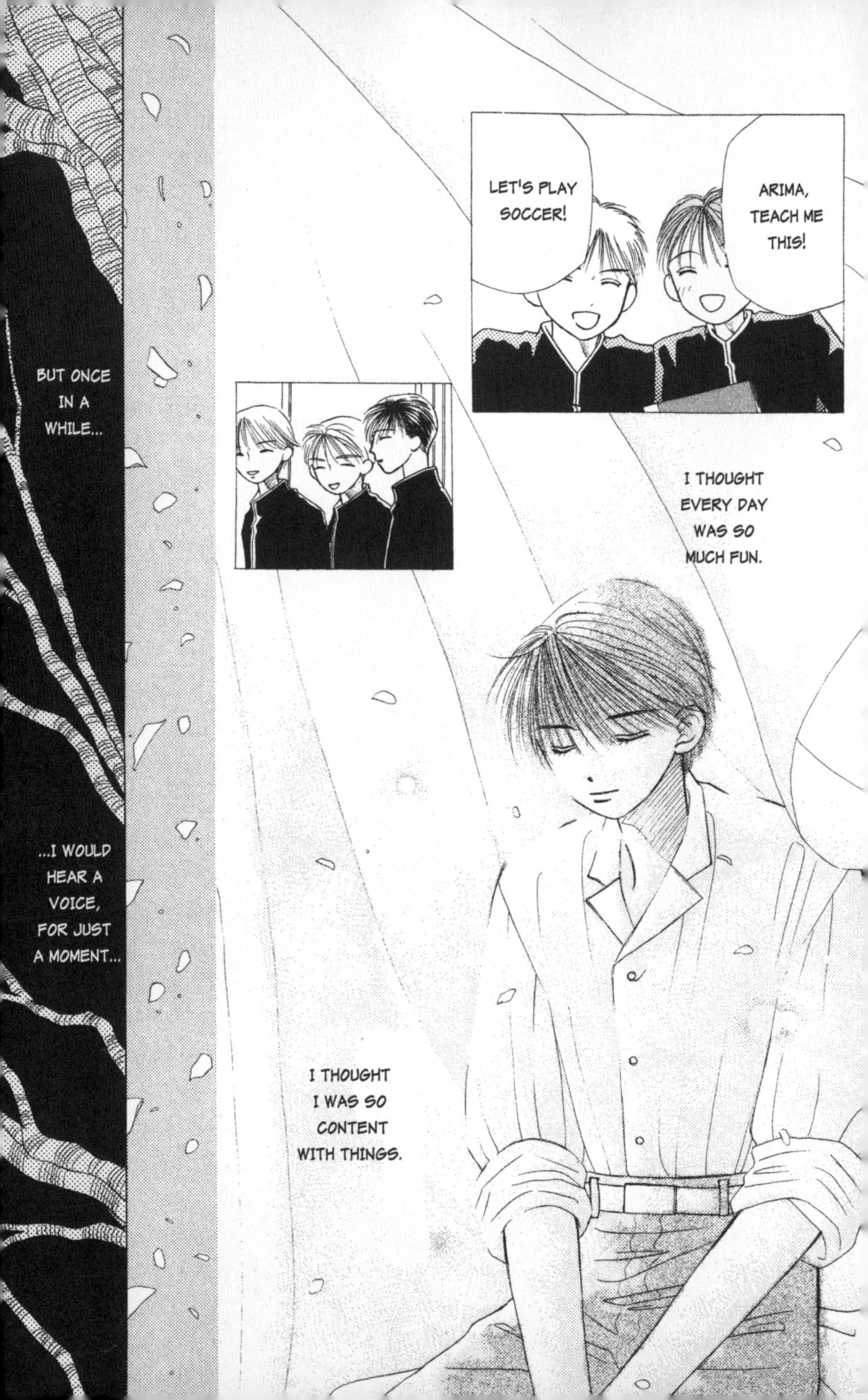
ARIMA, TEACH ME THIS!
LET'S PLAY SOCCER!
I THOUGHT EVERY DAY WAS SO MUCH FUN.
I THOUGHT I WAS SO CONTENT WITH THINGS.
BUT ONCE IN A WHILE...
...I WOULD HEAR A VOICE, FOR JUST A MOMENT...

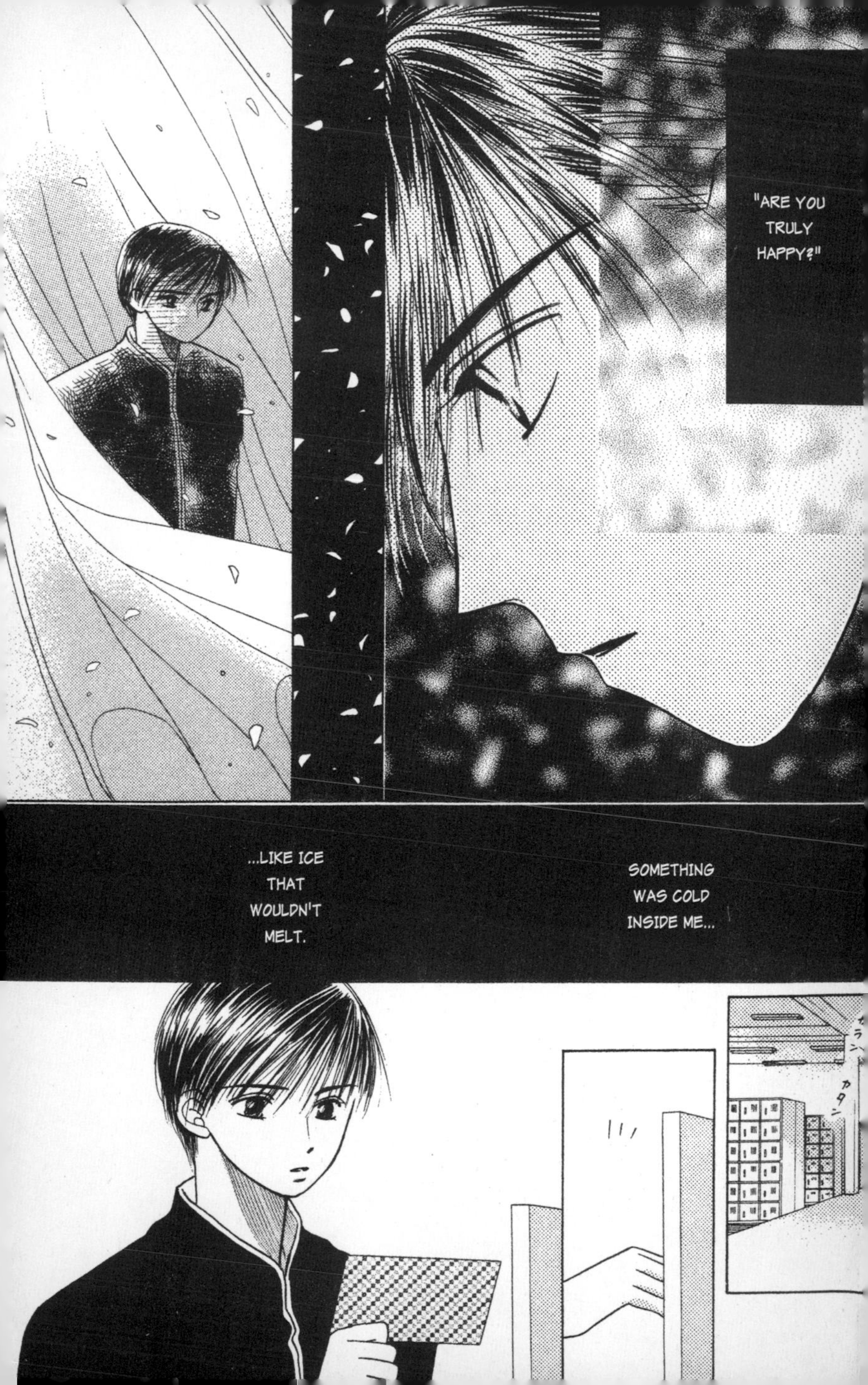
"ARE YOU TRULY HAPPY?"
SOMETHING WAS COLD INSIDE ME...
...LIKE ICE THAT WOULDN'T MELT.
カラン、
カタン

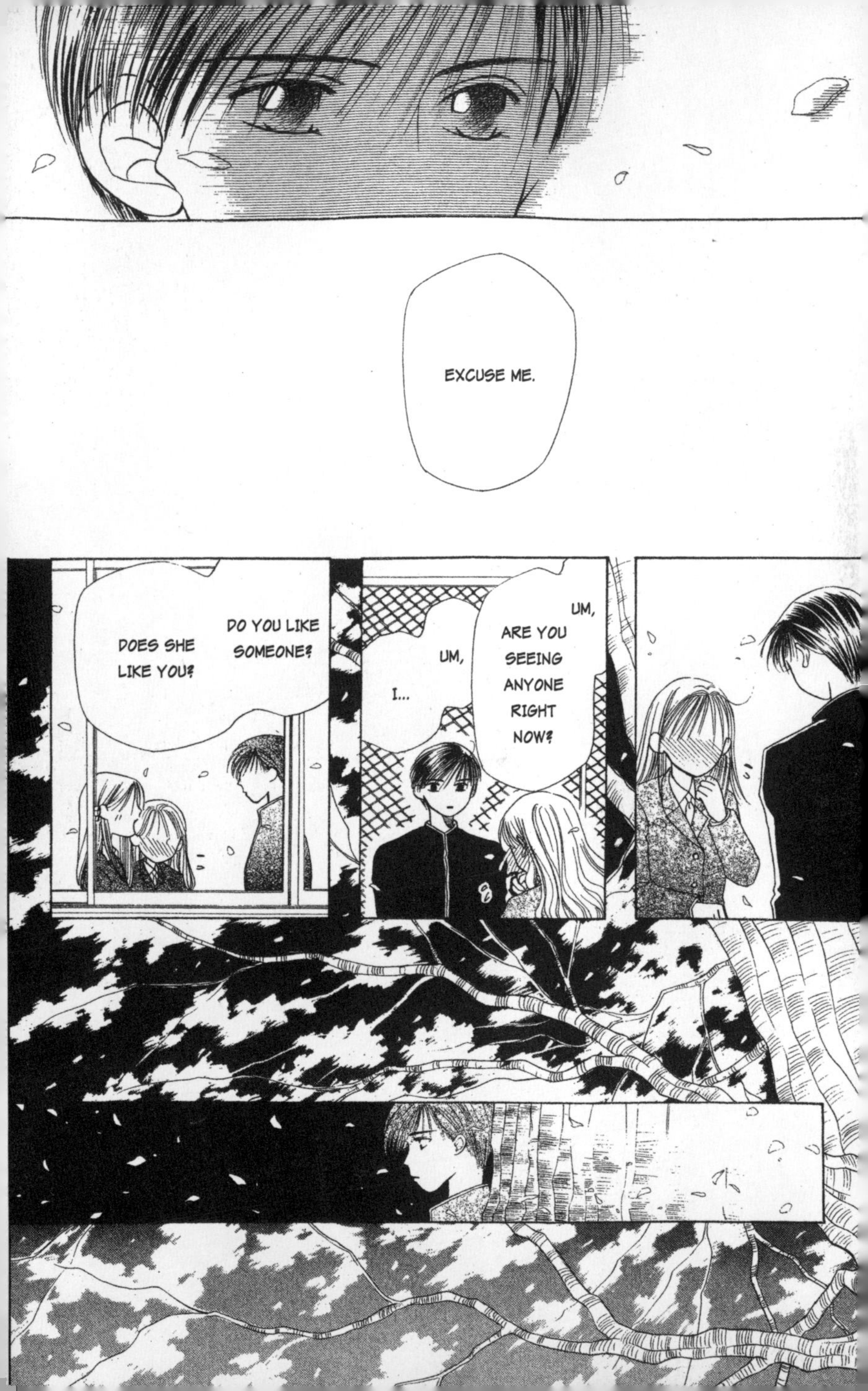
EXCUSE ME.
UM, ARE YOU SEEING ANYONE RIGHT NOW?
UM, I...
DO YOU LIKE SOMEONE?
DOES SHE LIKE YOU?

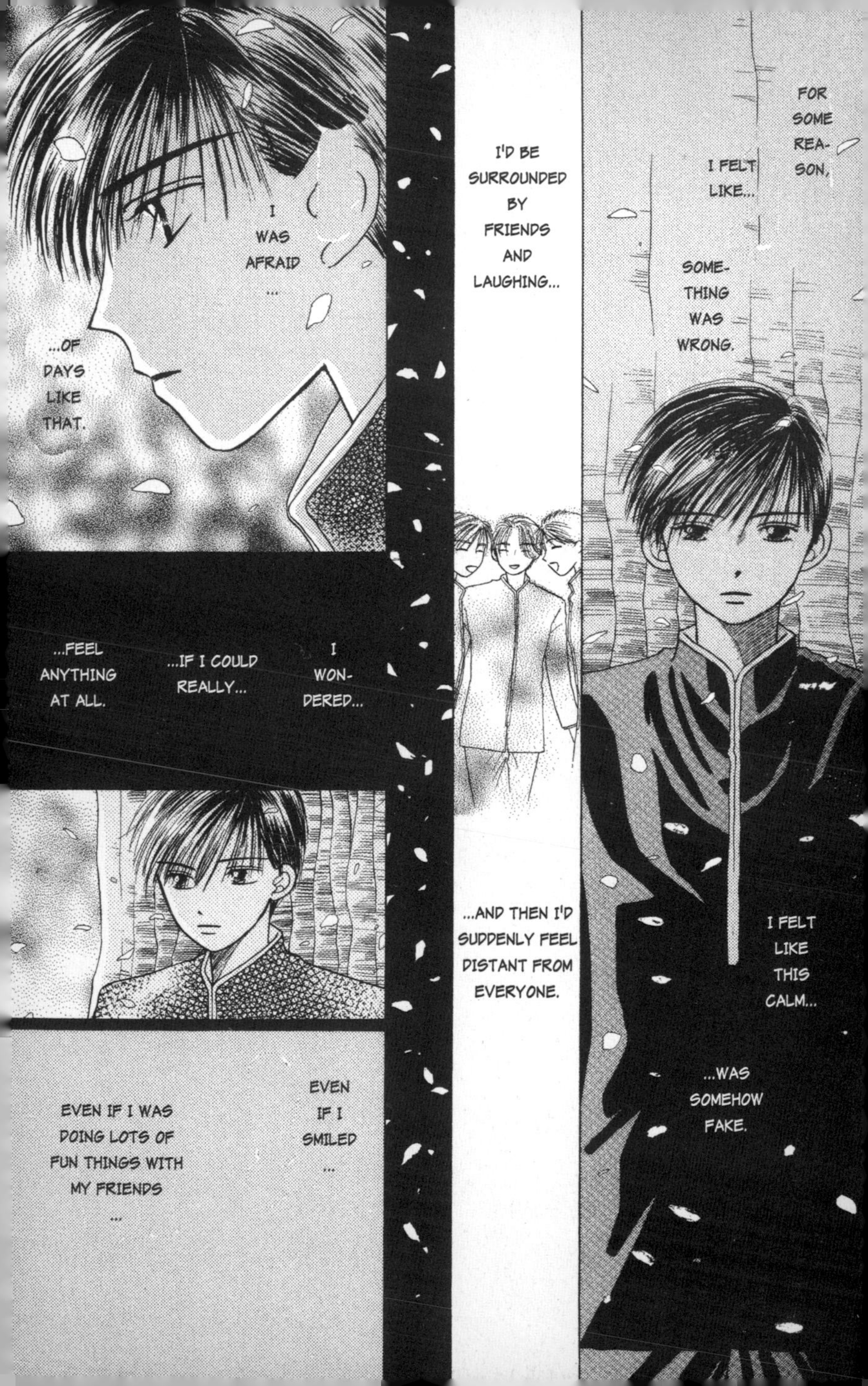
FOR SOME REA-SON,
I FELT LIKE...
SOME-THING WAS WRONG.
I FELT LIKE THIS CALM...
...WAS SOMEHOW FAKE.
I'D BE SURROUNDED BY FRIENDS AND LAUGHING...
...AND THEN I'D SUDDENLY FEEL DISTANT FROM EVERYONE.
I WAS AFRAID ...
...OF DAYS LIKE THAT.
I WON-DERED...
...IF I COULD REALLY...
...FEEL ANYTHING AT ALL.
EVEN IF I SMILED ...
EVEN IF I WAS DOING LOTS OF FUN THINGS WITH MY FRIENDS ...

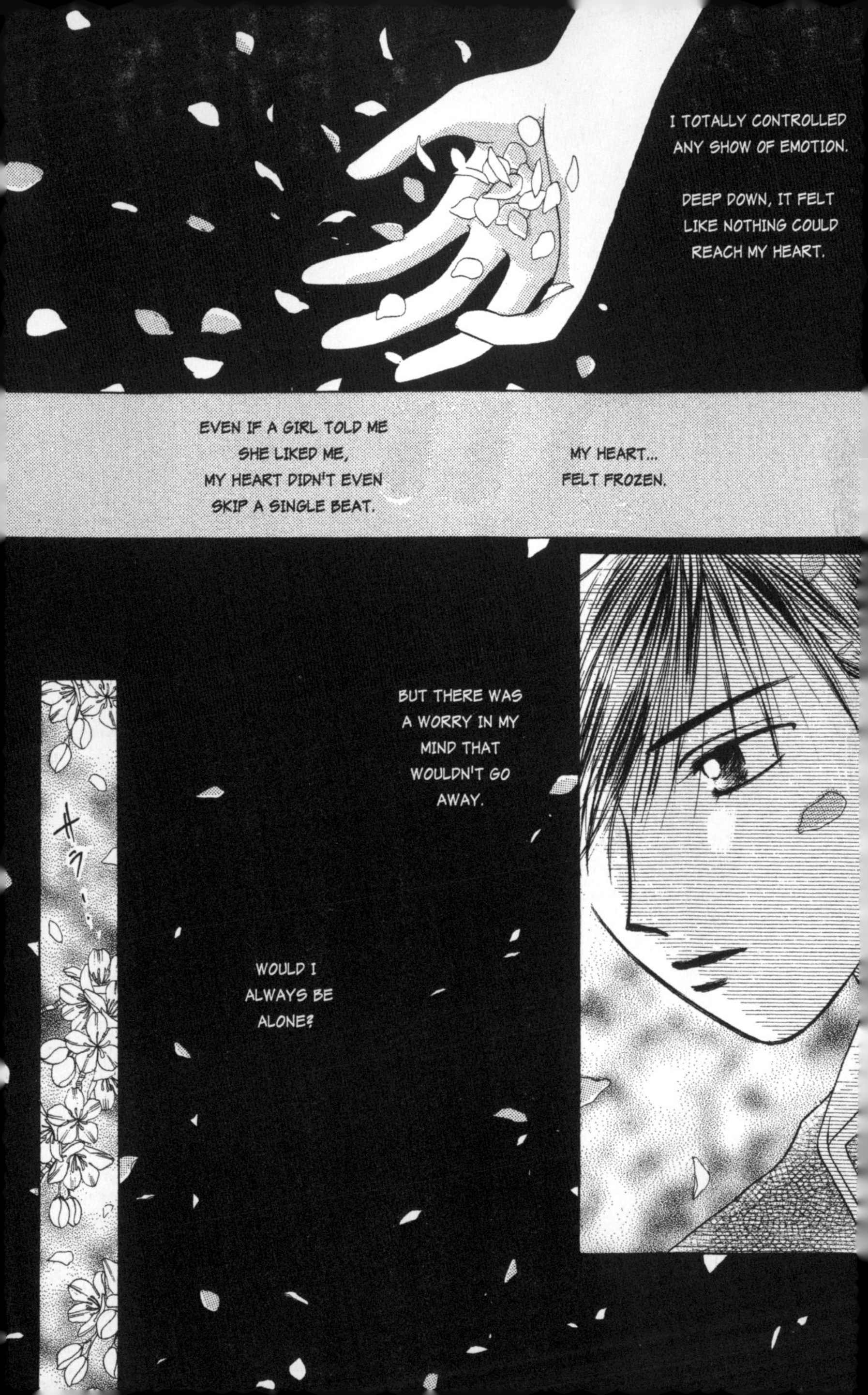
I TOTALLY CONTROLLED ANY SHOW OF EMOTION.
DEEP DOWN, IT FELT LIKE NOTHING COULD REACH MY HEART.
EVEN IF A GIRL TOLD ME SHE LIKED ME, MY HEART DIDN'T EVEN SKIP A SINGLE BEAT.
MY HEART... FELT FROZEN.
BUT THERE WAS A WORRY IN MY MIND THAT WOULDN'T GO AWAY.
WOULD I ALWAYS BE ALONE?

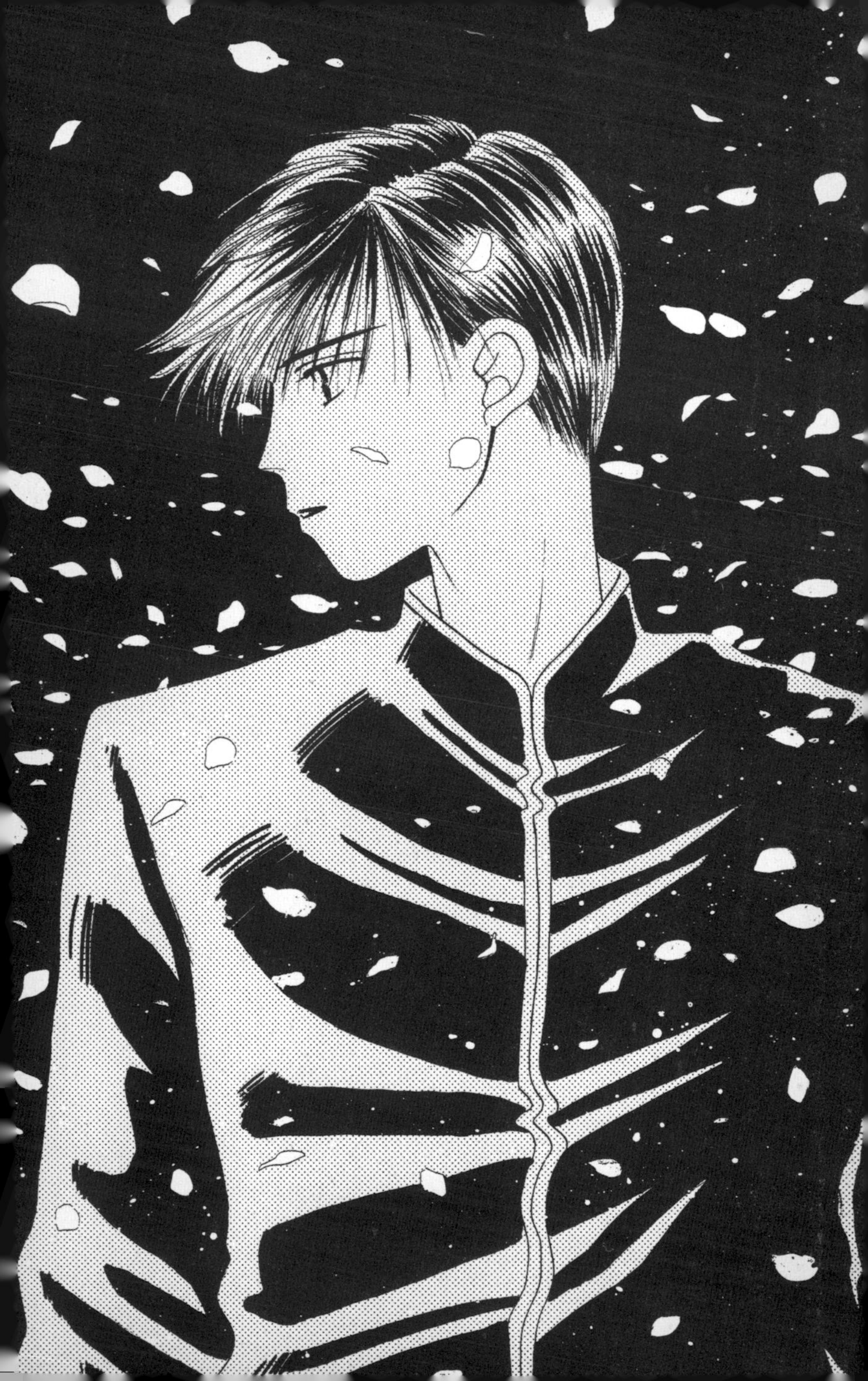

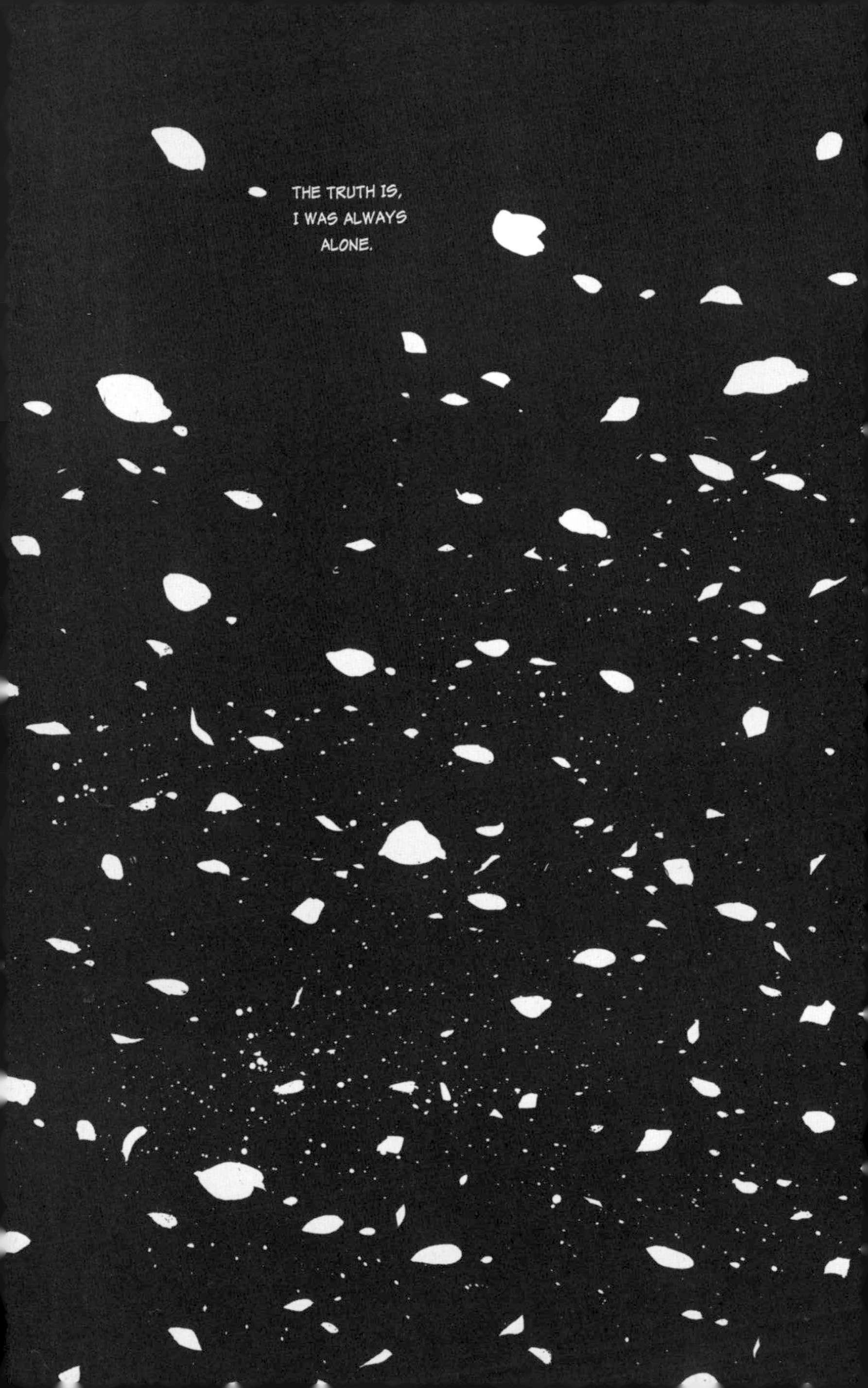
THE TRUTH IS,
I WAS ALWAYS
ALONE.

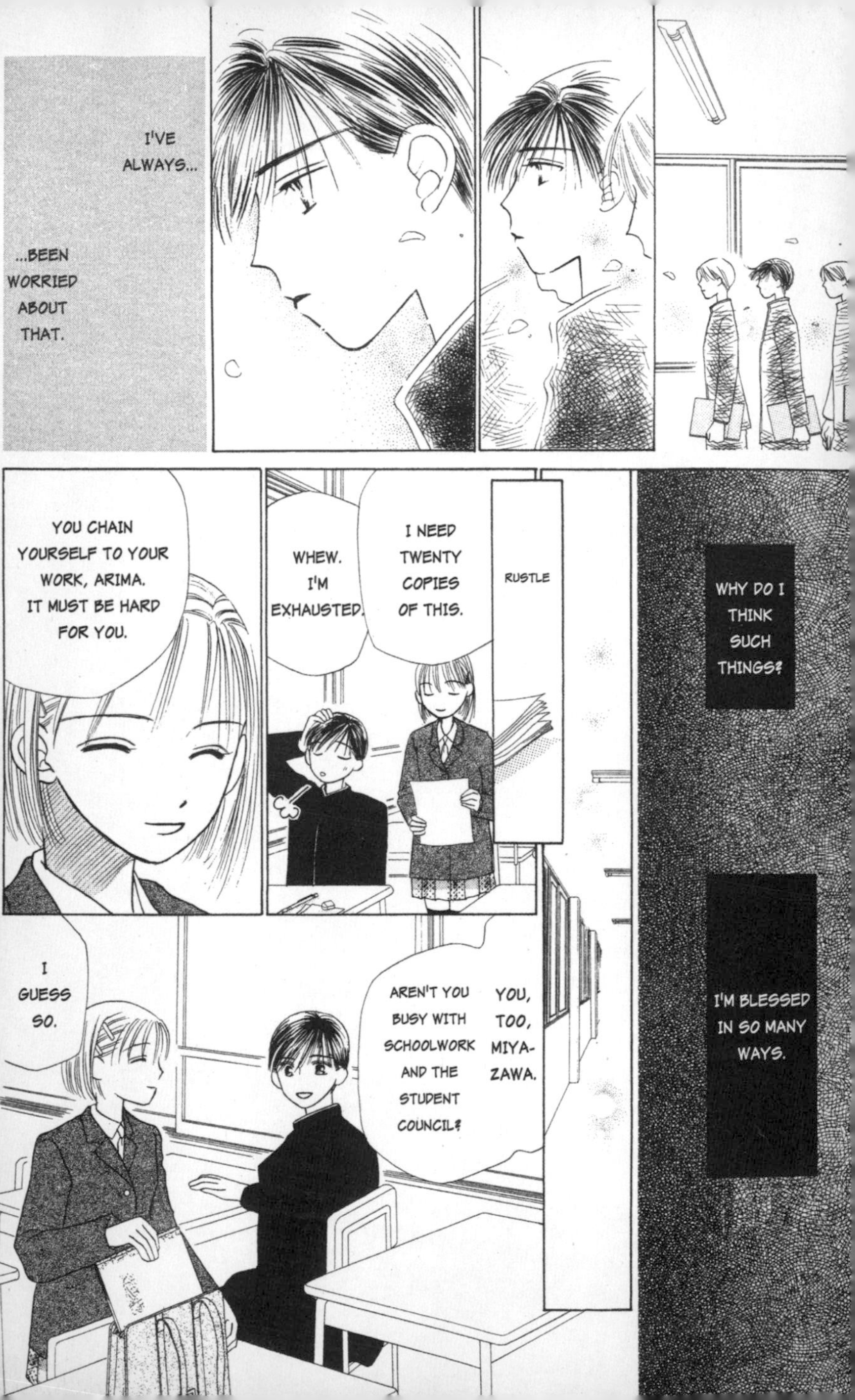
I'VE ALWAYS...
...BEEN WORRIED ABOUT THAT.
WHY DO I THINK SUCH THINGS?
I'M BLESSED IN SO MANY WAYS.
RUSTLE
I NEED TWENTY COPIES OF THIS.
WHEW. I'M EXHAUSTED.
YOU CHAIN YOURSELF TO YOUR WORK, ARIMA. IT MUST BE HARD FOR YOU.
YOU, TOO, MIYA-ZAWA.
AREN'T YOU BUSY WITH SCHOOLWORK AND THE STUDENT COUNCIL?
I GUESS SO.

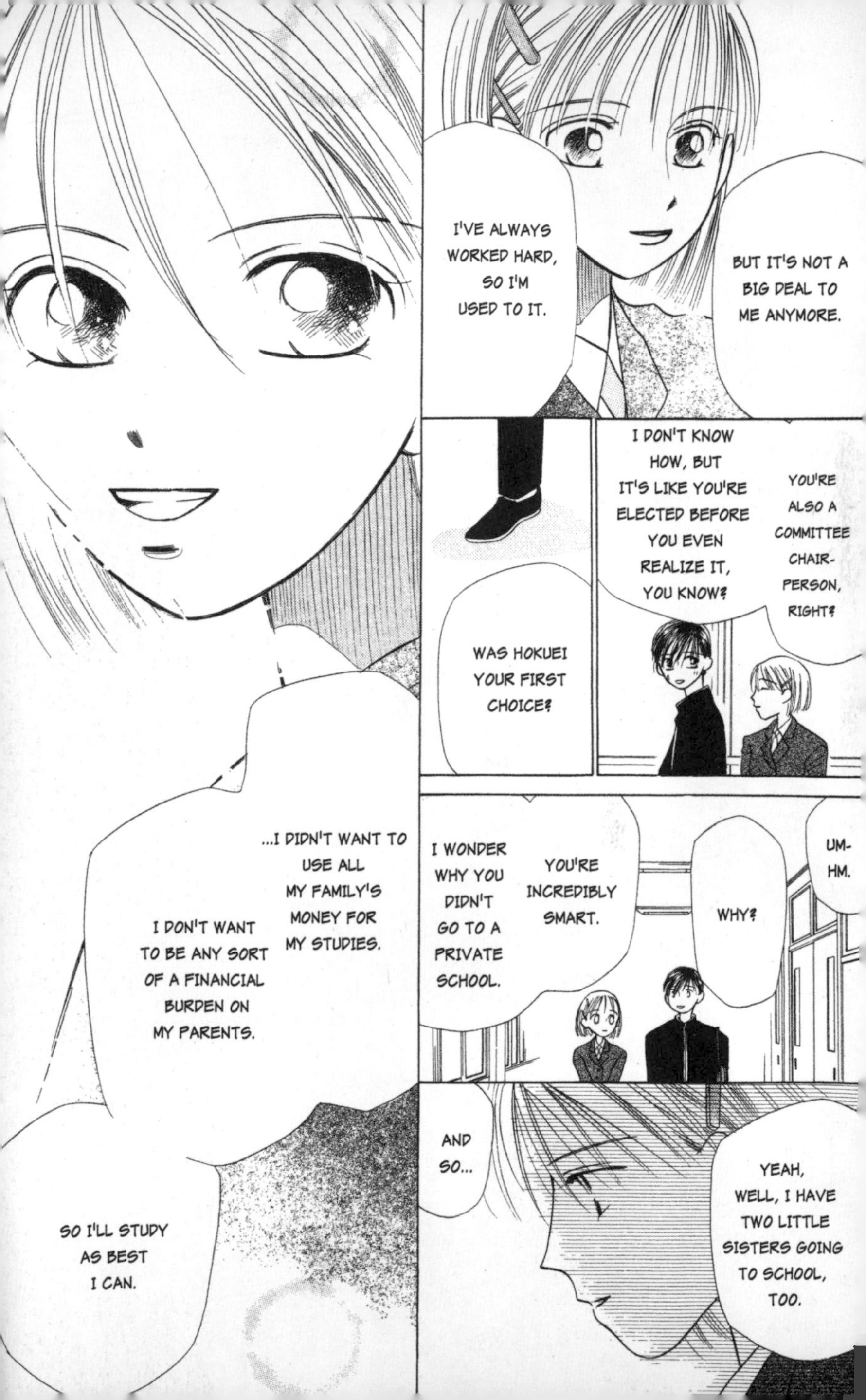
BUT IT'S NOT A BIG DEAL TO ME ANYMORE.
I'VE ALWAYS WORKED HARD, SO I'M USED TO IT.
YOU'RE ALSO A COMMITTEE CHAIR-PERSON, RIGHT?
I DON'T KNOW HOW, BUT IT'S LIKE YOU'RE ELECTED BEFORE YOU EVEN REALIZE IT, YOU KNOW?
WAS HOKUEI YOUR FIRST CHOICE?
UM-HM.
WHY?
YOU'RE INCREDIBLY SMART.
I WONDER WHY YOU DIDN'T GO TO A PRIVATE SCHOOL.
YEAH, WELL, I HAVE TWO LITTLE SISTERS GOING TO SCHOOL, TOO.
AND SO...
...I DIDN'T WANT TO USE ALL MY FAMILY'S MONEY FOR MY STUDIES.
I DON'T WANT TO BE ANY SORT OF A FINANCIAL BURDEN ON MY PARENTS.
SO I'LL STUDY AS BEST I CAN.

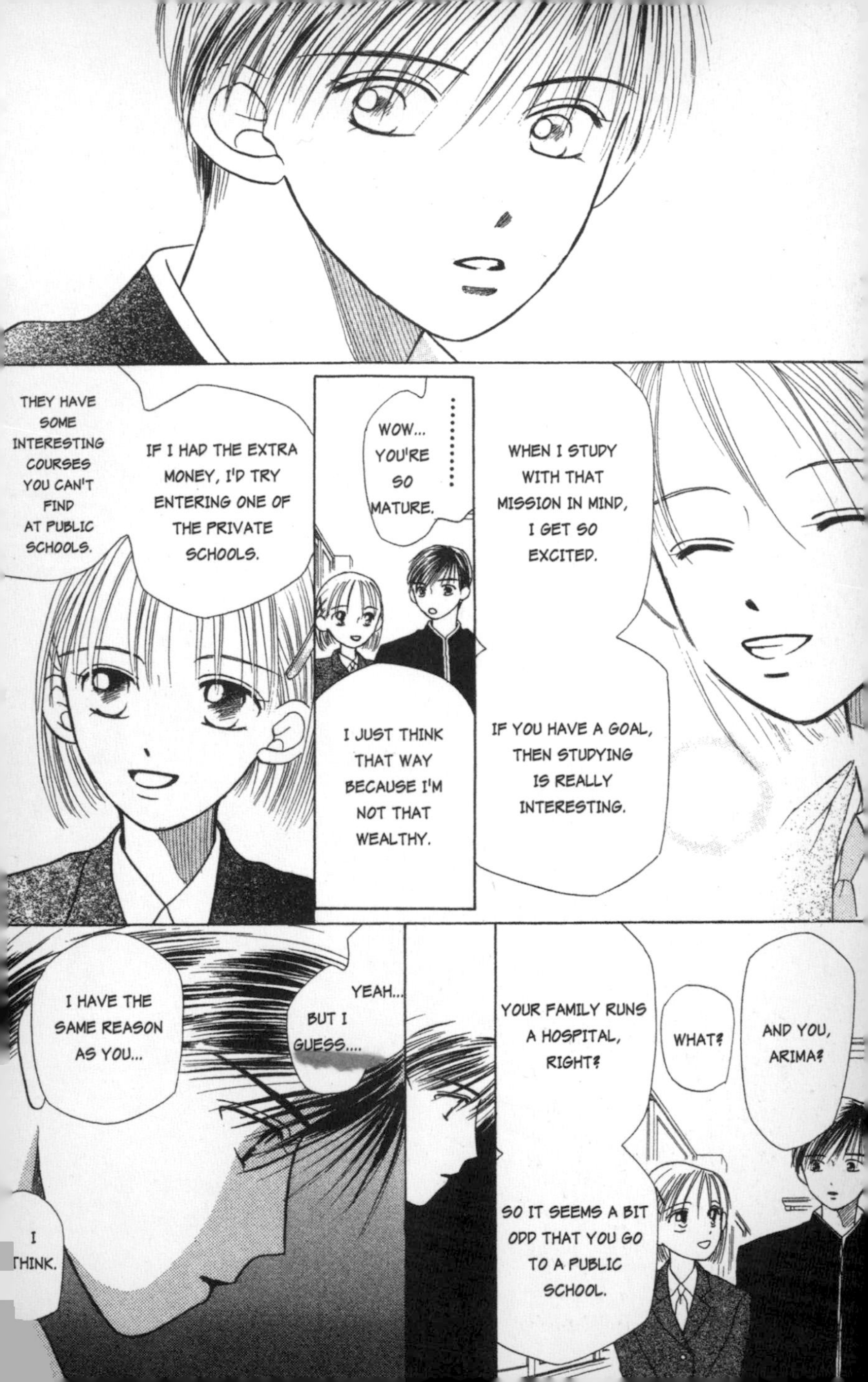
WHEN I STUDY WITH THAT MISSION IN MIND, I GET SO EXCITED.
IF YOU HAVE A GOAL, THEN STUDYING IS REALLY INTERESTING.
....
WOW... YOU'RE SO MATURE.
I JUST THINK THAT WAY BECAUSE I'M NOT THAT WEALTHY.
IF I HAD THE EXTRA MONEY, I'D TRY ENTERING ONE OF THE PRIVATE SCHOOLS.
THEY HAVE SOME INTERESTING COURSES YOU CAN'T FIND AT PUBLIC SCHOOLS.
AND YOU, ARIMA?
WHAT?
YOUR FAMILY RUNS A HOSPITAL, RIGHT?
SO IT SEEMS A BIT ODD THAT YOU GO TO A PUBLIC SCHOOL.
YEAH... BUT I GUESS....
I HAVE THE SAME REASON AS YOU...
I THINK.

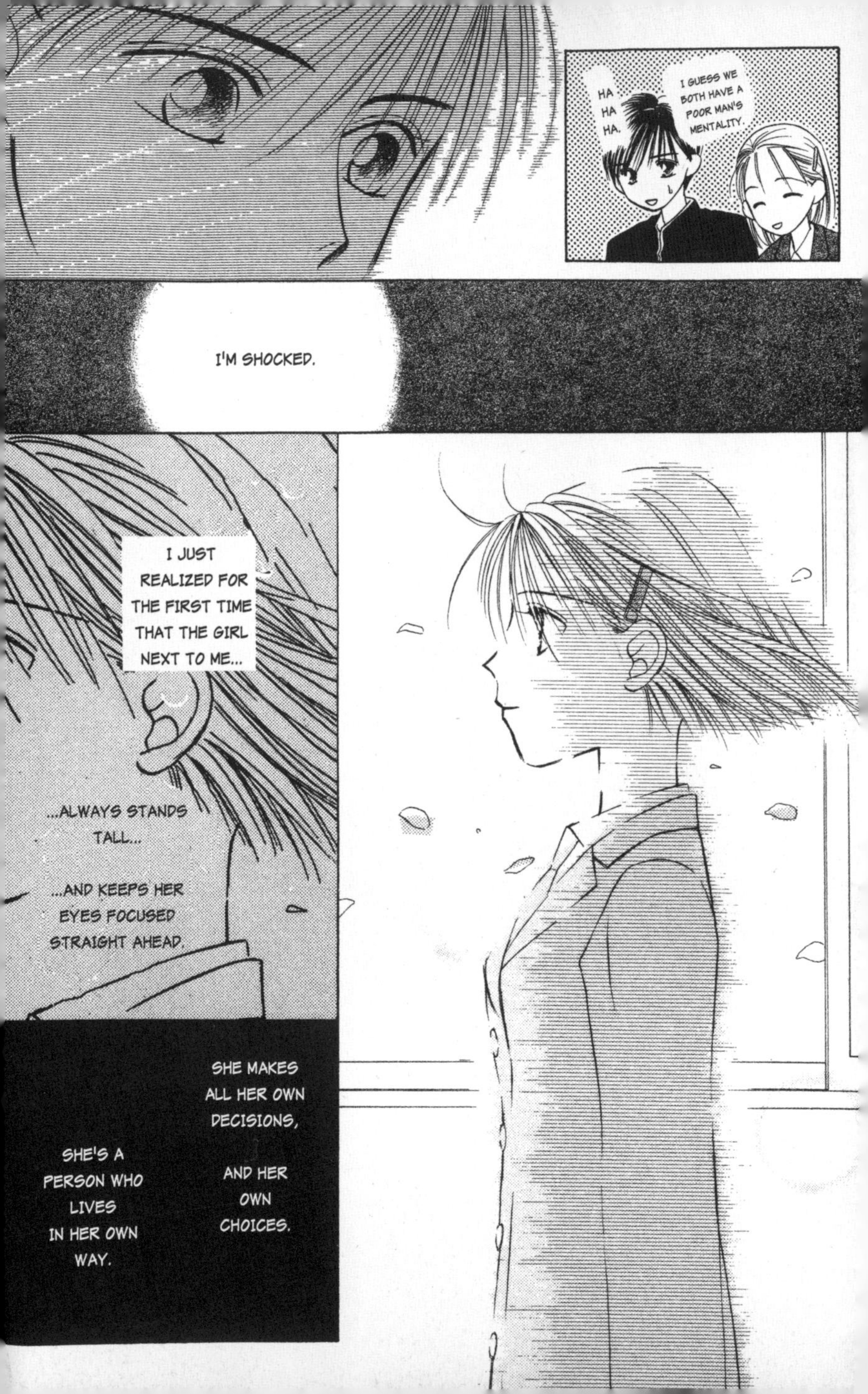
I GUESS WE BOTH HAVE A POOR MAN'S MENTALITY.
HA HA HA.
I'M SHOCKED.
I JUST REALIZED FOR THE FIRST TIME THAT THE GIRL NEXT TO ME...
...ALWAYS STANDS TALL...
...AND KEEPS HER EYES FOCUSED STRAIGHT AHEAD.
SHE MAKES ALL HER OWN DECISIONS,
AND HER OWN CHOICES.
SHE'S A PERSON WHO LIVES IN HER OWN WAY.

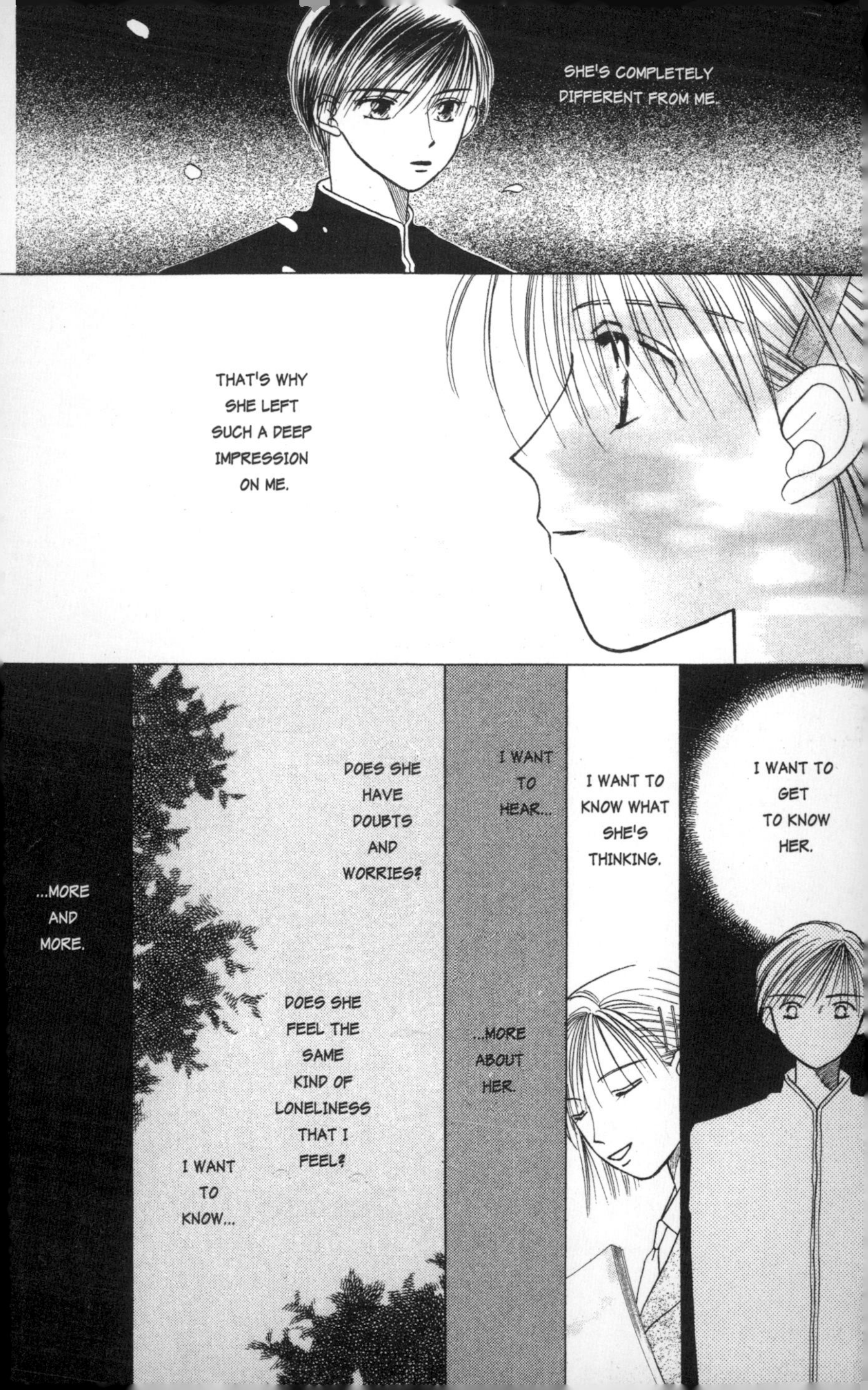
SHE'S COMPLETELY DIFFERENT FROM ME.
THAT'S WHY SHE LEFT SUCH A DEEP IMPRESSION ON ME.
I WANT TO GET TO KNOW HER.
I WANT TO KNOW WHAT SHE'S THINKING.
I WANT TO HEAR...
...MORE ABOUT HER.
DOES SHE HAVE DOUBTS AND WORRIES?
DOES SHE FEEL THE SAME KIND OF LONELINESS THAT I FEEL?
I WANT TO KNOW...
...MORE AND MORE.

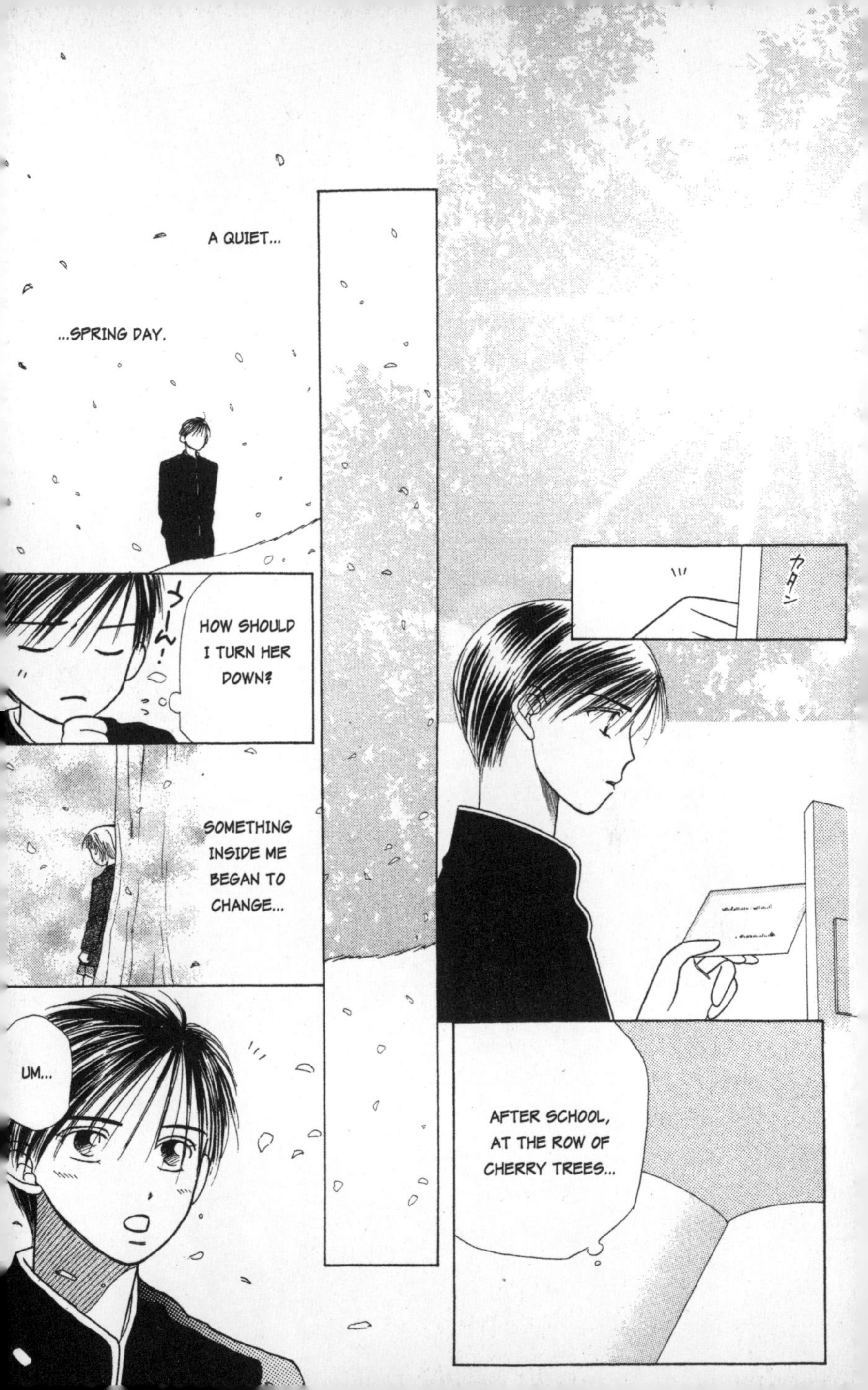
カタン
AFTER SCHOOL, AT THE ROW OF CHERRY TREES...
A QUIET...
...SPRING DAY.
うーん！
HOW SHOULD I TURN HER DOWN?
SOMETHING INSIDE ME BEGAN TO CHANGE...
UM...

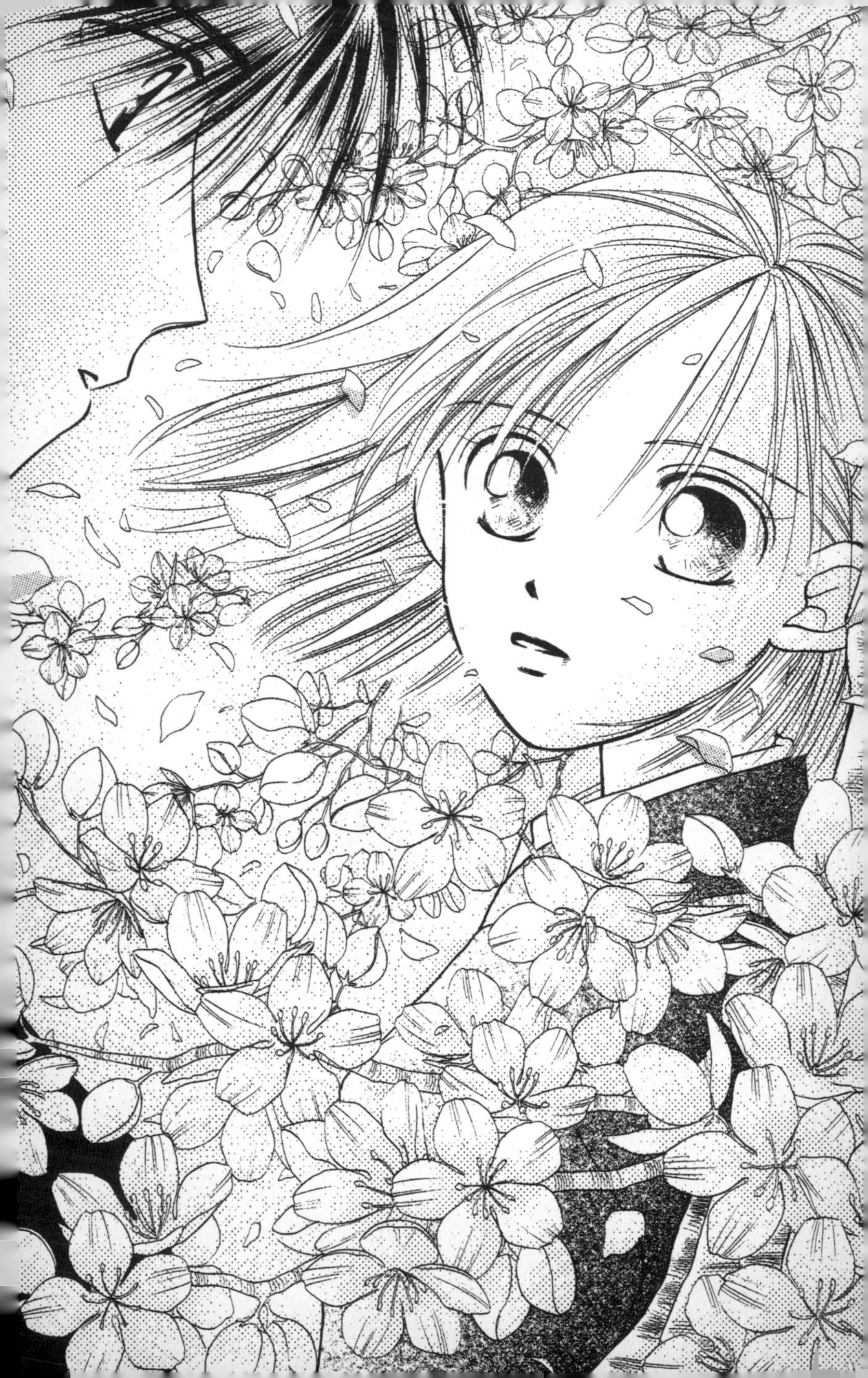

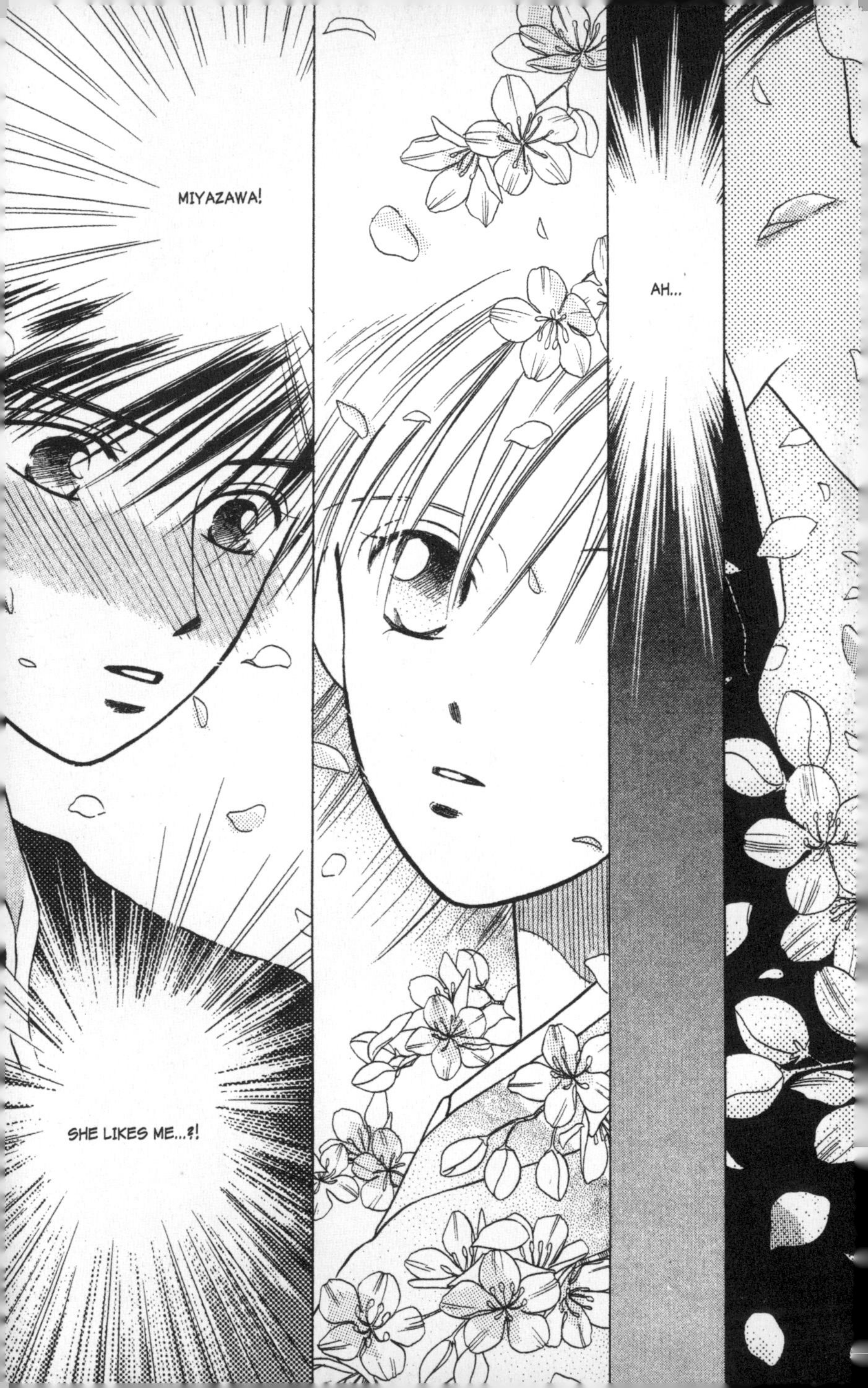
AH...
MIYAZAWA!
SHE LIKES ME...?!

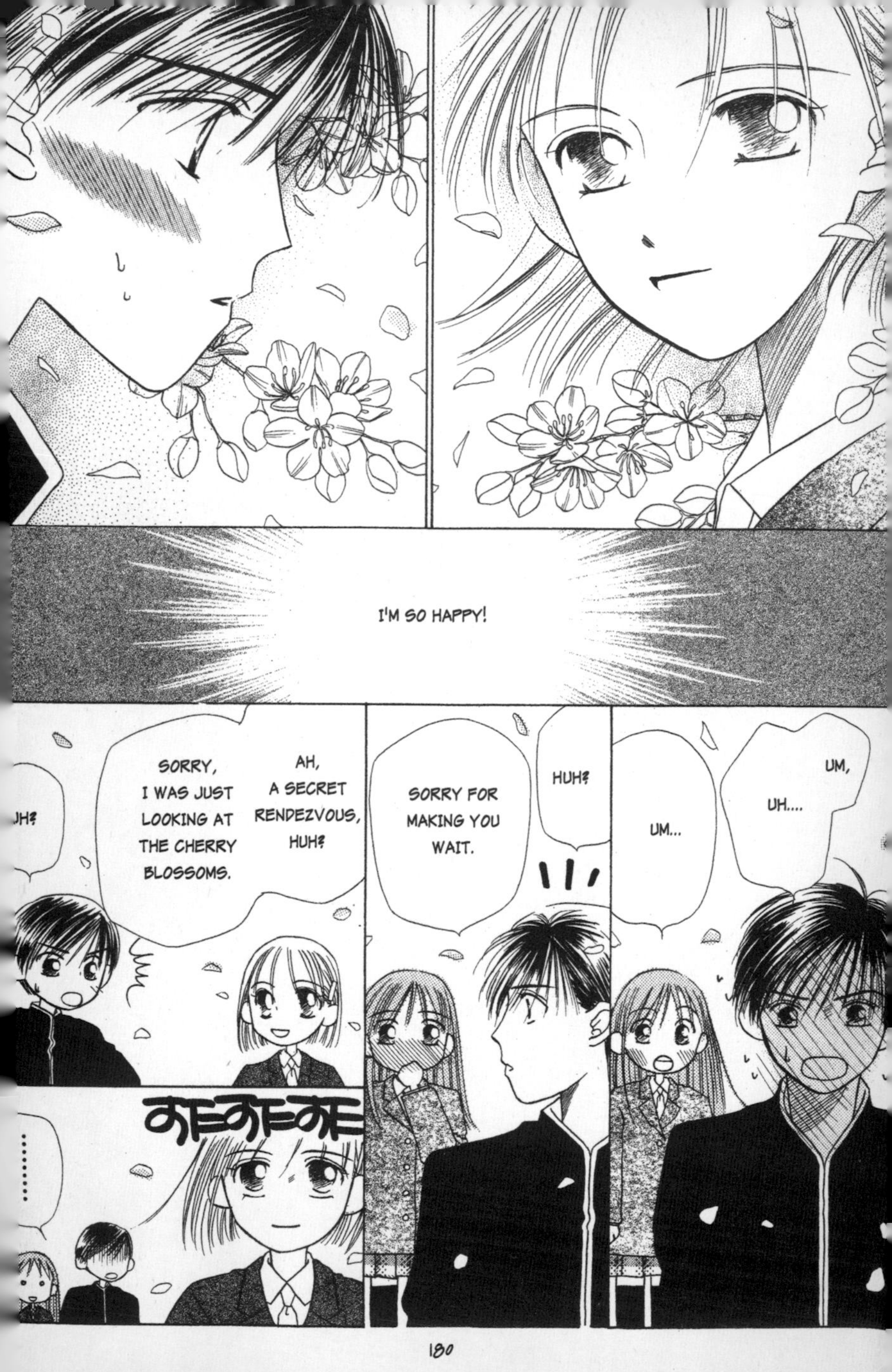
I'M SO HAPPY!
UM, UH....
UM...
HUH?
SORRY FOR MAKING YOU WAIT.
AH, A SECRET RENDEZVOUS, HUH?
SORRY, I WAS JUST LOOKING AT THE CHERRY BLOSSOMS.
おたおたおた
......

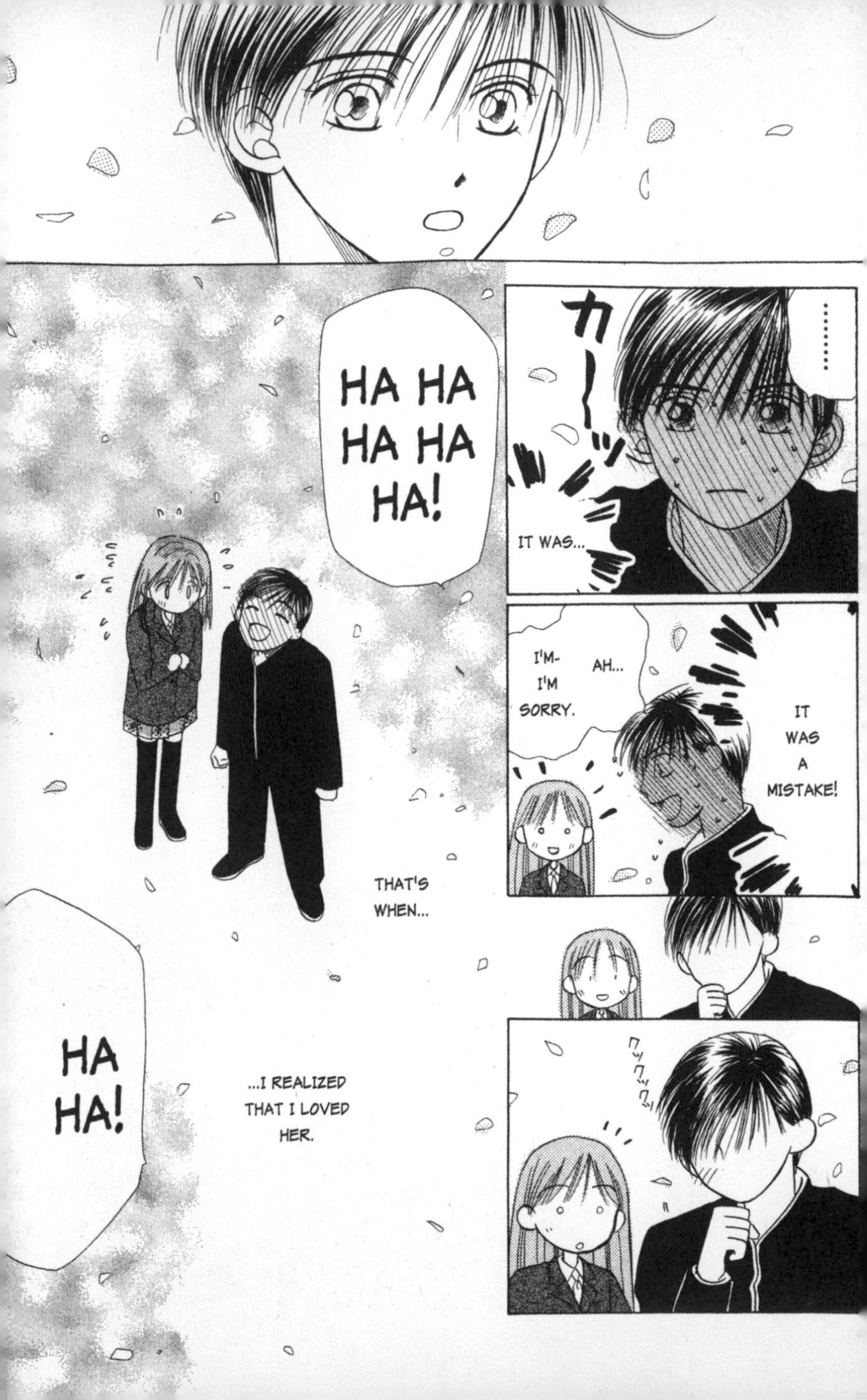

カーッ
....
IT WAS...
IT WAS A MISTAKE!
AH...
I'M- I'M SORRY.
HA HA HA HA HA!
THAT'S WHEN...
HA HA!
...I REALIZED THAT I LOVED HER.

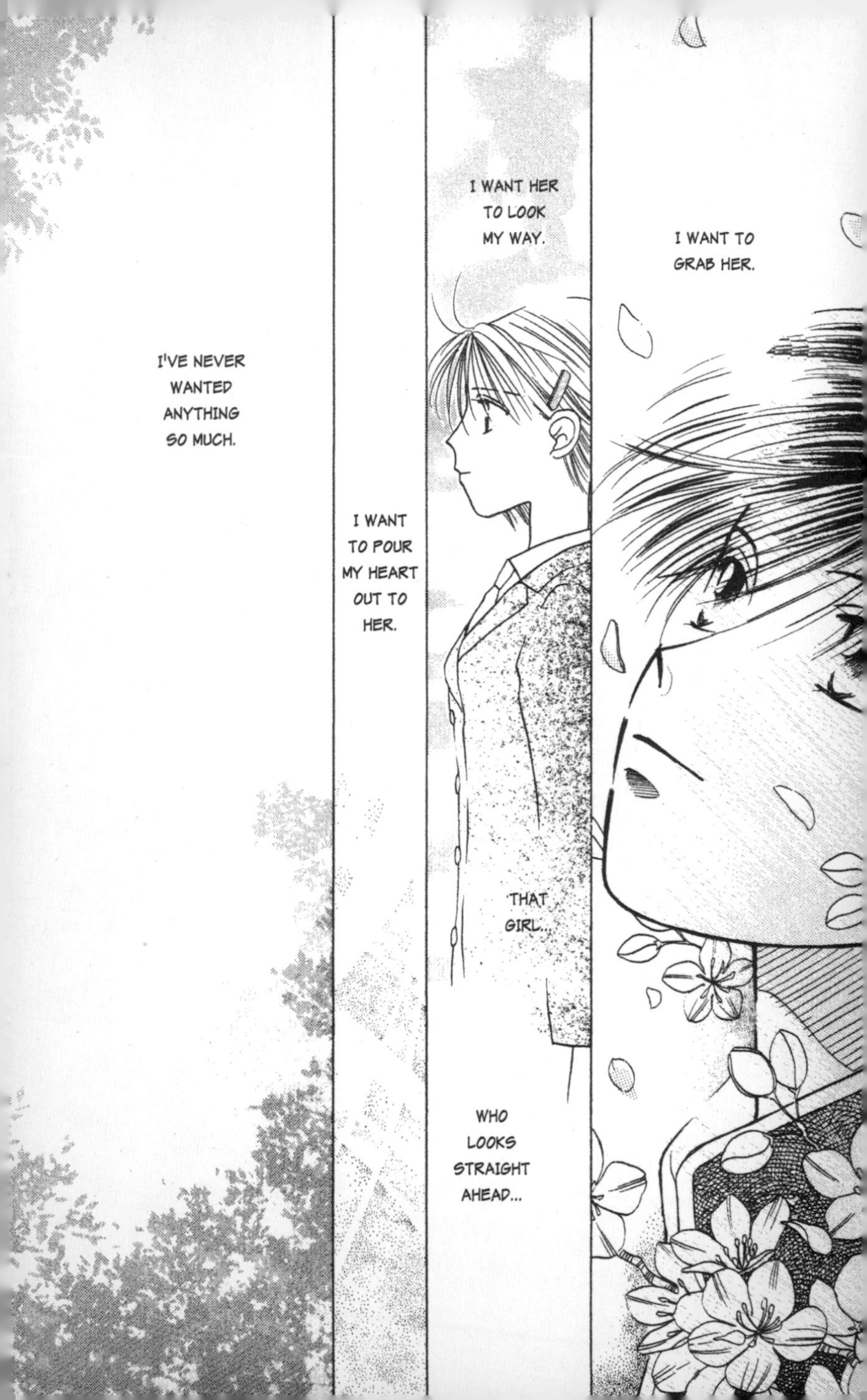
I WANT TO GRAB HER.
I WANT HER TO LOOK MY WAY.
THAT GIRL...
WHO LOOKS STRAIGHT AHEAD...
I WANT TO POUR MY HEART OUT TO HER.
I'VE NEVER WANTED ANYTHING SO MUCH.

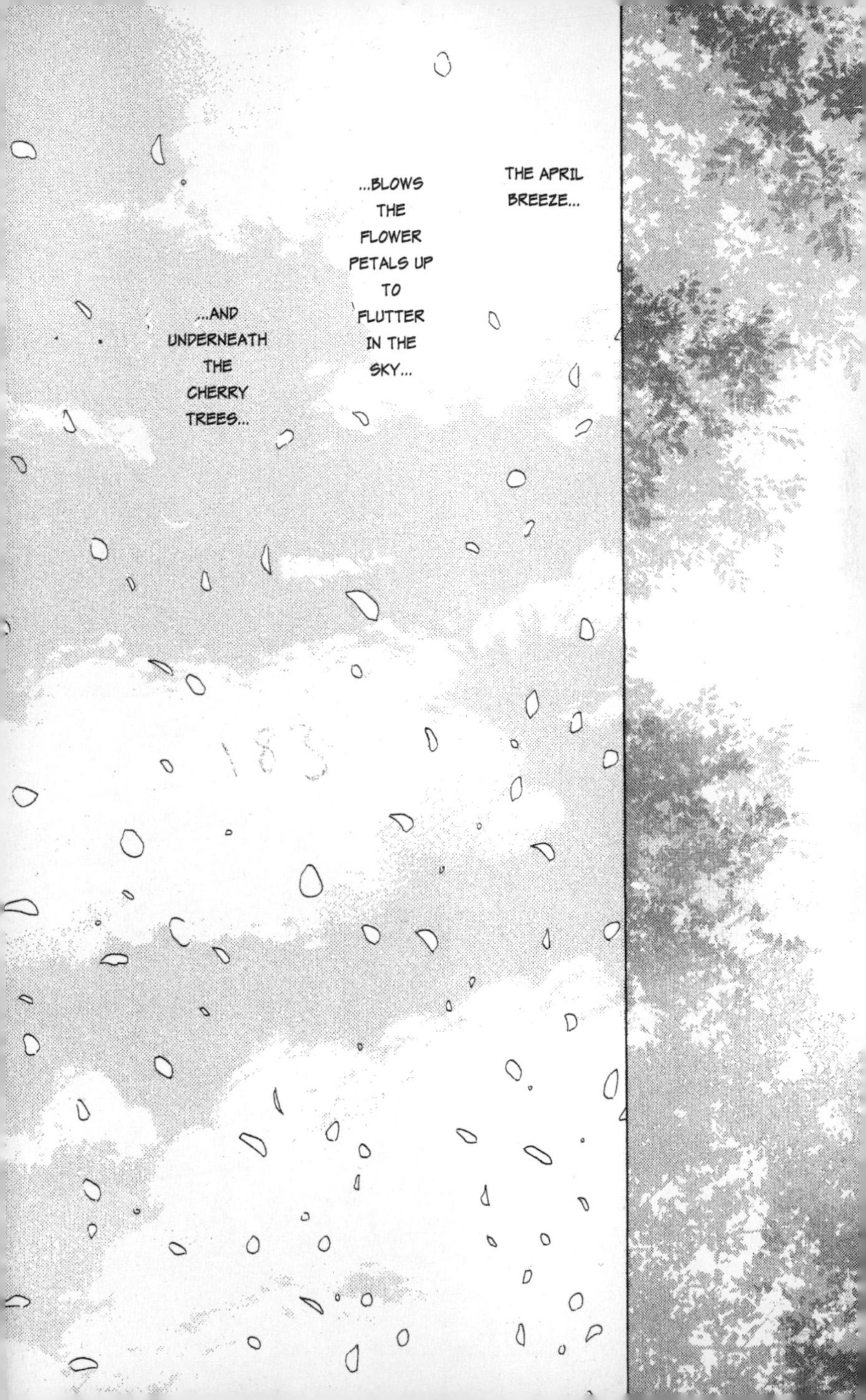
THE APRIL BREEZE...
...BLOWS THE FLOWER PETALS UP TO FLUTTER IN THE SKY...
...AND UNDERNEATH THE CHERRY TREES...

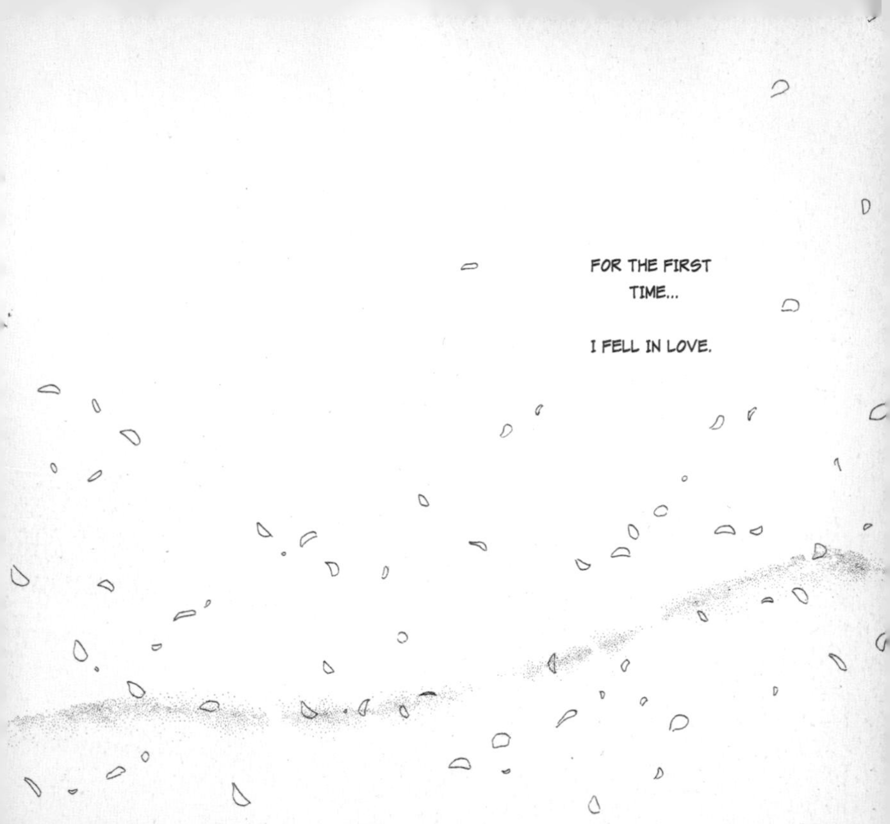
FOR THE FIRST TIME...
I FELL IN LOVE.

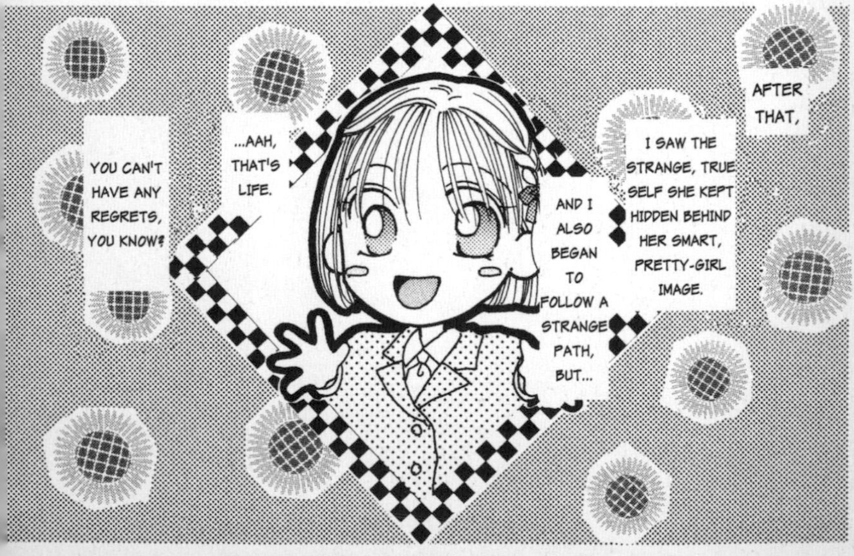
AFTER THAT,
I SAW THE STRANGE, TRUE SELF SHE KEPT HIDDEN BEHIND HER SMART, PRETTY-GIRL IMAGE.
AND I ALSO BEGAN TO FOLLOW A STRANGE PATH, BUT...
...AAH, THAT'S LIFE.
YOU CAN'T HAVE ANY REGRETS, YOU KNOW?

EXTRA * UNDER THE CHERRY TREES - THE END

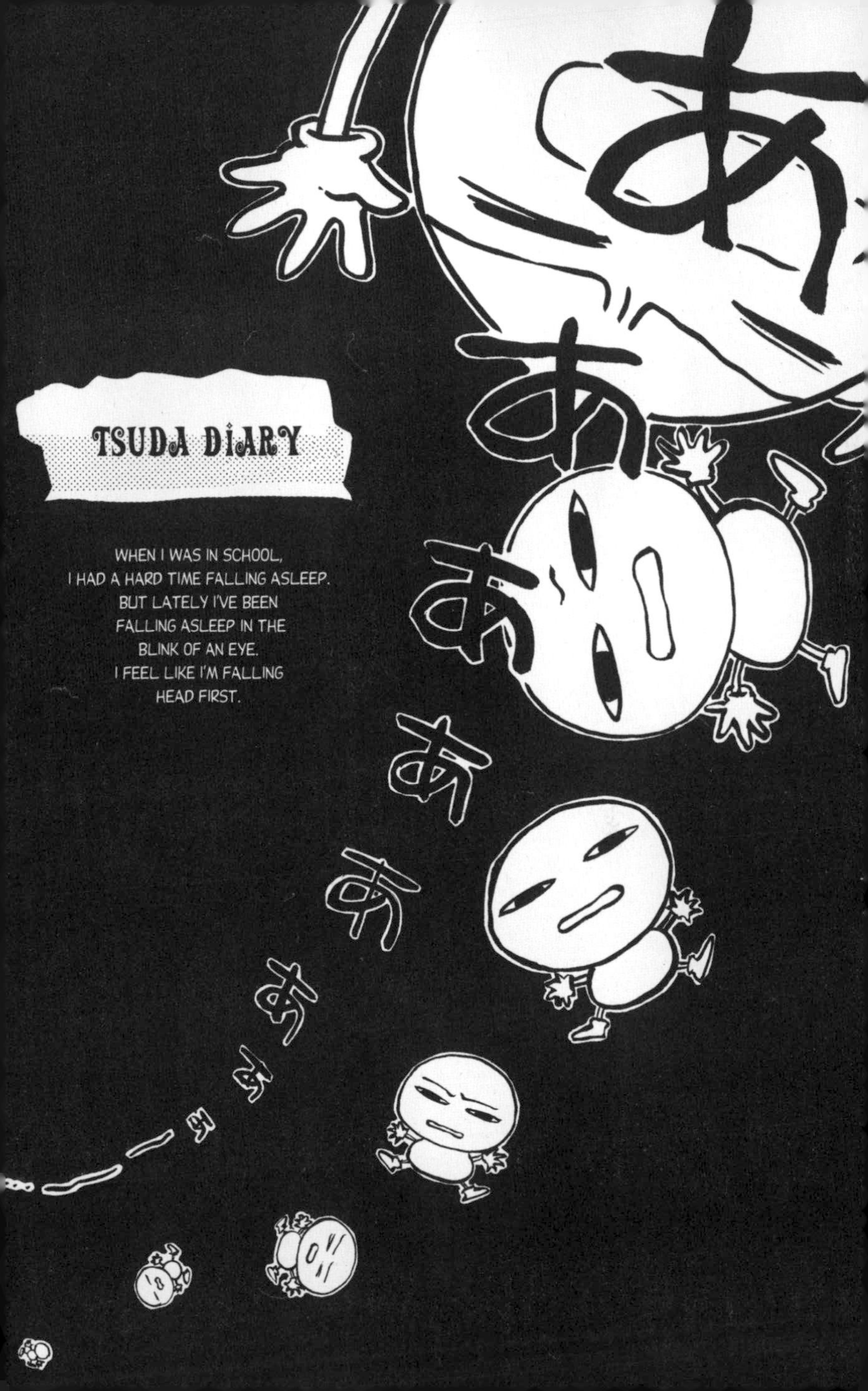
ああああああああーー

TSUDA DIARY

WHEN I WAS IN SCHOOL,
I HAD A HARD TIME FALLING ASLEEP.
BUT LATELY I'VE BEEN
FALLING ASLEEP IN THE
BLINK OF AN EYE.
I FEEL LIKE I'M FALLING
HEAD FIRST.

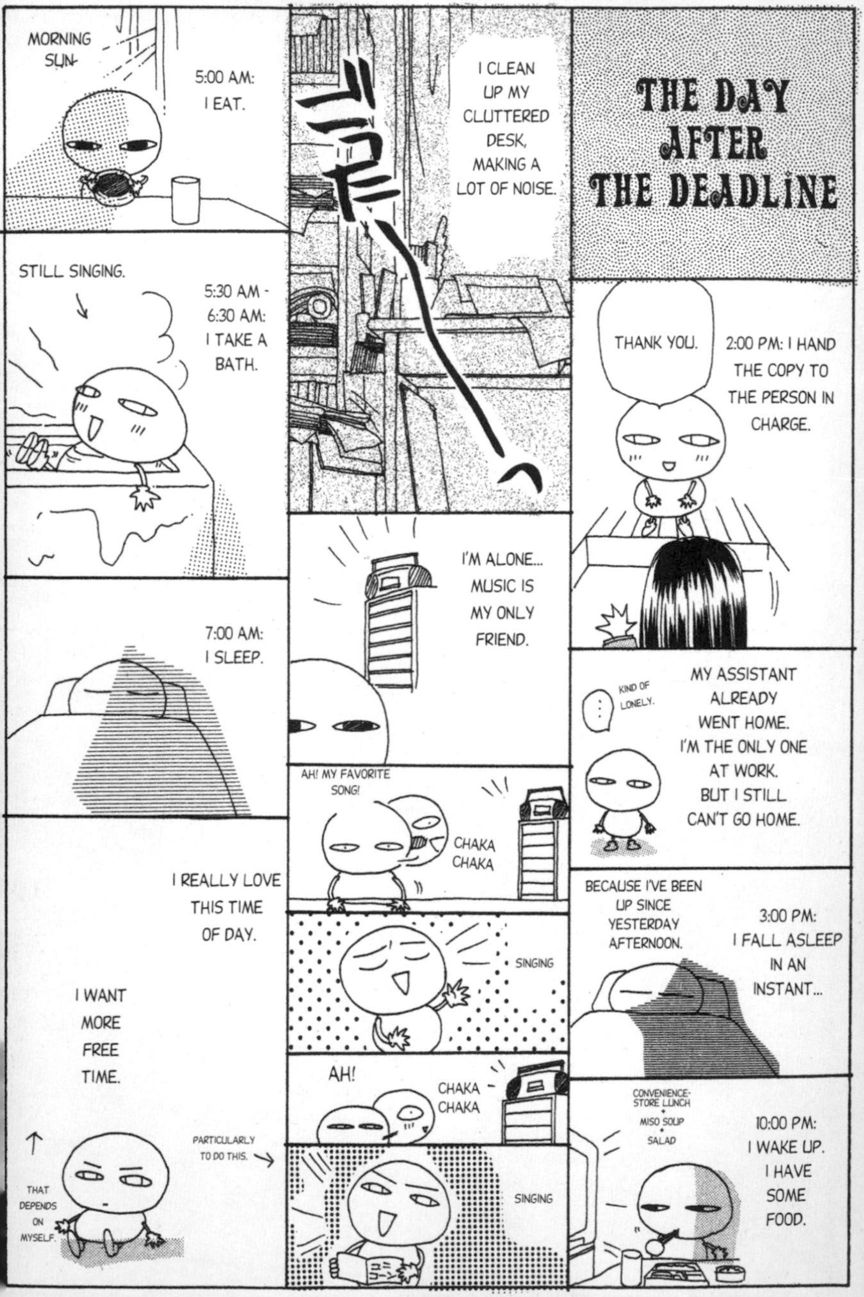
THE DAY AFTER THE DEADLINE
THANK YOU.
2:00 PM: I HAND THE COPY TO THE PERSON IN CHARGE.
MY ASSISTANT ALREADY WENT HOME. I'M THE ONLY ONE AT WORK. BUT I STILL CAN'T GO HOME.
KIND OF LONELY.
...
BECAUSE I'VE BEEN UP SINCE YESTERDAY AFTERNOON.
3:00 PM: I FALL ASLEEP IN AN INSTANT...
10:00 PM: I WAKE UP. I HAVE SOME FOOD.
CONVENIENCE-STORE LUNCH + MISO SOUP + SALAD
I CLEAN UP MY CLUTTERED DESK, MAKING A LOT OF NOISE.
I'M ALONE... MUSIC IS MY ONLY FRIEND.
AH! MY FAVORITE SONG!
CHAKA CHAKA
SINGING
AH!
CHAKA CHAKA
SINGING
MORNING SUN
5:00 AM: I EAT.
5:30 AM - 6:30 AM: I TAKE A BATH.
STILL SINGING.
7:00 AM: I SLEEP.
I REALLY LOVE THIS TIME OF DAY.
I WANT MORE FREE TIME.
PARTICULARLY TO DO THIS.
THAT DEPENDS ON MYSELF.

↗ 3:00 IN THE MORNING...

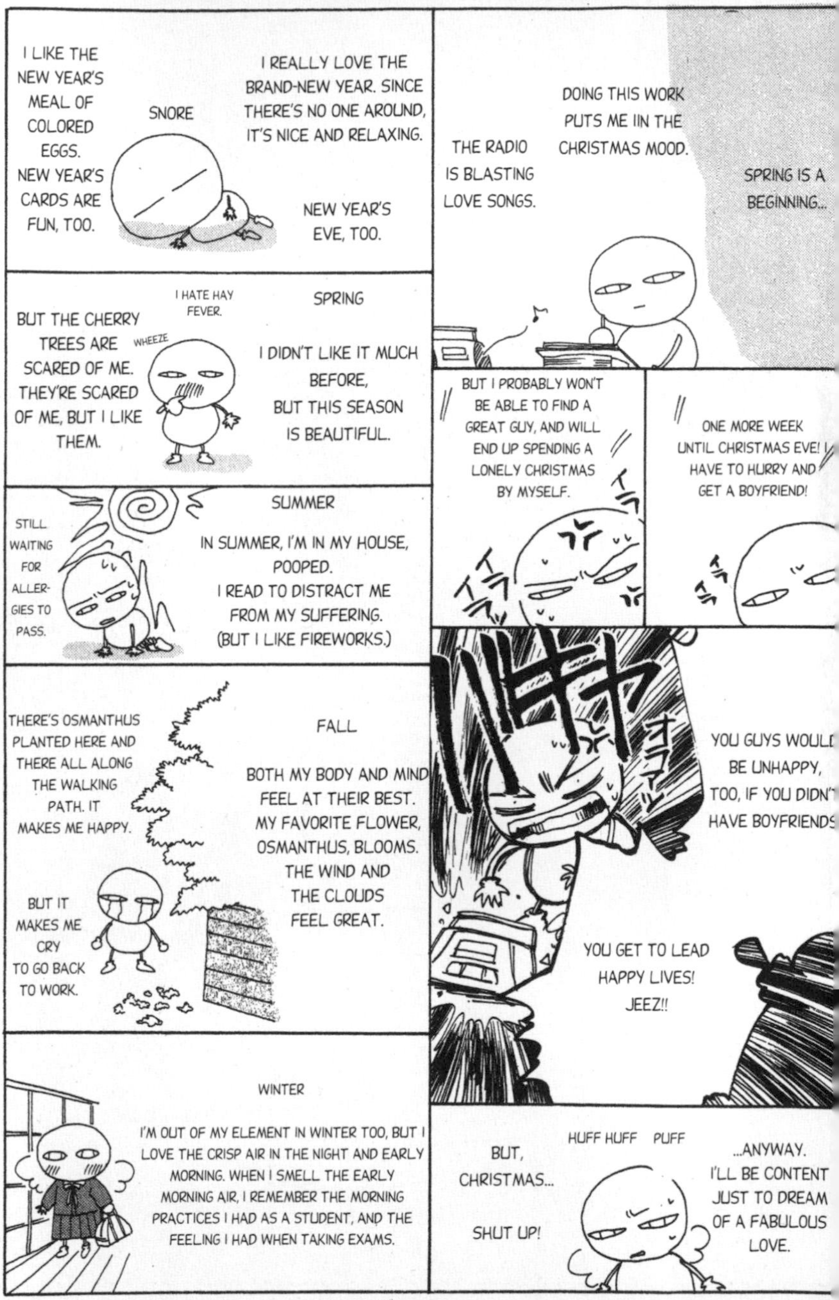
SPRING IS A BEGINNING...
DOING THIS WORK PUTS ME IIN THE CHRISTMAS MOOD.
THE RADIO IS BLASTING LOVE SONGS.
ONE MORE WEEK UNTIL CHRISTMAS EVE! I HAVE TO HURRY AND GET A BOYFRIEND!
BUT I PROBABLY WON'T BE ABLE TO FIND A GREAT GUY, AND WILL END UP SPENDING A LONELY CHRISTMAS BY MYSELF.
YOU GUYS WOULD BE UNHAPPY, TOO, IF YOU DIDN'T HAVE BOYFRIENDS
YOU GET TO LEAD HAPPY LIVES! JEEZ!!
...ANYWAY. I'LL BE CONTENT JUST TO DREAM OF A FABULOUS LOVE.
HUFF HUFF PUFF
BUT, CHRISTMAS...
SHUT UP!
I REALLY LOVE THE BRAND-NEW YEAR. SINCE THERE'S NO ONE AROUND, IT'S NICE AND RELAXING.
NEW YEAR'S EVE, TOO.
SNORE
I LIKE THE NEW YEAR'S MEAL OF COLORED EGGS. NEW YEAR'S CARDS ARE FUN, TOO.
SPRING
I DIDN'T LIKE IT MUCH BEFORE, BUT THIS SEASON IS BEAUTIFUL.
I HATE HAY FEVER.
WHEEZE
BUT THE CHERRY TREES ARE SCARED OF ME. THEY'RE SCARED OF ME, BUT I LIKE THEM.
SUMMER
IN SUMMER, I'M IN MY HOUSE, POOPED. I READ TO DISTRACT ME FROM MY SUFFERING. (BUT I LIKE FIREWORKS.)
STILL WAITING FOR ALLER-GIES TO PASS.
FALL
BOTH MY BODY AND MIND FEEL AT THEIR BEST. MY FAVORITE FLOWER, OSMANTHUS, BLOOMS. THE WIND AND THE CLOUDS FEEL GREAT.
THERE'S OSMANTHUS PLANTED HERE AND THERE ALL ALONG THE WALKING PATH. IT MAKES ME HAPPY.
BUT IT MAKES ME CRY TO GO BACK TO WORK.
WINTER
I'M OUT OF MY ELEMENT IN WINTER TOO, BUT I LOVE THE CRISP AIR IN THE NIGHT AND EARLY MORNING. WHEN I SMELL THE EARLY MORNING AIR, I REMEMBER THE MORNING PRACTICES I HAD AS A STUDENT, AND THE FEELING I HAD WHEN TAKING EXAMS.

FROM THE READERS

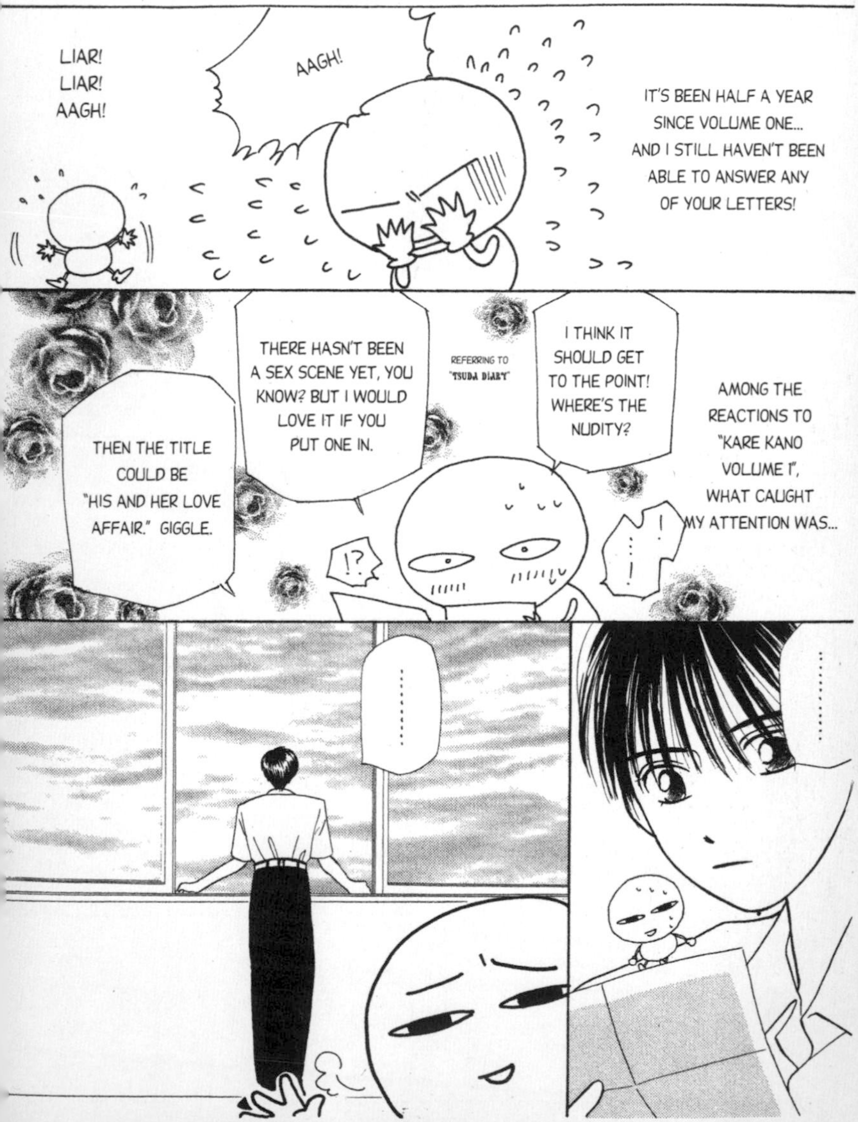
IT'S BEEN HALF A YEAR SINCE VOLUME ONE... AND I STILL HAVEN'T BEEN ABLE TO ANSWER ANY OF YOUR LETTERS!
AAGH!
LIAR! LIAR! AAGH!
AMONG THE REACTIONS TO "KARE KANO VOLUME I", WHAT CAUGHT MY ATTENTION WAS...
I THINK IT SHOULD GET TO THE POINT! WHERE'S THE NUDITY?
REFERRING TO "TSUDA DIARY"
THERE HASN'T BEEN A SEX SCENE YET, YOU KNOW? BUT I WOULD LOVE IT IF YOU PUT ONE IN.
THEN THE TITLE COULD BE "HIS AND HER LOVE AFFAIR." GIGGLE.
!?

THERE ARE A LOT OF ADULTS READING MY WORK. O-HO-HO!

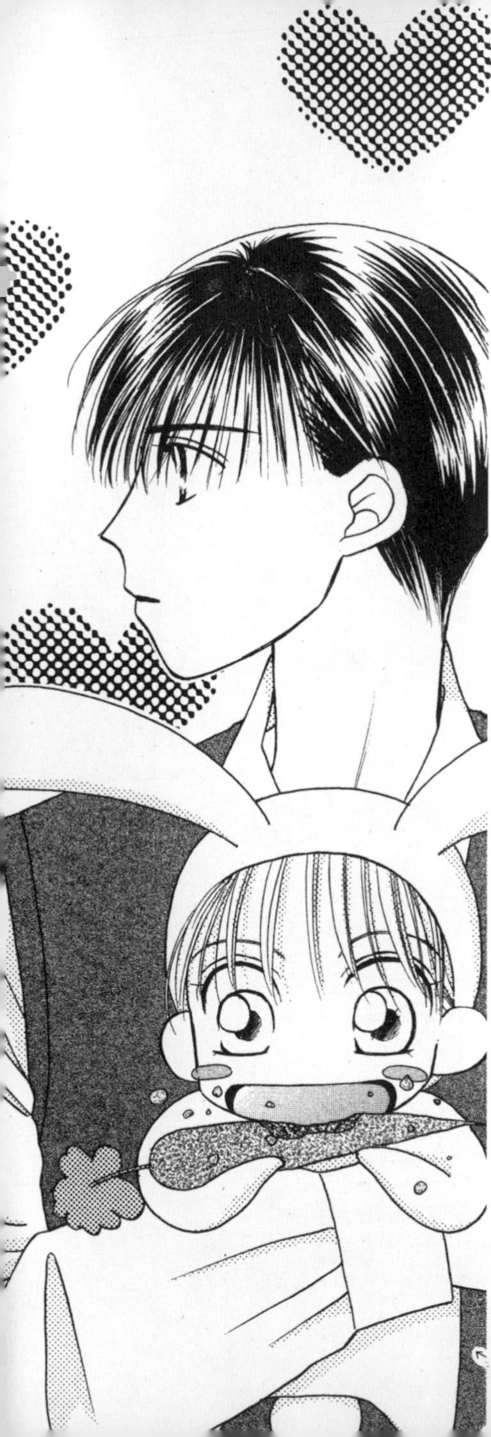

Hello. It's Tsuda!

Thank you very much for spending time with me. I said during volume one that the next would be a "lovey-dovey" version, but ultimately only "Crazy For You" was that way. Dang. And I wanted it to be more lovey-dovey, too. This volume is my first real series. (The first volume was written more as three separate parts, and seemed to me like a short story.) As I was writing, I thought, "How in the world do I write a series?" Lately, I've begun to realize that writing a series is like running a marathon. (I realized this too late.) It's mostly a battle with my own inexperience. Every time, I feel like a boxer getting into the ring—a marathon-running boxer! I really don't understand it. I'm a "boxer," but really, ideally, it's my dream to take it easy and leave myself to writing comics at a leisurely pace. I think it would be great if I was able to do that someday. I'm still learning. I'm doing my best!

Thank you for reading.

My readers are my greatest encouragement!

This Yukino rabbit was drawn for this magazine's reader's 'art corner.' I like it.

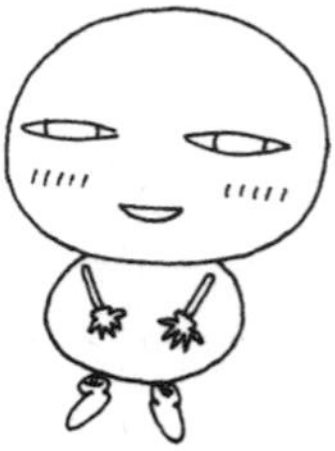

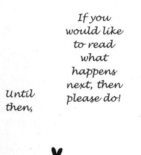

Thank you for reading.

If you would like to read what happens next, then please do!

Until then,

Masami Tsuda

SPECIAL THANKS TO:

S. TANEOKA

N. SHIMIZU

S. YOSHIKUNI

THANKS.

TSUDA DIARY / THE END

coming soon

kare kano

his and her circumstances

volume three

Things are going well for Yukino and Soichiro. They have accepted each other for who they are, and have truly become boyfriend and girlfriend. But they've been concentrating more on each other than on their schoolwork. When the two best students in school suddenly let their grades drop, it draws the attention and concern of one of the teachers. He wants Yukino and Soichiro to break up so they can concentrate on their schoolwork again! And he even calls a dreaded parent-teacher conference to tell their parents his concerns. Will they really make Yukino and Soichiro break up?

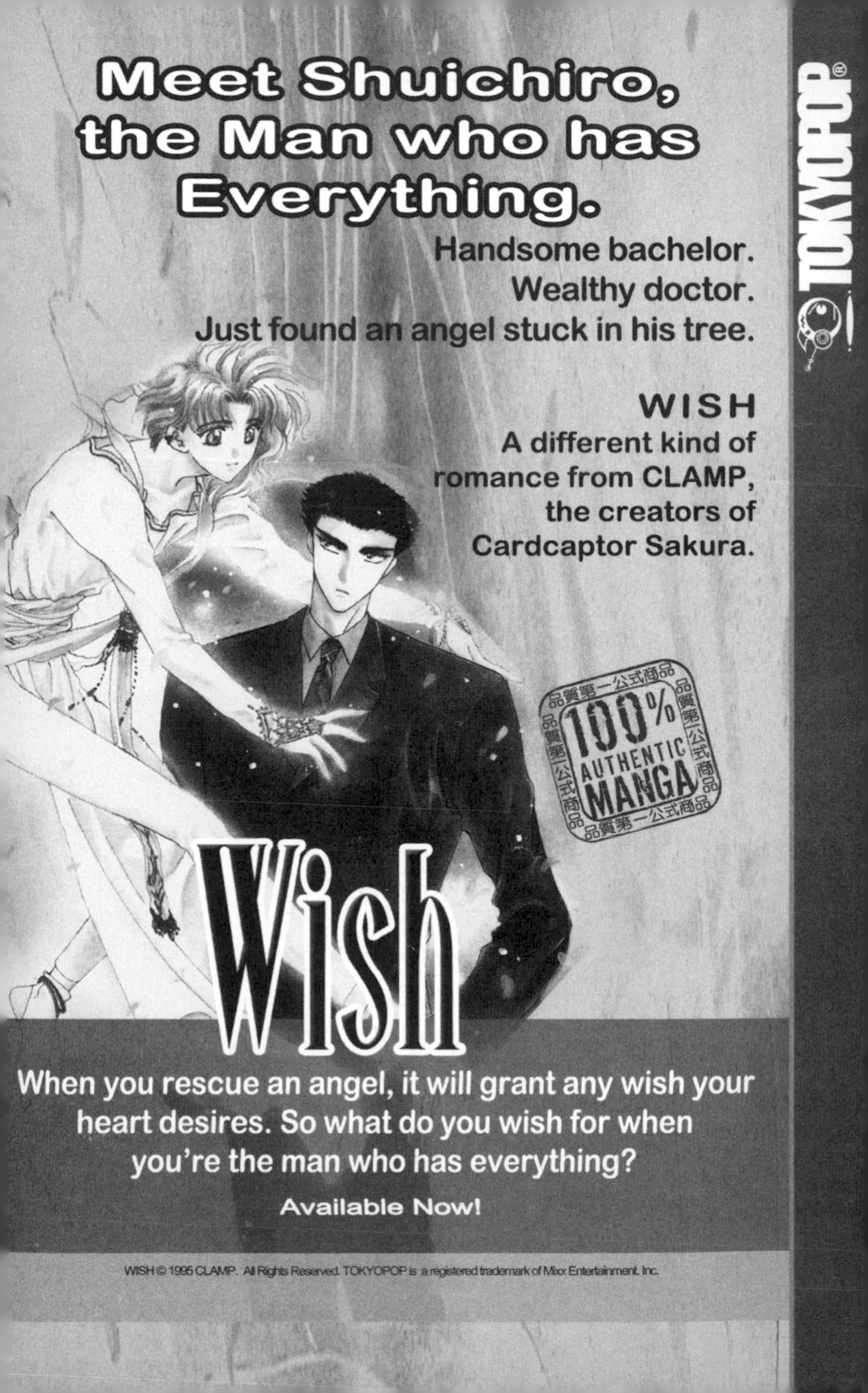
Meet Shuichiro, the Man who has Everything.
Handsome bachelor.
Wealthy doctor.
Just found an angel stuck in his tree.
WISH
A different kind of romance from CLAMP, the creators of Cardcaptor Sakura.
品質第一公式商品
100% AUTHENTIC MANGA
Wish
When you rescue an angel, it will grant any wish your heart desires. So what do you wish for when you're the man who has everything?
Available Now!
WISH © 1995 CLAMP. All Rights Reserved. TOKYOPOP is a registered trademark of Mixx Entertainment, Inc.
TOKYOPOP®

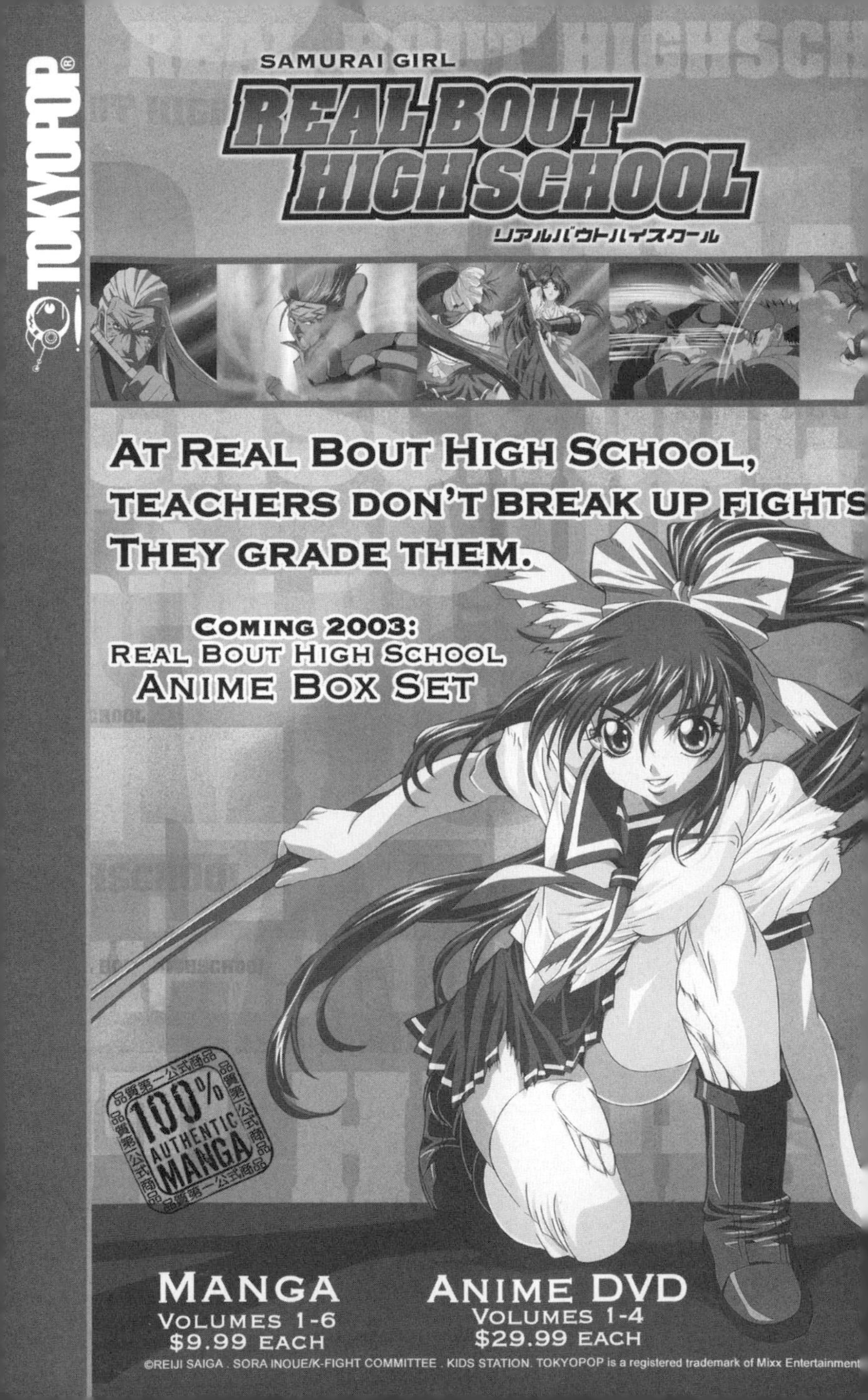
TOKYOPOP
SAMURAI GIRL
REAL BOUT HIGH SCHOOL
リアルバウトハイスクール
AT REAL BOUT HIGH SCHOOL,
TEACHERS DON'T BREAK UP FIGHTS
THEY GRADE THEM.
COMING 2003:
REAL BOUT HIGH SCHOOL
ANIME BOX SET
100% AUTHENTIC MANGA
MANGA
VOLUMES 1-6
$9.99 EACH
ANIME DVD
VOLUMES 1-4
$29.99 EACH
©REIJI SAIGA . SORA INOUE/K-FIGHT COMMITTEE . KIDS STATION. TOKYOPOP is a registered trademark of Mixx Entertainment

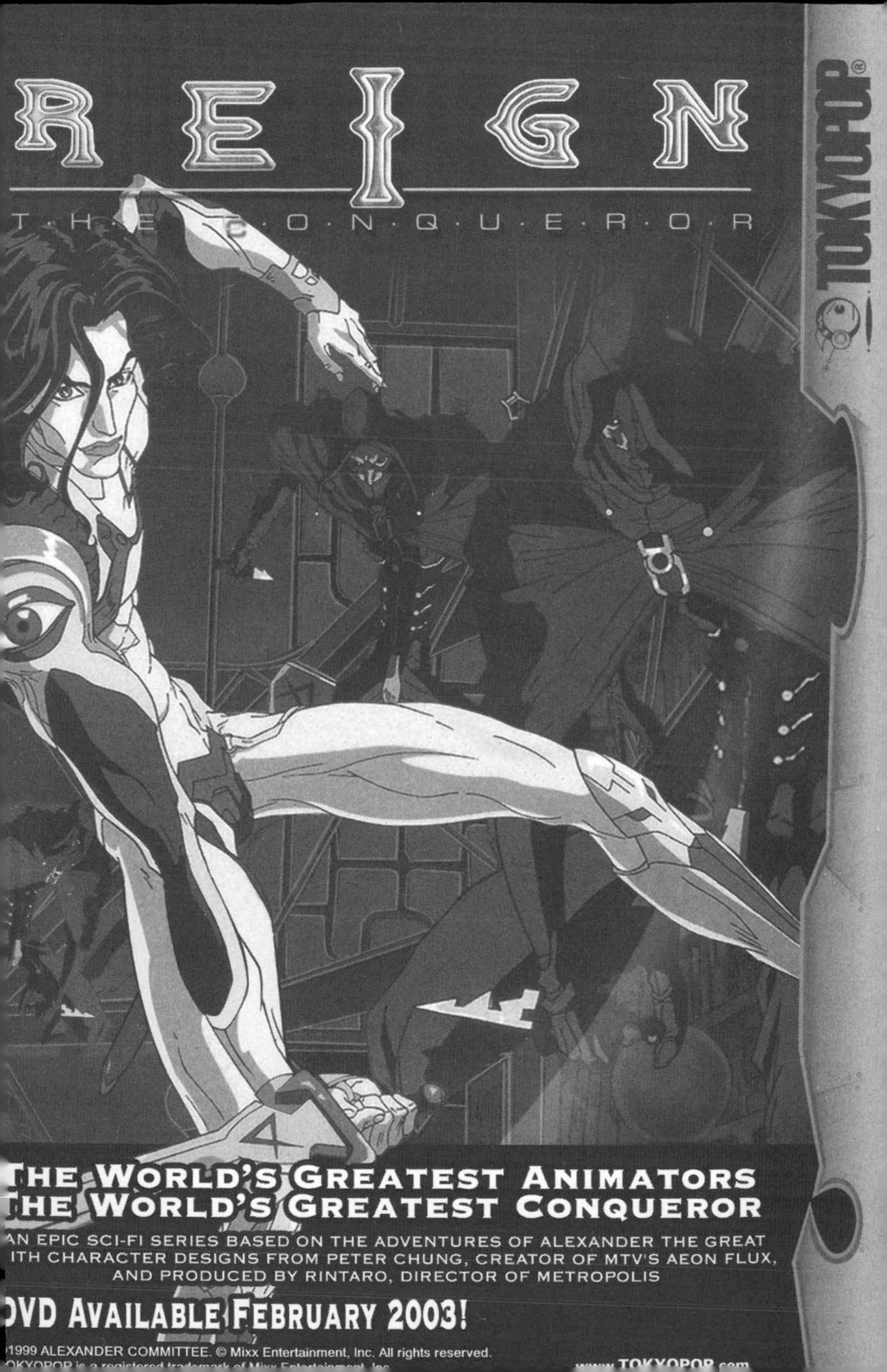
REIGN
T·H·E C·O·N·Q·U·E·R·O·R
TOKYOPOP
THE WORLD'S GREATEST ANIMATORS
THE WORLD'S GREATEST CONQUEROR
AN EPIC SCI-FI SERIES BASED ON THE ADVENTURES OF ALEXANDER THE GREAT
ITH CHARACTER DESIGNS FROM PETER CHUNG, CREATOR OF MTV'S AEON FLUX,
AND PRODUCED BY RINTARO, DIRECTOR OF METROPOLIS
DVD AVAILABLE FEBRUARY 2003!
1999 ALEXANDER COMMITTEE. © Mixx Entertainment, Inc. All rights reserved.

STOP!

This is the back of the book.
You wouldn't want to spoil a great ending!

This book is printed "manga-style," in the authentic Japanese right-to-left format. Since none of the artwork has been flipped or altered, readers get to experience the story just as the creator intended. You've been asking for it, so TOKYOPOP® delivered: authentic, hot-off-the-press, and far more fun!

DIRECTIONS

If this is your first time reading manga-style, here's a quick guide to help you understand how it works.

It's easy... just start in the top right panel and follow the numbers. Have fun, and look for more 100% authentic manga from TOKYOPOP®!